Al Hannex
1994

THE GETTYSBURG SOLDIERS' CEMETERY
AND
LINCOLN'S ADDRESS:
ASPECTS AND ANGLES

BY

FRANK L. KLEMENT

INTRODUCTION BY

STEVEN K. ROGSTAD

WHITE MANE PUBLISHING COMPANY, INC.

This White Mane Publishing Company, Inc. publication
was printed by
Beidel Printing House, Inc.
63 West Burd Street
Shippensburg, PA 17257 USA

In respect for the scholarship contained herein, the acid-free paper used in this book meets the guidelines for permanence and durability of the Committee on Production Guidelines for Book Longevity of the Council on Library Resources.

For a complete list of available publications
please write
White Mane Publishing Company, Inc.
P.O. Box 152
Shippensburg, PA 17257 USA

Library of Congress Cataloging-in-Publication Data

0-942597-61-3

PRINTED IN THE UNITED STATES OF AMERICA

DEDICATION

To three sons who shine brightly in my world —

1. Paul [and Kathy and their four:
   Kristine (and Marty), Mark (and Melissa), Vicki,
   and Steven]

2. Rick

3. Ken [and Deborah and their two: Kevin and
   Krystal]

TABLE OF CONTENTS

Author's Comments and "Thank Yous"

In September of 1992, Steven K. Rogstad (Secretary of the Lincoln Fellowship of Wisconsin and editor of that organization's newsletter, *The Lincoln Ledger*) called me long-distance with the suggestion that I "collect" my published articles dealing with the soldiers' cemetery at Gettysburg and Lincoln's address, write two or three new ones, and have all published as a book. This seemed to be a viable idea, and when Dr. Martin K. Gordon of White Mane expressed an interest, I decided to go ahead with the project. First of all, I asked Mr. Rogstad to write an "Introduction." Then I rounded up nine of the published articles, secured the permissions to republish, and wrote three new articles. The three are, in my opinion, the most intriguing, two dealing with controversial issues.

My indebtedness extends to many: (1) Professor Thomas Hachey, chairman of the Department of History at Marquette University, for endorsing the project by having his secretarial staff do the typing, (2) Ms. Mary F. Dunnwald, Assistant to the Chair (History Department), for supervising the typing, doing much of it herself, and taking a personal interest in the project, (3) Mr. Steven K. Rogstad for providing the idea of this book, (4) Dr. Nicholas J. Contorno, director of Marquette University bands and an authority on Civil War music, for his help with the final chapter, and (5) editors and others who gave permissions to republish articles as chapters in this book.

Readers, I hope, will find the various chapters scholarly, readable, and interesting.

Frank L. Klement
Emeritus Professor of History
Marquette University
November 19, 1993
(130th Anniversary of
Lincoln's Gettysburg Address)

INTRODUCTION

BY STEVEN K. ROGSTAD

Abraham Lincoln's historic trip to Gettysburg, Pennsylvania, in late 1863 occupied slightly more than thirty-seven hours of the 1,504 days he served as President of the United States.[1] Yet in the six score and ten years since he delivered it, the Gettysburg Address has enthralled scholars, authors, artists, actors, and film producers. It has become the subject of several books, innumerable pamphlets, booklets, articles, and two motion pictures. Historians have scrutinized virtually every aspect of Lincoln's short sojourn in that small Pennsylvania city and debated over just what he said and did while there. Did Lincoln compose his speech in the White House, en route to the ceremonies, or in Gettysburg shortly before its delivery? What did he actually say on the speaker's platform? Did he read his remarks or recite them from memory? Did he gesture while speaking or remain somber and stationary? Was the conclusion of the address met with thunderous applause or embarrassing silence? Where in the cemetery did Abraham Lincoln stand when he explained why the Civil War was being fought? "No single episode has presented so many divergent opinions as the incidents associated with writing, presentation, and evaluation of the remarks at Gettysburg," one historian has noted.[2] While many of the mysteries surrounding the event have been clarified by over a hundred years of scholarship, others still remain and continue to attract further attention.

When Lincoln rose from his chair to speak to those assembled around him, he made history. Unknowingly, the crowd was witnessing what would become the most famous public address of Lincoln's career. Although he had given much thought and preparation to his role in the program, Lincoln did not expect his remarks to be recalled for any significance, at any time, by any person, for any reason. Indeed, he made the greatest understatement in American history when he said "the world will little note, nor long remember what we say here." It was the only occasion where he dedicated anything, and the circumstance warranted simple words, not the campaign rhetoric which marked most of his political life in Illinois. The President understood his role would be momentary and told a friend what he intended to say would be "short, short, short."[3] As one of the most renowned orators of his day, Edward Everett was assigned the task of delivering the main address at the ceremony and was invited over a month before Lincoln was formally asked to attend. The President was simply called upon to say "a few appropriate remarks" of consecration over the graves of the Union dead who fell in the Gettysburg battle and he was happy to comply with the request.[4] But the 272 words Lincoln spoke at the Soldiers' National Cemetery that day have achieved greater fame than any others spoken by an American chief executive.

Almost as soon as Lincoln finished speaking and returned to his seat, individuals began writing about his speech. The first impressions were printed by newspapers, who sent correspondents to record the special event. While few reprinted his remarks, many editorialized about them. The larger metropolitan newspapers did neither. Party politics often influenced press reaction and Democratic papers were caustic in evaluating Lincoln's words. The *Patriot and Union* of Harrisburg, Pennsylvania, said: "The President succeeded on this occasion because he acted without sense and without constraint in a panorama that was gotten up more for the benefit of his party than for the glory of the nation and the honor of the dead . . . . We pass over the silly remarks of the President; for the credit of the nation we are willing that the veil of oblivion shall be dropped over them and that they shall no more be repeated or thought of."[5] However, most of the comments rendered by members of the press were very complimentary as exemplified by those published in Boston's *City Document.* "Perhaps nothing in the whole proceedings," the paper said, "made so deep an impression on the vast assemblage, or has conveyed to the country in so concise a form the lesson of the hour, as the remarks of the President. Their simplicity and force make them worthy of prominence among the utterances from high places."[6]

Another group of writers who also recorded their impressions did so for personal reasons and did not intend to have their comments publicly known. John Hay, Lincoln's secretarial assistant, was near the President and heard what Lincoln said. Not overly impressed, he wrote in his journal upon returning to the White House that "the President, in a firm, free way, with more grace than is his usual wont, said his half-dozen lines of consecration, — and the music wailed, and we went home through crowded and cheering streets."[7] Edward Everett's reaction to those "half-dozen words of consecration" was very different. They so moved him that he felt compelled to write Lincoln a day after the event, saying "I should be glad if I could flatter myself that I came as near to the central idea of the occasion in two hours as you did in two minutes."[8]

Lincoln's assassination in 1865 forever changed the perception of his ten short sentences at Gettysburg cemetery. That event made him the nation's first martyr, and biographers hurriedly assembled the events of his life to satisfy public demand. Many of those early chroniclers still only referred to the speech as a common "dedicatory address," but others seemed to recognize the power and beauty of its words and gave unprecedented praise to most of Lincoln's written record. Joseph H. Barrett concluded that while Edward Everett's "elaborate eloquence" contributed "solemn grandeur to the ceremonies of the day . . . no fitter or more touching words were spoken than those of Mr. Lincoln."[9] The most popular of the early biographers, Josiah G. Holland, wrote: "Surprisingly fine as Mr. Everett's oration was in the Gettysburg consecration, the rhetorical honors of the occasion were won by President Lincoln. His little speech is a perfect gem, deep in feeling, compact in thought and expression, and tasteful and elegant in every word and comma . . . . Strong feelings and a large brain were its parents — a little painstaking its accoucheur." He later added that the President's remarks "were very effective, and betrayed a degree of literary ability quite unexpected to those who read only his formal state papers."[10]

As the importance of the address increased over time and Abraham Lincoln became more and more venerated, people associated with the Gettysburg event came forward with recollections that often contradicted established facts or differed from the reminiscences of other individuals who witnessed the same occurrences. But having their statements recorded in newspapers and magazines forever linked them in history with Lincoln and one of his more famous public appearances. These remembrances occasionally coincided with the fact that the person had a biography about Lincoln published a short time before or had one pending publication. These press releases were an early form of "sneak previews" and good advertising for their larger works. One such person was Ward H. Lamon, a friend of Lincoln's who introduced the President to the audience that day at Gettysburg. After twenty-three years had passed, he wrote an open letter to the *Chicago Tribune* where he repeated from memory entire conversations that he had on that occasion with Lincoln, Everett, and Secretary of State William H. Seward about the effectiveness of Lincoln's words and how all three dubbed them a failure. Not only were these gentlemen disappointed in it, Lamon said, but so were those assembled to hear it and nobody applauded at its conclusion. Lamon's contributions to the history of the document were considered important, for they were some of the earliest statements about Lincoln's delivery of the speech and Lincoln's personal opinion of it. His friendship with the President and his presence on the speaker's platform seemed to place his credibility above reproach. Nevertheless, virtually all of his recollections would eventually be disproved. Unfortunately, he reiterated them later in a book which greatly influenced other writers and public feeling about how Lincoln's speech was received.

In 1894, *Century Magazine* published an article by John G. Nicolay, Lincoln's private secretary who traveled to Gettysburg with the President. Entitled "The Gettysburg Address," Nicolay's monograph intended to destroy the myth that had been circulated — that Lincoln wrote his address on the train en route to Gettysburg — and to give his and John Hay's new book, *Abraham Lincoln: Complete Works*, some publicity. Like Lamon, the former secretary recalled happenings many years after the events took place, but his close working relationship with Lincoln gave his story credence. Nicolay gave conclusive evidence that the Gettysburg Address was begun in the White House and finished in David Wills's home on the morning of November 19th. The publication of his dissertation marked the first time a periodical printed anything concerning the composition of the address and, coupled with Lamon's published works, became a primary source of information for future scholars.

Three publications appeared in 1906. Clark E. Carr published his personal recollections about the Gettysburg proceedings in a pamphlet, *Lincoln at Gettysburg* (a reprint of his address in Springfield that year before the Illinois State Historical Society). Carr was the Illinois representative at the ceremonies and made several contradictory statements years later about how Lincoln came to be invited for the occasion. As a member of the Commission of the National Cemetery at Gettysburg, his remembrances were prompted by that organization's official report and the recent works of Lamon and Nicolay. This treatise was reprinted as a small book and increased the confusion surrounding the claim that President Lincoln spoke at the spot where the Soldiers' National Monument was dedicated on July 1, 1869.

The second title was Mary Raymond Shipman Andrews' fictional tale "The Perfect Tribute," which appeared in the July issue of *Scribner's Magazine*. She based her information about the speech on the false recollections of her son's history teacher, who claimed his father was informed by Edward Everett that Lincoln composed his address on the train. According to Andrews, Lincoln realized he was expected to say something "brilliant, eloquent, strong" the following day and decided to work on his composition during the "leisure of the journey." Not finding any writing paper, he grabbed some brown wrapping paper that was lying on the floor of the train, "torn carelessly in a zigzag." With the stub of a pencil he wrote the address on the paper and dropped it to the floor, deeming it a failed effort. Later, he retrieved and folded the torn bit of paper and placed it in his coat pocket — still convinced of its inadequacy. The following day Lincoln delivered the speech in his "queer, squeaking falsetto" voice. The effect on the audience was ghastly and a titter of laughter ran through the crowd. At the conclusion of the speech, "not a hand was lifted in applause," nor was there any sign of approval. "His speech had been," Andrews wrote, "as he feared it would be, a failure."[11]

A month after its appearance, the story was published as a forty-seven page booklet by Charles Scribner's Sons, which sold over 500,000 copies by 1937 in five different editions.[12] Reviews of the story were very flattering, one newspaper hailing it as one of the "greatest stories" that had appeared in recent years.[13] Soon, high schools throughout the country placed *The Perfect Tribute* on required and recommended reading lists for English courses because of its brevity. Although it generated further appreciation for Lincoln's speech and was admired for its fine literary qualities, the little book was historically incorrect and kept generations of Americans away from the truth about how Lincoln wrote it. "It is to be regretted," one historian wrote, "that American youth for over half a century have received the impression that the finest oration in our language, was belatedly, hurriedly, and even slovenly written on a railroad train. The story is a travesty on how masterpieces are created.''[14] Mary Andrews was not the first person to say Lincoln wrote the Gettysburg Address on a train. But she crystallized the myth so well through her story that the book became an instant "best seller" and the subject of two motion pictures.[15]

Gettysburg and Lincoln by Henry Sweetser Burrage also was published that year. It was the first objective, book-length account of the Gettysburg experience. Burrage relied primarily on materials found in the *Official Records of the Union and Confederate Armies*, but also depended on Nicolay's 1894 article and information gleaned from Nicolay and Hay's 1890 monumental ten-volume biography of Lincoln. Slightly less than a fifth of the book's content was devoted to the President's participation in the dedication ceremony because the author wanted to record the "principal facts covering the period from the commencement of the Gettysburg campaign to the present time," which included lengthy portions about the battle and the origins of the cemetery and National Park.[16] Although influenced by prevalent traditions concerning the address, Burrage's work was the best historical treatment that had been published up to that time. Unfortunately, it was overshadowed by Mary Andrews' fiction and was soon forgotten.

The next thirty-eight years added four more works to the Gettysburg bibliography. Two were Orton H. Carmichael's *Lincoln's Gettysburg Address* (1917) and Henry Eyster Jacobs' *Lincoln's Gettysburg-World Message* (1919). Both were perfunctory studies at best. Carmichael simply attempted "to state briefly in logical order" the Gettysburg story in order to halt the growing misapprehension of facts concerning when and where Lincoln wrote his speech. Alluding to Mary Andrews' widely accepted account, he warned readers that "erroneous ideas widely prevail" and said that Lincoln's beautiful words were "the natural and logical product of his methods of thought and of his genius of spirit.''[17] Henry Jacobs was a student at the Lutheran Seminary at the time of the Gettysburg battle, as well as an eyewitness to the dedication. Aside from his first-hand recollections, he devoted a large part of his small book in discussing Lincoln's principles of statesmanship.

The first thorough study was William E. Barton's *Lincoln at Gettysburg* (1930). Reviewers praised it and prophesied that it would stand as the most comprehensive study of all phases of Lincoln's address for years to come.[18] The book's sub-title described its scope: *What He Intended to Say; What He Said; What He Was Reported to Have Said; What He Wished He Had Said.* Barton was a recognized authority on Lincoln's early life and "was at home," one scholar noted, "with the detailed analysis of some brief episode encrusted with myth over the years.''[19] He lent his talents to the Gettysburg Address after producing long, impressive treatises on Lincoln's religion, lineage, parentage, romances, and the famous letter of condolence to the Widow Bixby. His goal was to "tell the whole story of Lincoln's trip to Gettysburg" and collect all the known material on the subject.[20] He sought to differentiate between truthful and spurious information to be able to tell just what took place during those two days in 1863. Described as "a great historical detective," Barton traced the evolution of Lincoln's address, hinted at possible sources of inspiration for it, analyzed the contents of it, investigated the statements of those who heard it, and chronicled press reaction to it.[21] For good measure, he added Everett's oration and illustrations of the five handwritten copies of Lincoln's speech then available. The publishers of *Lincoln at Gettysburg* thought the 263-page volume "a pretty long book about a very short speech, important as that speech is."[22] He said so much so convincingly about the document that Lincoln scholar Benjamin P. Thomas admitted seventeen years later that "little can be added about the Gettysburg Address."[23] His book removed much of the uncertainty and disagreement over many aspects of Lincoln's Gettysburg trip and set a standard that stood for many years.

F. Lauriston Bullard's work, *A Few Appropriate Remarks*, was almost a condensation of Barton's work. Still, the book did have some merit as it questioned Clark E. Carr's credibility as a source of information and showed conclusively that the myth about Lincoln writing the speech on the way to Gettysburg originated as early as 1865.

The one hundredth anniversary of the speech prompted two more publications. The Library of Congress published *Long Remembered: The Gettysburg Address in Facsimile* in 1963, which simply reproduced the five then extant copies of the address with explanations and included an introductory essay by David C. Mearns and Lloyd A. Dunlap concerning how it was written. A year later, the Lincoln National Life Foundation published Louis A. Warren's exhaustive *Lincoln's Gettysburg Declaration: "A New Birth of Freedom,"* which one historian called "the definitive volume of Lincoln's Gettysburg Address and a work that is destined to take an honored place on the shelf of basic books dealing with the life and writings of Abraham Lincoln."[24] Throughout his long tenure as Director of the Lincoln National Life Insurance Company's major Lincoln research center in Fort Wayne, Warren developed a fascination for the Gettysburg Address. As editor of *Lincoln Lore* for twenty-seven years, he devoted eighteen issues to the subject and wrote two booklets about it before expanding his material into book form.[25] Two decades had passed since Bullard's study, and Warren felt enough new facts had been uncovered to justify another book on the subject. He presented new information, challenged established ideas, and supplied superb documentation for his findings. Warren broke away from tradition when he argued that the speaker's platform was not located where the Soldiers' National Monument stands today. It sparked a controversy that still lingers.

Almost twenty years elapsed before Philip B. Kunhardt, Jr., wrote an entertaining volume for the general audience in 1983 with *A New Birth of Freedom: Lincoln at Gettysburg.* Kunhardt boasted that his was "the most thoroughly researched and accurate account of Lincoln's trip to Gettysburg, the days preceding the trip, and the writing of the famous speech, I could make 120 years after the events took place."[26] Although well written and profusely illustrated, it was severely criticized for "omitting the appendages of scholarship," while including "unsubstantiated stories" and "embarrassing inaccuracies."[27] A lengthy appendix, however, provided facsimiles of the five variant versions of the address and provided a line-by-line analysis of the differences in text between each.

Nearly another decade passed before the Gettysburg theme again surfaced in 1992 with the publication of Garry Wills's *Lincoln at Gettysburg: The Words That Remade America.* While deemed "both exhaustive and irresistible," only two of the three appendices deal with details about the festivities themselves.[28] The balance of the text is a rhetorical study of Lincoln's words and an examination of the speech as a literary wonder and radical political discourse. "This is a book about language," one reviewer has said. "On this subject, Wills is at his best, and his best may be the best that has ever been written about the Gettysburg Address as literature."[29]

In 1970, Frank L. Klement was doing research in Ohio's State Historical Society for his biography of Clement L. Vallandigham, the noted Ohio Copperhead Democrat of the Civil War. While studying Governor David Tod's papers, he "came across all kinds of letters to and from David Tod . . . all leading up to Ohio's role in the dedication of the Soldiers' Cemetery."[30] Intrigued, Klement took time out from the Vallandigham work to write a lengthy monograph about Ohio's involvement in the Gettysburg program. It was the beginning of an interest in Lincoln's famous address which resulted in ten articles over the next twenty years. But the Gettysburg essays were "a kind of 'side road' from my main work," Klement explained, "which really has to do with Lincoln's Democratic critics in the Upper Midwest."[31]

Thomas R. Turner, editor of the *Lincoln Herald* and distinguished Lincoln scholar and author, has called Klement "a leading American historian" and "expert on the Copperheads and dissenters during the Civil War."[32] In 1960, Klement produced his first work, a landmark volume, *The Copperheads in the Middle West.* He continued his study of northern politics in his 1970 book, *The Limits of Dissent: Clement L. Vallandigham and the Civil War.* Fourteen years later a third volume, *Dark Lanterns: Secret Political Societies, Conspiracies, and Treason Trials in the Civil War*, "transformed the image of wartime Democrats and their activities" and was submitted for consideration for the 1985 Pulitzer Prize in history as well as that year's Bancroft Prize.[33] Aside from these classics, Klement has authored a fourth book about Wisconsin's role in the Civil War, sections in six others, and nearly a hundred articles that deal with the political scene during the Civil War, Lincoln's role as President, and how he outmaneuvered his Democratic critics. So influential has been his work that renowned Pulitzer Prize winner Mark E. Neely, Jr., has stated that "the works of Frank L. Klement in the 1950s, 1960s and 1970s would demolish the myth of a large secret, well-organized disloyal Northern opposition to the Lincoln administration."[34]

Thirty years have passed since the appearance of the last major work on the Gettysburg Address and, with the exception of Garry Wills's recent examination of Lincoln's eloquence, all previous titles are obsolete and out-of-print. The smaller volumes by Andrews, Carr, Carmichael, Jacobs and Bullard are no longer read by serious students and are sought mainly as collector's items. Burrage's and Barton's books are biased interpretations and rarely cited. Of the more modern studies, only Warren's book adequately addresses the topic and even his findings are now dated and incomplete.

The essays contained in this volume clearly show that there is still more to learn about Abraham Lincoln's immortal address. Klement once again recreates the activities at Gettysburg through the stories of its participants and a re-examination of some of the more interesting sidelights associated with Lincoln's visit. "Part One" describes the activities of the dedication festivities through the involvement of three individuals closely connected with the event. Chapter One, " 'Those Honored Dead': David Wills and the Soldiers' Cemetery at Gettysburg," is the result of Klement's original research in the David Tod Papers. It is the most complete account yet of Wills's idea for the cemetery and its dedication. Lincoln's friend and self-appointed bodyguard Ward H. Lamon was marshal-in-chief on that historic day — supervising the procession to and from the cemetery while also serving as master of ceremonies for the occasion. Tapping primary sources, Klement tells his story in Chapter Two, "Ward H. Lamon and the Dedication of the Soldiers' Cemetery at Gettysburg." Benjamin B. French has remained almost a footnote in the volumes of pages that have been written about the Gettysburg Address. Commissioner of Public Works and personal confidant to Mary Lincoln, French was one of the distinguished personalities on the speaker's stand and composed a special "Consecration Hymn" that was chanted just before Lincoln rose to speak. Now, after years of receiving only cursory mention, Klement tells the full extent of French's activities at Gettysburg in Chapter Three, "Benjamin B. French, the Lincolns, and the Dedication of the Soldiers' Cemetery at Gettysburg."

The second section reveals two isolated and unrelated topics connected with the solemn occasion. Ohio sent more representatives and sponsored more events than any other state involved in the program. The complete story is told in Chapter Four, Klement's first Gettysburg essay, "Ohio and the Dedication of the Soldiers' Cemetery at Gettysburg." One of Abraham Lincoln's lesser known utterances is described in Chapter Five, "Lincoln's First Gettysburg Address: A Little Known Impromptu Speech Perhaps Best Forgotten."

The four chapters of "Part Three" concern the composition and delivery of the address. In Chapter Six, "Lincoln, the Gettysburg Address, and Two Myths," the author shows that the published works of Mary Andrews and Ward H. Lamon, along with others, contributed largely to the modern misconceptions about how Lincoln authored his stirring words. Klement successfully refutes the notion that his ten sentences were jotted down hastily and without hardly any preparation. Chapter Seven, "Seven Who Witnessed Lincoln's Gettysburg

Address," and Chapter Eight, "The Ten Who Sat in the Front Row During the Dedication of the Soldiers' Cemetery at Gettysburg," survey who was near Abraham Lincoln on the crowded platform during the program and describe what they saw and heard. The unique story about William Yates Selleck, a State Military Agent during the Civil War who represented Wisconsin on the committee to develop the Soldiers' National Cemetery, is told in Chapter Nine, "A Milwaukeean Witnesses Lincoln's Gettysburg Address: W. Yates Selleck and the Soldiers' Cemetery at Gettysburg."

"Part Four" carefully examines two controversies and one minor theme associated with the Gettysburg experience. Since Lloyd Ostendorf's 1991 claim to have acquired the second page of the third or "lost draft" of the address written by Lincoln for David Wills at Wills's request, attention has again focused on the known copies of the speech Lincoln penned himself. Klement becomes the first historian to officially take sides in the recent quarrel involving the authenticity of Ostendorf's manuscript. In Chapter Ten, "The Six Copies of the Gettysburg Address in Lincoln's Own Hand," the author details the history of each of the six holographs and asserts that the document owned by the Dayton, Ohio artist is indeed "the very page that the President held in his hand while reciting his lines on the twelve foot wide and twenty foot long platform atop Cemetery Hill." The dispute over where Lincoln actually stood when he spoke has engaged historians since Louis Warren questioned the traditional site in 1964. Here, Klement gives a balanced overview of the debate in Chapter Eleven, "The Dispute Over the Site of the Platform." The author discusses "The Music at Gettysburg" in Chapter Twelve, a subject which has not appeared in any previous book about the Gettysburg Address. Extensive appendices conclude the volume, they include the oration of Edward Everett and other important information relating to the dedication.

Authors David C. Mearns and Lloyd A. Dunlap expressed their belief many years ago that, because of sparse evidence and conflicting testimonies of those involved, "the definitive story of Lincoln and the writing of the address has not been told, nor is it likely that it ever can be."[35] Despite the large quantity of misleading information, we have come significantly closer to learning how Lincoln brought together words that defined democracy and represented "the world's model of eloquence, elegance and condensation."[36] No author has studied the history of the Gettysburg Address more in the last quarter of a century than Frank L. Klement. He brings to this volume, dealing with one of the most familiar episodes in the life of Abraham Lincoln, fresh insights and vital new information. Expertly researched, extensively documented, and well written, this most readable collection of essays will entertain readers of all backgrounds and elicit further appreciation for President Lincoln's most inspiring document.

Steven K. Rogstad
Racine, Wisconsin
November, 19, 1993

David Wills, Ward H. Lamon, and Benjamin B. French had active roles in the Gettysburg soldiers' cemetery story. All three were involved in planning the program, took an active part in the proceedings, and had a place on the twelve foot wide and twenty foot long platform when Edward Everett orated and President Abraham Lincoln made his "few appropriate remarks." So the three chapters dealing with Wills, Lamon, and French fit together.

Wills, of course, was the central figure. He suggested a soldiers' cemetery on the battlefield to his governor, Andrew G. Curtin, and Governor Curtin in turn, put him in charge of the project — including the planning of the dedication program. The Wills story is based upon the David Wills Papers (a rather meager collection) in the Library of Congress, Wills's extensive published reports on the cemetery, the Andrew G. Curtin Letterbooks, 1861-1865, in the Pennsylvania State Archives (Harrisburg), and a variety of other sources. Four newspapers were most helpful: (Gettysburg) *Adams County Sentinel*, a Republican newspaper edited by David Wills's neighbor; Gettysburg *Compiler*, Democratic-oriented; the Washington *Daily Morning Chronicle*; and the Cincinnati *Daily Commercial*. The Wills chapter gives that worthy Gettysburg resident his day in court.

Wills asked Lincoln's bodyguard, Ward H. Lamon, to serve as Marshal-in-Chief during the procession (from the city of Gettysburg to the cemetery site) and to act as master of ceremonies during the program. Lamon also helped Wills plan the procession and the program. The extensive Ward H. Lamon Papers in the Huntington Library, San Marino, California, provide the starting point for the story about Lamon and the soldiers' cemetery in Gettysburg. It is a story that needed to be told.

Lamon, in turn, invited Benjamin B. French to be his "first assistant." French, Lincoln's Commissioner of Public Buildings, therefore accompanied Lamon to Gettysburg to meet with Wills to plan the procession and program. A "Consecration Hymn," composed by French, was chanted by a Baltimore choir as part of the program. Furthermore, French was seated in one of the ten front row chairs on the platform during the program. Since French kept both a diary and a journal, his insights and comments give a fresh look at the events of November 19, 1863. The Benjamin B. French Papers, available via inter-library loan from the Library of Congress, serve as the basic source for the story of French and the soldiers' cemetery.

There is bound to be some repetition when Wills, Lamon, and French have their stories told. All three stories have the same base, but each is told from a different perspective.

CHAPTER I

"THESE HONORED DEAD:" DAVID WILLS
AND THE SOLDIERS' CEMETERY AT GETTYSBURG*

Edward Everett's well-known but dreary oration and Abraham Lincoln's brief and memorable address helped to make the dedicatory program at the soldiers' cemetery at Gettysburg on November 19, 1863, a notable and oft-discussed event. Yet David Wills, the Gettysburger who conceived the idea of transforming a portion of the battlefield into a cooperative eighteen-state cemetery, converted that idea into a reality, and invited Everett and Lincoln to participate in the program, has passed into history almost unknown and unnoticed. Without Wills's perception, promotion and planning there would have been no Gettysburg-based oration by Everett nor address by Lincoln.

The story of the soldiers' cemetery at Gettysburg really goes back to the battles fought in the fields and woods near Gettysburg on July 1-3, 1863. After the rebel invaders withdrew to return to Virginia and the Union forces tardily followed, Gettysburg witnessed the influx of thousands: doctors by the dozens and nurses by the score, employees of the Christian Commission and the U.S. Sanitary Commission, state agents and representatives, relatives and friends of wounded or dead soldiers, and a horde of sightseers. "Hundreds and thousands of people," wrote a resident of Harrisburg, "are daily pouring through this city en route for the battlefield at Gettysburg."[1] Many were no more than "morbid curiosity seekers" who found "a sort of pleasure in beholding the ravages and misery of war."[2]

Visitors noticed the "unwearied labors of the people of Gettysburg" in tending the wounded and alleviating the suffering in spite of the "most inadequate supplies of course food, and none of suitable and delicate food, within reach of hospitals."[3] A few Gettysburgers, unfortunately, took advantage of the pilgrims and sightseers, charging "10 and 15 cents per quart" for milk and "$1 and even $1.50 per loaf" for bread, manifesting a "sordid meaness and

---

*Reprinted (with permission) from the *Lincoln Herald* , 74 (Fall, 1972), pp. 123-135.

[an] unpatriotic spirit."[4] Visitors also noticed that from 1,000 to 1,200 "walking wounded" were shipped out to Washington and Baltimore daily, reducing the number confined in the makeshift hospitals in and near Gettysburg.

Those who toured the battlefield were shocked to see the manner in which some of the dead had been buried, often no grave being dug and the body merely covered with spadefuls of earth. Heavy rains washed away some of the ground, exposing legs, arms, and heads. "I saw one entire skull above the ground," wrote one witness, "and in many instances hands & feet are sticking through."[5] The summer heat and the burning sun hastened the decomposition of the portions exposed and, along with the bloated and decaying carcasses of artillery horses, filled the air with a sickening stench, especially in the areas where the first day's fighting had been heaviest. "The atmosphere is truly horrible," one woman wrote, "and camphor and smelling salts are prime necessities for most persons, certainly for ladies."[6]

Governor Andrew G. Curtin, in the midst of troop-raising responsibilities and busy with his campaign for reelection, did not arrive in Gettysburg until late in the afternoon of July 10.[7] He toured some of the hospitals and portions of the battlefield, most of the time with thirty-two-year-old David Wills as his guide and companion.

Wills, an aggressive young lawyer who had come to Gettysburg only nine years earlier, was well-known in both Republican and community circles.[8] Transferring his allegiance from Whiggery to the newly organized Republican party, he became a local political leader as well as the superintendent of schools for Adams County. Success in law prompted him to buy a fine house, at the corner of York Street and the public square, centrally located in the small city of 3,000.

Before Governor Curtin returned to Harrisburg, he designated David Wills as his "agent" in matters having to do with the removal of Pennsylvania's dead from the battlefield. "Governor Curtin," the neighbor who edited the *Adams County Sentinel* reported, "has made arrangements with David Wills, esq., of this place for the removal of all Pennsylvanians killed in the late battles, furnishing transportation for the body and one attendant at the expense of the State."[9]

Wills's work as Governor Curtin's agent brought him an avalanche of work. He helped friends and relatives of dead soldiers locate graves scattered over the far-flung battlefield, hired undertakers to exhume the bodies, secured coffins, and sent the remains to their home communities — always with "one attendant at the expense of the State."[10] Wills noticed that many of the markers over the graves were temporary and the names half legible. " . . . three thousand men lie in and about Gettysburg," one observer wrote, "in cornfields, in meadows, in gardens, by the way-side, and in the public road, buried hastily where they fell, and others in long rows, with a piece of box lid or board of any kind, with the name of the person and the day he died written with lead pencil, ink, or whatever they had to make a mark with."[11] Time, aided by the elements, made some of the inscriptions illegible and many bodies, decaying and covered with maggots before dirt was spaded over them, had no headboards at all. Even worse, reports reached Wills that hogs, rooting in portions of the battlefield, were desecrating some of the graves.

Wills became acquainted with a score of state agents, like W.[illiam] Yates Selleck of Wisconsin and Henry Edwards of Massachusetts, giving them considerable advice and assistance in regard to their work. Edwards and other Bay State agents proposed that Massachusetts buy a portion of the battlefield, collect the decomposing bodies scattered in graves on the battlefield, and inter them in a plot somewhere atop Cemetery Hill. Wills also became acquainted with Andrew B. Cross, who, as head of the Christian Commission of Pennsylvania, pursued duties which at times overlapped with those of Governor Curtin's agent. Wills and Cross exchanged views about the desirability of transforming a portion of the battlefield into a cemetery and getting all of the eighteen states that had lost sons at Gettysburg to cooperate in the venture. Wills decided to present the case to Governor Curtin, with Cross taking it to the newspapers.[12]

Wills's letter of July 24, 1863, to Curtin suggested that the state of Pennsylvania purchase about 8 acres ("3½ acres belonging to Mr. Raffensberger and 4½ to Mr. Menchy") for a cemetery. Other states, he was sure, would partake in the cemetery project. He made a stirring plea: "Our dead are lying in the fields unburied (that is no graves being dug) with small portions of earth dug up alongside of the body and thrown over it. In many instances arms and legs protrude and my attention has been directed to several places where hogs were actually rooting out the bodies and devouring them — and this on Pennsylvania soil and in many cases the bodies of the patriotic soldiers of our State. Humanity calls on us to take measures to remedy this . . . ."[13]

Governor Curtin, busy campaigning for reelection, promptly authorized Wills to purchase the acreage deemed necessary, contact representatives and governors of the other states, make arrangements for the reburials, and supervise the project.[14] Andrew B. Cross, meanwhile, carried the campaign for the soldiers' national cemetery to the public press, creating grassroots support for the project.[15]

Three developments affected the success of the project. In the first place, Colonel Henry C. Alleman, in command at Gettysburg, issued an order prohibiting the further exhuming of bodies and shipping them to home communities. Although the order was based upon a fear of a "pestilence,"[16] it directly aided Wills's project, for it would assure more reburials in the proposed soldiers' cemetery. In the second place, Wills disagreed with Massachusetts's representatives over reburial policy, Curtin's agent wanting the reburials to be "promiscuous" while Bay State agents adamantly demanded that all of their dead soldiers be reburied in an allotted section of the proposed cemetery. At the urging of Governor Curtin, Wills bowed to the wishes of Massachusetts. The third controversy took place with officers of the Evergreen Cemetery Association, who made a persistent effort to have the soldiers buried in grounds controlled by that organization. They proposed that the reburials be made at a stipulated price, to be paid the cemetery association. Failing in that, they endeavored to connect the two cemeteries, so that both would be within one enclosure and all under the control, supervision, and management of the local cemetery association.[17]

Agents for some of the states threatened to withdraw from the cooperative cemetery venture if the project was turned over to the Evergreen Cemetery Association.[18] Wills, sparring with the cemetery officials, succeeded in sidetracking their project. He took steps to purchase the necessary land, convince more states to support the proposal for the cooperative cemetery, and compose a circular letter to the governors involved. Then Wills wrote a brief report to Governor Curtin on July 30. "There is no doubt," he stated, "[that] all the States will unite if made a national exclusive burial ground for soldiers." Eight state agents had been "consulted" and each "semi-officially" endorsed the project. "The site selection," Wills added, "contains twenty-four acres." The asking price was about $3,000, but "all of the twenty-four acres need not be taken."[19]

The next day Wills sent a telegram to each of the seventeen other governors whose troops had fought and died at Gettysburg. "By authority of Governor Curtin," the telegram stated, "I am buying ground on or near Cemetery Hill in trust for a cemetery for the burial of the soldiers who fell here in the defence of the Union." Would their state cooperate in "the project for the removal of her dead from the field?" "Signify your assent to Governor Curtin or myself," he instructed each state's chief executive, "and details [will] be arranged afterwards."[20]

Some of the governors replied promptly, others, like David Tod of Ohio and Richard Yates of Illinois, tardily or not at all, necessitating further prodding and prompting on Wills's part. Meanwhile Curtin's agent negotiated for the purchase of five different plots totaling seventeen acres; he bought two plots at $225 per acre, one at $200, another at $150 and the fifth at $135. The cost of the seventeen acres ran to $2,475.87.[21] He talked to state agents of Wisconsin and Connecticut, securing their aid in drafting a circular letter to each of the governors supposedly interested in the project.[22] He also took steps to compose "specifications" regarding the reburial of the dead soldiery and advertised for bids — exhuming the bodies from their scattered graves over the battlefield and near the hospitals and reburying them in reserved sections of the new soldiers' cemetery.[23] Wills also contacted William Saunders, an employee of the Department of Agriculture and a well-known landscape gardener, asking him to come to Gettysburg and lay out the proposed soldiers' cemetery.[24]

Wills's carefully composed "circular letter," printed and dated August 12, 1863, stated that Pennsylvania had purchased a portion of the battlefield "to be devoted in perpetuity" for a soldiers' cemetery, that the dead would be buried in sections assigned to each state, that "the grounds would be tastefully laid out, and adorned with trees and shrubbery," and that the "whole expense," not to exceed $35,000, would be apportioned among the cooperating states — each "to be assessed according to its population, as indicated by its number of representatives in Congress." Wills closed his "circular letter" with a request, that each governor appoint "an agent" or commissioner in carrying out the reburial project.[25]

Wills also wrote a short personal note to accompany each "circular letter." This brief letter asked each governor if he desired "a conveyance, in fee simple," for his state's portion of the ground within the soldiers' national cemetery. Pennsylvania, Wills wrote, would be willing to make out a deed for it, otherwise she would "hold the title in trust for the purposes designated in the circular." He added a note of urgency. "It is desirable," he stated, "to have as little delay as possible in getting your reply, as the bodies of our soldiers are, in many cases, so much exposed as to require prompt attention, and the ground should be speedily arranged for their reception."[26]

Wills, conscientious and concerned, made another progress report to Governor Curtin on August 17. He was pleased that fifteen out of the seventeen governors had already responded, "pledging their state to unite in the movement." He reported on the exact location of the seventeen acres, "fronting on the Baltimore turnpike, and extending to the Taneytown road," which he had purchased for the soldiers' cemetery. Will explained: "It is the spot which should be specifically consecrated to this sacred purpose. It was here that such immense quantities of our artillery were massed, and during Thursday and Friday [July 2-3] of the battle, from this most important point on the field, dealt out death and destruction to the Rebel army in every direction of their advance."[27]

Pleased with the cooperation of the governors and their agents, Wills was most anxious to move ahead with the project. He felt, however, that it was not desirable to begin the reburials until November. "I think it would be showing only the proper respect for the health of this community not to commence the exhuming of the dead, and removal to the cemetery," he added, "and in the meantime the grounds should be artistically laid out, and consecrated by appropriate ceremonies."[28]

When William Saunders, charged with laying out the grounds, arrived in Gettysburg late in August, he called at Wills's home, and the two then followed the dusty pike southward to the top of Cemetery Hill. Saunders walked over the seventeen acres purchased for the cemetery, studying the high and low portions of the ground. He recommended that a monument be placed at the central point on the highest reach of ground and that the parcel allotted to each state run toward the common center, fitting together in a semicircular arrangement. Saunders promised the services of a government surveyor to mark off the twelve-foot wide semicircular parallels, allowing five feet for a walk between parallels and seven feet for each grave.[29]

Wills's reference to the "consecration" of the grounds by "appropriate ceremonies" caught Governor Curtin's attention, and the state's chief executive promptly wrote to his agent at Gettysburg to compliment him for his labors and to urge early consideration of an appropriate program. "The proper consecration of the grounds," he wrote to Wills, "must claim our early attention;

and, as soon as we can do so, our fellow purchasers should be invited to join with us in the performance of suitable ceremonies on the occasion."[30] Curtin, aware of past disagreements between Wills and representatives of Massachusetts, added words of advice, asking his agent to yield "in every reasonable way, to the wishes and suggestions, of the States who join with her [Pennsylvania] in dedicating a portion of her territory to the solemn uses of a National sepulchre:"[31] Massachusetts, it seemed, had wanted to rebury its own dead and had turned the grisly task over to a private contractor.[32] The earlier argument between Bay State representatives and Wills, whether the reburied soldiers should be segregated by state or interred "promiscuously," evidently encouraged Massachusetts to go off on a tangent.

Wills's quarrel with Massachusetts did not prevent him from inviting that state's most famous orator, Edward Everett, to be the chief speaker for the proposed ceremonies. When Wills had stated his preference to other state agents, they had endorsed the suggestion most enthusiastically. This endorsement permitted Wills to write to Everett that he was the unanimous choice of "the several States interested" as the orator at the proposed dedication of "the 23rd day of October next." "I am therefore instructed, by the Governors of the different States interested in this project," Wills stated, "to invite you cordially to join with them in the ceremonies, and to deliver the oration for the occasion."[33]

Earlier Wills had stated his preference to Curtin, and now he wrote to each of the other governors of the states expected to cooperate with Pennsylvania in the cemetery project. He reported that satisfactory progress had been made, that October 23 had been selected as the day for the consecration of the grounds, and that Edward Everett had been invited to give the day's oration. Wills hoped, of course, that all the governors could attend the ceremonies in person and help to dedicate the sacred soil.[34]

Edward Everett replied promptly to Wills's invitation to give the oration. Yes, he felt obliged to accept the invitation, regarding acceptance as "a duty." But other commitments plus the time needed to compose and memorize the oration would not permit him to agree to an earlier time "than the 19th of November."[35]

Everett rather than Wills, thus, set the date of the dedication of the cemetery grounds. The date was later than Wills wished, but if he wanted Everett as his orator, he had to shift the proposed date from October 23 to November 19 and gamble on the weather. "The time for the exercises," noted an observant editor, "have been delayed longer than was originally intended, in order to secure the services of Mr. Everett, whose engagements prevented him from attending at an earlier day."[36]

The change in date from October 23 to November 19 necessitated another round of letters to the governors.[37] The change in dates also made it necessary to start the reburial of the dead in the soldiers' cemetery before rather than after the dedication ceremonies. Consulting several of the state agents still in Gettysburg, Wills rewrote and finalized the "specifications" for the removal of the bodies of the Union soldiers from their scattered graves to the designated plots in the new cemetery and invited bids for that unpleasant chore. The "specifications" not only set standards for the procedure of exhuming the bodies, but limited the number of reburials to one hundred per day. Everything would be done with care and under close supervision. The bids must be submitted no later than October 22.[38]

In all, Wills received thirty-four bids. He opened these proposals during the evening of October 22, noting that the bids ranged from a low of $1.59 per body to a high of $8.00. He promptly awarded the contract to the lowest bidder, Frederick W. Biesecker, and instructed him to begin work the following Monday (October 26).[39] Wills also hired Samuel Weaver, a onetime photographer in Baltimore and Gettysburg, to oversee the exhumation and identification of the Union dead.[40] "This work is to begin immediately," wrote Wills's neighbor, "the Cemetery grounds having been appropriately laid out for the purpose."[41]

After awarding the bid to Biesecker, Wills wrote another progress report to his Governor. Biesecker's bid, he stated, was much lower than he had expected. Wills suggested that Pennsylvania pay for the reburials promptly and then bill each state involved in the project for its share. Most of the state agents with whom he had consulted were most pleased with the design of the grounds and the general plans. Soon it would be necessary to finalize "arrangements" for the consecration of the grounds. Wills concluded, " . . . and I wish to consult with you about them."[42]

Earlier, Wills had invited President Lincoln to be present and participate in the ceremonies.[43] He also intended to invite Vice President Hannibal Hamlin, all the members of Lincoln's cabinet, foreign ministers, and a large number of army generals. He wrote to Henry W. Longfellow, "the distinguished poet," asking him to compose an ode or dirge for the occasion.[44] He invited the Rev. Thomas Stockton, chaplain of the House of Representatives, to give the invocation and the Rev. Henry L. Baugher, president of the Gettysburg (Lutheran) Seminary to give the benediction. He contacted several musical organizations, including Birgfield's Band (Philadelphia), the National Brass Band (Washington), the Marine Band, and the Maryland Musical Association (Baltimore) to participate in the procession and program.[45]

Gettysburgers shared Wills's enthusiasm and some dreamt that a crowd of fifty thousand or more would attend the ceremonies and put their small city on the map. "It is expected," wrote one enthusiastic editor, "this will be one of the most imposing and interesting occasions ever witnessed in the United States."[46]

The days that followed were indeed busy ones for David Wills. On October 27, for instance, he attended a flag-raising on Round Top, more than three miles south of Gettysburg. That evening he held a conference with four state agents, several of whom were new arrivals. He explained his "operations and plans in relation to the cemetery grounds and the removal and burial of the dead."[47]

The next morning the agents accompanied Wills to that portion of the battlefield where Biesecker and his crew were exhuming bodies of soldiers, searching the clothing for clues of identification, and putting the decomposed remains in makeshift hearses to convey them to their final resting place. Next, Wills took his guests over that part of the battlefield where General John F. Reynolds had fallen, the victim of a sharpshooter's bullet. Then they retraced their steps and headed for Cemetery Hill "to witness the work going on there." In the afternoon, Wills accompanied Ohio's agent to the Hospital to attend the funeral of Enock M. Deddy, "the first of Ohio's braves" to be reburied in that portion of the soldiers' cemetery reserved for "that State's heroes." It was, incidently the first military funeral at the new cemetery. The affair, conducted with solemnity and decorum, impressed Ohio's state agent and intensified his respect for David Wills, and furthered that state's cooperation in the cemetery project.[48]

David Wills's selection of Ward H. Lamon, Lincoln's bodyguard and U.S. Marshal in the District of Columbia, to take charge of the civil portion of the procession and program proved to be a stroke of genius. In the first place, Lamon's concern for organization and detail would assure a smooth and well-planned operation. In the second place, it intensified Lincoln's interest in the project and practically assured his participation in the ceremonies, even though his son was ill, and he was busy with his annual message to Congress, several special proclamations, and other problems.

Although Lamon had orally assured Wills that President Lincoln would be glad to participate, the resourceful Gettysburger formalized the invitation. "I am authorized by the governors of the different States to invite you to be present," Wills wrote to the President, "and to participate in these ceremonies, which will doubtless be very imposing and solemnly impressive." In the next sentence Wills defined and delimited Lincoln's exact role: "It is the desire that, after the oration, you, as Chief Executive of the nation, formally set apart these gounds to their sacred use by a few appropriate remarks."[49]

Wills concluded a personal note with his formal invitation to the President. He not only expressed the wish that Lincoln could be present, but invited him to be his house guest, along with Edward Everett and Governor Curtin, saying that the hotels in the town would be "crowded and in confusion."[50]

While awaiting replies to his letters and invitations, the busy Gettysburger wrote a rather long report to Governor Curtin. Frederick H. Biesecker and his crew were exhuming and reburying "about sixty bodies daily." The task was in good hands. "It is done with the greatest care and under the strictest supervision," Wills stated, "so as to avoid the possibility of an error in the marked graves." Wills next listed many to whom invitations to attend the dedication ceremonies had been extended and expounded upon plans for both the procession and program. Railroad companies, urged to arrange for excursion trains, were busy with extensive arrangements to afford "proper traveling facilities" for "the immense concourse of people, which will assemble on this memorable day." Mistakenly, Wills supposed that most of the governors whose states had plots in the soldiers' cemetery would be present in person, with large delegations.[51]

Soon after Wills made his progress report to Governor Curtin, Ward H. Lamon arrived from Washington[52] to report that President Lincoln would attend the ceremonies and to finalize plans for the procession and ceremonies. Wills spent considerable time with Lamon ironing out the details. After several conferences, Lamon, as "chief marshal for the ceremonies," issued instructions regarding the dress and duties of his assistants and the order and arrangement of the procession.[53]

Wills's high hopes ebbed in the days which followed. Only a half dozen of the eighteen governors promised to attend the dedication. One or two of the railroad companies hedged on their commitments to run special or excursion trains. Generals George B. Meade and Winfield Scott, among others, sent regrets: Meade wrote of his "duties" and Scott complained of "infirmities."[54] Admiral Charles Stewart failed to receive his invitation on time.[55] Secretary of the Treasury Salmon P. Chase sent his regrets.[56] Longfellow declined to compose an appropriate ode or dirge for the occasion, saying that he was too busy. There were other regrets and disappointments.

As the 19th of November approached, the residents of Gettysburg became caught up in the excitement, aware that distinguished visitors would gather for a momentous event in a onetime sleepy city. Thousands of persons arrived in Gettysburg several days before the scheduled program of the 19th. Every house and shed and stable was turned into a lodging house.[57] Most of the early arrivals wished to tour the battlefield and every conceivable wheeled vehicle which could carry passengers was put into operation.

Edward Everett was the first of Wills's notable guests to arrive in Gettysburg, coming two days early so he could tour the battlefield and gain inspiration for his oration. Wills and Everett met Lincoln's special train which arrived shortly after dusk on the evening of the 18th, and were members of the cortege which escorted the President (and his colored servant William) to the house where he would spend the night. Wills showed Lincoln to his second-floor bedroom with its washbasin and pitcher of cold water. Telegraphic dispatches reported that Governor Curtin's special train was delayed because of a balky engine and would not arrive until about midnight.[58]

Mrs. Wills served a sumptuous supper to Lincoln, Everett and an array of other mealtime guests. During the supper a crowd collected in the public square in front of Wills's house. Later, the Fifth New York Artillery band and many in the milling crowd serenaded the President. Twice Lincoln left the table and the post-meal conversation to appear before the serenaders. The second time the President made a few rambling remarks, saying he had nothing to say in disorganized fashion.[59]

Later in the evening Lincoln retired to his room to rest and prepare for the morrow. Once Lincoln sent his colored servant to ask Wills for a pen and some paper. Later Lincoln again sent for Wills, this time asking his host to direct him to the house where William H. Seward was staying. In less than half an hour Lincoln returned from his meeting with his Secretary of State and retired for the night.[60]

Wills, meanwhile, greeted scores of callers while awaiting the belated arrival of Curtin's tardy train. Ward H. Lamon, Wills's right hand man, held

David Wills (of Gettysburg), central figure in the story of the soldiers' cemetery.

The Wills house where President Lincoln was a guest for the night of November 19, 1863. Lincoln's room, that night, was on the second floor — the right side of the house, fourth window from the left.

The Robert G. Harper house, where Secretary of State Seward and Benjamin B. French were overnight guests, is to the right of the Wills house.

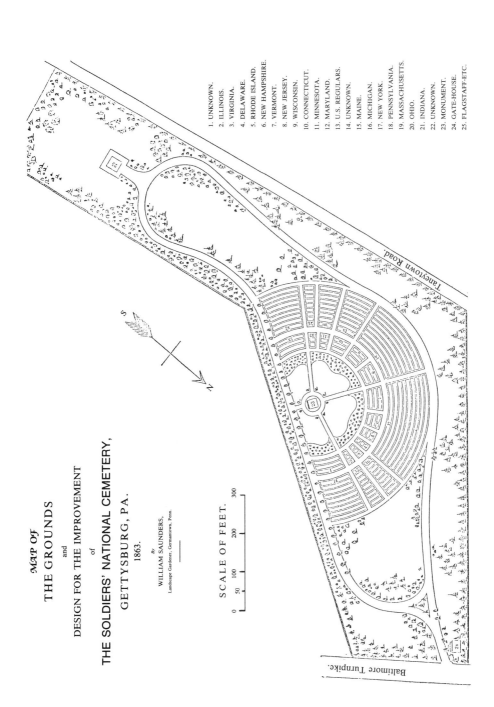

MAP OF
THE GROUNDS
and
DESIGN FOR THE IMPROVEMENT
of
THE SOLDIERS' NATIONAL CEMETERY,
GETTYSBURG, PA.
1863.

By
WILLIAM SAUNDERS,
Landscape Gardener, Germantown, Penn.

SCALE OF FEET.

0   50   100   200   300

1. UNKNOWN.
2. ILLINOIS.
3. VIRGINIA.
4. DELAWARE.
5. RHODE ISLAND.
6. NEW HAMPSHIRE.
7. VERMONT.
8. NEW JERSEY.
9. WISCONSIN.
10. CONNECTICUT.
11. MINNESOTA.
12. MARYLAND.
13. U.S. REGULARS.
14. UNKNOWN.
15. MAINE.
16. MICHIGAN.
17. NEW YORK.
18. PENNSYLVANIA.
19. MASSACHUSETTS.
20. OHIO.
21. INDIANA.
22. UNKNOWN.
23. MONUMENT.
24. GATE-HOUSE.
25. FLAGSTAFF-ETC.

Taneytown Road.

Baltimore Turnpike.

An artist's concept of Lincoln delivering his Gettysburg Address.

At Lincoln's right is Ward H. Lamon, marshal-in-chief of the day's program. John Hay, one of Lincoln's secretaries, sits behind Lamon. At Lincoln's left is Edward Everett, the day's orator. David Wills, organizer of the day's event, sits behind Everett. The artist is Lloyd Ostendorf and he gave his permission to reproduce this excellent drawing.

The Soldiers' National Monument at the central point of the cemetery. Tradition says that the platform on which Lincoln gave his address was located at the spot where the monument was later
erected. Four figures sit on the sides of the base; they are War, Peace, History, and Plenty. The
eighteen stars around the column represent the eighteen Northern States that lost sons in the Battle
of Gettysburg. The Goddess of Liberty stands majestically atop the monument.

a briefing session in the county courthouse for the "assistant marshals," giving them their assignments and instructions for the next day's affair.[61]

It was nearly midnight when a creaky engine pulled a half dozen passenger cars, including one for Governor Curtin and his guests, into the fringes of Gettysburg. Aides directed Curtin to Wills's house where the busy host then showed his last guest to his room. It was well after midnight before the last lamp was extinguished and restless sleep overtook the distinguished guests.

During the early hours of the morning of the 19th a shower or two dampened the ground and settled the dust. But before eight o'clock the skies cleared and the sun shone in autumnal splendor.[62] Special trains continued to arrive at the depot, discharging passengers who swelled the crowd in Gettysburg to "immense proportions." A local editor observed, "The streets swarmed with people from all sections of the Union, the number variously estimated from twenty to fifty thousand."[63]

The milling mass of humanity occupied every foot of each downtown street, making it difficult for Lamon and his assistant marshals, on horseback, to organize the procession. Each of Wills's three famous guests, meanwhile, pursued his own course. After an early breakfast, Lincoln and Seward took a bumpy ride around the Seminary grounds on a buckboard. Everett and several Massachusetts men took a leisurely walk over the surrounding countryside, the orator of the day still seeking the inspiration he had failed to find during earlier journeys over the fields. Curtin, last of the guests to arise, listened to Wills's account of his stewardship, trials and tribulations as well as successes and satisfactions.

Shortly before ten o'clock, the scheduled time for the procession to begin its trek southward to the top of Cemetery Hill, Lincoln emerged from the Wills house. He was dressed in black, wearing a frock coat and his well-known stovepipe hat, which had a wide mourning band around it. He carried white gauntlets or riding gloves. Scores of acquaintances and strangers stopped by to shake hands or exchange greetings. Even after the President belatedly mounted his "splendid black steed," scores stopped to offer best wishes and ask friendly questions, delaying the formation of the procession.

It was close to eleven o'clock before the impatient marshals put the show on the road. The Marine Band and a military escort led the way. Wills marched with the state agents or commissioners like a mother hen watching over her flock. Curtin shepherded the visiting governors and played the gracious host. Lincoln "rode easily, bowing to the right and left." Everett was not in the procession, for he had not yet returned from his morning tour of the battlefield.

It took more than an hour to seat the distinguished guests on chairs cluttering up the $12' \times 20'$ platform. The President, as the nation's chief mourner, sat in the middle of the front row, with Edward Everett to his right, and Secretary of State Seward to his left. Curtin, official host for the occasion — Wills had done the work and performed the responsibilities in the Governor's name — occupied the chair next to Seward. Wills supervised the comfort of the state agents while Lamon, serving as master of ceremonies, chose a place on the left side of the platform.

Wills, hopeful that the program would go off smoothly and impress the many who had assembled to honor the dead, watched and listened intently. Birgfield's Band, sponsored by the Philadelphia Union League, opened the formal program with a grand funeral march. Next the Rev. Thomas H. Stockton gave the invocation, "a prayer which thought it was an oration." The Marine Band performed next, playing Luther's hymn "Old Hundred."[64]

As the echoes of the music drifted toward the nearby hills, Ward H. Lamon introduced the orator of the occasion. Everett held the rapt attention of the vast audience but briefly as he recited his story about "the battles of Gettysburg." As he orated into the second hour the audience grew restless, and many who had formed the fringe of the crowd wandered off[65] to visit sections of the grounds consecrated by soldiers' blood. Lincoln listened intently while Seward, bothered by the bright sun, sat with his arms folded and his hat "drawn down over his eyes."[66]

After Everett, rather exhausted from his two-hour ordeal, finished with a flourish and returned to his chair, Lincoln, Seward, and Curtin offered their hands as a gesture of courtesy. Everett's speech did not scour. It was too long. It was merely a detailed account of the various battles which made up the whole, recited without emotion or imagination.

The crowd shuffled restlessly while the twelve members of the Maryland Musical Association chanted an original number written for the occasion by Benjamin B. French. It spoke of "holy ground," "our glorious dead" and "Freedom's holy cause," thrilling the audience and recreating interest in the program.

As the applause for French's words and the chant in unison gave way to expectation, Lamon introduced "the President of the United States." Wills watched apprehensively as Lincoln unwound himself from his uncomfortable chair, stepped toward the front of the platform, and delivered those "few appropriate remarks." The crowd, responding to Lincoln's inspirational words, interrupted five times with applause and complimented him with "tremendous applause" when he finished his address. Then the responsive crowd gave three cheers for Lincoln and three more for the governors.[67]

Wills who had shaped the program and invited all the participants, knew that only two numbers remained. He listened as a chorus of Gettysburgers, both men and women, sang a doleful dirge and then the Rev. Henry L. Baugher, head of the local seminary, ended the formal program with a brief benediction.

Marshal Ward H. Lamon stepped forward to announce that the formal program was over, but he invited all who were interested to hear the Hon. Charles Anderson, Lieutenant Governor-elect of Ohio, deliver an address at the Presbyterian church at five o'clock.[68]

After a battery of the Fifth New York Artillery fired a salute of eight rounds, the military portion of the mourning procession reformed and escorted the President back to the Wills house while the civilian portion dispersed in all directions.[69]

It was nearly three o'clock in the afternoon when President Lincoln, orator Everett, and Governor Curtin arrived back at the Wills house in Gettysburg. Mrs. Wills supervised the serving of a well-planned meal for "a very large company." Wills then transformed his house into a reception center, placing Lincoln in the hall opening on York Street where he greeted guests as they entered and placing Governor Curtin at the door fronting on the public square to shake the guests' hands as they were leaving.

At the conclusion of the reception, President Lincoln, flanked by Secretary of State Seward and John L. Burns, an aged civilian who had fought with the Union troops in the great battle, walked to the Presbyterian church to take in the "Ohio program." After the program Lincoln returned to the Wills house to pick up his carpetbag and express his personal thanks before going to the railroad depot to board the presidential special and return to Washington. Later Governor Curtin's special departed for Harrisburg and other excursion trains departed for their diverse destinations.

The hubbub and excitement of the day gave way to silence and solitude. "All is now quiet in the streets of Gettysburg," a newspaperman observed shortly before midnight, "the imposing ceremonies of the day having been completed in admirable order and without being marred in any respect."[70]

David Wills received accolades for a job well done, his program proving to be a memorable one. Editor Robert G. Harper of the *Adams County Sentinel* characterized the activities of the 19th "a perfect success," lauding the "systematic arrangements, the beautiful order which prevailed throughout the ceremonies."[71] Even the Democratic editor of the Gettysburg *Compiler*, fearing that Republicans might use the ceremonies for political gain, had only praise for David Wills and the dedication program.[72]

Wills's responsibilities did not end when Everett returned to Boston, Curtin to Harrisburg, and Lincoln to Washington. Biesecker and his crew, who had suspended operations on the 19th, returned to their gruesome task the next day. On November 25, Samuel Weaver, who supervised the exhumations and reburials, reported that 1285 bodies had been transferred to the new cemetery, "If the weather remains favorable," he wrote to his brother, "I think that I can have them all sent in by the first of Jan[uary]."[73]

Early in December, Wills wrote a final round of letters to the cooperating governors. He set December 17 as the meeting date of the "commissioners" of the new cemetery, expressing the hope that each of the eighteen states would have representatives present at the Jones House in Harrisburg to devise "a plan for the protection and preservation of the grounds near Gettysburg," provide for expenses already incurred, complete the work already begun, and arrange for the proper adornment and care of the grounds.[74]

On December 17 twelve commissioners representing ten states met in Harrisburg. As the first order of business, these representatives formally organized the soldiers' cemetery association with Wills as president and W. Yates Selleck of Wisconsin as secretary. The commissioners adopted five resolutions, all concerned with the completion and operation of the cooperative "Soldiers' National Cemetery." One commissioner then introduced a resolution which provided for the appointment of a committee "to procure designs of a monument to be erected in the cemetery." After the resolution was adopted unanimously, Wills appointed a five-member committee to implement the proposal.[75]

The failure of ten states to have commissioners present at the December 17 meeting made it necessary for Wills to write letters of information to their governors. Wills reported that 2271 reburials had been made, and he enclosed a copy of the proceedings of the commission which had met in Harrisburg two days earlier. He again begged the delinquent governors to appoint a trustee to the board charged with managing the new soldiers' cemetery.[76]

The approach of freezing weather nullified Samuel Weaver's hopes to have the interments completed before the end of the year. Biesecker and his grave diggers had to wait until the bleak winter had passed and the frozen ground had thawed before they could return to their grisly task. The Biesecker-Weaver duo completed their work on March 18, 1864, and reported that 3354 reburials had been tabulated — in addition, a private contractor reburied 158 Massachusetts soldiers. "And I here most conscientiously assert," Weaver wrote to Wills with an air of finality, "that I firmly believe that there has not been a single mistake made in the removal of the soldiers to the cemetery by taking the body of a rebel for a Union soldier."[77]

The completion of the reburials in the early spring of 1864 served as an excuse for David Wills to write a long report on his role in the establishment of the Soldiers' National Cemetery. "The estimated expenses of finishing the cemetery are $63,500," Wills stated, "and it is proposed to divide this sum among the different States having lots in the cemetery, in the ratio of their representation in Congress." He concluded with the hope that the state legislature would indemnify his work and fulfil the state's commitment to the project, so it could be completed and the grounds cared for fully.[78]

In time, the special committee that Wills had appointed on December 17 approved the design of a proposed monument, a sixty foot high memorial consisting of a massive pedestal twenty-five feet square at the base and crowned with a colossal statue representing the Genius of Liberty. Wills witnessed the laying of the cornerstone of this national monument on July 4, 1865, knowing that his two-year responsibility as Curtin's agent was about at an end.

David Wills lived to see his dream come true. His wish to transform a portion of the battlefield, consecrated by the blood of brave men, into a national cemetery reached fruition. The cemetery is as much a memorial to David Wills of Gettysburg as it is a burial ground for those whom Lincoln called "these honored dead."

CHAPTER II

WARD H. LAMON AND THE DEDICATION OF THE SOLDIERS' CEMETERY AT GETTYSBURG*

Ward H. Lamon's relationship with President Abraham Lincoln gave him the opportunity to play an important role in the dedication of the soldiers' cemetery at Gettysburg on November 19, 1863. Serving as Marshal-in-Chief for the day's events, Lamon supervised the procession which preceded the program and then served as master of ceremonies aboard the 12 ' × 20 ' platform during the dedication exercises.

Lamon's acquaintanceship with Lincoln dated back to the autumn of 1847. Earlier that year, the twenty-one-year-old Lamon left his home in Berkeley County, Virginia, and emigrated to Danville, Vermilion County, Illinois. One day at the county courthouse, John T. Stuart introduced Lamon to Lincoln. The two promptly exchanged quips and banter in a friendly fashion. After Lincoln learned that the former Virginian also possessed antislavery views, the acquaintanceship blossomed into a friendship. "Until the day of his death," Lamon later wrote, "it was my pleasure and good fortune to retain his confidence unshaken, as he retained my affection unbroken."[1]

Recognizing Lincoln's courtroom capabilities, Lamon promptly developed a working relationship with him, even though Lincoln was eighteen years his senior. Later Lamon stated, "I was his local partner, first in Danville, and afterward in Bloomington. We rode the circuit together, traveling by buggy in the dry seasons and on horse-back in bad weather, there being no railroads then in that part of the State."[2] Lamon's marriage to the daughter of Stephen T. Logan, Lincoln's law partner at that time, cemented their friendship. Both Lincoln and Lamon were good storytellers, the former appreciating the latter's quaint accent. Both excelled in the art of applying old anecdotes to new situations. In addition, Lamon had a good voice, especially suited to singing sad ballads. Lamon often sang at Lincoln's prodding, a favorite being a ballad entitled "Twenty Years Ago."

---

*Reprinted (with permission) from *Civil War History*, 31 (December, 1985), pp. 293-308.

Yet, in a way, the two gave substance to the old saying that opposites attract. Lamon was stout, most handsome, and possessed of a swashbuckling air; Lincoln was tall, lean, nearly ugly, and modest in a strange way. Lamon was an extrovert, Lincoln an introvert. Lamon was both a boozer and brawler; Lincoln preached temperance and was gentle and soft-hearted. It was said that Lamon spent more time in a downstairs barroom than in his upstairs law office. Anyway, both enjoyed life on the circuit and the repartee and storytelling which took place around the wood stoves in the boardinghouses and inns.

Later, Lamon worked for Lincoln's nomination at the Chicago-based Repubican national convention of 1860. In fact, Lamon is sometimes credited with printing an extra set of tickets for some of the seats inside the Wigwam and filling them with Lincoln supporters while William H. Seward's supporters paraded outdoors.

After the election, Lamon became president-elect Lincoln's unofficial bodyguard. He accompanied Lincoln on the long train trip from Springfield to Washington. On that strange midnight ride from Baltimore to Washington, amidst rumors of an assassination plot, Lamon was constantly at Lincoln's side, armed with two revolvers, two pistols, and two big knives.

Soon after the inauguration, the president gave Lamon a fancy title, "United States Marshal for the District of Columbia."[3] Although Lincoln occasionally sent Lamon on special missions, the impressive-looking marshal was usually handy and constantly concerned with the president's safety. At White House receptions, Marshal Lamon always stood at Lincoln's left, closer to the entrance door, keeping a watchful eye upon all visitors as they stood in the reception line.

Lamon developed an interesting circle of friends — most of whom would be involved in the dedication of the soldiers' cemetery at Gettysburg. One was Benjamin B. French, whom the president appointed Commissioner of Public Buildings. French's and Lamon's paths crossed often, especially when French acquired books for the library in the executive mansion or when he had unpleasant encounters with a very demanding first lady. Another was Judge Joseph Casey, a former congressman from Pennsylvania whom Lincoln had appointed as the first chief justice of the reorganized court of claims. Casey, too, was a good storyteller and his close ties to Gov. Andrew G. Curtin of Pennsylvania served Lincoln in good stead. Then there was John W. Forney — Secretary of the U.S. Senate, newspaper owner (the *Philadelphia Press* and the *Washington Chronicle*), and Lincoln disciple. Forney, like Lamon, drank his whiskey straight and enjoyed sentimental and bawdy ballads as well as companionship and repartee. There were others like Solomon Newton Pettis and John Van Riswick; both had been political appointees and lived in Washington. It was Van Riswick who earlier had pressured Lincoln to name Lamon as United States Marshal for the District of Columbia. All five accompanied Lamon to Gettysburg for the dedication ceremonies, several serving as aides.[4]

After Union victories at Gettysburg and Vicksburg enhanced Lincoln's re-election possibilities, Lamon's original plan had been to return to Illinois in

mid-November 1863 in order to bring his wife to Washington. This plan suffered a setback when Lamon received a letter from David Wills, the Gettysburg
citizen most responsible for the establishment of a soldiers' cemetery out of
a portion of the famous battlefield. Wills, at the direction of Governor Curtin,
also was responsible for planning the dedication program, asking the famous
orator Edward Everett to give the day's oration and inviting President Lincoln
to "formally set apart" the grounds "by a few appropriate remarks." In his
letter, Wills asked Lincoln's bodyguard to serve as Marshal-in-Chief on
November 19, acting as a supervisor of the procession preceding the program
and as master of ceremonies aboard the platform. "We have agreed upon you,"
Wills stated in his letter to Lamon, "as the proper person, and therefore extend to you an invitation to act as Marshal . . . on that day." Wills asked for
an early reply and expressed the hope that Lamon would "feel it his duty" to
accept the invitation.[5]

Vacillating between his personal wants and a civic responsibility, Lamon
took his problem to Lincoln. "He came to me," the president wrote several
days later to Lamon's father-in-law, "and I told him I thought that in view
of his relation to the government and to me, he could not well decline."[6]

After accepting the assignment, Lamon set to work with a will. He prepared
a printed letter which invited all U.S. marshals in the eastern half of the country to be his assistants on November 19, helping to organize and direct the
"gigantic procession" which would trek from Gettysburg to the cemetery site
atop a hill half a mile south of the city.[7] Then Lamon wrote to every one of
the eighteen Northern governors whose states had lost sons at Gettysburg; he
asked each to appoint two assistant marshals who would help to organize and
supervise the planned procession. Lamon must have been disappointed that so
many of the U.S. marshals turned down his invitation to serve as his assistants
and that so many of the eighteen governors failed to acknowledge his request.
In several cases the governors had good excuses, for they did not receive Lamon's
request until it was too late to act or until after the ceremonies were over.[8]

There were other responsibilities. Lamon received permission from three
different telegraph companies to frank messages relating to the dedication of
the Gettysburg cemetery. The president of the Western Telegraph Company,
for example, notified his superintendent: "We take pleasure to do Mr. Lamon's
business free."[9]

There was a need to obtain more horses than the one hundred that Wills
promised to have available in Gettysburg. At Lamon's request, Brig. Gen.
George H. Stoneman authorized the sending of thirty horses from camps around
Washington to Gettysburg — providing that Lamon provide the transportation. It was then necessary to contact military units to participate in the procession. Some generals not only promised to provide military units, but gave Lamon
advice. Arguing that military units should lead the procession, one general wrote,
"The Military placed in advance gives *effect* and ensures more *regularity* . . . and
on this occasion it would be particularly appropriate."[10]

Two weeks before the dates of the dedication, Lamon received a progress report from Wills, who wrote that he anticipated a "tremendous crowd" and "an impressive procession," with many dignitaries participating. An army quartermaster assured Wills that the one hundred horses, promised earlier, would be available. Railroad companies were scheduling excursion trains "for the transportation of the people." Wills ended his letter by asking Lamon to come to Gettysburg several days in advance of the dedication date. Would Lamon prefer a room in a hotel or in a private house?[11]

Lamon recruited Benjamin B. French as his first assistant and the two left Washington on November 13 for Gettysburg and a meeting with David Wills, where they learned some of the problems facing the organizer. Henry Wadsworth Longfellow had turned down Wills's invitation to compose a special hymn or ode for the dedication program. French, imaging himself to be a poet of sorts, offered to compose an ode that very night and present it to Wills the next morning. Then Wills turned the discussion in the direction of plans for the procession. They decided to organize the procession into three sections: the military force (including infantry, cavalry, and artillery units as well as the Marine Band), the Marshal-in-Chief's contingent (including the dignitaries), and the civic group (including fraternal and civic organizations, as well as ordinary citizens).[12]

Lamon and Wills decided to put the principals upon horses rather than in carriages; perhaps the fact that Lincoln's bodyguard was a good horseman may have had something to do with that decision. Lamon also decided to put his many assistant marshals and aides on horseback, supposedly giving them a better chance to carry out their responsibilites. In addition, he devised a distinctive uniform or dress code for his assistants:

1. Plain black suit (preferably a frock coat), black hat, and white gloves.

2. White satin scarf, five inches wide, to be worn over the right shoulder and carried across the breast and back to the left hip, and there fastened with a rosette, the ends to be fringed, and to extend to the knee. At the center on the shoulder the scarf would be gathered and mounted with a rosette.

3. Rosette, four inches and raised in center to be made of black and white ribbon, the outer circle only to be white.

4. Rosette of red, white, and blue on left breast. The initials of a state in center for identification. The saddle cloths on their horses, of white cambric bordered with black.[13]

On Monday, November 16, Lamon was back in Washington. He recruited nine friends as aides, ensuring a free train trip to Gettysburg for them.[14]

That evening Lamon met with his newly recruited aides and others interested in going to Gettysburg. In a room at the city hall, Judge Silas Carey presided and Col. John H. Puleston served as secretary. Lamon, of course, pulled the strings. He told the assemblage that the president of the Baltimore & Ohio Railroad had placed "a special car" at his disposal "free of charge." The North

Central Railroad, Judge Carey added, had also promised "a special car" for the second leg of the journey, from Baltimore to Hanover Junction. No arrangements had been made as yet for the final part of the trip from Hanover Junction to Gettysburg; negotiations, however, were in progress. Lamon promised to have all travel details verified and posted in his office by eleven o'clock the next morning. He circulated a paper headed "The undersigned wish to signify their intention of accompanying Marshal Lamon to Gettysburg tomorrow — leaving this city at the hour named."[15]

The Baltimore & Ohio train, with Lamon's special car attached, was fifteen minutes late in leaving the Washington depot. It arrived in Baltimore at one o'clock in the afternoon. The occupants of the special car then repaired to the Eutaw House for a sumptuous dinner, served with the compliments of the president of the Baltimore & Ohio Railroad company. At three o'clock that afternoon Lamon and his group entrained for Hanover Junction in a special car provided by the North Central Railroad company. The travelers were detained in Hanover Junction before the railroad company provided a train for their use on the Gettysburg spur.[16] Eventually the train reached Gettysburg and the travel-weary members of Lamon's party sought quarters for the night. Lamon took a room at the Eagle Hotel, not far from the Wills's house where quarters had been reserved for President Lincoln.

On the next day, November 18, most of Lamon's friends and aides toured various parts of the vast battlefield. Lamon had work to do. He met with David Wills to finalize plans for the procession and programs. Horses needed to be assigned to the principals and some special arrangements had to be made for Edward Everett — he wanted to make the trip from Gettysburg to Cemetery Hill by carriage, and he wanted a tent set up adjacent to the platform being built for the program. Tickets also had to be provided for those who would have reserved places atop the platform, and seating arrangements had to be determined, especially for the three front rows of ten chairs each.[17]

They took time from their attention to details to attend a flag-raising in the center of the village square. Citizens of Gettysburg had erected a sixty-foot flagpole, and a large audience gathered to watch as a huge flag was hoisted to the very top to unfurl in a gentle breeze.

Lamon, along with Wills and Edward Everett, met President Lincoln's special train when it arrived about dusk at the depot in Gettysburg. Assisted by an army unit (the First Regiment of the Invalid Corps), the three escorted the president to the Wills's house where he would spend the night. Later in the evening, Lamon held a briefing session for his aides and assistant marshals in a room at the courthouse. He explained their duties and responsibilities and specified on what street corners each state's delegation was supposed to gather. The military portion of the procession, Lamon explained, would gather along Carlisle Street, north of the public square, and the civic portion on York Street.[18] Benjamin B. French, Lamon's first assistant, helped with the details. With all of the instructions spelled out, little more was to be done before retiring for the night and hoping for good weather for the next day's activities.

Thursday, November 19, dawned bright and clear, the rising sun aglow with life and warmth on this fine fall day. The early morning frost disappeared as the sun's rays warmed the autumn air. The city of three thousand souls came to life, with hundreds of visitors already present and thousands more streaming toward the center of a web of country roads and well-traveled turnpikes. "At an early hour, long before sunrise," a newspaperman reported, "the roads leading to Gettysburg were crowded by citizens from every quarter thronging into the village in every kind of vehicle — old Pennsylvania wagons, spring wagons, carts, family carriages, buggies, and more fashionable modern vehicles, all crowded with citizens — kept pouring into the town in one continual string, while the roads were constantly dotted with pedestrians by twos, by threes, singly, in companies, all facing towards the village." Meanwhile, "the railroads disgorged their eager crowds, while the streets ever filling, overflowed with the invading host."[19]

Apprehensive, Lamon arose at dawn. After an early breakfast at the Eagle Hotel, he walked over to the Wills's house, anxious about the president's welfare and desirous of meeting with Wills to iron out last-minute details. The huge flag atop the sixty-foot flagpole was lowered to half-mast.

When Lamon arrived at the Wills's house, he learned that Lincoln was still upstairs in his room with his personal secretary, John G. Nicolay, who was making a morning call to see if his services were needed.[20] Soon the two came downstairs, and Secretary of State William H. Seward, who had spent the night at a neighbor's house, also arrived to pay a call. Seward and Lamon spoke briefly with the president. Soon after, Lincoln and his Secretary of State left for a morning carriage ride. They drove over to the area of the Lutheran church and seminary where the fighting had raged hottest on the first day of the three-day battle; there Maj. Gen. John F. Reynolds had fallen, victim of a sharpshooter's bullet. Lamon, meanwhile, had a morning conference with David Wills.

After Lamon came out of the Wills's house, he met and conferred with some of his aides and assistant marshals. All were dressed in the distinctive garb that Marshal-in-Chief Lamon had earlier prescribed. All were anxious to secure their mounts and transform the rapidly growing crowd into a procession.

After returning from his carriage ride, President Lincoln went back to his second-floor room to dress for the occasion. He emerged from the Wills's house at about ten o'clock, the hour the procession was supposed to form and take off on its southward journey. The president was dressed in black, with a frock coat and a stovepipe hat which had a wide mourning band about it — in memory of his son Willie who had died the previous year in the White House. Lincoln carried white gauntlets or riding gloves. He seemed to be sad and serious, perhaps concerned with his day's responsibilities.[21]

When Lincoln came out of the Wills's house, the huge crowd that had been gathering in the central square came to life. Those who sighted the president greeted him with "three hearty cheers." Scores tried to crowd around him, either to shake his hand or gawk at him. Someone called for three cheers for "Father Abraham" — they were given with a will. Soon after, some Republican party member, injecting partisanship into the affair, called for three cheers for "the next president of the United States." Again the crowd responded with alacrity and "with no less enthusiasm." As things were starting to get out of hand, with the president becoming a prisoner of the mob, Lamon came to Lincoln's rescue. Serving again as the president's bodyguard, Lamon ordered the crowd back in a loud and firm voice. He asked Lincoln to mount his horse, hoping it would be easier to isolate the president from friends and from the curious. The strategy failed to bring order. An observant reporter described the scene: "In the meanwhile the President had mounted and was besieged by an eager crowd thronging around him, and anxious for the pleasure of taking him by the hand, while he sat pleasantly enjoying the hearty welcome thus spontaneously accorded, until the marshals, having mercy on his oft-wrung arm and weary exertions, caused the crowd to desist and allow the President to sit in peace upon his horse. But the people, not yet satisified, must have another three cheers for honest Old Abe, and they fairly eclipsed all the others." Lincoln, looking out over the countryside and talking to his three cabinet members and to Marshal Lamon, remarked that he was surprised that the cultivated areas were so expansive and the forested areas so small in number.[22]

Finally, about 10:30 in the morning, Lamon's assistant marshals began the procession when the military units, led by the Marine Band, moved southward along the road toward Cemetery Hill. Then came a squadron of cavalry, two batteries of artillery, and a regiment of infantry.

Lamon, bedecked in his colorful costume, led the marshal's section. A newspaperman described the scene: "Next came Marshal-in-Chief, Ward H. Lamon, Esq., and his numerous staff of Aides, wearing yellow and white scarfs, with tri-colored rosettes on the breast, and black and white shoulder knots." President Lincoln, "riding easily," was flanked by three members of his cabinet and by Nicolay. An observer wrote, "I must do the President justice to say that his awkwardness, which is so often remarked, does not extend to his horsemanship."[23] Other notables included several generals, nine governors, several members of Congress, three foreign ministers, members of the cemetery commission, and some guests of honor. Edward Everett was not in the procession; he was somewhere touring the battlefield and still seeking inspiration for his oration.

The civic portion, far and away the largest, included citizens of the eighteen states involved in the cemetery project as well as fraternal and benevolent orders and service and civic organizations. "Pennsylvania furnished the largest numerical representation," a newspaperman wrote, "Ohio next, Wisconsin third, and Massachusetts fourth." Lamon deserved some of the credit for "the impressive sight." Everything was in perfect order as "the military mass rolled on as waves of the ocean."[24]

When the military units reached the dedication site, they formed lines, both to salute the president as he passed and to protect him from the crowd. Escorted by Lamon, Lincoln walked slowly toward the speaker's platform. He was received by the enormous crowd "with marked respect and a perfect silence due to the solemnity of the occasion, every man among the immense gathering uncovering at his appearance."[25]

WARD HILL LAMON

Lamon served as President Lincoln's bodyguard with a colonelcy in hand and the fancy title United States Marshal for the District of Columbia. He was Marshal-in-Chief during the procession and master of ceremonies during the three-hour dedication program.

The procession started on its southward trek from Gettysburg to Cemetery Hill. Matthew Brady took this picture and it is in the Brady Collection, Library of Congress.

Lamon escorted the president up the steps, located at the front of the platform, to the extreme left. Lincoln, the governors, and others on the platform had a chance to visit while the tail-end of the procession reached the hilltop and thousands in the audience formed a half-circle in front of the stand. Eventually, Lamon directed Lincoln toward the front-row chair reserved for him.

Lamon and Wills had decided earlier who would occupy each of the ten front-row chairs. Everett, as the honored orator of the day, would sit at Lincoln's right, then two clergymen and Benjamin B. French and William Saunders. Each of the clergymen was scheduled to offer a prayer, one the invocation, the other the benediction. French not only was Lamon's first assistant for the day's affair, he was also the author of an ode that would be recited by a choral group. Saunders was the Washington-based landscape gardener who had planned the cemetery, laying out the plots, rows, and parallels in a half-circle pattern.

Lamon and Wills had reserved the chair at Lincoln's left for Secretary of State Seward. The three chairs to Seward's left would be occupied by three governors — Curtin, Horatio Seymour of New York, and David Tod of Ohio. Governor Curtin, in reality, was the host of the whole affair. Governor Seymour, a Democrat, had earlier argued with President Lincoln over draft quotas and there was a need to regain his good will. Governor Tod earned Lamon's favor by sponsoring a special train from Columbus to Pennsylvania; furthermore, Ohioans had organized a special afternoon program in downtown Gettysburg.[26]

Chairs were reserved for others including six more governors, four generals, three foreign ministers or secretaries, two other cabinet members, Everett's daughter and son-in-law, and nine of Lamon's aides.[27] Lamon, as master of ceremonies, preempted a spot where the steps led up to the left front corner of the platform.

Three or four bands took turns playing appropriate music while everyone awaited the start of the formal program and the arrival of the orator of the day. After Everett returned to the Wills's house from a leisurely walk over a part of the battlefield, he found a carriage ready to take him to the site of the new cemetery. When the carriage arrived atop Cemetery Hill and near the assembled audience, Everett dismounted and walked over to a tent which had been set up at his request near the back of the platform.[28] Like a true Boston Brahmin, he took his time resting and refreshing himself while the assembled throng waited and all else was in readiness.

When Everett finally emerged from his tent, David Wills and Governor Seymour went down to meet him and escort him to the chair at Lincoln's right. Everyone on the platform stood up as the aging orator, seventy winters old, walked slowly to be greeted by the president and take his allotted chair.

It was past time for the program to begin. Marshal-in-Chief Lamon stepped forward to read some regrets. Gen. Winfield Scott had written that "increasing infirmities" made it impossible to attend. Gen. George G. Meade had written that his army had "duties to perform" that demanded his full time and attention. Secretary of the Treasury Salmon P. Chase had used the excuse of "imperative public duties."[29]

Lamon was away from his place on the platform when it was time to begin the formal program, so his first assistant (Benjamin B. French) instructed Birgfield's Band to play its "introductory dirge." Next, Lamon, having returned to the platform, motioned to Rev. Thomas H. Stockton, chaplain of the House of Representatives in Washington, that he should arise and present the invocation. Reverend Stockton recited an overly long and highly emotional opening prayer — one writer characterized it as "a prayer which thought it was an oration." It brought tears to many eyes and neither Everett nor Lincoln made an effort to hide their emotions.[30]

After Reverend Stockton's long invocation ended, Lamon instructed the Marine Band to play; it responded with Luther's hymn "Old Hundred," "in all its grand and sublime beauty."[31]

Lamon, back on his spot on the platform, stepped forward to introduce the orator of the day. After the introduction, there was a tense moment. "Some idiot in the crowd," a reporter noted, "at once proposed three cheers for Everett, which the good sense of the people decided to irreverent upon such an occasion that no one responded, and Mr. Idiot subsided."[32]

Everett, sensing that his audience was ready and waiting, began his two-hour recitation. Although he delivered it "with his accustomed grace," the topic was dull, dealing in the main with the strategy and tactics of the half dozen separate battles which had made up the whole. It was "smooth and cold," but lacking "one stirring thought, one vivid picture, one thrilling appeal." Another observer added a similar evaluation: "Everett's Gettysburg affair was painfully cold . . . with no sunbeam warmth. He seemed the hired mourner — the laureate chanting a funeral dirge to order, with no touch of 'in memoriam' about it. His monument was an iron statue with no glow or pulse or passion in it."[33]

President Lincoln, with his "thoughtful, kindly, care-worn face," listened intently. Secretary of State Seward, with "a wiry face" and "bushy, beetling eyebrows," sat "with his arms tightly folded and his hat drawn down over his eyes" — the day's bright sun bothered him. Reverend Stockton, "with lips as white as the wasted cheek" and with flowing white hair and chin whiskers, sat "impassively."[34] It must have been difficult for Marshal-in-Chief Lamon and others on the platform to keep their eyes and minds from wandering.

The scene itself was an impressive one. The audience surrounding the platform "stretched away in the distance, far out of the range of possible hearing." Many in the crowd were bedecked in mourning. For these people it was "a sad pilgrimage" to a place where loved ones had fallen. Military officers on horseback added distinction to the crowd. Lamon's assistants clad in their colorful dress provided "a pleasing variety to the scene." Then there were the members of the various fraternal organizations, dressed in their regalia. The multitude of banners, flags, and devices of regiments, associations, or delegations produced "a blending and contrast of colors highly pleasing to behold." Prominent in the foreground was a beautiful in memoriam banner held aloft by a group of forty soldiers from an army hospital in York, Pennsylvania. All had been wounded in the Battle of Gettysburg and all felt the emotion of the hour, for they were revisiting the ground where their comrades had fallen. Their banner drew much attention and interest. On one side was an urn and the inscription "Honor to our brave comrades;" on the other side were the words "In memory of those who fell at Gettysburg, July 1st, 2d, and 3d, 1863."[35]

Scattered over the landscape were thousands of sightseers, some of whom had wandered off from the fringe of Everett's audience — some bored with his lengthy oration and others despairing of obtaining a place within hearing distance of the speaker's voice. They were satisfying their curiosity and expressing their sentiments and sorrow in their own way.[36]

Those whose eyes wandered toward the horizon witnessed a grand sight. To the north lay Gettysburg, deserted but flag bedecked. The huge U.S. flag, half-mast on the sixty-foot flagpole, reacted to a gentle breeze. Stretching in every direction were the fields and farms and roads where many soldiers, whether clad in blue or gray, had died.

About a quarter-mile west of Gettysburg one could see the edifice of Pennsylvania College, a Lutheran seminary, and the steeple of an adjacent church. The seminary was "a chaste specimen of the Doric order," one hundred and fifty feet in length.[37] Near there the first day's fighting had raged hottest, and the Iron Brigade, on its way to becoming a legend, had been decimated.

Those on the platform who looked northeastward could see Culp's Hill, "precious in history." To the east lay valleys and hilltops which had been spared the destruction of battle. To the south, in the hazy distance, stood the victory-crowned summits of Big Round Top and Little Round Top. A sixty-foot flagpole on Big Round Top had its flag at the very top — someone had forgotten to put it at half-mast. Far to the west one could see the distant outlines of South Mountain, forming part of a dimly defined frame for the whole picture. The lofty chain of mountains swept northward and then eastward, forming the western and northern boundaries of Adams County.

Attention centered on orator Everett again as he closed his two-hour oration, blaming slavery for the war and treason for the nation's troubles. He seemed to discard his mechanical recitation and put more emotion into his closing paragraphs. He closed with the supposition that, in "the glorious annals" of the county, there would be "no brighter page than the one dealing with the Battles of Gettysburg." There was much stirring when Everett finished and bowed to the audience, "but little applause was given" — mostly of the polite variety. Perhaps many were "too solemnized by the associations and influence of the spot to be more demonstrative."[38] Perhaps some of the applause was given by those who were glad the oration was finally over. After all, many in the crowd had been standing for three hours and were anxious to hear their president.

After Everett sat down on his chair, Lamon motioned for the twelve-man chorus of Maryland Musical Association to proceed. In unison, they chanted the ode composed by Benjamin B. French. The Baltimore choristers performed admirably. The ode (sometimes characterized as a hymn) contained such phrases as "holy ground," "sacred blood," "our glorious dead," and "Freedom's holy cause." Hearty applause expressed the audience's appreciation.

Lamon stepped forward once again, this time to introduce the president of the United States. Lincoln waited for silence, adjusted his spectacles, looked down at the copy of his address which he held in his left hand, and then recited a short speech which he had memorized. The remarks won the crowd's favor. He was interrupted by applause five times, and at the end he received "long applause." For good measure, the audience gave Lincoln three cheers then three more for the governors.[39]

Following the president's brief but memorable address, a mixed chorus of Gettysburg citizens sang a dirge, this one of Percival's. Birgfield's Band accompanied the singers. Lamon nodded in the direction of Rev. Henry L. Baugher, president of the Gettysburg-based college and seminary. He stepped forward and recited the benediction, brief and well delivered.

The Marshal-in-Chief walked front and center on the stage for the last time. He announced that the formal program was over. At the request of Governor Tod he also announced that an Ohio-sponsored program would be held in the Presbyterian church at five o'clock that afternoon and that all who were interested were invited.[40] Then he "dismissed the assemblage" and asked his assistant marshals to reform the procession for the return trek to Gettysburg.

After a battery of the Fifth New York Artillery fired an eight-round salute, Lamon's assistant marshals directed the reforming of the procession. On the return trip to Gettysburg, Lamon again performed a double role, serving as Marshal-in-Chief of the procession as well as the president's bodyguard. Many who had participated in the first procession did not take part in the second. "Many lingered until the shades of the evening approached," one reporter wrote, "seemingly loath to leave the ground consecrated by the blood of those heroes who fought, died, and found a grave there."[41]

After the northward bound procession reached the city square, it quickly and quietly disbanded. Lamon escorted the president back to the Wills's house where competent helpers served a sumptous supper to selected guests.

Lamon still had some work to do. He had to arrange the details for shipping horses back to Washington. Then he met with his aides and assistant marshals in a room at the courthouse. Lamon thanked both his assistant marshals and his nine aides for performing their assignments well. He offered a resolution which he had written earlier for their approval: "*Resolved,* That we tender our heartfelt thanks to the Ladies and Gentlemen of Gettysburg for their generous hospitality and their many acts of courtesy and kindness extended to us during our sojourn in that town."[42]

Lamon returned to the Wills's house to supervise a reception by the president. Wills placed Lincoln in the hall opening on York Street and Governor Curtin at the door fronting on the public square. A parade of callers, all eyed by Lamon, entered the hall to shake hands with the president after they entered the Wills's house; they shook Governor Curtin's hand before exiting through the front door onto the public square.

In time, the president's special train with Lamon and his nine aides aboard departed for Washington. After a wearisome delay in Hanover Junction, the train reached Baltimore. All the travelers moved from one depot to another to complete their return trip. It was about one o'clock in the morning before the tired travelers reached their destination.[43]

Both Ward H. Lamon and David Wills received accolades. Editor Robert Harper of Gettysburg's Republican newspaper characterized the events of November 19 as "a perfect success" and he lauded "the systematic arrangements" and "the beautiful order which prevailed throughout the ceremonies." Even Editor Henry J. Stahle of the Democratic-oriented *Gettysburg Compiler* had words of praise for the procession and the program.[44]

The finest compliment of all came from the pen of Benjamin B. French. His relationship with Lamon had brought him honors and recognition. He not only had had a front-row seat on the platform at Gettysburg, but he also had had the thrill of listening to a choral group chant an ode which he had composed for the occasion. French wrote, "Never was the duty of Marshal-in-Chief performed by any one acting in that capacity better and more satisfactorily to all than it was performed by Marshal Lamon. He was earnest, indefatigable, and energetic from the very commencement of his duties, more than a week prior to the celebration, to its close. He did everything well, and left nothing undone. The celebration was a success in every particular."[45]

In Washington, Lamon resumed his duties as Lincoln's bodyguard and United States Marshal for the District of Columbia. He remained concerned about the president's safety. Occasionally, someone reminded him about his role in the dedication of the soldiers' cemetery at Gettysburg. In late December 1863, for example, he received a curt note from the superintendent of the metropolitan police in the District: "Do me the favor to send me the pistol I loaned you when you were about to leave for Gettysburg."[46]

Meanwhile the war ground down to a close as Gen. U.S. Grant came to Washington to assume control of all the armies. It had evolved into a war of attrition. On April 9, 1865, Gen. Robert E. Lee surrendered the remnant of his once notable army. Lamon was on special mission to Richmond on the night President Lincoln was shot at Ford's Theater.

Lamon returned to Illinois soon after, resuming the practice of law. At times, editors and others urged him to write an article or a book about his friendship with Lincoln and his experiences in Washington. John P. Usher, Lincoln's second Secretary of the Interior who attended the dedication ceremonies at Gettysburg, urged Lamon to put his recollections on paper — "commit to writing your recollections of him [Lincoln], his sayings, and doings." "I venture to say," Usher stated in his letter, "[that] there is now none living than yourself in whom he so much confided, and to whom he gave free expression of his feelings toward others, his trials and troubles in conducting his great office."[47]

Lamon took Usher's advice. His reminiscences were published in 1895, edited by a daughter and entitled *Recollections of Abraham Lincoln, 1847-1865*. He entitled chapter 11 "The True Story of the Gettysburg Speech." In this strange chapter, Lamon made no mention of his role as Marshal-in-Chief at

Gettysburg. He did, however, provide some substance to the myths already in circulation — one was that Lincoln had gone to Gettysburg unprepared and the other that Lincoln's address was poorly received by the audience. Lamon made up a quotation and attributed it to Lincoln: "He said to me on the stand, immediately after concluding the speech 'Lamon, that speech won't *scour*. It is a flat failure, and the people are disappointed.' "[48]

One lie led to another. In the manner of Baron Munchhausen, Lamon embroidered upon his tale:

> On the platform from which Mr. Lincoln delivered his address, and only a moment after it was concluded, Mr. Seward turned to Mr. Everett and asked him what he thought of the President's speech. Mr. Everett replied, "It is not what I expected from him. I am disappointed." Then in his turn Mr. Everett asked, "What do you think of it, Mr. Seward?" The response was, "He has made a failure, and I am sorry for it. His speech was not equal to him." Mr. Seward then turned to me and asked, "Mr. Marshal, what do you think of it?" I answered, "I am sorry to say that it does not impress me as one of his great speeches."[49]

Lamon felt the need to restate his the-speech-was-a-failure prevarication again. He wrote, "Mr. Lincoln said to me after our return to Washington, 'I tell you, Hill, that speech fell on the audience like a wet blank. I am distressed about it. I ought to have prepared with more care.' "[50]

Lamon's letters and handwritten recollections offer no clues which would explain why he fabricated quotations that he attributed to others. Perhaps he thought he needed to enliven his written memoirs in order to ensure their publication. Perhaps, as he aged, his mind twisted facts which had occurred many years earlier. Perhaps he really came to believe several of the myths about the Gettysburg Address which were gaining popularity during the 1890s while he was putting pen to paper. The 1890s were, after all, years which witnessed the apotheosis of Lincoln and transformed him from a historical figure into a demigod.

Lamon deserved little credit for furthering and fostering myths about Lincoln's Gettysburg Address — some have been debunked time and again.[51] On the other hand, Lamon deserves some of the credit for making the Gettysburg cemetery observance a most memorable event. He was a central figure in the oft-discussed events of November 19, 1863, supervising the processions and serving as master-of-ceremonies during the three-hour program. His role as Marshal-in-Chief on that day, as well as his work as President Lincoln's bodyguard, have earned him more than a footnote in his country's history.

BENJAMIN B. FRENCH, THE LINCOLNS, AND THE DEDICATION OF THE SOLDIERS' CEMETERY AT GETTYSBURG*

Benjamin Brown French's working relationship with Abraham Lincoln and Ward H. Lamon, the President's bodyguard, fashioned an opportunity for him to play a major role in the dedication of the soldiers' cemetery at Gettysburg. French, a native of Chester, New Hampshire, served as Marshal-in-Chief Lamon's first assistant during the procession and the program, and helped Lamon plan both. He had one of the front-row chairs on the 12 ′ × 20 ′ platform when Edward Everett recited his two-hour oration and Lincoln delivered his "most memorable address." Furthermore, French listened to a chorus chant an ode that he had composed especially for the occasion. Later the New Hampshire native wrote that memories of the affair would be "forever precious."[1]

French first met Lincoln in early December of 1847. At the time French, a Democrat, was serving as clerk of the House of Representatives in Washington and Lincoln was a newly-elected Whig congressman from Illinois. French hoped that members of the new House would re-elect him to a second term as clerk and expected behind-the-scenes bargaining to give him the much-sought sinecure. But French lost the clerkship to Thomas Jefferson Campbell, a Whig from Tennessee, by a 113 to 109 vote. Lincoln cast one of the decisive votes for French's opponent.[2]

In the years that followed, Lincoln and French went their own ways. Lincoln did not seek re-election and established himself as a leading lawyer and a leading Whig in the state of Illinois. In the 1850s he left the dying Whig party and joined the surging Republican Party, debated Stephen A. Douglas in a bid for a U.S. Senate seat, won his party's presidential nomination in June of 1860, and defeated three other contenders in the November election that followed. He returned to Washington in February, 1861.

---

*Reprinted (with permission) from *Historical New Hampshire*, 42 (Spring, 1987) pp. 36-63.

French had an up-and-down career before he met Lincoln again. Between 1847 and 1853 he was associated with Samuel F. B. Morse in promoting the Magnetic Telegraph Company and practiced law in Washington, D.C. When Franklin Pierce emerged as a presidential candidate in 1852, French slighted his law and business interests to work long hours for his old New Hampshire friend. "I have devoted pretty much of the last six months," he wrote to a brother, "to the nomination and election of Pierce...."[3]

Pierce's victory gave French claims for an office in the new administration. He walked off with a good prize, the office of Commissioner of Public Buildings in the District of Columbia. It did not take French long, however, to become disillusioned with the Pierce administration. There was much political infighting and the President seemed to be a servant of the Southern slavocracy. Urged by his half-brother, Henry Flagg French, to bring his anti-slavery sentiments into the open, French resigned his post and wrote a letter to Pierce renouncing his allegiance to a party that had "lost its devotion to democratic principles."[4] During the months that followed, French, like so many other anti-slavery Democrats, drifted into the Republican party. Soon a Republican activist, he became head of the Republican Association of Washington in 1857. French's involvement in the Knights Templars of the United States (he served as Grand Master from 1859 to 1865) and in the Masons gave him valuable contacts.

During the election of 1860 French and his Republican Association did noble work on Lincoln's behalf. Soon after President-elect Lincoln came to Washington to be bombarded by office-seekers, French called on him to press his claims for some worthy office. Named Marshal-in-Chief for the inauguration ceremonies, French had a good chance to gain Lincoln's good will and enhance his chances for a federal office. On March 1, 1861, three days before inaugural day, French met with the President-elect to discuss details and ascertain wishes. After talking with Lincoln on March 1, French wrote in his journal: "I had considerable conversation with Mr. Lincoln and was very much pleased at his off-hand, unassuming manner, and I believe he will make a first-rate President."[5]

March 4 was a busy day for Benjamin B. French. He was on horseback "from half-past eight in the morning until late afternoon." The parade was most impressive — "went off gloriously." No more "imposing or more orderly pageant" ever "passed along Pennsylvania Avenue." French stood near the President as he delivered his inaugural address. "I got a position," French wrote that evening, "where I could hear every word and was delighted."[6]

After the inauguration ceremonies were over, Marshal-in-Chief French escorted the new President to the White House, where Lincoln received "all comers with that cordial welcome that so strongly marks the sincerity of the man." Later French escorted thirty-four young women into the Blue Room of the White House. French explained: "In the procession was a sort of triumphal car, splendidly trimmed, ornamented and arranged, in which rode thirty-four young girls. On our return, the girls all alighted, and I took them in and introduced them to the President. He asked to be allowed to kiss them all, and he did so. It was a very interesting scene, and elicited much applause.'''[7]

The fact that affairs on inaugural day "went off without an accident or blunder," strengthened French's claim to a worthy federal office, but as the days passed he despaired of getting his "just dues." He expressed his disappointment in a letter to a brother: "I am again disgusted with politics. I have withdrawn from being a candidate for office, and it seems to me as if I never again shall enter the political arena for anybody. Pierce cheated me and 'Abe' ignores me. 'Let her rip.' ''[8]

The despair gave way to hope when the President mentioned that French "had claims [to an office] which should not be forgotten."[9] The office — clerk of the Court of Claims — did not satisfy French long because the work was tedious and the pay meager. French was used to a high standard of living, having a fine home, several servants, and other amenities. At every opportunity French begged for a better position with better pay. Finally, opportunity knocked when the Senate refused to confirm the President's first choice for Commissioner of Public Works, and he offered the post to French.[10] French had held the same position under Pierce.

On Sunday, September 8, French called on the President and First Lady to discuss his work. Pleased with their friendliness and affability, he confided to his journal:

> I was at the President's and saw Mrs. Lincoln and the President. Mrs. L. expressed her satisfaction at my appointment, and I hope and trust she and I shall get along quietly. I certainly shall do all in my power to oblige her and make her comfortable. She is evidently a smart, intelligent woman, and likes to have her own way pretty much. I was delighted with her independence and her lady-like reception of me. Afterwards I saw the Presdient and he received me very cordially.[11]

The President's cordiality continued as the weeks went by. Although he addressed French rather formally by his last name, he always showed his warmth by telling a story. The First Lady, on the other hand, mixed cordiality and discourtesy according to her moods when French consulted her about various matters. "The Republican Queen," French wrote to a brother, "plagues me half to death with wants with which it is impossible to comply . . . ."[12]

One of French's responsibilities was to attend White House receptions. If it was a regular public reception, French stood between the President and the First Lady, introducing each guest to her. If it was Mrs. Lincoln's levee, French had a dual responsibility — companion as well as receptionist.[13]

By the end of the year, French imagined that he was "on the most cosey terms" with Mrs. Lincoln. "We introduced *each other* to the callers every Saturday afternoon and on reception evenings," he wrote to a sister, adding, "There is no denying the fact that she is a curiosity, but she is a lady and an accomplished one too. But she does have money, aye, better than I do and a great deal better than her honored spouse." Later, in this letter, he both defended and criticized the First Lady, writing, "They tell a great many stories about Mrs. Lincoln,

NHHS COLLECTIONS; PHOTO BY BILL FINNEY

BENJAMIN B. FRENCH

French was the "first assistant" to Marshal-in-Chief Ward H. Lamon and helped to plan the Gettyburg proceedings. He had a front-row chair on the platform and composed a "Consecration Hymn" that was chanted by a Baltimore choir as part of the formal dedication program.

but I do not believe them — indeed I know many of them are false . . . . She is a very imprudent woman in many things."[14]

The monotony of French's assignment was broken with the death of Lincoln's son Willie. The President was overcome with grief and the First Lady was disconsolate. U.S. Senator Orville H. Browning, a friend of Lincoln, called on French to tell him that the President and Mrs. Lincoln wanted French to take "the entire charge of funeral arrangements at the White House."[15]

During the weeks that followed, French cemented his relationship with the President and the First Lady. Yet there were trying times, and the Commissioner of Public Buildings confided his problems in letters to a brother. "She is not easy to get along with," he wrote on March 23, 1862, "though I succeed pretty well with her."[16] Although French's regard for Mrs. Lincoln was gauged by her moods, his feelings for the President evolved from respect to reverence. "The more I see of him," French once wrote in his journal, "the more I am convinced of his superlative goodness, truth, kindness, and patriotism."[17]

French frequently made "business calls" upon the President. Once Lincoln authorized French "to draw on the sum appropriated at the last session of Congress, of $250 for Books for the Executive Mansion, for the sum of ($125.90) one hundred twenty-five dollars ninty [sic] cents."[18] Another time he sought Lincoln's support in a plan to move the army bakery out of the Capitol basement.[19] On another occasion French asked the President, at a tearful request of the First Lady, to approve a one thousand dollar overrun for White House furnishings.[20] Then early in November of 1863, both Lincoln and French were invited to have important roles in the dedication of the soldiers' cemetery at Gettysburg.

French's "working relationship" with Ward H. Lamon began shortly before the inauguration. As Lincoln's bodyguard, Lamon was interested in planning for the President's safety during the day's events. Fench and Lamon were similar. Both were lawyers. Both possessed antislavery sentiments. Both worked for the President. And both sought well-paying federal jobs from Lincoln. Both first met Lincoln in 1847, French when the freshman congressman presented his credentials to the clerk of the House of Representatives in early December, Lamon when a lawyer acquaintance introduced him to Lincoln in a county courthouse in Illinois.

In time Lamon's acquaintance with Lincoln blossomed into a friendship. "Until the day of his death," Lamon wrote years later, "it was my pleasure and good fortune to retain his confidence unshaken, as he retained my affection unbroken." Recognizing Lincoln's courtroom abilities, Lamon often asked his eighteen-year senior to help with cases. Lamon explained his relationship: "I was his local partner, first in Danville, and afterward in Bloomington. We rode the circuit together, traveling by buggy in the dry seasons and on horseback in bad weather, there being no railroads then in that part of the state."[21]

Like French, Lamon worked for Lincoln's election in 1860 and then served as the President-elect's bodyguard on the trip from Springfield to Washington. Armed with two pistols, two derringers, and two large knives,

Lamon was constantly at Lincoln's side during that strange midnight ride from Philadelphia to Washington amidst assassination rumors.

Lamon and French were strange bedfellows. The forty-year old Lamon was stout, handsome, and a heavy-drinking swashbuckler; French was sixty, fair-skinned, nearly bald, and a slight well-bred gentleman. Lamon liked bourbon, risque stories, bawdy ballads, and seldom read a book; French preferred wine, enjoyed euchre and cribbage with friends, loved opera and the theater, and read voraciously, having memorized hundreds of quotations from the classics. Lamon was a Western roughneck, French an Eastern elitist. The two moved in different social circles, French mingling with the best in Washington society, Lamon an outsider.

Both gained official appointments early in the Lincoln administration, French as Commissioner of Public Buildings, Lamon as Marshal for the District of Columbia. Both had a place in the reception line during the President's and Mrs. Lincoln's first levee, early in December of 1861. The four stood in the middle of the Blue Room, Lamon first in line — between the President and the door. He introduced the callers to the President, who turned them over to French who, in turn, introduced them to the First Lady. The next evening French recorded his thoughts about the first White House levee to his journal:

> It was a jam and well might the President exclaim "jam satis!" My particular duty consisted in introducing the guests to Mrs. Lincoln, and I found it no sinecure. For two mortal hours a steady stream of humanity was passing on, and there *we* stood, I saying "Mr. or Mrs. or General or Col. or Gov. or Judge, so & so, Mrs. Lincoln," and she curtseying and saying "How do you do," and sometimes to a particular acquaintance, "I am so glad to see you," and giving the tips of white-kidded fingers in token of that gladness. She bore herself well and bravely, and looked queenly.[22]

French's abilities evidently impressed Lamon. When David Wills, promoter of the idea of a soldiers' cemetery on the Gettysburg battlefield and responsible for the dedication ceremonies scheduled for November 19, 1863, asked Lamon to serve as the day's Marshal-in-Chief, Lamon invited French to be his first assistant. French agreed to help and noted in his journal: "This will be a task. But we are all in for doing what we can to show our Patriotism, and I should not think I was doing my duty were I to decline. If alive and well, I shall be there."[23]

The story of the soldiers' cemetery at Gettysburg goes back to the battles fought in the fields and woods about Gettysburg on July 1-3, 1863. After Gen. Robert E. Lee's Confederate troops retreated to Virginia, relatives and friends of the Union dead rushed to Gettysburg to claim bodies placed in shallow graves scattered over the battlefield. Many of the dead were sent back to their home towns and buried in local cemeteries. Others, however, were not claimed by relatives or friends, and their decaying bodies lay rotting in thousands of improvised graves. At times no grave had been dug and the body had merely been covered with spadefuls of earth. Heavy rains washed the ground away, exposing legs or arms or heads. "I saw one entire skull above ground," one witness wrote, "and in many instances hands and feet are sticking through."[24]

Noting that hogs were desecrating some of the soldiers' graves, David Wills wrote to Andrew Curtin, governor of Pennsylvania, suggesting the purchase of part of the battlefield and transforming it into a soldiers' cemetery. The eighteen states that had lost sons at Gettysburg would participate in the project.

> "Our dead are lying in fields unburied (that is no graves being dug), with small portions of earth dug up alongside the body and thrown over it. In many instances, arms and legs protrude and my attention has been directed to several places where hogs were actually rooting out the bodies and devouring them — and this on Pennsylvania soil and in many cases the bodies of the patriotic soldiers of our State. Humanity calls on us to take measures to remedy this . . . ."[25]

Governor Curtin endorsed the cemetery proposal. He promised to seek the support of the Pennsylvania stated legislature, instructed Wills to buy the acreage deemed necessary, invite the other seventeen states to take part, and proceed with plans for the reburials. As the project moved forward, Wills suggested that it was time to plan for the "consecration" of the cemetery "with appropriate ceremonies." Curtin authorized Wills to plan an appropriate program, set a date for the dedication, and invite the other seventeen governors to the affair.[26]

Wills proceeded to carry out his governor's wishes and envisioned an event that would turn the national spotlight upon Gettysburg. He visualized "an impressive procession" and an outstanding dedication program. After setting the date of November 19 for the ceremonies, Wills asked Edward Everett to be "the orator of the day," invited President Lincoln to "formally set apart these grounds to their sacred use by a few appropriate remarks," and arranged for some proper prayers and some musical numbers. Then he asked Lamon to serve as Marshal-in-Chief for the day's activities — supervise the procession and serve as master-of-ceremonies during the program. This was clever, for it ensured President Lincoln's participation in the program.[27]

After consulting with Lincoln, Lamon accepted the responsibility.[28] Marshal-in-Chief Lamon set to work with a will. He requested that each of the eighteen governors involved in the event appoint two assistant marshals to help supervise the activities, and he invited all the United States marshals of "the eastern half of the country" to serve as his aides.[29]

He also had the good sense to appoint French to be his assistant, recognizing that the latter's work as Marshal-in-Chief for Lincoln's inauguration gave him experience that could be put to good use.

Lamon and French left Washington for Gettysburg on the morning of November 13 for a meeting with Wills to discuss plans and arrangements concerning the dedication program. When they missed the regular connection at Hanover Junction, as French recalled, "a special train was sent on with us . . . ." They arrived in Gettysburg late in the afternoon and went to the Eagle Hotel. Wills called upon the two soon after their arrival and took them to his law office, where they spent the rest of the afternoon and early evening discussing plans and details. They decided to put the principals on horses rather than securing scores of carriages. They also decided to organize the procession — they anticipated more than 10,000 marchers — into three sections. The military section under Gen. Darius N. Couch would include infantry, cavalry, and artillery units as well as the Marine Band. The Marshal-in-Chief's section would include "the dignitaries" — the President, his personal secretaries, members of the President's cabinet, congressmen, governors, foreign ministers, the cemetery commissioners, special guests, and others. The civic section would include fraternal, benevolent, and service organizations as well as ordinary citizens, grouped by states. It was also decided that all assistant marshals and aides would be on horseback and dressed in distinctive garb — white satin shoulder sashes, rosettes, and white gloves. There was need to print programs, publicize the order of the procession, obtain enough horses, build a $12' \times 20'$ platform near the cemetery, plan the seating on the platform, assure security for President Lincoln, and verify other details.[30]

Wills reported that he had invited Henry Wadsworth Longfellow, William Cullen Bryant, John Greenleaf Whittier and George H. Boker — in that order — to write an ode or a hymn for the dedication program, but all had turned him down.[31] On the spur of the moment, French offered to write something suitable and have it ready the next morning. "My muse volunteered," he later said.[32] They agreed to meet the next day to complete their work.

French mulled over some thoughts and phrases before he fell asleep, exhausted from the day's ordeal. Next morning he arose at daybreak, put pen to paper, and composed an ode of five six-line stanzas. He entitled his handiwork "Consecration Hymn" and after reworking it, made copies for Wills and Lamon. After a visit to the newly surveyed soldiers' cemetery and a discussion about the route of the procession and the precise location of the $12' \times 20'$ platform, Lamon and French returned to Washington.

On Monday evening, November 16, three days before the dedication, Marshal-in-Chief Lamon called a meeting of all available aides, assistant marshals, and some friends, in a room of the city hall. Lamon reported that the president of the Baltimore & Ohio Railroad had promised "a special car" for the first leg of the journey and that the president of the North Central Railroad (Baltimore to Hanover Junction) had followed suit. No definite arrangements had yet been made for the Hanover Junction-to-Gettysburg portion of the journey. Lamon promised to have all travel information posted in his office before noon of the next day. He said he had prepared a paper entitled "The undersigned wish to signify their intention of accompanying Marshal Lamon to Gettysburg tomorrow — leaving this city at the hour named."[33] All who wanted a free ride were invited to sign.

Then it was necessary to set the time of departure. Lamon suggested three o'clock the next afternoon. French cast the lone dissenting vote, arguing for a morning departure. Engines were often balky and train schedules unreliable. If any "train trouble" developed it could mean that the travelers "would probably be out all night." Lamon stubbornly chose to ignore French's suggestion.

French, nonetheless, decided to leave next morning. Accompanied by a family friend, Dr. John Stevenson, French took an early train (6:30 o'clock) on the 17th for Gettysburg, via Baltimore and Hanover Junction. The Baltimore-to-Hanover Junction train was overcrowded, most passengers Gettysburg bound. Yet, overall, the cheerful French declared it "a very pleasant trip."[34]

When French and Dr. Stevenson arrived in Gettysburg about 1:30 p.m., they walked to the Eagle Hotel, where Dr. Stevenson had a confirmed reservation. When the proprietor would not promise French a room, French then proceeded to the residence of Robert G. Harper, a fellow Mason. Harper, editor of the city's Republican newspaper, assured French that he was welcome to be his guest; Marshal-in-Chief Lamon's first assistant, thus, would spend several days with the Harpers. It turned out to be a fine experience. Later, French wrote, " . . . and to him and his excellent wife and daughters I am indebted for as much comfort and happiness as any man in Gettysburg enjoyed from 2 o'clock on Tuesday [November 17] until 10 o'clock, p.m., on Friday [November 20] . . . . The whole family was remarkably hospitable and pleasant."[35]

French spent most of the afternoon and evening visiting with the Harpers, mainly listening to Mrs. Harper's account of the battle and many incidents connected with it. Her husband was out of the city at the time. During the battle the large Harper house became a makeshift hospital. Two bullets came into the house through the windows; one bullet struck a crib at the bedside of a wounded Union officer while the other passed within a few inches of Mrs. Harper. An artillery shell fell in the garden, within a few feet of the house, but it did not explode. Some soldiers later removed "the charge," and the undetonated projectile became a dining-room ornament.[36]

French found the sixty-four year old Harper a most interesting and remarkable fellow — one who moved about "with the elasticity of a boy." He was the father of twelve children — two by his thirty-two year old third wife. Perhaps French felt kinship with Harper. As a sixty-two year old widower, French had married a thirty-one year old woman on September 9, 1862, a little more than a year before.

Early the next morning, French walked to the Eagle Hotel to meet Lamon. But Lamon's train, delayed again and again, did not reach Gettysburg until half past nine that morning. French gloated; he had warned Lamon that they might spend the night on trains.

Later in the morning, French and Lamon met again with David Wills, this time to finalize plans for the procession and the program. Horses had to be assigned to individuals and chairs on the platform to the principals. Everett, ever the Boston Brahmin, wanted a tent set up for him near the platform and he also wanted a carriage for his trip from Gettysburg to the top of Cemetery Hill. French also learned that the verses that he had composed would be recited, in unison, by a choral group from Baltimore as part of next day's program.[37]

Early in the afternoon, Wills, Lamon, and French attended a flag-raising ceremony. A sixty-foot flagpole had been erected in the central square, and there was much excitement as a huge flag moved toward the top to wave gently in a western breeze. Then, with matters seemingly in hand, Lamon and French visited several sectors of the expansive battlefield. They were especially interested in the spot where Gen. John F. Reynolds had fallen, victim of a sharpshooter's bullet, and where Gen. George E. Pickett's assault against Federal troops atop Cemetery Hill and Cemetery Ridge had ended disastrously in dramatic fashion.

Shortly before 6:00 p.m., Wills, Lamon, French, Everett and others walked over to the railway depot to meet the President's incoming train. A regiment of the Invalid Corps also arrived to form an escort for Lincoln as he walked about a block to the Wills's house.

While Wills hosted Lincoln and Everett, Lamon and French held a briefing session for the assistant marshals and aides in a room of the county courthouse. Lamon and French explained plans that had been made, recited responsibilities, and specified on what streets the various sections of the procession should assemble next morning. Later, in his journal, French commented upon the briefing session: "The Marshal had a meeting at the Court House, which I, of course, attended. We made all the necessary arrangements for the following day, and contributed $160 to purchase food for our starving prisoners at Libby Prison, Richmond. I gave $20."[38]

After French returned to the Harper house, he told "the company" (it included Secretary of State William H. Seward) that Marshal-in-Chief Lamon and his assistants and aides "had raised" $160 to purchase food for Union officers held in Richmond prisons. Seward, very interested, said that "the Rebel government" would not permit food to be given to Yankees held as prisoners. French said that they would — "if it came from individuals, but not the Government." Seward then handed French ten dollars saying "Put that down from *Marshal* Seward, an individual."[39] Seward, that evening, made an indelible impression on French.

On retiring for the night, French was kept awake by noise from the public square, which was filled with people in a festive mood, who sang, "hallooed," and cheered. "Among other things," French wrote, "they sang, in full chorus and admirably, the whole of that well-known production whose refrain is 'We are coming Father Abraham, three hundred thousand more.'" Finally, sometime between one and two o'clock, French fell asleep. Next morning, after breakfast, French sought out an army quartermaster in order to procure his horse. It was "a shaggy, unpromising-looking nag." But upon mounting the horse, and using the spurs "pretty freely," he found the animal to be "a spirited and easy-going beast" that performed "admirably." He directed his horse toward the public square where a crowd was gathering. Scores of French's assistant marshals arrived, "with sashes on and batons in hand." They were, more or less, under French's supervision, for Lamon's responsibility was to be at Lincoln's side. French and his assistants had the task of transforming an ever-growing crowd into a procession.[40]

Shortly before ten o'clock, the scheduled time for the procession to begin its southward trek to Cemetery Hill, President Lincoln emerged from the Wills's house. He was dressed in black, wearing a frock coat and his well-known stovepipe hat, with a wide mourning band about it. Many acquaintances and strangers crowded around. When the situation was getting out of hand, Marshal-in-Chief Lamon ordered the crowd back and instructed the President to mount his horse. The crowd, uncowed, gave repeated cheers for Lincoln, once, at the suggestion of a Republican partisan, even giving three cheers for "the next president of the United States."[41] Meanwhile the crowd increased in size, finally numbering seven or eight thousand.

About 10:30, French and his assistant marshals started the procession. The Marine Band, playing marching music, led the way. Next came the military units, consisting of a squad of cavalry, two batteries of artillery, and a regiment of infantry. Lamon led "the Marshal's section;" it included President Lincoln, two of his personal secretaries, three members of Lincoln's cabinet, nine governors (the governor of New Hampshire failed to attend), a few congressmen, and other dignitaries or guests-of-honor. The civic section included members of benevolent and fraternal organizations (some in their colorful regalia), hundreds of civilians, and a number of soldiers recovering from wounds received in the three-day battle. "Pennsylvania furnished the largest numerical representation," one newspaperman noted, "Ohio next, Wisconsin third, and Massachusetts fourth."[42]

It was an impressive procession. "Never was a procession better formed," French contended, "or more orderly."[43] An observer seconded French's contention, writing, "This was a grand and magnificent sight. I have no language to depict it as the mighty mass rolled on like waves of the ocean, everything was in perfect order."[44]

When the military units reached the dedication site they formed lines so the President would have a lane to the platform steps. Lamon escorted the President up the steps and onto the platform. Lincoln visited with the governors and others while French and his assistant marshals arranged the procession participants into a half-circle audience in front of the platform.

Earlier, French had been involved in assigning the platform seats. There were three rows of ten chairs each, then scattered chairs and a small table at the back of the 12' × 20' platform. Lincoln and Everett, of course, had the two middle chairs in the front row, the orator of the day seated at the President's left. Secretary of State Seward, beetle-browed and squinting because of the noonday sun, sat at Everett's left, then three govenors — Curtin (Pennsylvania), David Tod (Ohio), and Horatio Seymour (New York), in that order. Two clergymen, one scheduled to give the invocation and the other the benediction sat at Lincoln's immediate right, then French, and William Saunders. French had a front row chair because he was Lamon's chief assistant as well as composer of an ode which would be recited as part of the program. Saunders deserved a front row chair because he was the landscape gardener from Washington who had planned the cemetery with its half-circle of plots, paths, and parallels.[45]

After the procession had become an audience, Lamon, who was at the left corner of the platform next to the steps, walked forward to read some regrets. French heard him say that General Winfield Scott was unable to attend because of "increasing infirmities;" General George G. Meade had "duties to perform" and Secretary of the Treasury Salmon P. Chase used the excuse of "imperative public duties." There were others.

Birgfield's Band opened the formal program with appropriate music, "an introductory dirge." Next the Marshal-in-Chief called on the Rev. Thomas H. Stockton, chaplain of the House of Representatives, to give the opening prayer. According to Lincoln's sarcastic secretary, John Hay, the loquacious Reverend Stockton offered up "a prayer which thought it was an oration."[46] French, however, characterized it as "one of the most impressive and eloquent prayers I ever heard."[47]

Lamon, as master-of-ceremonies, next called on the Marine Band to play its chosen number; it responded with Martin Luther's hymn "Old Hundred" — "with great effect" and "in all its grand and sublime beauty."[48]

Lamon then introduced "the orator of the day," the Hon. Edward Everett. Without notes of any kind the experienced Everett delivered a two-hour oration. French described it as "one of the greatest, most eloquent, and appropriate orations to which I ever listened."[49] French, carried away by the emotions of the hour, was overly generous with his praise. One critic characterized Everett's presentation as "cold and smooth," but lacking "one stirring thought, one vivid picture, one thrilling appeal."[50] Another listener offered a similar critique, writing, "Everett's Gettysburg affair was painfully cold . . . with no sunbeam warmth. He seemed the hired mourner — the laureate chanting a funeral dirge to order, with no touch of 'in memorium' about it. His monument was an iron statue with no glow or pulse or passion in it."[51]

After Everett finished his oration and shuffled back to his chair, French apprehensively awaited the chanting of his recently composed poem which he had entitled "Consecration Hymn." Ironically, the printed program merely listed it as an "Ode," without mention of the composer or the chorus of the Maryland Music Association. It was chanted "beautifully and with much effect." French listened to the words, chanted in unison:

> *'Tis holy ground —*
> *This spot, where, in their graves*
> *We place our Country's braves,*
> *Who fell in Freedom's holy cause*
> *Fighting for Liberties and Laws —*
> *Let tears abound.*
>
> *Here let them rest —*
> *And Summer's heat and Winter's cold,*
> *Shall glow and freeze above this mould —*
> *A thousand years shall pass away —*
> *A nation still shall mourn this clay,*
> *Which now is blest.*

Here, where they fell,
Oft shall the widows' tears be shed,
Oft shall fond parents mourn their dead,
The orphans here shall kneel and weep,
And maidens, where their lovers sleep,
Their woes shall tell.

Great God in Heaven!
Shall all this sacred blood be shed —
Shall we thus mourn our glorious dead,
Or shall the end be wrath and woe,
The knell of Freedom's overthrow —
A Country riven?

It will not be!
We trust, Oh, God! Thy gracious Power
To aid us in our darkest hour,
This be our Prayer — "Oh, Father! save
A people's Freedom from its grave —
All praise to Thee." [52]

The applause which followed was loud and long. French was pleased. "I can say *here*," he wrote in his journal several days later, "that I was never so flattered at any production of my own, as in relation to that same Hymn. All who heard it seemed to consider it most appropriate and most happily conceived."[53]

Lamon then announced, "Ladies and Gentlemen, the President of the United States." Lincoln stepped forward, waited for silence, put on his spectacles, and then "in a few brief, but most appropriate words, dedicated the cemetery." The President's well-chosen words won the crowd's favor. He was interrupted by applause five times, and when he finished, received "long applause." Then, for good measure, the crowd gave Lincoln three cheers and added three more for the governors.[54] French, later, added his own compliment:

> Abraham Lincoln is the idol of the American people at this moment. Anyone who saw and heard, as I did, the hurricane of applause that met his every movement at Gettysburg would know that he lived in every heart. It was no cold, faint shadow of a kind reception — it was the tumultuous outpouring of exultation, from true and loving hearts, at the sight of a man whom everyone knew to be honest and true and sincere in every act of his life and every pulsation of his heart. It was the spontaneous outburst of heartfelt confidence in *their own* President.[55]

After the cheers and applause for Lincoln had subsided, a local chorus sang a dirge, accompanied by Birgfield's Band. Next the Rev. Henry L. Baugher, president of the Lutheran seminary near Gettysburg, recited a brief and appropriate closing prayer. In declaring the formal program over, Lamon added that the Ohio delegation would sponsor a program at the Presbyterian church at five o'clock. Then Lamon instructed his assistant marshals to reform the procession for the return trip to Gettysburg. After the parade participants reached the village square they scattered in all directions. Lamon, French, and the assistant marshals escorted the President to the Wills's house where a three o'clock dinner awaited him and Everett.

While Lincoln was dining, Lamon met with the assistant marshals and aides in the courthouse. He thanked all for their help — it was a difficult job well done. Lamon read a resolution which thanked "the Ladies and Gentlemen of Gettysburg" for their generous hospitality "and their many acts of courtesy and kindness" which they had extended to all. The resolution, adopted unanimously, was later published in Gettysburg newspapers.[56]

After President Lincoln had partaken of dinner and finished "receiving guests" at the Wills's house, Lamon, French, and the assistant marshals escorted him to the Presbyterian church and later to the railway depot where he boarded his Washington-bound train at six o'clock.

Lamon accompanied Lincoln back to Washington. French and most of the assistant marshals, however, stayed over an extra day. Next morning, at ten o'clock, they procured horses and "rode out to, and over the Battlefield, in a body." They were escorted by a man who was preparing a map of the battlefield and who was well acquainted with the many separate battles which made up the whole. While atop Cemetery Ridge, French went off on his own, intent upon visiting the house which had been General Meade's headquarters during the battle. As chance would have it, Alexander Gardner, a well-known Washington photographer, arrived on the scene to take a picture of the famous farmhouse. "At his urgent request," French wrote two days later, "I walked back to the house and took a position on the porch where I was . . . photographed with the house. There were, then, two children on the porch with me."[57]

French returned to Gettysburg about noon, and soon thereafter, boarded a special car to take him as well as Lamon's assistant marshals and aides back to the nation's capital. The return trip was "very pleasant." Later French wrote, "The Marshal's car was crowded from Gettysburg to Baltimore, but its inmates were joyous. We had conversation, singing, and merriment. The Star Spangled Banner and other patriotic songs were sung in full chorus."[58] The train arrived at Baltimore "at ½ past 5" and most of the occupants of the Marshal-in-Chief's special car repaired to the Eutaw House to partake of "an excellent supper." At eight o'clock they left for Washington and arrived there about ten.

Buoyed by feelings that he had participated in a memorable event at Gettysburg, French wrote: "The whole affair from commencement to close was conducted in the most admirable manner, and without a single accident or baulk. It was most creditable to all concerned, and the memory of it will be forever precious."[59] French was, of course, complimenting Marshal-in-Chief Lamon, David Wills, and himself.

The next day French read the account of the dedication of the Gettysburg cemetery which appeared in the *National Intelligencer*. He wrote a letter to the editors to correct several misstatements. " . . . I am mentioned as having introduced Mr. Everett to the audience, and it is also said that I announced the receipt of General Scott's letter. This is an error. Marshal Lamon made all the introductions and announcements from the stand, with the single exception of calling upon the band [Birgfield's] to play the opening music, which I did in consequence of the temporary absence of the Marshal-in-Chief." For good measure, French added a compliment for the man who asked him to be his top assistant: " . . . never was the duty of Marshal-in-Chief performed by any one acting in that capacity better and more satisfactorily to all than it was performed by Marshal Lamon. He was earnest, indefatigable, and energetic from the very commencement of his duties, more than a week prior to the celebration, to its close. He did everything well, and left nothing undone. The celebration was a success in every particular."[60]

French, retaining his position as Commissioner of Public Buildings until 1867, continued to carry out the bidding of President Lincoln and the First Lady. In the election year of 1864, he characterized Lincoln as "the noblest Roman of them all," deserving of re-election. "I almost idolized him," French wrote to his brother, "he is so honest and so true . . . God Bless Abraham Lincoln."[61]

That same year when rumors made the rounds that Lincoln's enemies intended to criticize the First Lady for political gain, French wrote a strong defense of her:

Rumors are about, that the Democrats are getting up something in which they intend to show up Madame Lincoln. Thank Heaven I know no more *of my knowledge*, of her doings than any one else — in deed I do not *know* that she has ever done a wrong act, and I think an appeal to the people, in good set terms to pour down such ungallant and mean conduct as an attack on a *woman* to injure her husband, would be met, as it should be, with a curse on the movers, and do the getters of *vile slander* more harm than their *effort would do good.*[62]

French was shocked when an assassin shot his beloved president. In the days which followed, Mrs. Lincoln returned to Springfield, Illinois. So did Ward H. Lamon, thus ending his four-year relationship with French. The tragedy of Lincoln's death did not erase French's faith in the future. He wrote a valedictory:

God is taking care of us well. The Nation has come out of the furnace of Rebellion and Treason and War and murder and assassination unscathed, and with renewed youth and vigor, and will show all Creation, "and the rest of mankind," that it can stand anything, and *lick* the universe.[63]

The two chapters put together in Part Two seem to have little in common, yet both deal with aspects of the Gettysburg cemetery story. The chapter about Ohio's role in the dedication of the soldiers' cemetery is one of the longer ones; the chapter dealing with President Abraham Lincoln's impromptu speech the evening before the dedication program is by far the shortest. The Ohio story is heavily footnoted and was written for a scholarly journal; the story of Lincoln's brief impromptu speech was written as a human interest account for a popular bimonthly usually devoted to battlefield articles.

The story of Ohio's role in the establishment of the soldiers' cemetery and the dedication program offers insights and angles not available in the other chapters. The Buckeye State was the only one to send "a special train" to the Pennsylvania-based ceremonies. No state had more dignitaries on the platform than Ohio. The state also sponsored "an Ohio program" after the dedication ceremonies were over — at Gettysburg's Presbyterian Church at five o'clock. President Lincoln, Secretary of State William H. Seward, and John Burns attended this Ohio-sponsored program.

The short account dealing with Lincoln's impromptu speech is based upon solid research but written for public consumption — it is without footnotes. It was sent to David Roth, editor-publisher of *Blue & Gray Magazine*. He was kind enough to publish it, but he added three words of his own to the title. "Lincoln's First Gettysburg Address: A Little Known Impromptu Speech" became "Lincoln's First Gettysburg Address: A Little Known Impromptu Speech Perhaps Best Forgotten."

CHAPTER IV

OHIO AND THE DEDICATION OF THE
SOLDIERS' CEMETERY AT GETTYSBURG*

Ohioans had more than a passing interest in the dedication of the Soldiers' Cemetery at Gettysburg on November 19, 1863. A decisive three-day battle, fought in the surrounding countryside on July 1-3, 1863, had claimed the lives of many of the state's soldiers, some of whom were hurriedly buried in shallow graves or merely covered with spadefuls of dirt where they had fallen. No other governor, not even Pennsylvania's Andrew Curtin, did as much as Ohio's David Tod to encourage officials and citizens of his state to journey to Gettysburg to witness the dedication ceremonies. No other state had an ex-governor, a governor, and a governor-elect present on the central platform during the program. In fact, Ohio had more citizens seated on the platform than any other state. No other state, not even Pennsylvania, had as many newspapermen in attendance, one of whom wrote far and away the most detailed eyewitness account of the day's proceedings. One of the three major generals who marched in the procession and had a seat of honor on the platform was an Ohioan. Furthermore, the man who gave the second formal oration of the day, drawing more applause and presenting a more appropriate message than the first speaker, Edward Everett, claimed Ohio as his home.

The story behind the dedication of the Soldiers' Cemetery goes back to late June 1863 when General Lee's forces, with morale high and with Confederate flags and regimental banners waving in the summer breeze, crossed the Potomac and moved up into Pennsylvania. Since Ohio adjoins Pennsylvania, Lee's invasion of that state gave rise to much speculation and many rumors. Ohioans read the telegraphic accounts of the invasion and fighting at Gettysburg with interest and apprehension during the first week of July 1863. Pro-Lincoln groups feared that a notable Confederate victory might adversely affect the fall gubernatorial contest in which the Unionist party candidate, John Brough,

---

*Reprinted (with permission) from *Ohio History*, 79 (Spring 1970), pp. 76-100.

opposed Clement L. Vallandigham, the Peace Democratic nominee then in exile in Canada. Furthermore, many Ohio soldiers belonged to the Army of the Potomac and each military encounter generated anxiety back home.

After the battle was over and Robert E. Lee led his defeated army back across the Potomac, Ohioans pieced together the events of the bloody three days. They learned that their soldiers had performed heroically in various parts of the vast battlefield. Five infantry regiments and two of the four artillery batteries suffered heavily during the first day's action when the Confederates overpowered the Eleventh Corps on the plain north of Gettysburg. Three regiments and three batteries, reinforced by six other Ohio units played a decisive part in the fierce hand-to-hand fighting for Culp's Hill late on the second day, completely destroying the famous Louisiana "Tigers" in General Harry Hays's brigade. On the third day Ohio soldiers and batteries defended the Union flanks from positions on Cemetery Hill and on Little Round Top during Pickett's gallant but futile assault against the center of General Meade's defenses built along Cemetery Ridge. Ohio units numbering 4327 men counted their losses: 171 killed, 754 wounded, and 346 missing, totaling 1271 casualties, or nearly one in three engaged.[1]

Many Ohioans, informed of the death of a son, brother, or husband, journeyed to Gettysburg to claim the bodies and brought them home to be buried in local cemeteries.[2] Others only knew that their loved ones were among the missing or were not even informed that they were lying somewhere on the baneful battlefield. Some of the dead soldiers were buried hurriedly or carelessly and, in some cases, only shovelfuls of earth were tossed over the lifeless bodies by weary survivors. Heavy rains washed off some of the soil which had covered the dead, exposing portions of arms or legs, and sickening stench hovered over the areas where the first day's fighting had been heaviest.

While Ohio residents were reclaiming their dead and mourning the loss of loved ones, David Wills, a community leader in Gettysburg, took the initiative in urging the governor of Pennsylvania to purchase a portion of the battlefield, "the ground on which the centre of our line of battle rested July 2 and 3rd," for a cemetery and to rebury the patriotic soldiers who had fallen there. He stated that hogs were desecrating some of the graves and that "propriety and humanity" dictated that Pennsylvania should "take measures" to remedy the situation. Wills added that he was sure "other States which had lost sons at Gettysburg" would be willing to share the expenses in establishing a national cooperative cemetery to be administered by "the States interested."[3]

Governor Andrew G. Curtin, in turn, authorized Wills to buy whatever acreage he deemed necessary and to pursue the idea of a cooperative cemetery further, giving assurance of his own endorsement as well as that of the Pennsylvania legislature. Wills then sent a telegram on August 1, 1863, to each of the seventeen governors whose states had furnished the various Union forces which had fought with those from Pennsylvania on the battlefield of Gettysburg. His three-sentence telegram to Governor David Tod read:

By authority of Gov. Curtin, I am buying ground on or near Cemetery Hill, in trust for a cemetery for the burial of the soldiers who fell here in defense of the Union.

Will Ohio co-operate in the project for the removal of her dead from the field? Signify your assent to Gov. Curtin or myself, and details will be arranged afterwards.[4]

Governor Tod did not reply to Wills's telegram and follow-up letters on the question of Ohio's participation in the cemetery venture until August 23. He wanted to consult with members of his party's hierarchy:

Your letter of the 12th instant, giving plans, &c., for the place of rest of the gallant dead who fell in the battle of Gettysburg, is before me.

Heartily approving, as I do, of the project, I can only now promise that I will commend the same to the coming General Assembly.[5]

After state representatives from Wisconsin and Connecticut had assured David Wills that his project was a worthy one, he purchased twelve acres atop Cemetery Hill, secured the assistance of a landscape gardener to design the burial grounds, and composed some guidelines for the cooperative cemetery, including them in a circular letter he sent to each governor. Wills's carefully drafted circular letter on August 12 stated that he had purchased "about twelve acres" of the battlefield "to be devoted in perpetuity" for a soldiers' cemetery, that the dead would be buried in sections assigned to each state, that "the grounds to be tastefully laid out, and adorned with trees and shrubbery," and that the "whole expense," not to exceed $35,000, would be apportioned among the cooperating states — each "to be assessed according to its population, as indicated by its number of representatives in Congress." The letter closed with the request that each governor appoint "an agent" who would assist in the carrying out of the reburial project.

Wills also sent a short personal note to Governor Tod along with the printed circular letter. He said, if Ohio desired "a conveyance, in fee simple," for her share of the "burial ground in this cemetery," Pennsylvania would make a deed for it — otherwise she "will hold the title in trust for the purposes designated in the circular." "It is desirable," Wills noted, "to have as little delay as possible in getting your reply, as the bodies of our soldiers are, in many cases, so much exposed as to require prompt attention, and the ground should be speedily arranged for their reception."[6]

The Ohio governor, however, was dilatory in naming the state's agent expected to go to Gettysburg to work with Wills and other agents on the cemetery project. Waiting until October 25, Tod finally named Daniel W. Brown, a Republican judge who had once served as warden of the State Penitentiary, as the Ohio agent and instructed him to remain in Gettysburg as his representative until November 19, the day of the dedication ceremonies.[7]

Wills, meanwhile, had taken other steps to carry out the project. He purchased several adjoining plots of ground to bring the cemetery area to seventeen acres. He worked with William Saunders, who was a landscape gardener in the Department of Agriculture and was from Germantown, Pennsylvania, "to lay out the ground in State lots, apportioned in size according to the number of marked graves each state had on this battle field." He also invited bids for "disinterring, removing and burying in the National Cemetery, all the Union dead on the battle field." Thirty-four bids were received, ranging from the low of $1.59 to $8.00 per body; the contract was awarded to Frederick W. Biesecker, the lowest bidder. Wills, in turn, hired Samuel Weaver to superintend the exhuming of the bodies of Union soldiers. His duties included identifying the bodies in all the graves opened by Biesecker's crew and keeping careful record of all items found therein, and then seeing that the bodies were carefully placed in a coffin and reburied. In cases where Confederate bodies were uncovered, they were reburied where they were found.[8]

By mid-August Wills again wrote to Governor Curtin, outlining the progress being made and suggesting that the grounds be "consecrated by appropriate ceremonies." The Pennsylvania governor agreed with Wills's suggestion. "The proper consecration of the grounds must claim our early attention," Curtin replied, "and, as soon as we can do so, our fellow-purchasers should be invited to join with us in the performance of suitable ceremonies on the occasion." He then instructed Wills to set the date for the event and to plan the day's program.

Wills first set October 22 as the day for the dedication of the burial grounds as "sacred soil," and wrote to all the governors asking them to attend the ceremonies and help consecrate the grounds. He also invited the Honorable Edward Everett, the scholar-statesman who recently had changed from condoning secession to all-out support of the Union cause, to be the orator for the occasion. Everett accepted the honor but begged for a later date — his commitments would prevent him from being ready before November 19. Since Wills had his heart set on getting Everett, he had to change the dedication date from October 22 to November 19.

The change in dates necessitated another round of letters to the governors, Wills's letter to Tod being dated October 13. The Ohio governor, dilatory once more, delaying his answer for twelve days, promised that he and "a large number of our State officials" would be in Gettysburg for the dedication ceremonies. He also informed Wills that Daniel W. Brown had been named as the state agent "to look especially after the removal of the dead of our State . . . . He is a worthy gentleman, and I beg you to receive and treat him kindly."[9]

Tod's agent, with a letter of introduction and a draft for $100 in his pocket, left for Gettysburg on October 26. After a three-hour delay in Harrisburg and four at Hanover Junction, agent Brown arrived in Gettysburg. He walked directly to Wills's house, but the busy promoter had gone to a flag-raising on Round Top, about three miles south of the small town. Brown decided to walk over to witness the ceremonies. When he introduced himself to Wills, he received "a kind reception" and was then conducted on a tour of Cemetery Ridge before returning to Gettysburg. In the evening Wills held an informal reception for Brown and three other state agents, briefing them on action already taken and

COURTESY OF OHIO HISTORICAL SOCIETY

GOVERNOR DAVID TOD

Governor Tod arranged for a special train to take more than a hundred Ohioans to the dedication program at Gettysburg. He also arranged a special "Ohio program" after the dedication ceremonies.

explaining plans for the cemetery and its dedication. All of those already buried in the new cemetery were the unknowns killed north and west of town in the first day's fighting. These were not identifiable because they had lain out in the hot sun until the rebels retreated, so they could not be recognized and their shallow graves were unmarked.[10]

The next morning agent Brown accompanied David Wills on a tour of the fields where the rival armies had clashed in the first day's fighting. They visited the spot where Major General John F. Reynolds, General Meade's most trusted subordinate, had fallen and other points of interest, presumably the battle-scarred woods around McPherson's Ridge, the railroad cut, and the Middleton Road north of town where several Ohio regiments had suffered heavy losses. They also visited the new cemetery grounds to witness "the work going on there." In the afternoon Brown went to the "Hospital" to attend the funeral services for Enoch M. Detty, Company G, Seventy-Third Ohio Volunteer Infantry Regiment — the first known Union soldier reburied in the new cemetery. The funeral was conducted with military honors, and the ceremonies, symbolism, and scenery deeply impressed the Ohio agent. In reporting to his governor, Brown described the cemetery site as "one of the most beautiful as well as most appropriate places that could have been selected."[11]

Governor David Tod, meanwhile, composed a circular letter inviting "the officers of the State," which in terms of the invitation included state officials, members and members-elect of the state legislature, several newspaper editors, and a handful of military officials, to join him in witnessing the dedication of the Soldiers' Cemetery in Gettysburg on November 19. He wrote that the state would pick up the tab for the excursion to Gettysburg. "Upon being advised of your willingness and ability to participate in the ceremonies," the closing sentence of the letter read, "I will send you transportation at the expense of the State."[12]

The favorable response to Tod's invitation was overwhelming. About one hundred thirty wrote letters of acceptance, even though not that many actually attended. The list included such notables as Governor-elect John Brough, Colonel Edward A. Parrott, State Treasurer G. Volney Dorsey, and many others. It also included a surprising number of state legislators — nearly all Republicans.[13]

Two groups sent regrets. The first included those Ohio notables, like Major General William S. Rosecrans and United States Senator John Sherman who had already accepted an invitation to attend the opening of the Cleveland-Meadville (Pennsylvania) branch of the Atlantic and Great Western Railroad. This rival event of November 18 featured a free ride from Cleveland to Meadville, "a splendid lunch" there, the return trip to Cleveland, "a magnificent supper" at the Angier House, and an evening of entertainment and oratory.[14]

The second set of regrets came from Democrats, some of whom tried to make political capital out of Governor Tod's promise to provide free transportation to Gettysburg. George L. Converse, Democratic spokesman in the lower house of the state legislature the previous session, wrote a scurrilous letter declining Tod's invitation and circulated it in his party's newspapers. Converse said he did not want to accept any favor from a bitter political opponent who had been guilty of spreading "falsehoods and misrepresentations of me personally" during the recent hotly contested Brough-Vallandigham campaign. He also did not want to be "a party to the fraud and larceny of taking money from the Public Treasury to pay" for his trip to Gettysburg. The incensed Democratic critic asked a series of pointed and insulting questions:

> Will you allow me to inquire of your Excellency why it is that this "transportation at the expense of the State" is furnished to men who are generally able to pay their own expenses? Would it not be more prudent as well as more patriotic to furnish it to the poor widows and orphans, and childless mothers who have been made such by the great battle in July, that they might visit at the expense of the State the graves of their husbands, fathers and sons, and moisten the dry earth that covers the gallant dead, with the copious tears of affliction and affection that are now falling in silence and seclusion all over the land.

Converse asked other questions too. Could not the money, spent on an excursion to Gettysburg, be better spent by "purchasing clothing, fuel, and food for the suffering poor who have been made such by that great battle?" Was it proper for Tod to "unceremoniously thrust your [his] arm into the state treasury?" or "Was this a raid upon the treasury for the benefit of the Rail Roads?"[15]

Nearly every Democratic editor in Ohio published Converse's critique, some with and some without editorial comment. It appeared first in the *Crisis* in Columbus on November 4, 1863, along with editor Samuel Medary's comment to the effect that "it is gratifying to know that there is one man left bold enough to cry out against a system of the wildest extravagance which ever cursed any people." The editor of the Hillsboro *Weekly Gazette* added his own carping criticisms to those of Converse:

> We would like to know where Tod the thief got his authority to issue "transportation" to the amount of $15,000 to transport "officials" to Gettysburg! He addressed communications to Democrats offering to pay their expenses if they wo'd condescend to honor the brave dead at Gettysburg, by being present at the dedication of the Soldiers' Cemetery. Several refused, we notice, to have any complicity in the high-handed robbery of the Treasury. That's right. If any Democrat accepted Tod's pilfering "transportation," we are in favor of reading them out of the party.[16]

George W. Manypenny of the Democratic-oriented *Ohio Statesman* (Columbus) asked questions like Converse's: "The taxpayers will have to foot the bills; but what care these gentlemen [Tod & Company] for that? Does the State also pay for the Champaign [*sic*] and other luxuries that accompanied the 'expedition'?" James J. Faran of the Cincinnati *Enquirer* told his readers that Tod was guilty of violating the state constitution, citing the section which read: 'No money shall be drawn from the treasury, except in pursuance of a specific appropriation made by law.' Archibald McGregor of the *Stark County Democrat* (Canton) published Converse's letter in the same issue in which he featured an editorial comparing the "reign" of Lincoln to that of Oliver Cromwell and criticizing both for their use of force in an effort to gain the "allegiance" of conquered peoples. Some other Democratic state officials also felt the same as Converse and declined Tod's invitation *"to accept a gratuitous passage at the expense of the State."*[17]

Many Unionists, on the other hand, assured Tod that posterity would express its thanks and rewards for his efforts to honor the fallen soldiers. "If the living do not," wrote one, "the dead will bless you, for your affectionate care of Ohio soldiers." Isaac Jackson Allen of the *Ohio State Journal* (Columbus) said in his letter of acceptance to Tod's invitation: "Permit me to add that posterity will surely award both praise and blessings to the men, who, with yourself, have been instrumental in securing this solemn, appropriate, and honorable testimonial of an admiring Nation's gratitude to that *'noble Army of Martyrs'* who fell at Gettysburg! — Geo. Convers' [sic] infinitessimal [sic] soul to the contrary notwithstanding!"[18]

While the partisan controversy over the use of state funds for "Tod's excursion" continued, the reburial of the dead from shallow battlefield graves to the semi-circular landscaped cemetery went on at a steady pace. Daniel W. Brown, Tod's agent in Gettysburg, however, expressed his concern about the many Ohio soldiers whose remains were being exhumed and shipped back to Ohio. "Hundreds [of bodies]," Brown wrote late in October, "have been removed and friends are here constantly removing." He believed that most of these bodies being shipped back would have been left at Gettysburg to be reburied into the new soldiers' cemetery if only their friends and relatives had known of "the arrangements" being carried out. "The time for removing has about passed by," the solicitous agent added, "and those who may come here for friend who are marked [in marked graves], may find them already deposited in the cemetery, after which it will be very difficult to remove them without disarranging the whole plan."[19]

Samuel Weaver, the superintendent of the reburial work, sought to remove many bodies before the fall weather gave way to winter's cold, for spades and shovels were ineffective in frozen ground. Most of the battlefield graves were singles, but occasionally Weaver's men found the dead buried in trenches or shallow ditches, in which the decaying corpses laid side by side — in several instances the numbers in a single trench "amounted to sixty or seventy bodies." Weaver explained why some bodies were in an advanced stage of decomposition: "On the battle field of the first day, the rebels obtained possession before our men were buried, and left most of them unburied from Wednesday [July 1] until Monday [July 6], following when our men buried them. After this length of time . . . heat, air, and rains causing rapid decomposition of the body, they could not be identified."[20]

When it became apparent that many of the state's notables and citizens would attend the dedication ceremonies at Gettysburg, Governor Tod decided to arrange for a special Ohio program to be held in the late afternoon so that these gentlemen could "hear an address from one of their own number." After consulting with his friends, Tod invited Colonel Charles Anderson to give the oration. Anderson was an excellent choice — he was lieutenant governor-elect and had an outstanding reputation as a public speaker. Both his speeches and pamphlets had proved him "a good Union man." Since he had supported the Bell-Everett ticket in 1860, he was regarded as less a partisan than most Unionists — the term used for Republicans in Ohio during the Civil war. Furthermore, he had won praise for his bravery at Chickamauga, where he had been wounded. He was the brother of Major Robert Anderson, whose name had become a household word after the Fort Sumter attack of April 1861. Colonel Anderson accepted Tod's invitation, promising to do his best, and immediately set to work writing and memorizing an appropriate oration.[21]

Governor Tod, seeking to assure an excellent turnout for the dedication ceremonies and for the Ohio program, instructed the state's agent in Washington, D.C., to seek furloughs for Ohio troops in the area so that they might attend the Gettysburg affair on November 19.[22]

David Wills, meanwhile, expressed satisfaction with the progress of reburying soldiers and the transformation of a portion of the battlefield into a cemetery and with the cooperation he had received from the governors. President Lincoln had also helped by sending his bodyguard, Ward H. Lamon, to Gettysburg to give Wills whatever help he needed. In turn, Wills named Lamon the marshal for the dedication ceremonies. Wills and Lamon, discussing the organization of the procession and the program of November 19, decided to ask each of the cooperating states to name "two suitable persons" to help organize the procession and to supervise the day's affairs.[23] They also exchanged views about musical organizations and names of those who might be invited to give the benediction and invocation.

Wills, consequently, wrote to several musical organizations, inviting each to take part. He asked the Reverend Thomas H. Stockton, chaplain of the House of Representatives, to give the invocation and the Reverend Henry L. Baugher, president of Gettysburg Seminary, to close the dedication program with a benediction. Wills also invited President Lincoln, Vice-President Hannibal Hamlin, all Cabinet officials, heads of foreign legations, and members of Congress to attend. And after Wills received word from Lincoln that he would attend, the promoter had the foresight to ask the President to "formally set apart these grounds to their sacred use by a few appropriate remarks."[24]

As the day to entrain for Gettysburg approached, there was a flurry of activity in Columbus and Washington. President Lincoln, sensing the importance of the occasion, "strongly urged" his Cabinet members to attend "the ceremonials" at Gettysburg. Nevertheless, the two Ohioans in the Cabinet, Edwin M. Stanton, Secretary of War, and Salmon P. Chase, Secretary of the Treasury, found good excuses to spend the day in Washington. Both had earlier sent their regrets to David Wills. Chase, in a letter of November 16, asked to be excused because of his "imperative public duties." In reference to the fallen soldiers, he said, "It consoles me to think what tears of mingled grief and triumph will fall upon their graves, and what benedictions of the country, saved by their heroism, will make their memories sacred among men." The President, however, continued to twist Chase's arm. "I expected to see you [Chase] here at [the] Cabinet meeting," Lincoln wrote in his note of November 17, "and to say something about going to Gettysburg. There will be a train to take and return us,"[25] but Chase still ignored the President's request. Perhaps the fact that Secretaries William H. Seward, John P. Usher, and Montgomery Blair had decided to go was enough of an excuse for Chase to stay home — all were members of the rival faction within the Cabinet. So another of Ohio's most illustrious sons was not present at the ceremonies of November 19.

And still another, Stanton, offered the same excuses as Chase. He said that the duties of his office were too pressing to admit his absence from Washington, but he did make the transportation arrangements for the President. Stanton first arranged for a special train to leave Washington early on the morning of the dedication, arriving just in time for the ceremonies, and then for the train to return the same evening. Lincoln did not like this plan. A slight accident or delay would cause him to miss the program — it seemed "a mere breathless running of the gauntlet."[26] The Secretary of War then scheduled the President's party to leave Washington at noon on November 18, arriving at Gettysburg the evening before the ceremonies.

While Lincoln was still urging members of his Cabinet to accompany him to Gettysburg, Governor Tod's large entourage boarded the cars of the "Steubenville Short Line" (the Pittsburgh, Columbus & Cincinnati Railroad) on the morning of November 16 and waved good-bye as they headed for their destination via Steubenville, Pittsburgh, Harrisburg, and Hanover Junction. An accident about two miles east of Coshocton, the result of a collision of two freight trains, delayed Tod's train for seven hours. The impatient travelers spent the long hours playing euchre or spinning yarns. After clean-up crews removed the debris from the tracks and effected repairs, Tod's train resumed its journey toward Steubenville, arriving there an hour and a half past midnight.[27]

The train left Steubenville for Pittsburgh at six-thirty the next morning (November 17). When the Ohio delegation arrived, they found that Pennsylvania's Governor Curtin had placed "a beautiful and most commodious car" at their disposal. At Harrisburg a large number of Ohioans, including Governor-elect and Mrs. Brough and Colonel Charles Anderson, joined Tod's party. There Tod met Governor Andrew Curtin, his host, and boarded "the Governor's Special." Tod also met two other governors on this train, Oliver P. Morton of Indiana and Horatio Seymour of New York.

Bad luck seemed to dog Tod's delegation. About fifteen miles out of Harrisburg the locomotive "gave out" and the travelers lost three more hours, much to the embarrassment of Governor Curtin. The delay threw the train way off schedule and the overly cautious engineers proceeded at what seemed like a snail's pace, more anxious to get the passengers safely rather than speedily to

Gettysburg. It was nearly midnight when the creaky steam engine brought its train of special cars into the station.[28]

Agent Brown met the special train and escorted the dignitaries in the Ohio delegation to hotels or houses where he had reserved rooms. He had arranged for "suitable accommodations, although the town was crowded to excess by the throng of visitors seeking rooms and shelter." All Ohioans were not as fortunate as the important members of Tod's delegation. William T. Coggeshall of the Springfield *Republic*, for example, had to try to sleep "upon boards laid upon trussels, in the kitchen of a 'hospitable' Gettysberger."[29]

While directing the Tod party to quarters reserved for them, Brown reported on the progress of the reburials and on his own activities as the state's agent. The work of exhuming the bodies of the Union soldiers and reburying them in the new cemetery had proceeded satisfactorily, being about one-third completed by November 14. Twenty-four of the 1188 interred had been identified as Ohioans and had been reburied in that section reserved for the state. In addition, some of the 582 who had been buried in the section reserved for the "unknown" had belonged to Ohio regiments, but no one could hazard a guess as to how many. (The total number buried between October 27, 1863, and March 18, 1864, was 3564; Ohio's known dead was 131). Brown also reported that Ward H. Lamon, chief marshal for the ceremonies, had held a meeting with the assistant marshals who were present in the courthouse to give instructions regarding the next day's procession and plans. Since both of Ohio's assistant marshals, Colonel Gordon Lofland of Cambridge and Colonel George B. Senter of Cleveland, had been aboard Tod's train, they had missed Lamon's briefing session, so Brown informed them that the governors of the states and their staffs had been placed in the front section of the procession directly behind the speaker of the day and the chaplain, but that the Ohio delegation's place was at the end — a mile away. Brown also said that he had arranged for the use of a large Presbyterian church for the special Ohio program which would follow the cemetery dedication ceremonies.[30] Then, since it was very late and everyone was tired, members of Tod's large delegation sought sleep and rest, knowing that November 19 would be a strenuous day.

During the early hours of the morning of the 19th, successive showers of rain fell, but by eight o'clock the skies had brightened and the sun shone in all its autumnal splendor. The assistant marshals, under Lamon's supervision, made the rounds, instructing the states' delegations as to their places in the procession, scheduled to leave downtown Gettysburg at ten o'clock. Colonels Lofland and Senter, the assistant marshals representing Ohio, were decked out in "sashes of white and straw-colored ribbon, caught at the shoulders by mourning rosettes, Union rosettes upon their breasts, and saddle-cloth of white cambric, bordered with black."[31]

The presence of so many strangers and the steady arrival of sightseers made the task of the assistant marshals more difficult and delayed the departure of the procession for the new cemetery more than an hour. Many of the persons, coming on foot, horseback, carriage and train, were fathers, mothers, brothers,

or wives of the dead who had come from distant parts to weep over the remains of their fallen kindred and to witness the dedication or a portion of the
battlefield as holy ground.[32]

While Colonels Lofland and Senter tried to round up Ohioans and direct
them toward the street corner designated as the state's place in the procession,
thousands of visitors wandered around various portions of the huge battlefield.
Several members of the Ohio press corps, including Martin D. Potter of the
Cincinnati *Commercial* and Isaac Jackson Allen of the *Ohio State Journal*, joined some of the pilgrims on the country road leading to Cemetery Hill, half a
mile south of Gettysburg, where the ceremony was to be held. When Potter
reached the top of the hill, he noticed that the new cemetery (located adjacent
to the old) was "laid out in a semi-circular form, each State being allotted ground
in proportion to its dead .... The lines dividing these allotments are the radii
of a common center, where a flag-pole is now raised, but where it is proposed
to erect a national monument. The trenches follow the form of the circle, and
the head of each is walled up in a substantial manner [to hold the headstones
to be erected later]. The bodies, enclosed in neat coffins, are laid side by side,
where it is possible, the fallen of each regiment by themselves, the heads toward
the center. Boards bearing the name, regiment, and company are put up tem-
porarily."[33]

Newspaperman Isaac Jackson Allen, from his position atop Cemetery Hill,
observed the panoramic view of the countryside and was deeply stirred. "From
this point," he wrote with feeling, "the landscape is beautiful ... and as the
undulating valley, rich with fertile fields and dotted with glistening white farm-
houses, goes rolling on and on towards the distant mountains, that stand like
a giant framework to this lovely picture of peacefulness, and quietude, we could
scarce comprehend that all this had so recently been the theater where was
enacted one of the great tragedies of war."[34]

As the sentimental scribe looked northward, he saw the town of Gettysburg,
a beehive of activity, encompassed in the morning's sunlight. Northward also
lay the rolling countryside where many Ohio soldiers had given their lives in
the first day's fighting on July 1. West of Gettysburg he could see the outline
of McPherson's Ridge near which Major General John F. Reynolds had fallen,
victim of a well-aimed sharpshooter's bullet. When Allen turned his eyes south,
he saw the Union line's earthworks before which Pickett's Confederate division had made its fateful assault in the face of murderous musket and artillery
fire on the third day's fighting. Allen noticed that Cemetery Ridge, even yet,
was "grim and ghastly with the mute memorials of strife and carnage." He
saw the "soiled fragments of uniforms in which heroes had fought and died,
remnants of haversacks and cartridge-boxes, and other mementoes of that terrible conflict, still lay strewn about ... still lower down the hill side, is seen a
mound of earth covering the decaying remains of the artillery horses which were
slain by the side of the masters whom they served on that dreadful field."[35]

Newspaperman Allen then took a leisurely walk to Culp's Hill where nine
Ohio regiments and two batteries had fought heroically to repulse Confederate

attempts to capture that stronghold on the second day of fighting. While musing on "the tragic scenes" which had transpired there, he was joined by a soldier who had stood behind those rude breastworks and battled bravely in defending the hill against the persistent rebel attacks. He pointed out the places "where heroes fought and fell," and the trees "scarred and marred with ball and shell."[36]

After a brief visit to the small farmhouse which had been General Meade's headquarters, Allen hurried back to the platform which had been erected near the new cemetery especially for the dedication ceremonies. The sound of martial music greeted the ear, and when he looked northward he could see the long procession moving along the road toward the point he occupied. The military escort consisting of one regiment of infantry, one squadron of cavalry, and two batteries of artillery moved toward the platform to the blaring music of the Marine Band, which held second spot in the long procession. Allen noticed that "President Lincoln had joined in the procession on horseback . . . and is the observed of all the observers."[37] Riding with the military escort was General Robert C. Schenck. The Ohio officer had fought valiantly at Second Bull Run until he was wounded and sent to the rear to have his injury bandaged. Even more important, perhaps, he had bested Clement L. Vallandigham, a pro-peace crusader and critic of the Lincoln administration, in a hotly contested congressional election the previous fall. The general and his staff had boarded the President's special train in Baltimore, and, after his arrival in Gettysburg, Ward H. Lamon gave him a prominent place in the procession. Another Ohio newspaperman, witnessing Schenck and his steed, characterized the congressman-elect as "the finest looking officer of them all."[38]

Next came the "marshal's division commanded by Lamon. This group included President Lincoln, three members of his Cabinet, and two of his personal secretaries. On reaching the grounds, the President, dressed in black and wearing a crepe band around his stovepipe hat, dismounted, and marshal Lamon escorted him and his party to the platform. Dozens of persons, including ex-Governor William Dennison of Ohio, exchanged greetings or comments with Lincoln. While the President visited briefly with the many distinguished guests as he made slow headway toward his chair, the remainder of the long drawn-out procession moved toward the hilltop. When some members in the Ohio delegation, commanded by Colonel Lofland and last in the procession, realized that they would have little chance to see and hear the speakers, they "broke ranks and charged indiscriminately upon the crowd in front of the stand," creating consternation and confusion. A few secured good places near the platform, but the majority were so far from the speakers that they could see or hear little — "and soon wandered off to ramble over the battlefield."[39]

It required almost half an hour to arrange the multitude around the platform. Both Governor Tod, "gruff" and disgruntled, and Governor-elect Brough, of "massive frame" and self-confident demeanor, took seats in the second row of chairs on the huge platform — right behind the place reserved for the President. Members of Ohio's press corps, designated by Tod as members of his staff, "pro tempore," had places on the stage, but mostly in the back rows.

General Schenck and ex-Govenor Dennison had seats on the north end and were not seated with Tod and Brough. Ohio had more honored guests than any other state, so the state's representatives had an excellent chance to hear every speaker.[40]

It was about 11:30 a.m. before the President, accompanied by Secretaries Seward, Blair, and Usher, was able to ascend the steps leading to the platform and make his way toward his chair, in the front row and near the center of the stage. Tod and Brough, who had already been escorted to their seats by marshals Earl Bill and George Senter, stood up, obeying protocol. When Lincoln came near, Tod in hearty manner, said, "Mr President, I want you to shake hands with me." Lincoln cordially acquiesced. Then Tod introduced Governor Brough to the President, who said, "Why, I have just seen Governor Dennison of Ohio — how many more Governors has Ohio?" "She has only one more, sir," replied Brough, "and he's across the water."[41]

President Lincoln, in turn, introduced Tod and Brough to Seward. Tod told Seward that he had called on him earlier in the morning but did not find him. Seward replied that he and the President had visited the battleground west of Gettysburg early in the morning. "Well, Governor," Seward added, "you seem to have been to the State Department and to the Interior, I will now go with you to the Post Office Department." Whereupon Seward turned to Montgomery Blair and "introduced Governors Brough and Tod to him."[42]

After all those on the platform were seated, Birgfield's Band opened the formal program with a grand funeral march.[43] Next, Rev. Thomas H. Stockton, chaplain of the House of Representatives, gave the invocation — "a prayer which thought it was an oration," by one account. The Marine Band then played a number, during which the dignitaries alternately listened and visited.[44]

As the melodies of martial music drifted over the nearby hills, the Honorable Edward Everett arose to deliver his scholarly oration, replete with copious historical allusions. As he spoke into the second hour, many in the audience grew restless and "bits of the crowd" broke off to wander over the battlefield.[45] Those seated on the platform stared off into space or studied the expressions of the other guests who were waiting for the rambling, two-hour address to end. Martin D. Potter of the Cincinnati *Commercial* registered his observations for posterity. He saw the President, with his "thoughtful, kindly, care-worn face," listening intently. He observed Seward, with "a wiry face" and "bushy, beetling eyebrows," sitting with arms tightly folded and his hat "drawn down over his eyes." He noted the "absolutely colorless" face of Rev. Stockton with his "lips as white as the wasted cheek, and the flowing hair, and tuft of whiskers under the chin, as snowy white as wool." Potter also looked at Tod and Brough, fidgeting on their uncomfortable chairs. He characterized the former as "good-humored, florid, and plump" and the latter as "the Aldermanic Governor-elect of Ohio."

When Everett, exhausted ("the two-hour oration telling on him"), finished, applause was slight, "the audience being solemnized too much by the associations and influence of the spot to be more demonstrative." Also, quite possibly, the abstract character of the speech was inappropriate for the audience assembled. President Lincoln and Secretary of State Seward offered Everett their hands in congratulations. The crowd shuffled about restlessly; then twelve men of the Union Musical Association of Maryland sang a hymn written especially for the occasion by Benjamin B. French. This was an exceptional number, emotional and well rendered — it spoke of "holy ground," "Freedom's holy cause," and "mourn our glorious dead."[46]

As applause diminished, Ward H. Lamon introduced Lincoln. The President arose, took a "thin slip of paper" out of his pocket, and proceeded to the front of the stage. There was a rustle of expectation and a visible attempt of many to get nearer the stand. Those on the outer fringes, including some Ohioans, pushed to get nearer the President, trying "to make two corporeal substances occupy the same space at the same time."[47]

After first adjusting his glasses, but then discarding them and the paper because he seemed unable to focus his eyes in the bright sunlight, the President delivered his address unaided by notes. Though short, the Washington *Chronicle* said it "glittered with gems, evincing the gentleness and goodness of heart peculiar to him, and will receive the attention and command the admiration of all the tens of thousands who will read it." Isaac Jackson Allen of the *Ohio State Journal* noted that Lincoln was interrupted by applause five times. He also noticed that when the President uttered the words, "The world will little note, nor long remember what *we say* here, but it can never forget what *they did* here," a stalwart officer, wearing a captain's insignia and with one empty sleeve, buried his face in his handkerchief and "sobbed aloud while his manly frame shook with no unmanly emotion." After "a stern struggle to master his emotions, he lifted his still streaming eyes to heaven and in low and solemn tones exclaimed, '*God Almighty bless Abraham Lincoln.*'" Allen thought it was evident that Lincoln's appropriate remarks "had touched the responsive cords [of] feeling, that Everett's finished oratory had failed to reach."

When the President finished his short address, the audience gave him a "long applause," followed with three cheers for Lincoln and three more for the governors.[48]

Next came a dirge, followed by the benediction pronounced by the Reverend Henry L. Baugher, president of the Lutheran seminary located on the outskirts of Gettysburg. Marshal Ward H. Lamon then arose, stepped to the front of the platform, and announced that the Honorable Charles Anderson, Lieutenant Governor-elect of Ohio, would deliver an address at the Presbyterian church in Gettysburg at five o'clock. Lamon, speaking for Governor Tod, invited the President and members of his Cabinet, and all others, to attend the "Ohio program." He then proclaimed the assemblage dismissed.[49]

While the marshals reformed the procession, a battery of the Fifth New York Artillery fired a salvo of eight rounds. William T. Coggeshall of the Springfield *Republic* watched the reforming of the procession. He thought the

President "a timorous, but respectable horseman," and that Seward seemed "much more at home with a pen in his hand than with a bridle rein."[50]

After the procession reached Gettysburg and dispersed, most of the notables, including Dennison, Tod, and Brough, assembled at David Wills's home for a three o'clock dinner, followed by an hour-long reception. During the reception President Lincoln took his place in the hall opening on York Street and greeted guests as they entered. While the reception was in progress, a side show took place before the residence where Horatio Seymour of New York was staying. The Fifth New York Artillery Regiment marched in review as Governor Seymour and Major General Schenck stood on the front porch. Seymour presented the unit with the new silk regimental banner, a gift of the merchants of New York City. He also made a three-minute speech advocating a vigorous prosecution of the war and asking the artillerymen to bring added honors to the banner. He then called upon General Schenck for a few words. The eminent Ohioan spoke briefly and eloquently, thanking the regiment for past heroics and challenging the proud soldiers to win further honor and glory for themselves and their state.[51]

Shortly before five o'clock a large crowd assembled at the Presbyterian church to hear Colonel Anderson's oration. Ex-Governor Dennison presided over the meeting while Isaac Jackson Allen served as secretary. Dennison, as prearranged, called on Tod to say a few words. Aware that Ohio Democrats had abused him for dipping into state funds to subsidize the "junket" to Gettysburg, Tod defended his actions in cooperating with the sponsors of the new cemetery. He was happy to know that "one and all" in the Ohio delegation approved of his decisions relating to the state's participation in the day's proceedings. The respect paid to "the honored dead would be gratefully remembered by their kindred," giving cheer to the grief-stricken mothers and friends of "those who had fallen here." These bereaved would be heartened to know that "the virtuous and the good of their immediate neighborhood" fully appreciated the cause for which they had died.[52]

Dennison then invited General Schenck to give a short impromptu, speech, but he declined the honor in a few brief words. Just then John Burns, "a grave and venerable old man of seventy, clad in the common costume of a country farmer" in the company of President Lincoln, Secretary Seward, and Secretary Usher, entered the hall. Burns was there as the President's "honored guest," and the audience seemed more interested in him than in the three important public figures.[53]

After order was restored, Dennison introduced Colonel Anderson as not only a well-known orator but also "as a soldier who at the head of his regiment, in the Battle of Stone [Stones] River, had shed his blood in the cause of his country."[54] The speaker began by acknowledging the role of Ohio troops in the battles of Gettysburg, and, as Lincoln had earlier done, paid tribute to the gallant soldiers who had died for "the cause." He characterized the Confederate invaders turned back at Gettysburg as "the army of treason and despotism." "That host of rebels," Anderson asserted, "deluded and sent hither by conspirators and traitors, was vanquished, and fled cowering in dismay from this land of Penn and Franklin, of Peace and Freedom, across the Potomac, into the domain of Calhoun and Davis, of oligarchic rule and despotic oppressions.'' A rebel victory would have turned back civilization and set back the ideals of freedom and democracy. Then, turning his face upward, he spoke as if he heard the voices of the dead Union soldiers, their mute lips conveying the message:

> We have died that you might live. We have toiled and fought — have been wounded and suffered in keenest agonies, even unto death, that you might live — in quietude, prosperity, and in freedom. Oh! let not such suffering and death be endured in vain! Oh! let not such lives and privileges be enjoyed in ungrateful apathy toward their benefactors! Remember us in our fresh and bloody graves, as you are standing upon them. And let your posterity learn the value in the issues of that battlefield, and the cost of the sacrifice beneath its sod.[55]

Along with other topics Anderson discussed the factors and forces which had brought a new nation into being and lauded the ideals of this nation, "God's best hope on earth." Dwelling upon the consequences of disunion, he scolded the Peace Democrats, couching his criticism in rhetoric and metaphors. He borrowed from the abolitionists when denouncing slavery as an evil and the slave-catchers as devils incarnate. After defending Lincoln's emancipation policy, Anderson tried to convince northern workingmen that the freed blacks would not compete with them for jobs nor create social problems in the northern cities because "climate, custom, and society with their likes and equals will conspire to withhold the absent and withdraw from us those who are now here."

Anderson closed his discourse with an oratorical flourish. Yes, he wanted these honored dead remembered for all time. They, like the founding fathers of the nation, had striven to enthrone and enshrine American liberty. These soldiers had not died in vain; they were martyrs to a cause and their blood sanctified the country's ideals. The orator took his seat amidst resounding applause. The *Ohio State Journal* reported that "Both the President and Mr. Seward expressed great satisfaction with Col. Anderson's effort, and complimented the Ohio delegation upon the spirit and energy displayed by the earnest manner in which they had joined in the work of securing and dedicating the National Cemetery." The speaker gloried in the compliments and praise heaped upon him. Actually, he had made a more effective speech in forty minutes than Edward Everett had in two hours.

After Anderson's speech, Isaac Jackson Allen introduced three resolutions:

> *Resolved*, That the thanks of the Ohio delegation be tendered to the citizens of Gettysburg for the generous hospitality extended to us on the occasion of our present visit.
>
> *Resolved*, That the thanks of the delegation be tendered to Col. Anderson for his able and eloquent Address, and that he be requested to publish the same.
>
> *Resolved*, That the thanks of the delegation be extended to the officers of the Presbyterian Church for the favor conferred by the use of their church building on this occasion.[56]

After the Ohio program ended, many of the visitors headed for the railroad station to await their respective trains. The President's train, with Colonel Anderson, Governor-elect Brough, and General Schenck aboard, left for Hanover Junction at eight o'clock. The "Governor's Special," carrying Tod and most of the members of the Ohio delegation, moved off an hour later. At the Junction, while awaiting the arrival of the east and westbound trains, the passengers spent time in "easy conversation" as the governors and members of the Ohio delegation gathered around Mr. Lincoln. Writing later, Allen of the *Ohio State Journal* said he had a seat very near and could see that the President "was suffering from a grievous headache from sitting with his head bared in the hot sun during the exercises of the day. Resting his elbow on the arm of his chair, he leaned his head on his hand, listened and smiled at the quaint sayings of those around him, but joined sparingly in their conversation."[57] The President's train came to the Junction about midnight, bringing the storytelling session to an end. Brough, Anderson, and Schenck climbed aboard the Washington-bound train — Brough for meetings with the President and Secretary of War Edwin M. Stanton next day, and Schenck to return to Baltimore and the command of the Middle Department. Tod and members of the Ohio delegation had to wait for their train until eight o'clock the next morning, taking part in some "tall cussing" during the interim. "The amount of blasphemy manufactured at the little hotel [in Hanover Junction] was considerable," wrote an interested observer, "and contrasted very harshly with the solemn events of the day." "A good deal of indignation is manifested by people at the poor railroad accommodations," wrote Martin D. Potter of the Cincinnati *Commercial*, "and the Northern Central is in worse repute than ever."[58]

Every Ohioan, however, did not leave Gettysburg on the evening of the nineteenth. Several reporters, some soldiers on furlough, and parents or brothers of the reburied dead, stayed over to tour the battlefield and dream of other days. Editor John S. Stephenson of the Cleveland *Plain Dealer* — he was one of the few Democratic (with Unionist tendencies) editors who had made the pilgrimage to Gettysburg at the state's expense — spent two days visiting the various areas where war god Mars had reaped the heaviest harvest. On the twentieth he and two Cleveland soldiers, recuperating from wounds received during the battle, as guides, and the many sightseers visited those sectors where the Ohio regiments had fought so well. Stephenson collected some relics or mementoes: a bloody handkerchief, a soldier's cap pierced by a ball, a handful of round and conical bullets, and a skull bleached by the sun.[59]

"A great many citizens of Gettysburg," also noted Potter of the Cincinnati *Commercial*, "are in the relic business, and sold immense numbers of shot and unexploded shell, during the day, at stiff prices." Editor Stephenson, a man of considerable foresight, predicted that the battlefield would become "an American mecca," to which "thousands of sorrowing parents and others" would make "annual pilgrimages, to visit the last resting places of the loved ones." More than that, future generations would visit the grounds in great numbers, out of curiosity and respect, paying tribute to the brave, "who gave their lives that the nation might live."[60]

The story of the dedication ceremonies did not end with Lincoln's return to Washington and Tod's to Columbus. Most Unionists newspapers published Lincoln's brief address and Everett's long oration in full. The editors of these papers, still concerned about the Converse letter, went out of their way to praise Tod for his role in honoring Ohio's and the nation's dead. W. H. Foster of the Columbus *Express*, for example, saw the furthering of the democratic ideal in the Gettysburg ceremonies which witnessed the gathering of the great and lowly, the chief of state and yeomen farmers, famous generals and unknown privates, residents of the nearby towns and the "scholars, poets and artists of New England." "It was good to be there," he added, "and to be rebaptised in the spirit of patriotism, and devotion to human liberty."[61]

Most Democratic newspapers, on the other hand, either played down the events of November 19 and did not publish the text of the speeches, or openly criticized the speeches and belittled the Republicans' efforts. The *Crisis* (Columbus) and the Circleville *Democrat*, for example, published in full the speech which Clement L. Vallandigham, in Windsor (Canada West) as an exile, gave to a visiting delegation of students from the University of Michigan. The *Crisis*, in a discussion of the general topic of states' rights, criticized Lincoln's Gettysburg speech in regard to his division of power: '*of* the people, *by* the people, and *for* the people,' but said no more about the ceremony; and the Circleville *Democrat* described the ceremony in only one paragraph.[62] James A. Estill of the *Holmes County Farmer* (Millersburg) regretted the "bitter partizanship" which "was evinced by the abolitionists," especially before and after the dedication ceremonies. "The abolition leaders," Estill added, "acted more like wild enthusiasts in attendance at an excited political meeting than like men paying the last tribute of respect to those who have left the scenes of life forever."[63]

William H. Munnell of the Hillsboro *Gazette* viewed the Gettysburg gathering as a strictly partisan session "*to make Abolition nominations for the next Presidency*" and "*to harmonize if possible certain unruly elements that threaten the dissolution of the party.*" He believed that "these nominations," secretly agreed upon, would be publicly ratified later "to keep up a show." He ended his critical comments upon a bitter note:

> It is thus the memories of the dead are mocked by these Jacobin Infernals. What care they about the dead? They have made too many dead to honor them. Their business is to butcher men, not mourn over dead men. Show us the honor of robbing the State of Ohio of $15,000 to transport a pack of politicians to Gettysburg, who were amply able to pay their own expenses, if perchance honor of the dead prompted them in that direction. How many of the [Union] *Leaguers* would have been present, if they had to pay expenses out of their own pockets? Who is it that cannot afford to honor the dead and ride over the country, if their expenses are paid? We wonder how much champaign [sic] and bad whiskey was drank [sic]? Why was not this money expended in transporting the widows, mothers, and fathers, of the lamented dead, who were not able to pay their own expenses to Gettysburg?[64]

James J. Faran of the Cincinnati *Enquirer* did not have much to say about the Ohioans at Gettysburg, but used considerable newspaper space to criticize the speaker, Edward Everett, who was once a constitutionalist and a conservative but had become a radical and a Republican. Portions of speeches he had made in 1859, 1860, and 1861 were quoted in which the orator had stated his opposition to war as a means to national unity: "To expect to hold fifteen States in the Union by force is preposterous. . . . If our sister States must leave us, in the name of Heaven let them go in peace." Contrasted to this position, portions of the Gettysburg speech were quoted in which Everett criticized the principle of states' rights. " . . . to speak of the *right* of an *individual* State to secede, as a *power* that could have been, though it was not delegated to the *United States*, is simple nonsense." Faran thought the reader could draw his own conclusions about the integrity of the speaker who would hold such contradictory views within such a short span of time.[65]

Governor David Tod, on the other hand, expressed himself "particularly gratified" with the work of agent Daniel W. Brown in "the work of consigning the remains of our gallant dead to this their final and honored resting place." About three weeks after the dedication the governors received from David Wills to name two commissioners to meet at the Jones House in Harrisburg to devise "a plan for the protection and preservation of the grounds near Gettysburg" — to provide for expenses already incurred, to complete the work already begun, and to make provisions for the proper adornment and care of the grounds. Governor Tod again looked to Daniel W. Brown and Colonel Lofland for assistance and appointed them to be the state's commissioners, instructing them to attend all necessary meetings.[66] The two met with representatives of nine of the eighteen states on December 17, taking prominent roles in the deliberations. On a motion of Colonel Lofland, David Wills was elected chairman, an honor he had richly earned. The commissioners adopted five resolutions, all concerned with the establishment of a corporation for the completion and operation of the cooperative "Soldiers' National Cemetery."

On the motion of Mr. Levi Scobey of New Jersey a five-member committee was set up by the chairman "with a view to procure designs of a monument to be erected in the Cemetery." Wills named Brown to this special committee. Before adjourning the commissioners voted their thanks to Mr. William Saunders "for the designs and drawings furnished gratuitously for the SOLDIERS' NATIONAL CEMETERY." Then Brown offered the following resolution:

> *Resolved,* That MR. WILLIAM SAUNDERS be authorized to furnish forty photographs of the plan of the SOLDIERS' NATIONAL CEMETERY, for the use of the States having soldiers buried there.[67]

Ohio's share of the estimated $63,500 "expenses of finishing the cemetery" came to $7834.46. Brown, as a member of the battlefield monument committee, helped to select the design of the national memorial, eventually erected. It was to be a superstructure sixty feet high, consisting of a massive pedestal twenty-five feet square at the base and crowned with a colossal statue representing the Genius of Liberty. Later the individual states erected monuments at appropriate places on the battlefield. Ohio's were dedicated on September 14, 1887, and all the units engaged in the three-day battle were honored.[68]

After the bleak winter passed and the frozen ground thawed again, Samuel Weaver and his crew returned to their grisly work, scouring every foot of the battlefield and exhuming and reburying the Union dead. They completed their work on March 18, 1864, and Weaver reported that 3354 Union soldiers had been reburied (979 were unknown) and that 158 Massachusetts bodies had been reburied by a private contractor from Boston. Ohio had 131 soldiers occupying graves in the state's section of the half-circle cemetery.[69]

Democratic threats to censure Tod for spending state funds for the "junket" to Gettysburg came to naught. No such motion or resolution was even introduced into the legislature. Democrats held a minority of the seats in both houses and the many Unionist legislators who made the trip at state expense considered the money well spent. A handful of die-hard Democrats, however, obtained a modicum of revenge by voting against resolutions introduced by Republicans in both houses of the state legislature complimenting and thanking the out-going governor for his "able, self-sacrificing and devoted manner in which he has discharged all the duties of Chief Magistrate of this State," including "the enduring memorials to the dead of the *rank and file* in the cemeteries of Spring Grove and Gettysburg."[70]

The failure of dissident Democrats to introduce censure resolutions was, in effect, an admission that the public supported the state's participation in the dedication of the Soldiers' Cemetery at Gettysburg. Ohio did play an important role in that historic event, thanks largely to Tod's initiative and energy. The governor's foresight enabled him to realize the meaning of the second stanza of the ode which he had heard at the November 19 ceremonies:

> *Here let them rest;*
> *And summer's heat and winter's cold*
> *Shall glow and freeze above this mould —*
> *A thousand years shall pass away —*
> *A nation still shall mourn this clay,*
> *Which now is blest.*[71]

CHAPTER V

LINCOLN'S FIRST GETTYSBURG ADDRESS: A LITTLE KNOWN IMPROMPTU SPEECH PERHAPS BEST FORGOTTEN*

Most high school students know that President Abraham Lincoln delivered "a most memorable address" in Gettysburg as part of a program dedicating a portion of the famous battlefield as a soldiers' cemetery. Some even know that the nine-sentence address was delivered on a 12' × 20' platform on November 19, 1863. Few, however, know that the evening before, while a guest at the home of David Wills, the Civil War president responded to a serenade with a seven-sentence, impromptu speech that can properly be called "Lincoln's First Gettysburg Address," and one of the worst of his career.

When David Wills agreed to serve as Gov. Andrew G. Curtin's "agent" to buy a portion of the Gettysburg battlefield and transform it into a cemetery, he became the central figure in a saga rich in irony and famous in history. Wills, a 32-year old Gettysburger, had a solid reputation as a lawyer and civic leader, as well as one of the small city's leading Republicans. In time, Wills purchased 17½ acres (costing $2475.87) atop Cemetery Hill, near the Evergreen Cemetery already there, and comprising a portion of the ground where Pickett's famous charge had tried to penetrate the Union lines.

Wills wrote several rounds of letters to the governors of the other 17 states whose sons had fought and died on the famous battlefield, seeking their cooperation in the cemetery project. Dead Union soldiers whose bodies had not been shipped back to their hometowns and were still buried in various parts of the far flung battlefield would be reburied in allotted sections in the new cemetery. Wills secured the services of William Saunders, a well-known landscaper, who recommended that a monument be placed at the central point on the highest reach of ground in the new cemetery, and that the parcel allotted to each state run toward the common center, fitting together in a semicircular pattern. Wills

---

*Reprinted (with permission) from *Blue & Gray Magazine*, 8 (December, 1990), pp. 36-38.

awarded the contract for opening the battlefield graves, identifying the decaying corpses, inventorying contents of the pockets, and reburying the bodies in new graves in the soldiers' cemetery to a local resident, Frederick W. Biesecker, "at $1.59 per body."

As the project made headway, Wills suggested to his governor that it was time to be concerned with "appropriate ceremonies" and "the proper consecration of the grounds." Gov. Curtin, in turn, asked Wills to take over the responsibility of planning a proper program.

David Wills set to work with a passion. He invited Edward Everett to give the oration for the occasion, he asked President Lincoln to "formally set apart these grounds to their Sacred use by a few appropriate remarks," and requested Ward Hill Lamon's services as Marshal-in-Chief — supervising the proposed procession and serving as master-of-ceremonies during the program. The formal program would also include some musical numbers, opening and closing prayers, and an ode, which its author had entitled "Consecration Hymn." Wills invited President Lincoln, orator Everett, and Gov. Curtin to he his household guests before and after the dedication exercises, for he expected that the hotels in town would be "crowded and in confusion."

Lincoln's special train arrived in Gettysburg about dusk on the evening of November 18, 1863; one imaginative newspaperman said that it was "in shimmering moonlight." David Wills and Edward Everett, among others, were at the railroad station to meet and greet their president. An honor guard, consisting of members of the Invalid Corps, escorted Lincoln to the Wills's house, located on the central square with an entrance on York Street. Lincoln's black servant, William, tagged along, carrying the president's carpetbag. In the left hand pocket of the president's long black frock coat was a copy of the address he was scheduled to give the next day. It was not yet in its final form, as Lincoln planned to rework and rewrite that long, long last sentence — it carried over from page one to page two on White House stationery that was neatly folded in thirds.

Wills escorted Lincoln and his servant to a second floor bedroom. In addition to the bed, which was hardly long enough for the six-foot-four president, the room held two tables — one had a chair next to it and the other held a water basin and a pitcher. After Lincoln refreshed himself he went downstairs to partake in a sumptuous supper that Mrs. Wills was preparing.

Several telegrams arrived. One stated that Gov. Curtin's special train was delayed by a balky engine and a freight train. Another one, sent by Secretary of War Edwin M. Stanton, stated that all was quiet on the military front. And another, sent by Mrs. Lincoln, reported that "Tad" (the nickname for son Thomas), who was quite seriously ill when the president left Washington, was feeling better.

Host David Wills and his gracious wife seated the guests at the dining room table. Lincoln sat at the head of the table; Everett sat at the president's right. Everett, who several years earlier had imagined that Lincoln was some kind of a Western boor, was soon engaged in a lively conversation with the president. Later Everett would write that he found the president "the peer of any man at the table" in "gentlemanly appearance, manners, and conversation."

Wills's guests could hear music and shouts from the crowd gathered on the central square. Earlier in the day thousands had arrived in the small city of 3000 souls. Some had come by train or horse-drawn carriages; others on horseback or afoot. Some were "morbid curiosity seekers" who found "a sort of pleasure in beholding the ravages and misery of war" — this was the opinion of a newspaperman. Some had come to see and hear their president, or listen to the country's foremost orator (Everett), or walk over ground consecrated by the blood of those who had died on the battlefield.

As the day wore on every house and shed and stable had been turned into a lodging place. Gettysburgers, caught up in the excitement, had raised a 60-foot flagpole in the center of the square and recognized that their city was in the national spotlight. "It is expected," the editor of the city's Democratic newspaper wrote, that "this will be one of the most imposing and interesting occasions ever witnessed in the United States."

During the evening meal at the Wills's house, the 5th New York Artillery band left the pavilion in the public square to serenade the president. The crowd, growing by leaps and bounds, then centered its attention upon the house where Lincoln and Everett were eating and conversing. The calls for the president grew louder and more frequent. Lincoln excused himself from the table, walked to the front entrance of the house, stood in the doorway, and saw an audience that responded with shouts and cheers. "Abraham Lincoln is the idol of the American people at this moment," one observer wrote, adding, "Anyone who saw and heard, as I did, the hurricane of applause that met his every movement at Gettysburg would know that he lived in every heart."

After bowing, time and again, the president returned to the dinner table to finish his meal. The band, assembled close to the front door, continued to play, giving way once to a male quartet that sang several numbers, and again to an impromptu chorus that sang "We are coming, Father Abraham, three hundred thousand strong." The crowd chanted for the president — "continuously and vociferously."

Lincoln, reacting to instinct, returned to the front entrance to pay his tribute to the hundreds assembled there. Bows and nods and waves of the hand did not satisfy the crowd; bolder spirits called for a speech. Hesitantly, and in "a high treble voice," he offered his tribute:

> I appear before you, fellow citizens, merely to thank you for this compliment. The inference is a very fair one that you would hear me for a little while at least, were I to commence to make a speech. I do not appear before you for the purpose of doing so, and for several substantial reasons. The most substantial of these is that I have no speech to make. (Laughter) In my position it is somewhat important that I should not say any foolish thing. (A voice — "If you can help it.") It very often happens that the only way to help it is to say nothing at all. (Laughter) Believing that is my present condition this evening, I must beg of you to excuse me from addressing you further.

It was a disorganized, repetitious, jumbled, third-rate speech — undoubtedly the poorest of Lincoln's life. One reporter who listened to the seven-sentence speech wrote, "He said nothing, but he said it well." Evidently Lincoln's first Gettysburg address was flat and uninspiring, far less than an eager crowd on the eve of such an auspicious occasion had anticipated from their president.

Disappointed that Lincoln had let them down, the crowd centered its attention next door to serenade Secretary of State William H. Seward, who was an overnight guest of Robert G. Harper, editor of the city's Republican newspaper. Seward acknowledged the serenade and gave a brief but emotional speech, blaming slavery and the South for the war and paying a tribute to those who fought and died on nearby battlefields. It was far superior to Lincoln's redundant remarks a short time earlier. The crowd broke into segments, each seeking diverse excitement. Lincoln would have a chance to redeem himself.

As the clock approached the hour of ten the president expressed a desire to retire to his upstairs bedroom. The others awaited the long delayed arrival of Gov. Curtin — his train would not arrive until about midnight. Lincoln wanted to rework and rewrite that long last sentence of the address that he would be giving on the morrow. About ten minutes later Lincoln's servant William came downstairs to tell Wills that his master wanted a pencil and some writing paper. Wills gave William a pen and several sheets of bluish-gray foolscap and the latter hurried back upstairs. Lincoln reshaped and rewrote that long last sentence, this time finishing it on the foolscap that Wills provided. After rereading it several times — it evidently finally met his exacting literary standards — the president came downstairs with his two-page manuscript in hand and told his host that he wanted to see his Secretary of State. Wills offered to fetch Seward. "No," Lincoln said, "I'll go and see him." With Wills leading the way the two set out for Harper's house next door. As they walked the short distance they were serenaded by the Union Glee Club of Philadelphia. A newspaperman noted that Lincoln and Wills moved slowly through the crowd "while the singing was in progress." Apparently Seward read and approved of the brief address. As Lincoln returned "the crowd called upon him for another speech, and he told them he would see them tomorrow. The crowd then gave him three cheers . . . ." Wills later wrote, "In less than half an hour, Mr. Lincoln returned with the same paper in hand." The address still needed to be memorized and recited.

After spending some time trying to imprint the finely tuned address in his memory, the president retired for the night, tired and exhausted and evidently oblivious to the noise and commotion still continuing outdoors. Members of the crowd seemed to be in "a festive mood" as they sang and cheered and "hallooed." The moon did not seem to fit with the dedication ceremonies planned the next day.

* * * * *

During the very early hours of the next morning, November 19, 1863, a shower dampened the grass and the dusty roads, but before eight o'clock the skies cleared and "the sun shone in autumnal splendor." During the morning hours special trains arrived to swell the crowd "to immense proportions." The roads swarmed with travelers. "At an early hour, long before sunrise," a reporter wrote, "the roads leading to Gettysburg were crowded by citizens from every quarter thronging into the village in every kind of vehicle — old Pennsylvania wagons, spring wagons, carts, family carriages, buggies, and more fashionable modern vehicles, all crowded with citizens — kept pouring into the town one continual string, while the roads were constantly dotted with pedestrians by twos, by threes, singly, in companies, all facing toward the village."

After an early breakfast the president returned to his room to review and finish memorizing his nine-sentence address (the long last sentence consisted of 82 words). John Nicolay, the president's competent secretary, called on Lincoln — as Nicolay later wrote "to report for duty." Nicolay found the president sitting at a table in his room, with a pencil in his right hand and his address laid out before him. Nicolay noted that the first page, in ink, was White House stationery while the second page, in pencil, was bluish-gray foolscap.

With his address fully memorized, and ready to redeem himself, Lincoln, Seward, and William McDougall (the president's Canadian guest) took a carriage ride westward toward the Lutheran Seminary where some of the first day's fighting was fiercest. After an hour or so the carriage brought Lincoln back to the Wills's house so that he could ready himself for the procession and the program dedicating the new soldiers' cemetery.

Lincoln did redeem himself atop the $12' \times 20'$ platform on Cemetery Hill, a scant half-mile south of Gettysburg. Without a single gesture and with great confidence he recited his two-page address without once referring to the manuscript that he held in his left hand. The audience interrupted with applause five times and when Lincoln finished there was "long continued applause." Then the appreciative audience gave the president "three cheers" and added three more for the eight governors who were in attendance.

When Lincoln returned to his chair Everett arose to greet him, supposedly saying, "Mr. Lincoln, allow me to congratulate you on those noble sentiments . . . there was more in your twenty lines [Everett erred by eleven] than in my twenty pages." Later, in a letter, Everett complimented Lincoln again: "Permit me also to express my great admiration of the thoughts expressed by you, with such eloquent simplicity & appropriateness, at the consecration of the cemetery. I should be glad, if I could flatter myself that I came as near to the central idea of the occasion, in two-hours, as you did in two minutes. My son who parted from me in Baltimore & my daughter, concur in this sentiment . . . ." It was the case of a Boston Brahmin paying a sincere compliment to a son of the Western prairies.

Everett's compliments were matched by others. Robert Ingersoll, one of the most famous orators of the post-Civil War era said: "The oration of Lincoln will never be forgotten — it will live until languages are dead and lips are dust." A contemporary wrote, "It ought to be remembered as long as the language lasts in which it was spoken." Lord Curzon, English statesman and man-of-letters, regarded Lincoln's nine-sentences one of the three great orations delivered "in the mother tongue." Curzon wrote: "The Gettysburg Address is far more than a pleasing piece of oratory. It is a marvelous piece of English composition. It is a pure well of English undefiled . . . . The more closely the address is analyzed the more one must confess astonishment at the choice of words, the precision of the thought, its simplicity, directness and effectiveness . . . . Above all, it was a declaration of America's fundamental principles."

Ironically, Lincoln's best address followed his worst by but half a day. One is revered and memorized; the other is ignored and forgotten. Truly, Lincoln redeemed himself so magnificently that his second practically relegated his first Gettysburg address to oblivion.

PART THREE: THE GETTYSBURG ADDRESS

These four chapters deal with Lincoln's Gettysburg Address in one way or another. Lincoln's two-minute speech has been regarded among the world's finest. Lord Curzon, an English statesman who was a great orator, said that the Gettysburg Address was one of the three greatest masterpieces of English eloquence. Lincoln's Secretary of War, Edwin M. Stanton, who gave us the words "Now he belongs to the ages," also had a compliment for the Gettysburg Address: "It will be remembered as long as anybody's speeches are remembered in the English language." Interesting too is a comment made by Herbert Hoover in 1930: "Greater than the tribute of granite or bronze remains that memorable message to the American people."

The first of these chapters deals with two of the most popular myths about Lincoln and the Gettysburg Address: 1) that Lincoln wrote it on the Gettysburg-bound train, either on the back of a yellowed envelope or on a bit of wrapping paper, and 2) that there was no applause during or after the speech. This chapter was originally presented as a paper at a national convention of the Military Order of the Loyal Legion of the United States — a convention held in Milwaukee. The eleven footnotes were dropped when a copy was sent to the editor of *Blue & Gray Magazine*. It was published soon after (in the November, 1984 issue).

The second chapter in Part Three resulted from an attempt to deal with an old topic in a unique way. Each of the ten in the front row received a hearing. Lincoln and Everett, of course, occupied the two middle chairs. Then there were three governors and two preachers. Finally we had William Saunders and Benjamin B. French — each of the two earned a front row chair.

The chapter entitled "Seven Who Witnessed Lincoln's Gettysburg Address" was first presented as a paper to the membership of the Lincoln Fellowship of Wisconsin. It was later published by that organization as *Historical Bulletin No. 40*. Because three of the seven who witnessed Lincoln's Gettysburg Address occupied front row chairs on the 12 ′ × 20 ′ platform, there is some repetition here.

The Milwaukeean who occupied a back-row chair on the speakers' platform at Gettysburg, and witnessed Lincoln's Gettysburg Address, was W. Yates Selleck. Later in life he wrote an 1800-word recollection that is an important primary source — thus incorporated into this chapter. It lists the thirty-eight persons who had places on that platform. Selleck was an astute observer, so his recollections should be of interest to every reader.

CHAPTER VI

*LINCOLN, THE GETTYSBURG ADDRESS, AND TWO MYTHS**

Time, circumstance, and nationalism have transformed Abraham Lincoln into a national hero, surrounding him with myths and legends. Debunkers and academic historians have chipped away at the myths and legends, but on the popular level, the stories continue to circulate and misrepresent history.

Two myths about the Gettysburg Address continue to make the rounds and, like the cat with nine lives, refuse to die. One is that Lincoln composed his short speech aboard the Gettysburg-bound train, writing it either on a brown piece of wrapping paper or a yellowed envelope. The second is that Lincoln's address either entranced his vast audience or fell on them like "a wet blanket" and that there was no applause — the spell of stunned silence leading the President to believe his performance was a disaster.

No book has contributed more to the fashioning of these two myths than Mary Shipman Andrews's *The Perfect Tribute* (1906). It is a little book — only forty-seven pages of text — which seemingly presented fiction as fact.

The book starts out by describing the scene aboard the special train taking President Lincoln and others to Gettysburg for the dedication ceremonies. Edward Everett, with his two-hour oration fully memorized, occupied a seat across the aisle from Lincoln (actually, Everett was already in Gettysburg). The President sat quietly, perhaps concerned with his role in the next day's program. There was the need, of course, to make some "appropriate remarks" dedicating a portion of the battlefield at Gettysburg as a cemetery. Thus Andrews wrote:

> And the work might as well be done now in the leisure of the journey. He put a hand, big, powerful, labor-knotted, into first one sagging pocket and then another, in search of a pencil, and drew one out broken across the end. He glanced about inquiringly — there was nothing to write upon. Across the car, the Secretary of State had just opened a package of books and their wrapping of brown paper lay on the floor, torn carelessly in zig-zag. The President stretched a long arm.

---

*Reprinted (with permission) from *Blue & Gray Magazine*, 2 (November, 1984), pp. 7-11.

"Mr. Seward, may I have this to do a little writing?" he asked, and the Secretary protested, insisting upon finding better material.

But Lincoln, with a few words, had his way, and soon the untidy stump of a pencil was at work and the great head, the deep-lined face, bent over Seward's bit of brown paper, the whole man absorbed in his task.

The words, according to Mrs. Andrews, came hard, being "colorless and wooden." Finally he finished with his scribbling, unhappy with the results. "It was," Mrs. Andrews added, "the best he could do, and it was a failure. So, with the pang of the workman who believes his work done wrong, he folded the torn bit of paper and put it in his pocket, and put aside the thought of it, as a bad thing which he might not better, and talked cheerfully with his friends."

Several pages later, Mrs. Andrews turns the scene to the $12' \times 20'$ platform atop Cemetery Hill, half a mile due south of the small town of Gettysburg. It was a day later — the early afternoon of November 19, 1863, with the dedication ceremonies in progress.

After a lengthy invocation, the Marine Band played Luther's hymn "Old Hundred." Then, as the music drifted over the valley and the hills beyond, it was Edward Everett's turn to shine. According to Mrs. Andrews, he orated in masterful fashion, thrilling the audience gathered in a half-circle before the platform. Cheers and applause paid honor to the speaker when he finished his memorized two-hour recitation and returned to his chair.

It was Lincoln's turn. He unwound from his chair, stepped forward hesitantly, and sized up the audience. After adjusting his spectacles and looking down at his two-page manuscript, he recited his piece — an address consisting of only nine sentences. The audience seemed lifeless. It failed to respond to his words. Mrs. Andrews wrote:

> There was no sound from the silent, vast assembly . . . . He stared at them a moment . . . . Not a hand was lifted in applause. Slowly the big, awkward man slouched back across the platform and sank into his seat, and yet there was no sound of approval, of recognition from the audience; only a long sigh ran like a ripple on the ocean through rank after rank. In Lincoln's heart a throb of pain answered it. His speech had been, as he feared it would be, a failure.

Mrs. Andrews's little book added another bit of fiction. In the last paragraph, Lincoln was visiting a soldiers' hospital near Washington and stopped at the bedside of a dying Confederate soldier. The soldier, not knowing who his visitor was, had high praise for LIncoln's Gettysburg Address, saying its words were magnificent and its sentiments enduring. He wished that someday he could shake the hand of the president whose words had seared his soul. As life ebbed away, the dying soldier reached out and grasped the hand of his strange caller. Holding Lincoln's hand, the soldier gasped and died — not knowing his deathbed wish had been realized.

Mrs. Andrews's contributions to Lincoln mytholody were matched by those of Ward Hill Lamon. Before his death, Lamon completed a manuscript entitled,

"Recollections of Abraham Lincoln, 1847-1865." Edited by his daughter, the manuscript evolved into a book published in Chicago in 1895.

Ward Hill Lamon's friendship with Lincoln dated back to their circuit-riding days in Illinois. Lincoln frequently served as co-counsel in cases which Lamon initiated in the state courts. In the book, Lamon explains his early relationship with Lincoln: "I was his local partner, first in Danville, and afterwards in Bloomington. We rode the circuit together, traveling by buggy in the dry seasons and on horseback in bad weather, there being no railroads then in that part of the state." The acquaintanceship was strengthened when Lamon married the daughter of Stephen T. Logan, Lincoln's law partner at the time.

Lamon and Lincoln developed a respect for one another despite the fact they were opposites in so many ways. Lamon was burly, gruff, handsome, and possessed a swashbuckling air. Lincoln was lean, tall, gentle, and modest in a strange sort of way. Lamon was a brawler and "a legendary boozer" who spent more time in a downstairs saloon than in his upstairs law office. Lincoln, on the other hand, was kindly and mild, abhorred violence, and preached and practiced temperance. Perhaps Lincoln, as far as Lamon was concerned, placed faith in an old Kentucky saying: "Folks who have no vices generally have few virtues."

When Lincoln sought the presidential nomination at the Republican National Convention in Chicago in June of 1860, Lamon was there actively working in his friend's behalf. In fact, he deserves some of the credit for printing a second set of tickets for seats in the convention hall and packing the place with Lincoln supporters. After Lincoln's nomination and election, Lamon became the President-elect's bodyguard. He was constantly at the side of the President-elect during the strange midnight ride from Philadelphia to Washington, supposedly to foil an assassination plot. Lamon was ready for action, armed with two revolvers, two pistols, and two big knives. Lincoln gave him a fancy title, "United States Marshal for the District of Columbia," and occasionally sent him on special missions.

Lamon had an important role in the ceremonies dealing with the dedication of the soldiers' cemetery at Gettysburg. He served as "grand marshal" for the day, supervising the procession from Gettysburg to the top of Cemetery Hill, and served as master of ceremonies during the formal program. He stood in the front and left corner of the 12' × 20' platform while Edward Everett recited his long, long, oration and Abraham Lincoln gave his brief address.

Lamon was on a special mission to Richmond on the night Lincoln was shot at Ford's Theatre, April 14, 1865. Soon after, Lamon returned to Illinois to resume his law career and write his memoirs. He quickly sloughed the veneer of respectability the Washington setting had imposed upon him. When writing his recollections he fabricated conversations, made up incidents, and told outright lies.

Several of the lies pertained to Lincoln's performance on the platform during the dedication ceremonies at Gettysburg. For example, Lamon fabricated this quotation and attributed it to Lincoln: "He said to me on the stand, immediately after concluding the speech, 'Lamon, that speech won't scour. It is a flat failure, and the people are disappointed'." For good measure, Lamon added another paragraph of make-believe:

> Mr. Seward turned to Mr. Everett and asked him what he thought of the President's speech. Mr. Everett replied, "It is not what I expected from him. I am disappointed." Then in his turn Mr. Everett asked, "What do you think of it Mr. Seward?" The response was, "He has made a failure, and I am sorry for it. His speech is not equal to him." Mr. Seward then turned to me and asked, "Mr. [Grand] Marshal, what do you think of it?" I answered, "I am sorry to say that it does not impress me as one of his great speeches."

Feeling the need to buttress his tall tale, Lamon added another lie in his hand-written recollections: "Mr. Lincoln said to me after our return to Washington, 'I tell you Hill, that speech fell on the audience like a wet blanket. I ought to have prepared it with more care'."

Ward Hill Lamon and Mary Shipman Andrews were not the only contributors to the two myths. Harriet Beecher Stowe, author of *Uncle Tom's Cabin*, stated that President Lincoln wrote his address aboard the Gettysburg-bound train. In a book entitled *Men of our Times*, published three years after Lincoln's death, Mrs. Stowe said:

> Perhaps in no language, ancient or modern, are any number of words found more touching and eloquent than his speech of November 19, 1863, at the Gettysburg celebration. He wrote it in a few moments, while on the way to the celebration, on being told that he would be expected to make some remarks.

But Mrs. Stowe was in Boston and not aboard the special train. She was only repeating rumors making the rounds in parlors and dining rooms.

Andrew Carnegie's contentions were even more preposterous. The story circulated that he was aboard the President's special train, visited with him, and even gave Lincoln the broken pencil with which the Gettysburg Address was written — this time on the back of a yellowed envelope. Though Carnegie got good mileage out of the story, he was in Pittsburgh at the time.

Historical evidence contradicts the myths devised or circulated that Lincoln wrote the Gettysburg Address aboard the Gettysburg-bound train the day before the ceremonies. The imposing evidence is that the first eight sentences of the nine-sentence address were written in Washington sometime before Lincoln went to Gettysburg. It is a fact that the first page of Lincoln's first draft of the Gettysburg Address was written in ink and on White House stationery. The ninth and last long sentence started on the same page of White House stationery, and was completed in pencil on a page of bluish-gray foolscap — it was probably reworked and rewritten in Gettysburg the evening before the dedication ceremonies.

Lincoln told journalist Noah Brooks, a close friend and confidant, that the address "was written, but not finished" several days before he left

Washington for Gettysburg. James Speed, a Kentucky friend who later became President Lincoln's Attorney General, also stated that he had been told, several days before the Gettysburg trip, that the address was "nearly done," needing only slight revision. Evidently, the first draft was down on paper, but Lincoln was not satisfied with that long, last sentence.

Lincoln wrote nothing on the train. John Nicolay, the President's personal secretary who *was* aboard the special train and always available to "the Tycoon" (a phrase of endearment Nicolay sometimes used), stated firmly and explicitly that Lincoln did not put pencil to paper on the Gettysburg-bound train. Recalling the journey, Nicolay wrote: "There is neither record, evidence, nor well-founded tradition that Mr. Lincoln did any writing, or made any notes, on the journey between Washington and Gettysburg."

In Gettysburg, the President (as well as Edward Everett) were the overnight guests of David Wills, the local Republican leader responsible for fashioning the dedication program — asking Edward Everett "to deliver the oration for the occasion" and inviting Lincoln to "formally set apart these grounds to their sacred use by a few appropriate remarks." Later in the evening, Lincoln retired to his upstairs bedroom to rework and rewrite that troublesome last sentence — this time in pencil and on a page of bluish-gray foolscap provided by his host. Satisfied at last, Lincoln came downstairs carrying this two-page address and asked David Wills to direct him to Secretary of State Seward's quarters.

Wills conducted Lincoln next door where Seward was staying at the home of Robert Harper, editor of the county's Republican newspaper. Lincoln evidently read his brief speech to the Secretary of State, who approved of the language and sentiments. When Lincoln returned to the Wills house he retired to his room, perhaps spending some time memorizing his address before going to bed.

After breakfast next morning, John Nicolay "reported for duty" to Lincoln's room. He found the President sitting at a table with a pencil in his hand, reviewing the remarks which he had committed to paper. Lincoln's personal secretary noticed that the first page was in ink on White House stationery and the second was in pencil on bluish-gray foolscap. After a while, fully satisfied that his speech was in its final form and fully memorized, the President folded his two-page manuscript in thirds and put it in the left-hand pocket of his black frock coat — the folds match and still show on the two pages, offering mute testimony that Lincoln had prepared well.

Historical evidence also contradicts the myth, stated by both Mary Shipman Andrews and Ward Hill Lamon, that Lincoln's speech at the dedication ceremonies was greeted by "stunned silence" or that the President regarded his performance as "a flat failure."

Edward Everett's two-hour oration, as tiring for the crowd as it was for the seventy-year old speaker, was followed by an ode superbly chanted by a twelve-man chorus of the Maryland Musical Association of Baltimore. The ode, replete with such terms as "holy ground," "sacred blood," "widow's tears," "our glorious dead," and "Freedom's holy cause," struck a responsive chord with the audience. Long and loud applause followed, indicating the crowd's appreciation.

Then it was Lincoln's turn. Slowly he untangled himself from his chair, pulled the two-page manuscript from the lefthand pocket of his frock coat, and shuffled forward two steps. He adjusted his spectacles and waited for silence. He sized up his audience, glanced down at his manuscript, and eyed the crowd again. In a firm and high pitched voice he began to recite the nine sentences he had committed to memory.

Newspaper accounts of the occasion, in both the Cincinnati *Commerical* and the Washington *Chronicle*, indicate that the audience interrupted Lincoln's recitation of his address five times. Then there was "Tremendous applause" when he finished with the words "that we here highly resolve these dead shall not have died in vain — that this nation, under God, shall have a new birth of freedom — and that government of the people, by the people, for the people, shall not perish from the earth." More than that, as Lincoln returned to his chair the appreciative audience gave "three cheers" for the President.

Both Edward Everett and Secretary of State Seward arose to meet Lincoln and compliment him, for he had caught the spirit of the occasion and touched the hearts of his audience. "Mr. Lincoln," Everett said as he grasped the President's hand, "allow me to congratulate you on these noble sentiments . . . there was more in your twenty lines than in my twenty pages." A day later, Everett wrote to Lincoln to compliment him again: "I should be glad, if I could flatter myself that I came as near the central idea of the occasion, in two hours as you did in two minutes. My son-in-law and my daughter [both had seats on the platform] . . . concur in this sentiment."

Benjamin B. French, who had a front-row chair on the platform and who had composed the ode so ably chanted by the Baltimore chorus, also recognized that Lincoln had excelled. He noticed Lincoln's empathy with his audience and the emotions of the crowd. He wrote his observations as a diary entry:

> Anyone who saw and heard, as I did, the hurricane of applause that met his every movement at Gettysburg would know that he lived in every heart. It was no cold, faint shadow of a reception; it was a tumultuous outpouring of exaltation from true and loving hearts . . . . It was the spontaneous outburst of the heartfelt confidence of the people in their President.

Lincoln's empathy with his audience was also revealed by the actions of a soldier who occupied a spot directly in front of the platform and who followed the proceedings with a passionate interest. This unknown soldier had an empty sleeve — he had lost an arm at Gettysburg. When Lincoln recited the sentence "The world will little note nor long remember what we say here, while it can never forget what they did here," the soldier's emotions nearly took over. An observant newspaperman reported what he saw:

> . . . a gallant soldier (a stout and stalwart officer bearing a captain's insignia) buried his face in his handkerchief [and] sobbed aloud while his manly frame shook with no unmanly emotion. In a few moments, with a stern struggle to master his emotions, he lifted his still streaming eyes to heaven and in low and solemn tones exclaimed "God Almighty, bless Abraham Lincoln."

This soldier's action, as well as the historical evidence offered by Benjamin B. French, Edward Everett, and a host of newspaper reporters, refute the myth that Lincoln's Gettysburg Address was met by "stunned silence" and that the Civil War President, ever the realist, believed his speech was "a disaster."

It is high time these two myths were laid to rest and the slanderous statement that Lincoln went to Gettysburg unprepared be again discredited. Lincoln performed well because he had prepared well and was able to sense public sentiment. He knew the age-old axiom: "Thorough preparation brings just rewards."

CHAPTER VII

THE TEN WHO SAT IN THE FRONT ROW ON THE PLATFORM DURING THE DEDICATION OF THE SOLDIERS' CEMETERY AT GETTYSBURG*

The scene of November 19, 1863 atop Cemetery Hill, half a mile due south of the small city of Gettysburg, was a most impressive one. A crowd of approximately nine thousand, formed as a half-circle, confronted a newly constructed platform. The eyes of the audience were focused on the overcrowded 12 ′ × 20 ′ platform, but especially upon the dignitaries seated on the chairs, arranged in three rows — ten chairs to a row.

The affair, the dedication of 17½ acres of a famous battlefield as a soldiers' cemetery, had been carefully planned. Every Northern state was represented in the audience. Some people had come because they sensed the importance of the occasion. Some, perhaps prompted by patriotism, wanted to visit the battlefield where the gray-clad Confederates had more than met their match in the most dramatic battle of the war. Others had come to see and hear their President, or listen to the nation's most distinguished orator, or gawk at the other notables having a place on the platform. "Perhaps on no other stage," a reporter for the *Cincinnati Commercial* wrote, "has there been such a conjunction of all that is distinguished by official position, statesmanship, learning, and eloquence."[1] Although most members of the vast assemblage were interested in the two principals sitting on chairs in the middle of the front row, some were anxious to view the three members of the Cabinet, the nine governors, or the five generals who had seats on the platform.

The seating as well as the day's program had been planned by David Wills, a thirty-two year old Gettysburger who was both a friend and political ally of Andrew Curtin, the governor of Pennsylvania. In fact, Wills was the central figure in the story of the soldiers' cemetery.[2] It was he who conceived the idea of transforming battlefield acreage into a soldiers' cemetery subsidized by the

---

*Reprinted (with permission) from the *Lincoln Herald* , 88 (Winter, 1985), pp. 106-113.

eighteen Northern states which had lost sons at Gettysburg. He then convinced his governor that the project was a worthy one and that Pennsylvania should lead the way. Acting promptly, Governor Curtin assured Wills that his state would advance whatever funds were necessary. Curtin then asked Wills to direct the project.[3]

As Governor Curtin's "agent," Wills purchased the land deemed necessary, secured a landscape gardener to plan the cemetery, wrote to the other seventeen governors to secure their cooperation, wrote specifications and let contracts for the reburials, and set November 19, 1863 as the date of the dedication of the grounds. More than that, he secured Edward Everett as the event's orator, asking President Abraham Lincoln to "formally set apart these grounds to their Sacred use by a few appropriate remarks," and invited Ward Hill Lamon (the President's bodyguard whose official title was United States Marshal for the District of Columbia) to serve as "grand marshal" for the day.[4] Securing Lamon's services was a stroke of genius. It practically insured Lincoln's acceptance of Wills's invitation although the President was very busy composing his annual message to Congress and a lengthy and complicated proclamation of amnesty and reconstruction. Lamon, whose role as "grand marshal" gave him the responsibility of overseeing the procession from Gettysburg to the top of Cemetery Hill and serving as master of ceremonies during the program, also helped David Wills decide who would occupy the ten front row chairs on the $12' \times 20'$ platform.

Lincoln, scheduled to make some dedicatory remarks, and Everett, prepared to give the day's oration, held down the two middle chairs in the front row.[5] Everett, properly, sat at the President's right and the two held center stage together. In a way, the two were as dissimilar as two prominent men could be. Lincoln was fifty-four and a politician evolving into a statesman; Everett was nearing his seventieth birthday and in the twilight of an illustrious career. Young Everett had attended a prestigious prep school and graduated from Harvard; young Lincoln had attended only three winter terms of a subscription school and garnered much of his education from newspapers and agitated discussions around pot-bellied stoves in country stores. At the age of nineteen, Everett had been ordained pastor of the Brattle Street Unitarian Church in Boston; during his nineteenth year Lincoln followed an iron-shod plow, cleared brush and trees to increase the size of a small farm, and rode a flatboat loaded with produce down the Mississippi River all the way to New Orleans. Everett piled honors atop honors: Eliot Professor of Greek Literature at Harvard (1820-1826), five terms in the House of Representatives in Washington, four years as governor of Massachusetts, president of Harvard (1848-1849), Envoy Plenipotentiary to Britain, Secretary of State in President Millard Fillmore's cabinet, and a stint as a U.S. Senator. Lincoln's ladder had ill-shaped rungs: a struggling surveyor, co-proprietor of a country store which went bankrupt, railsplitter and odd-job doer, member of a militia company involved in the futile chase of Black Hawk and his braves, three ineffective terms in the Illinois State legislature and one two-year term in the House of Representatives in Washington, and a most successful lawyer in Springfield.

After the death of Daniel Webster, Everett emerged as the best orator of his day; he delivered his well-known lecture on George Washington 122 times, receiving fees totaling more than $100,000. Lincoln, on the other hand, became best-known for his political speeches, giving scores of them, first as a Whig and then as a Republican. He received a mere $300 for his speeches — $100 for his lecture at the Wisconsin State Fair in Milwaukee and $200 for his Cooper Union address in New York City.[6] Everett was urbane and cosmopolitan, egotistical and aloof, well-read, and an intellectual who glorified in being a Boston Brahmin. Lincoln, constantly growing in stature as a worthy man, was a six-foot four-inch "gentle giant" — neighborly and friendly, a product of the prairies, self-educated, humble in a strange sort of way, and pragmatic to the nth degree.

Both, however, had prepared well for their different roles on the platform atop Cemetery Hill. Everett wrote out his two-hour oration as soon as he could and entitled it "The Battles of Gettysburg" — he correctly saw the three-day struggle as a series of separate encounters rather than as a single coordinated engagement. He devoted four-fifths of his two-hour oration to a description of the various battles, discussing strategy and tactics and the heroics of the brigades, divisions, and corps. The last fifth Everett devoted to the political background of the war — he put the blame upon slavery, the nefarious doctrine of states' rights, and errant Southern leaders.

After completing the first draft and a revision, Everett gave his composition to the editor of the *Boston Daily Advertiser*, so it could appear in print on the same day that he delivered it. In print, it covered six columns of fine type on a single page of newsprint. The editor gave Everett several copies of the printed oration, and the orator spent part of each day reading and re-reading it while committing it to memory. He wanted to give a flawless performance.

Everett knew that the President followed him on the program, so he extended him the courtesy of sending one of his printed copies of the oration. The President appreciated Everett's deference; he told a friend: "It was very kind of Mr. Everett to send me this. I suppose he was afraid I should say something he wanted to say. He needn't have been alarmed. My speech isn't long."[7]

Everett, it might be added, gave a mediocre performance. Although he did not skip a phrase or sentence of the two-hour composition, and the oration was given with "his accustomed grace," it lacked life and inspiration. The stream of eloquence was there, but the recitation was too mechanical. One newspaperman, bored by the long drawn-out descriptions of battles, stated that Everett's oration lacked "one strong thought, one vivid picture, one thrilling appeal." Another critic, the Democratic editor of the *Philadelphia Age*, wrote: "Seldom has a man talked so long and said so little. He told us nothing about the dead heroes, nothing of their former deeds, nothing of their glories before they fell like conquerors before their great conqueror, Death. He gave us plenty of words, but no heart. His flowers of rhetoric were as beautiful and as scentless and as lifeless as wax flowers. His style was as clear and cold like Croton ice. He talked like a historian, or an encyclopaedist, or an essayist, but not like an orator, but a great disappointment.'' Everett should have sensed that full audience interest was lacking, for those on the outer fringe drifted off to tour nearby sectors of the battlefield.[8]

Polite applause followed Everett's speech. After a graceful bow, the rather exhausted orator turned to go back to his chair. Lincoln arose and met him halfway and grasped Everett's hand warmly. Appreciating the part where the orator had denounced states' rights doctrine, Lincoln said, ''I am more than grateful, I am grateful to you.''[9]

After a twelve-man chorus representing the Maryland Musical Association chanted an ode, written especially for the occasion, it was President Lincoln's chance to shine. He arose from his chair, took a step forward, adjusted his spectacles, and recited his piece. He, too, had prepared well. After receiving Wills's invitation to make ''a few appropriate remarks,'' he had the responsibility to compose an address worthy of the office and the occasion. ''He probably followed his usual habit in such matters,'' the President's personal secretary [John Nicolay] wrote years later, ''using great deliberation in arranging his thoughts, and moulding his phrases mentally, waiting to reduce them to writing after they had taken satisfactory form.''[10]

About a week before the date of the dedication ceremonies at Gettysburg, Lincoln had put his thoughts down on paper — two pages of White House stationery. He was quite well satisfied with the first eight sentences, but displeased with the long and cumbersome final sentence which carried over to the second page. Two days before leaving Washington for Gettysburg, the President told a friend that his speech was ''written but not finished.''[11] That long last sentence still needed rephrasing and refinement.

The night before the ceremonies atop Cemetery Hill, Lincoln retired to his second floor room in the Wills's house — where both he and Everett were overnight guests — to rewrite the last sentence and finish the memorization of his address. Soon after, he sent his black servant (William) downstairs to ask his host for some writing paper. Wills, obligingly, sent up several pages of foolscap.[12]

Concentrating on the task at hand, Lincoln reworded and rewrote most of that last troublesome sentence — this on a page of paper which Wills had provided. Satisfied at last, Lincoln came downstairs and asked Wills to direct him to where his Secretary of State, William H. Seward, was staying. Lincoln evidently read his address to his Secretary of State, seeking comments and approbation. In less than half an hour, and carrying his composition in hand, the President returned and soon thereafter retired for the night.

Next morning, after breakfast, Lincoln's personal secretary reported to Lincoln's room ''for duty.'' John Nicolay found the President sitting at a table and holding a pencil in his right hand. He had his two-page address before him and he was evidently perusing it for last minute changes while memorizing it. Nicolay noticed that the first page was White House stationery with the handwriting in ink while the rewritten portion was in pencil and on "bluish-gray foolscap." When Lincoln was fully satisfied with his handiwork, he folded it in thirds and placed it in the left pocket of his black frock coat.[13]

The President's thorough preparation paid dividends. An appreciative audience interrupted his nine-sentence speech with applause five times and rewarded him with "tremendous handclapping" when he finished. The responsive crowd then gave three cheers for Lincoln and three more for the nine governors.[14]

As Lincoln returned to his chair, both Secretary of State Seward and orator Everett arose to grasp their President's hand and pay compliments. "Mr. Lincoln," Everett said, "allow me to congratulate you on these noble sentiments . . . there was more in your twenty lines than in my twenty pages.[15] The next day, in a letter to Lincoln, Everett expressed the same sentiments: "I should be glad, if I could flatter myself that I came as near the central idea of the occasion, in two hours as you did in two minutes."[16]

Like Lincoln and Everett, two others sitting on the ten front row chairs had parts in the formal program. The two were clergymen, one assigned the invocation, the other the closing prayer.

The Rev. Henry L. Baugher sat at Everett's immediate right. The learned Baugher, titled "Doctor," was president of Gettysburg College, a Lutheran seminary on the western outskirts of the town. The college buildings were in the center of some severe fighting during the first day's battle. General John F. Reynolds climbed up into the church's belfry to view the countryside and assess enemy positions. Shortly after descending, and while directing the brigades and divisions of his First Corps into line, he fell victim to a sharpshooter's bullet. Later in the day, as the Confederates pushed their blue-clad enemy eastward, through Gettysburg and toward Cemetery Hill, Confederate officers used the tower of Reverend Baugher's church as an observation post.

Dr. Baugher's role in the program was to give the benediction. It was brief, recited solemnly, and well received: "O Thou King of Kings and Lord of Lords, God of the Nations of the Earth, who permitteth them to do only whatsoever Thou willest, we beseech Thy blessing on these holy services. Bless this spot. Bless these holy graves. Bless the President of the United States and the Cabinet. Bless all governments of the earth. Bless the representatives of the States and bless those whose hands embroiled the nation in war — that their hearts might be influenced by Thy grace to return. Bless the efforts to subdue the Rebellion, that it may be overthrown. And now may the grace of our Lord Jesus Christ, the love of God, Our Heavenly Father and the fellowship of the Holy Ghost be with you all, Amen."[17]

The Rev. Thomas H. Stockton, who gave the opening prayer, occupied the chair to Reverend Baugher's right. One newspaperman noted his "absolutely colorless face," with "lips as white as the wasted cheek, and the flowing hair, and tuft of whiskers under the chin, as snowy white as wool."[18]

The ashen-faced Reverend Stockton was a native of Pennsylvania. An antislavery activist before the war, he was serving as chaplain of the House of Representatives during the Thirty-seventh Congress. He was a popular and respected preacher. Wills, perhaps at the urging of Lamon, invited Stockton to give the opening prayer. "Never was a man selected for any service," one Republican editor wrote, "so fit in every respect to perform it."[19]

The Reverend Stockton's prayer was a long, long one — a petition of about a thousand words. It was a fervent prayer, rendered by one emotionally affected by the setting in which it was given. Some of those who heard it passed out compliments. The editor of Gettysburg's Republican newspaper called it "a most impressive prayer;" he added that it "brought tears to many eyes."[20] Everett thought it "a highly rhetorical but otherwise extremely well written prayer."[21] John Hay, one of President Lincoln's secretaries thought it too long and he wrote rather sarcastically and irreverently: "Mr. Stockton made a prayer which thought it was an oration."[22]

Benjamin Brown French, who sat at the Reverend Stockton's immediate right, earned his front row seat by writing an ode which was recited as part of the formal program. Chance and circumstance brought him into the picture. He was a native of New Hampshire who had dabbled in politics and the antislavery movement before becoming obsessed with a new-fangled invention, the telegraph. He invested money in some of the new telegraph lines and lobbied in Congress for subsidies. He served a stint as clerk of the House of Representatives, presenting congressman Abraham Lincoln's credentials to the Speaker in December of 1847. In 1861, President Lincoln appointed him Commissioner of Public Buildings. Records show that he purchased a batch of books for the White House on August 26, 1862.[23] French developed a working relationship with Mrs. Lincoln, whose changing demands tested a flimsy friendship.

French also had developed a working relationship with Lamon, who agreed to serve as "grand marshal" for events associated with the dedication of the soldiers' cemetery at Gettysburg. On November 13, French accompanied Lamon to Gettysburg. Lamon was anxious to finalize plans for events of the 19th. In French's presence, Wills related some of his problems. He stated that he had asked Henry Wadsworth Longfellow, "the distinguished poet," to write an appropriate hymn or ode for the occasion, but had received a polite declination. French, who imagined he was a poet of sorts, then and there offered to work up something and promised to submit it to Wills the next morning.

Next day French handed Wills a five-stanza composition, entitled "Consecration Hymn." It fit in with the spirit of the dedication; it contained phrases like "holy ground," "our glorious dead," "sacred blood," "widow's tears," and "Freedom's holy cause." Wills liked it and, with Lamon's assistance, secured the Baltimore chorus to chant it as part of the formal program — sandwiched between Everett's oration and Lincoln's address.[24]

Wills repaid French by assigning him a front row chair on the platform. French, thus, sat as a witness who saw Everett in action and Lincoln's rendezvous with destiny. He had the right to feel proud when twelve members of the Maryland Musical Association chanted his ode in unison in a most impressive fashion. The hearty applause which followed the recitation of the ode should have warmed French's heart.

The last chair in the front row, to French's right, belonged to William Saunders, a well-known landscape gardener and a prominent member of Washington society.

After Wills got the cemetery project underway, he asked Saunders to come to Gettysburg to lay out the proposed burial ground. Saunders, it could be noted, had had an interesting career before Wills asked him to contribute his time and talents to a worthy cause. He was a Scottish-born horticulturist who had emigrated to the United States in 1848. In time, he became the best-known horticulturist and landscape gardener in the country. In 1862, he was named to a position in the department of agriculture in Washington. In the same year he imported twelve trees of the seedless orange from Bahia, Brazil — these trees became the bases for the Florida and California orange industry. He had a hand in selecting sites for parks and designing the grounds in the District of Columbia.

Late in August of 1863 Saunders took a trip to Gettysburg to meet with Wills. The two walked over the 17½ acres which had been purchased for the cemetery; they studied the lay of the land, noting the high and low areas. Saunders recommended that a monument be placed on the highest reach of ground and that it serve as the focal point for the half-circle in which the graves would be placed. Parcels allotted to each of the eighteen participating states would run toward the common center, fitting together in a semicircular arrangement. Saunders promised the services of a government surveyor to mark off the twelve-foot semicircular parallels, allowing five feet for a walk between parallels and seven feet for each grave. Saunders, it is evident, occupied a front-row seat because of his contributions to the planning of the soldiers' cemetery at Gettysburg.[25]

The chair immediately at President Lincoln's left — it was the fourth in the front row — belonged to Secretary of State William H. Seward. He was one of three Cabinet members to accompany Lincoln to Gettysburg aboard the special train the day before the dedication ceremonies.

Seward and Lincoln, it seemed, had developed a special relationship as the war increased the burdens of both. Seward was one of the first to recognize the genius in Lincoln, to sense his innate honesty, and to recognize his devotion to nationalistic principles. Seward often rode in the President's carriage, a morning practice that became a ritual. They plumbed each other's souls, empathized with each other's problems, and laughed at each other's risque stories or witticisms.

Wills arranged to have Seward quartered next door, at the home of Robert G. Harper, editor of the Republican-oriented *Adams County Sentinel*.[26] Next morning, Seward rode at Lincoln's right in the procession which moved along a dusty road southward to Cemetery Hill. A journalist, observing the two riders, noted, that the President was "a timorous but respectable horseman" while the Secretary of State seemed "much more at home with a pen in his hand than with a bridle rein."[27]

Most of the time during Everett's long oration, Seward sat with his arms folded and his hat "drawn down over his eyes" because of the bright autumnal sun.[28] When Everett finished, Seward offered him his hand as a silent form of compliment. He offered Lincoln the same courtesy at the end of his brief address. Bright, sedate, dignified, and somewhat mellowed, Secretary of State Seward watched as tradition and history were made on a platform at Gettysburg.

The chairs to Seward's left were occupied by three of the nine governors attending the ceremonies. Wills, perhaps with Lamon's help, decided who the three would be.

Pennsylvania's governor Andrew G. Curtin, sat at Seward's left. After all, Curtin was the host for the occasion, so it was fitting that he have a front row seat.

President Lincoln's relationship with Curtin, at least early in his administration, was somewhat frayed. Curtin was the recognized leader of one Republican faction in the State of Pennsylvania; Simon Cameron led the other. Curtin was not happy, after Lincoln's election, when Cameron received the Cabinet post promised to Pennsylvania. After Cameron resigned as Secretary of War in January of 1862, Lincoln made an effort to mend his fences with Curtin.

On August 28, 1863, Governor Curtin, worried that he might not be re-elected in October, visited Washington and the War Department to ask that Pennsylvania troops from Republican districts be furloughed so they could go home to vote. Curtin also had a conference with President Lincoln, presenting his case as a patriotic cause. It is presumed that Curtin, at this time, invited Lincoln to come to Gettysburg for the yet unplanned dedication exercises for the soldiers' cemetery.[29] The furloughing of scores of Pennsylvania regiments, it might be added, helped Curtin to carry the October gubernatorial election — making him indebted to Lincoln and the Secretary of War.

After the dedication services were set for November 19, Curtin invited all attending governors to come to Harrisburg to be his guests. He would have seats reserved for them, he wrote, aboard the special train which would go from Harrisburg, via Hanover Junction, to Gettysburg.[30]

Governor Curtin was a most solicitous host on the day of the dedication ceremonies. He shepherded his fellow governors, providing a steed for each in the procession. He saw that each had a seat reserved on the platform.

During the program, Governor Curtin was a model of decorum and attentiveness. He applauded when Everett recited his oration and again when Lincoln finished his brief address. Curtin's comments about Lincoln's performance testified to the fact that the President excelled: "He pronounced that speech in a voice that all the multitude heard. The crowd was hushed into silence because the President stood before them. But at intervals there were roars of applause. My God! It was so impressive! It was the common remark of everybody. Such a speech as they said it was! Everett and all went up and congratulated the President, shaking him by the hand."[31]

Horatio Seymour, New York's Democratic governor, had the chair at Curtin's left. During the prewar years, Seymour had denounced abolitionism and Republicanism as twin heresies. During the secession winter of 1860-61 he had openly advocated compromise as the rational alternative to military coercion. As a moderate and always dignified critic of the Lincoln administration, Seymour won the governorship in the 1862 election. Of course he disapproved of Lincoln's Emancipation Proclamation and the institution of federal conscription.

Seymour exchanged curt notes with the War Department regarding quotas assigned to Democratic districts. The New York antidraft riots of July 13-16 astounded Washington and Republican newspapers put the blame at Seymour's doorstep. Lincoln and Seymour exchanged tart letters as the two blamed each other for the violence. The President retreated before some of Seymour's sallies and the War Department eventually reduced quotas — excessive in the first place.

Seymour did not go to Harrisburg to ride aboard Governor Curtin's special train. He came directly from New York City and stayed at the home of one of Gettysburg's most prominent Democrats. The evening before the dedication ceremonies, standing on the front porch of the house where he was a guest, Seymour reviewed the 5th New York Artillery Regiment and its renowned band. He presented a new silk regimental banner to the unit's colonel and gave a three-minute patriotic speech.

Political deference, plus the prominent role of New York regiments in the Battle of Gettysburg prompted David Wills to assign Seymour a front row chair on the platform. The New York State governor applauded politely after each number on the program. When Ward Hill Lamon, as the day's "grand marshal," announced to the crowd that the formal program was over, Seymour watched intently as the 5th New York Artillery fired a salute of eight rounds. Then the procession reformed and Seymour mounted his horse to return to Gettysburg.

Governor David Tod of Ohio sat at Seymour's immediate left — on the first chair in the front row. Tod, a Democrat, had followed a zigzag course in Buckeye politics before the war. Twice, first in 1844 and again in 1846, he had been defeated by Whig candidates in the state's gubernatorial elections. Then he had served a stint (1847-1851) as U.S. minister to Brazil. During the years which followed he amassed a fortune in coal and iron and railroad investments and began to flirt with the Republican party. Evidently Tod felt uncomfortable in the Democratic party — it was devoted to low tariffs and catered to immigrant-American voters.

Republicans, needing public support to retain the state house in 1861, nominated David Tod as their candidate and raised the Union party banner. Democrats, viewing the ex-Democrat as a renegade and rank opportunist, waged a vicious campaign against him. Tod, nevertheless, won the governorship.

He served his state well — judiciously, honestly, impartially, and patriotically. He expected to be renominated and really deserved the honor. But members of the Republican hierarchy pulled the rug from under him, for the public associated Tod with arbitrary arrests which had been made and the institution of federal conscription. Brazenly, Republicans cast Tod aside and nominated another ex-Democrat, "Honest John" Brough. His pride pricked, Tod secretly blamed President Lincoln for not giving him open support, but the disheartened governor campaigned for Brough against Clement L. Vallandigham, "the notorious Copperhead" then in exile in Canada.

Lincoln was most anxious for Vallandigham's defeat and kept a wary eye upon the Ohio election scene. When word reached Washington that Vallandigham had been defeated, the President sent Tod a telegram: "Glory to God in the Highest! Ohio has saved the Union!"[32]

No state did more than Ohio to insure a crowd for the dedication of the soldiers' cemetery at Gettysburg. Tod arranged for a special train to leave Columbus and head for Harrisburg. He invited hundreds to accompany him and his aides even arranged for a special "Ohio program" for the evening of the dedication. Next to Pennsylvania, Ohio had more participants in the procession than any other state.[33]

Tod was already at his chair on the platform when President Lincoln ascended the stairs. Tod, in a hearty and brazen fashion stepped forward to greet him, saying, "Mr. President, I want you to shake hands with me." Lincoln cordially acquiesced and then introduced Tod to Secretary of State Seward.[34]

After the program began, Tod was at his best behavior. A newspaperman, studying those who held down the ten front row seats, characterized Tod as "good-humored, florid, and plump." Another described Tod as "aldermanic."[35]

Tod and the other nine who held down front row chairs were solemnized by the spirit of the occasion. This spirit of awe and reverence reached its climax during the chanting of the second stanza of French's ode:

> *Here let them rest;*
> *And summer's heat and winter's cold*
> *Shall glow and freeze above this mould —*
> *A thousand years shall pass away —*
> *A nation still shall mourn this day,*
> *Which now is blest.*

CHAPTER VIII

*SEVEN WHO WITNESSED LINCOLN'S GETTYSBURG ADDRESS**

Under a cloudless sky, with a bright autumnal sun warming the crisp November air, about five or six thousand spectators watched President Abraham Lincoln arise from a rickety chair, step forward toward the front edge of the platform, and recite a most memorable address.[1] The 12′ × 20′ platform, built especially for the occasion, stood on a portion of Cemetery Hill, about a half-mile due south of the small city of Gettysburg. The platform was overcrowded, some standing on the rear part of it while most sat on chairs provided for the dignitaries. It was a notable group. "Perhaps on no other stage," a reporter wrote, "has there been such a conjunction of all that is distinguished by official position, statesmanship, learning and eloquence."[2]

Seven members of the vast assemblage — presented here as witnesses — had an especial interest in the proceedings, several having an active role in the day's affair. Six of the seven sat on the 12′ × 20′ platform. The seventh, rescued from oblivion by an observant newspaperman, stood about five feet in front of the platform, almost lost in the sea of humanity.

The first of the seven witnesses was a thirty-two-year-old Gettysburger named David Wills. He had come to Gettysburg nine years earlier, after graduating from Pennsylvania College and reading law in Lancaster in Thaddeus Stevens's office. Stevens indoctrinated Wills with his political principles and a belief in the equality of all men, regardless of color.

After establishing his law office in Gettysburg, and transferring his loyalty from the dying Whig party to the rising Republican party, young Wills prospered. Personable and energetic, he became the superintendent of schools for Adams County as well as the city's No. 1 Republican. He purchased a large, three-story rectangular home fronting on York Street and with a side entrance on the city's central square.

---

*Reprinted (with permission) from Historical Bulletin No. 40 of the Lincoln Fellowship of Wisconsin, pp. 2-25.

During the three-day Battle of Gettysburg, Wills stayed out of sight, letting the city's Democrats negotiate "a ransom" — provisions and money which would save the city from pillage and destruction. After the defeated Confederate army retreated, Wills closed his law office for several days to minister to the thousands of wounded who lay in the makeshift hospitals in the Gettysburg area. In the days and weeks that followed, David Wills became the central figure in the story of the soldiers' cemetery and all of the events revolving around it.[3]

Meanwhile, thousands of outsiders poured into Gettysburg: employees of the Christian Commission and the United States Sanitary Commission, doctors by the dozen and nurses by the score, state agents, relatives and friends of the wounded and the dead, and hundreds of sightseers. Some were no more than "morbid curiosity seekers," interested in "the ravages and misery of war."[4] But most came to claim the buried bodies of loved ones. Each day hundreds of coffins containing the bodies of Union soldiers were loaded onto trains and shipped off to be buried in local cemeteries from Maine to Minnesota — eighteen Northern states had lost noble sons at Gettysburg.

Wills was busy, busy, busy. He helped fathers locate the corpses of their sons, conducted dignitaries on tours of the extensive battlefield, dispatched the walking wounded to Baltimore and Washington, distributed stores of food and medical supplies, and repeatedly met with Andrew B. Cross, head of the Christian Commission of Pennsylvania.[5]

Governor Andrew G. Curtin, the state's chief executive, was busy with troop-raising duties and re-election activities and so did not arrive at Gettysburg until the afternoon of July 10[6] — seven days after the battle. Wills met the governor's train at the depot and put him up for the night. The next day the two toured the battlefield and some of the hospitals. Before Governor Curtin returned to Harrisburg, he designated Wills as his "agent" in matters having to do with the removal of Pennsylvania soldiers from battlefield graves to home cemeteries. "Governor Curtin has made arrangements with David Wills, esq., of this place," the editor of the small city's Republican newspaper reported, "for the removal of all Pennsylvanians killed in the late battles, furnishing transportation for the body and one attendant at the expense of the State."[7]

Those who toured the battlefield were shocked at the manner in which some of the soldiers, whether rebel or Yankee, had been buried. In many cases no graves had been dug and the bodies merely covered with spadefuls of earth. Heavy rains had washed away some of the spaded soil and a searing sun had speeded up the decomposition of the corpses. Thus, arms and legs and maggot-infested heads were sometimes exposed. "I saw one entire skull above ground," one observer wrote, "and in many instances hands and feet were sticking through . . . . I saw so many masses of hair lying where the head had been — the body so decomposed that it had fallen off — one entire scalp of long, black and beautiful curls."[8] Worse than that, in the fields and woods where the heaviest fighting had occurred on the first day of the battle, hogs were rooting up the mounds which covered the bodies — desecrating the graves.[9]

On some sectors of the battlefield the exposed portions of human corpses and the bloated bodies of artillery horses filled the air with a sickening stench. "The atmosphere is truly horrible," one queasy woman wrote, "and camphor and smelling salts are prime necessities for most persons, certainly for ladies."[10]

David Wills's work with state agents and with Mr. Cross of the Christian Commission took him, time and again, over every portion of the far-flung battlefield. He noticed that many of the temporary markers placed over graves were often only half legible. "... three thousand men lie in and about Gettysburg," Cross of the Christian Commission wrote about two weeks after the battle, "in cornfields, in meadows, in gardens, by the way-side, and in the public road, buried hastily where they fell, and others in long rows, with a piece of box lid or board of any kind, with the name of the person and the day he died written with a lead pencil, ink, or whatever they had to make a mark with."[11] Time, aided by the elements, made many of the inscriptions illegible while many graves had no headboards at all.

Wills wondered about the possibility of reburying the Union dead, scattered over all sectors of the battlefield, together atop Cemetery Hill, perhaps next to the old graveyard already there. Cross of the Christian Commission endorsed the idea enthusiastically. So did several state agents. Henry Edwards, the state agent from Massachusetts, said that his governor had encouraged him to purchase an acre or two, collect his state's dead from scattered graves, and rebury them together somewhere on the battlefield. The three discussed the feasibility of "a cooperative cemetery," subsidized by all of the eighteen states which had lost sons in the three-day battle. Wills agreed to lay the idea before his governor and Cross agreed to promote it in the press.[12]

In a letter of July 24, 1863, Wills suggested to Governor Curtin that the state of Pennsylvania purchase about eight acres ("3½ acres belonging to Mr. Raffensberger and 4½ to Mr. Menchy") for a cemetery. Other states, Wills assured Governor Curtin, had expressed a willingness to partake in the cemetery project. He made a stirring plea: "Our dead are lying in the fields unburied (that is, no graves being dug) with small portions of earth dug up along side of the body and thrown over it. In many instances arms and legs protrude and my attention has been directed to several places where the hogs were actually rooting out the bodies and devouring them — and this on Pennsylvania soil and in many cases the bodies of the patriotic soldiers of our State. Humanity calls on us to take measures to remedy this . . . ."[13]

Governor Curtin, in turn, authorized Wills to buy the acreage deemed necessary, contact agents and governors of the other seventeen states, make arrangement for the reburials, and supervise the project.[14] Pennsylvania would supply the original funds and expect reimbursement from the other states.

In time, Wills bought five different plots totaling seventeen acres for $2,475.87.[15] He also wrote "specifications" for the reburial of the scattered corpses and let a contract to the lowest bidder — $1.59 a body for exhuming it and reburying in a designated plot in the new soldiers' cemetery,[16] adjacent to the old one operated by the Evergreen Cemetery Association of Gettysburg.

Wills wrote repeatedly to Governor Curtin to report progress. He was quite pleased with the cooperation of the other governors. William Saunders, a landscape gardener employed by the federal government, came from Washington to lay out the cemetery grounds.[17] It was time, Wills wrote to Governor Curtin, to plan "appropriate ceremonies" for the "consecration" of the grounds, after which the reburials could commence.[18]

The Governor replied promptly. He complimented Wills for his good work and urged him to plan an appropriate program. "The proper consecration of the ground," Curtin wrote to his protege, "must claim our early attention; and, as soon as we can do so, our fellow purchasers should be invited to join with us in the performance of suitable ceremonies on the occasion."[19]

Wills took steps to set a date for the dedication of the cemetery grounds and invite the orator of the day. He had his heart set on Edward Everett as the chief speaker and wrote to the well-known Massachusetts orator. The date: "the 23rd day of October next." Wills added, "I am therefore instructed, by the Governors of the different states interested in this project, to invite you cordially to join them in the ceremonies, and to deliver the oration for the occasion."[20]

Everett replied promptly. Duty, he said, called him to accept the honor and the invitation. But commitments, and the time required to write and memorize a two-hour oration, would prevent Everett from accepting such a responsibility earlier "than the 19th of November."[21]

Since Wills wanted Everett as his orator, he changed the proposed date of the dedication ceremonies from October 23 to November 19. The change in dates necessitated another round of letters to the governors. Through Governor Curtin, Wills invited President Lincoln to attend the ceremonies of November 19 and to visit the famous battlefield.[22] Also receiving invitations were: Vice-President Hannibal Hamlin, members of Lincoln's cabinet, congressmen, foreign ministers, and army generals. Among others, Wills also extended invitations to two clergymen to participate in the dedication program, one to give an opening prayer and the other the benediction. And, he asked four musical organizations to march in the procession and partake in the program. Finally, he invited Henry W. Longfellow, the distinguished poet, to compose a special hymn or ode for the occasion.[23]

The change in dates, from October 23 to November 19, made it necessary to start the reburials before rather than after the dedication of the cemetery grounds. The coming of winter and frozen ground would hamper the reburial crew. On October 28, Wills witnessed the first reburial, that of an Ohio soldier.[24]

Having an indirect assurance that Lincoln would attend the ceremonies of November 19, the perceptive Wills formalized the invitation and asked the President to participate: "It is the desire that, after the oration, you, as Chief Executive, formally set apart these grounds to their sacred use by a few appropriate remarks."[25] Wills included a personal note with the formal invitation, asking the President, "along with Edward Everett and Governor Curtin" to be his house guest — "the hotels in town would be crowded and in confusion."[26]

The next two weeks were hectic indeed. Wills supervised the building of a platform at the northwestern edge of the new reburial grounds. He had conferences with Ward Hill Lamon, who agreed to serve as marshal-in-chief. He watched bodies being exhumed and reburied in allotted graves in the new soldiers' cemetery. And he wrote again to the governors, urging them to be present in person with "large delegations."[27]

Wills greeted his famous guests when they arrived in Gettysburg. Everett came two days early in order to walk over the battlefield and gain inspiration for his oration. President Lincoln arrived shortly after dusk on the evening of November 18. Governor Curtin arrived shortly before midnight, delayed for four hours by a balky locomotive.

Mrs. Wills served a sumptuous supper to her guests who spent an interesting evening in discussing politics, plans for the morrow, and highlights of the three-day battle. Later in the evening, the President spent some time in his upstairs bedroom, reworking and rewriting a portion of his address and committing it to memory.

The procession was not scheduled to leave from the central square of Gettysburg for Cemetery Hill until ten o'clock on the morning of November 19. Shortly before the procession was supposed to start its southward trek, Wills and Lincoln emerged from the house. Wills showed the President the splendid black steed he would ride in the procession.

The assistant marshals were slow in getting the show on the road. Finally, about eleven o'clock, the military units at the head of the procession were ordered to move. The Marine Band led the way, followed by the others. Then came the Marshal's division with its collection of notables. The civic division, made up of civilian and fraternal orders, brought up the rear.

When the procession reached the top of Cemetery Hill, Wills escorted President Lincoln to his chair on the platform. He also seated the eight governors and other notables on the thirty chairs arranged in three rows. It took nearly an hour for the last units in the parade to arrive and their members to fan out as part of the audience.

Wills was more than interested in the program — after all, he had put it together. Birgfield's Band of Philadelphia opened the formal program with "a grand funeral march." The Reverend Thomas Stockton gave an impressive invocation, "a prayer which thought it was an oration."[28] Next the Marine Band played Luther's hymn "Old Hundred."[29]

As the echoes of the music drifted toward the nearby hills, Edward Everett arose and moved forward. After the audience gave him its attention, he began his recitation entitled "The Battles of Gettysburg." It was a story of attacks and counterattacks, of tactics and strategy, and the dozen separate battles which made up the whole. It was a dreary recitation—much too long and with few emotional aspects.[30] Wills noticed, as did others, that Lincoln listened intently while Secretary of State William H. Seward, bothered by a bright sun, sat with arms folded and hat "drawn down over his eyes."[31] Some, standing on the outer fringe of the crowd, drifted away.

When Everett finally finished, there was some applause, most of it of the polite category. Next came an ode chanted by the Maryland Musical Association, a chorus of twelve voices. Then it was Lincoln's turn to speak.

As a witness to an historic event for which he was chiefly responsible, Wills watched while Lincoln was introduced and as he arose to generous applause. The President then recited those "few appropriate remarks." Wills noticed that applause interrupted Lincoln's presentation five times and that, after the President finished, there was "tremendous applause." For good measure, the crowd gave three cheers for Lincoln and three more for the governors.[32]

Two numbers, arranged by Wills, remained. A mixed chorus of local citizens sang a dirge. Then the Reverend Henry L. Baugher, head of the local Lutheran seminary, ended the formal program with a brief benediction.

After the ceremonies, the military portion of the procession re-formed and escorted President Lincoln and the other notables back to Gettysburg. Mrs. Wills supervised the serving of "a well-planned meal" to "a very large company." After dinner, President Lincoln and Governor Curtin received "guests." Then, early in the evening, Wills escorted President Lincoln to the depot and watched as the special train pulled out of the station.

The next day was a quiet one in Gettysburg. David Wills, the central figure in the story of the soldiers' cemetery, received accolades.[33] Even the city's Democratic newspaper complimented Wills and praised the dedication program.[34]

There was more to be done. The reburial crew continued exhuming and reinterring corpses until winter weather froze the ground. In the spring, the reburial crew resumed its gruesome task. In his report of March 18, the chief of the crew stated that 3,354 Union soldiers had been buried in the new cemetery.[35]

Without Wills's perception, promotion, and planning there would have been no special soldiers' cemetery at Gettysburg. Nor would there have been an oration by Edward Everett and an address by Abraham Lincoln. Ironically, David Wills, as a witness to Lincoln's Gettysburg Address, left no written opinion as to the quality of the President's carefully chosen words.

Governor Curtin of Pennsylvania was another witness to Lincoln's most memorable address as well as an important man in the story of the soldiers' cemetery.

A native Pennsylvanian, Curtin was born in Bellefonte and educated at Milton Academy and Dickinson College. After gaining admission to the bar in 1837, he practiced law and let politics become an obsession. After stints as the state's secretary and superintendent of schools, he became governor on January 15, 1861 — three months before the start of the Civil War. After President Lincoln's call for troops, Governor Curtin raised and equipped one regiment after another — 270 in all. He was busy with re-election plans when General Robert E. Lee and his rebel army, seventy-five thousand strong, invaded Pennsylvania.

Curtin was tardy getting to Gettysburg after the three-day battle. But he had the good sense to make Wills his "agent" in all matters having to do with the dead Pennsylvania soldiers whose bodies were scattered over all sections of the battlefield. Curtin also deserved credit for endorsing Wills's idea of a cooperative state cemetery on a portion of the battlefield. He kept his finger in the pie, advancing state funds for the project and asking Wills to assume the responsibility for both the cemetery and the dedication program. The Governor was also responsible for bringing in William Saunders (an employee of the Department of Agriculture and a well-known landscape gardener) to lay out the cemetery.[36] Furthermore, Curtin asked Wills to go along with Massachusetts's insistence that each state's soldiers be buried together in an allotted section of the cemetery rather than "promiscuously" as Wills had proposed.[37] More than anybody else, Curtin was responsible for Lincoln's presence at the dedication ceremonies.[38]

Although Governor Curtin accepted Wills's invitation to spend the night of November 18 as his guest, he was also solicitous about housing for the other seven governors whom he considered his "guests" at the dedication. In fact, he arranged for the other governors to meet him in Harrisburg and ride a special train to Hanover Junction and Gettysburg.

According to Curtin's plans, the governor's special train would arrive in Hanover Junction before the President's — so Lincoln could be received with "becoming honors." Unfortunately, Curtin's train had engine trouble and did not arrive there until 10:30 p.m. It took another half hour to chug-chug the remaining twelve miles to Gettysburg. Wills and some state agents met the train and escorted the governors to their quarters — Curtin had an upstairs room in Wills's house awaiting him.

Early next morning, while Lincoln and Everett toured sections of the battlefield, Governor Curtin and Wills had a long conference. Wills reported at length on his role as "agent" and plans for the day.

The trek of the procession from downtown Gettysburg to the summit of Cemetery Hill was uneventful. Curtin watched over the governor-guests like a mother hen. When reaching their destination, Curtin guided his guests to the platform.

There was some disorder when President Lincoln ascended the steps leading to the platform. It seemed as if everyone already there wanted to greet the President and shake his hand. In time, the last units in the procession reached the hilltop and became part of the semicircular crowd. Those assigned to chairs on the platform took their seats and waited for the formal program to begin. Lincoln sat in the center of the first row. Secretary of State Seward sat at the President's left, then Governor Curtin, Governor Horatio Seymour of New York, and Governor David Tod of Ohio.

Edward Everett, the orator of the occasion, sat at Lincoln's right, then two clergymen (Reverend Thomas H. Stockton and Reverend Henry L. Baugher), Benjamin B. French, and William Saunders. The other five governors had chairs in the second row. Among other dignitaries also having seats were: Simon Cameron, once Lincoln's Secretary of War; John W. Forney, clerk of the United States Senate and owner of two newspapers; John Brough, governor-elect of Ohio; William Dennison, an ex-governor of Ohio; and Joseph A. Wright, a United States Senator from Indiana. A dozen newspapermen had chairs at a table. Two dozen others, mostly assistant marshals for the occasion stood in back, shifting their weight from one foot to the other. All were, in a sense, "guests" of Governor Curtin.

The governor of Pennsylvania was a model of attentiveness and decorum during the three-hour program. He tried to follow Edward Everett's account of the separate battles taking part here and there and making up the whole. Curtin applauded when Everett finished and returned to his chair. He bent an ear to Lincoln when he recited his words of dedication in a firm and steady voice, noting pauses for applause. Later, Governor Curtin, as an interested witness, stated his reaction to Lincoln's address: "He pronounced that speech in a voice that all the multitude heard. The crowd was hushed into silence because the President stood before them. But at intervals there were roars of applause. My God! It was so impressive! It was the common remark of everybody. Such a speech, as they said it was! Everett and all went up and congratulated the President, shaking him by the hand."[39]

After the ceremonies, Governor Curtin joined the procession which returned to Gettysburg. The three o'clock dinner served by Mrs. Wills to a sizable group, was heartily appreciated by the principals. Wills then transformed his house into a reception center. He placed Lincoln in the hall of the York Street entrance and Governor Curtin near "the exit door" opening on the central square. Then, early in the evening, Curtin's train left for Hanover Junction and Harrisburg.

In the days which followed, Governor Curtin and President Lincoln remained on amicable terms. The events at Gettysburg helped each develop more respect for the other. Curtin won his bid for re-election in the October 13, 1863, elections by a narrow margin, and after the war he served as minister to Russia (1869-1872) plus three terms in the lower house of Congress. Yet being present at the dedication ceremonies and witnessing Lincoln's Gettysburg Address should have been one of the highlights of a long public career.

The third witness, like the previous two, had an important role in the proceedings associated with the soldiers' cemetery at Gettysburg. He was Edward Everett, honored orator of the day.

At the time David Wills asked Everett to give the day's oration, the Massachusetts orator was approaching his seventieth birthday. He was, in many ways, the antithesis of Lincoln. Young Everett had attended a prep school and graduated from Harvard; young Lincoln had attended only three winter terms of an elementary school. At the age of nineteen, Everett had been ordained pastor of the Brattle Street Unitarian Church in Boston; at the age of nineteen, Lincoln had worked on a flatboat which went down to New Orleans and had done odd jobs in the community.

Climbing the academic ladder, Everett became Eliot Professor of Greek Literature at Harvard, 1820-1826; Lincoln, still drifting, attended "raisings," following the furrow of an ironshod plow, split wood and rails, and read a half-

Edward Everett.

Edward Everett with the manuscript of his oration. Both the signature and the "In Memory" comment are in Everett's hand. It is likely that Everett had this photograph taken shortly after he returned to Boston. This is a previously unpublished photograph in the possession of Lloyd Ostendorf and is reproduced here with his permission.

In Memory of the 19th November 1863.

WHIPPLE,
96 Washington Street,
BOSTON.

FOUND IN GETTYSBURG
PHOTOGRAPH, ALBUM

450.- '88

dozen books. While Everett served five terms in the House of Representatives at Washington, four years as governor of Massachusetts, and president of Harvard, Lincoln tended a store, read law, and tested his political wings by serving (rather ineffectively) in the Illinois State Legislature. Everett added to his laurels: Envoy Extraordinary and Minister Plenipotentiary to Britain; Secretary of State in President Millard Fillmore's cabinet; a stint as United States Senator; and unsuccessful candidate for vice-president on the Constitutional Union ticket in 1860. In contrast, Lincoln served two years in Congress, practiced his skills as a stump-speaker and politician, and grew in stature as a worthy man. Everett, by the 1850's, was recognized as the best orator of his day — he delivered his famous oration on George Washington 122 times and received lecture fees totaling more than $100,000. Lincoln, on the other hand, gave scores of political speeches, lectured three times on temperance, and received a mere $300 for two speeches — $100 for his speech in Milwaukee at the Wisconsin State Fair and $200 for his Cooper Union Address in New York City. Everett was urbane, egotistical, well-read, and an intellectual; Lincoln was a gentle giant — neighborly, self-educated, humble in a strange sort of way, and pragmatic to the nth degree.

After Lincoln's election to the presidency, some sedate Easterners wondered if democracy was the best political system. They noted that the speeches which the president-elect made on his way from Springfield to Washington were vague and unimpressive. Everett, evidently, regarded the president-elect as a Western boor. A diary entry reflected Everett's condescending attitude: "These speeches thus far have been of the most ordinary kind, destitute of everything, not merely of felicity and grace, but of common pertinence. He is evidently a person of very inferior cast of character, wholly unequal to the crisis."[40]

Everett did not meet President Lincoln personally until September 24, 1862. The famous orator was planning a trip to Europe and he called at the White House. Lincoln, in turn, wrote a tactful appropriate letter of recommendation: "Whom it may concern: Hon. Edward Everett goes to Europe shortly. His reputation & the present condition of our country are such, that this visit there is sure to attract notice and may be misconstrued. I therefore think fit to say, that he bears no mission from this government, and yet no gentleman is better able to correct misunderstandings in the minds of foreigners, in regard to American affairs. While I commend him to the consideration of those, whom he may meet, I am quite conscious that he could better introduce me than I him, in Europe."[41]

After his return from Europe, Everett immersed himself in Union League activities. He was, as before, much in demand as lecturer and orator. He felt obligated to give full support to the government although he disapproved of some of the measures of the Lincoln administration.[42]

Late in September, 1863, Everett received David Wills's letter asking him to give the oration at the dedication of the soldiers' cemetery at Gettysburg.[43] Everett replied promptly. Yes, he felt obligated to accept the honor and responsibility. He could not, however, prepare and memorize an oration earlier "than the 19th of November."[44]

Thus, it was Everett, rather than Wills, who set the date for the cemetery exercises. "The time for the exercises," an observant editor noted, "have [*sic*] been delayed longer than was originally intended, in order to secure the services of Mr. Everett, whose engagements prevented him from attending at an earlier day."[45]

While he was still composing his Gettysburg oration, Everett received another letter from David Wills. It stated that the Massachusetts orator, along with President Lincoln, Governor Curtin, and others, was invited to be Wills's overnight guest.

After finishing the composition early in November, Everett lent it to the editor of the Boston *Daily Advertiser* and several advance copies were printed — it covered six columns of fine print on a single page of newsprint.[46]

Everett sent Lincoln an advance copy of his oration. The President appreciated Everett's deference. Lincoln told a friend: "It was very kind of Mr. Everett to send me this. I suppose he was afraid I should say something he wanted to say. He needn't have been alarmed. My speech isn't long."[47]

A week or so before departing for Gettysburg, Everett asked Wills for a favor. Would Wills set up a tent near the platform — with chairs, a cot, and a basin of water?[48] It was the mind of a Boston Brahmin at work. Gentlemen were entitled to amenities.

Everett left for Gettysburg several days early. The North Central Railroad provided a special train — compliments of the railroad company. When he arrived at Gettysburg he was met by David Wills and Henry Edwards, the capable state agent from Massachusetts. They walked the short distance to the Wills house. Everett was not happy when told that he was expected to share a bed with Governor Curtin.[49]

The next day Everett and Henry Edwards, in charge of the reburial of Massachusetts soldiers in the cooperative state cemetery, walked over portions of the battlefield. They visited that part of the new cemetery where Massachusetts's dead were being reburied. They walked over the ground where Pickett's charge had taken place and they visited the spot where Union General John F. Reynolds had fallen. Evidently, Everett was still seeking inspiration for his oration from the battlefield environment.

Everett accompanied David Wills to the station to meet the President's special train when it arrived on the evening of November 18. At supper, Everett sat at Lincoln's right and the two engaged in an amiable conversation. Everett's earlier belief that Lincoln was a Western boor evaporated. Later, he said that he found Lincoln to be the peer of any man at the table "in gentlemanly appearance, manners, and conversation."[50]

Everett retired shortly before midnight. His diary revealed an apprehension: "I did not get to bed until ½ past 11 & the fear of having the Executive of Pennsylvania [i.e., Governor Curtin] tumble in upon me kept me awake until one."[51]

During the early hours of the morning of November 19, a light shower settled the dust. Then the sun came out in full glory to bless the day's events.

After breakfast, Everett and some friends went for a leisurely stroll over the countryside. Evidently, he was still seeking the inspiration he had been unable to find on earlier trips over the battlefield.

Everett was not in his place in the procession when it began its southward trek to the hilltop where the ceremonies would be held. He was still somewhere on the battlefield. When he finally returned to the Wills's house, he was provided transportation in a carriage. When he arrived near the platform he retired to his nearby tent to rest and relax before the formal progam would begin.

When the audience had settled in place and the other dignitaries had taken their assigned chairs on the platform, Everett emerged from his tent. Four governors went to meet him and escort him to his chair on the platform. The President arose to acknowledge Everett's arrival. The orator of the day then took the chair (at the President's right) which had been reserved for him.

After two musical numbers and the invocation, it was Edward Everett's turn to shine. He stood up, turned to his left, made a very low bow, and said, "Mr. President." Lincoln returned the salutation saying, "Mr. Everett." The orator then turned to the expectant crowd and began his oration with an impressive sentence or two:

> Standing beneath this serene sky, overlooking these broad fields now reposing from the labors of the waning year, them ighty Alleghenies dimly towering before us, the graves of our brethren beneath our feet, it is with hesitation that I raise my poor voice to break the eloquent silence of God and Nature. But the duty to which you have called me must be performed; grant me, I pray you, your indulgence and your sympathy.[52]

Then Everett launched into an extended description of the separate battles which had taken place over the three days. It was the story of attacks and counterattacks, of strategy and tactics, of the heroics of brigades, divisions, and corps. He spoke slowly and seemed to deliberate on each sentence. At times the recital seemed mechanical, without emotion and inspiration. As he orated into the second hour, most in the audience listened politely. Many on the outer fringes of the crowd shuffled off to tour the battlefield.

After Everett finished his description of the many separate battles, his oration took on more life. He blamed slavery and the South for the war. He denounced the states' rights theory as political heresy. He paid a tribute to "our noble women." And he concluded with "a benediction on the honored graves" saying in closing, " . . . in the glorious annals of our common country there will be no brighter page than that which related 'The Battles of Gettysburg.' "[53]

Polite applause followed Everett's speech. After a graceful bow, the rather exhausted orator returned to his chair. Lincoln met him halfway, grasped Everett's hand warmly, and said, "I am more than grateful, I am grateful to you."[54]

After another musical number, it was Lincoln's turn to speak and Everett's to listen and be witness to a most memorable address. Repeated applause told Everett that Lincoln had excelled. As Lincoln, amidst "three cheers for the President," turned to go back to his chair, Everett and Secretary of State Seward arose to shake the President's hand and tell him that he had done well. "Mr. Lincoln," Everett said, "allow me to congratulate you on these noble sentiments... there was more in your twenty lines than in my twenty pages."[55] Soon after a Pennsylvania politician complimented Everett, the orator said, "You are very kind, but Mr. Lincoln perhaps said more to the purpose in his brief speech than I in my long one."[56]

After the ceremonies, Everett returned to the Wills's house. He spent some time visiting with his daughter and son-in-law, both of whom had come from Washington on Lincoln's special train. Then, early the next morning, Everett's train departed for Boston. Always, courteous, Everett wrote a gracious note to President Lincoln. In part, he said, "I should be glad, if I could flatter myself that I came as near the central idea of the occasion, in two hours as you did in two minutes. My son-in-law any my daughter, who left me in Baltimore, concur in this sentiment."[57]

In late January of 1864, Everett wrote again to Lincoln. Sponsors of the Metropolitan Fair of New York City had asked Everett to give them the manuscript of his oration for an auction and asked him to request the same of Lincoln.[58] The President replied a few days later: "I send herewith the manuscript of my remarks at Gettysburg... you are at liberty to use for the benefit of our soldiers as you requested."[59]

Everett did not live to see the war's end nor Lincoln's Gettysburg Address glorified. He died in Boston on January 15, 1865 — preceding Lincoln's death by three months.

The fourth witness, like the previous three, also had an important part in events associated with the dedication of the soldiers' cemetery at Gettysburg. His name was Ward Hill Lamon and he directed events on the platform on that momentous day.

Lamon's acquaintanceship with Lincoln dated back to their circuit-riding days in Illinois. In fact, Lincoln and Lamon, then of Danville, had "a standing business association" — Lincoln served as co-counsel in cases which Lamon drummed up in Vermilion County. Later Lamon wrote, "I was his local partner, first in Danville, and afterward at Bloomington. We rode the circuit together, traveling by buggy in the dry seasons and on horse-back in bad weather, there being no railroads then in that part of the State."[60]

The two developed a mutual respect for each other despite the fact that they were as different as could be. The personal relationship was furthered when Lamon married the daughter of Lincoln's law partner, Stephen T. Logan. Lamon was stout, handsome, gruff, and possessed of a swashbuckling air. Lincoln was tall, lean, gentle, and modest. Lamon was "a legendary boozer" and a brawler; Lincoln preached and practiced temperance and went out of his way to avoid fisticuffs. It was said that Lamon spent more time in the downstairs saloon than in his upstairs law office.

Furthermore, Lamon liked lewd storied and dirty ditties. Perhaps Lincoln based his respect for Lamon upon a Kentucky axiom: "Folks who have no vices generally have few virtues."[61]

Later, Lamon worked for Lincoln's nomination at the Chicago Convention of 1860. In fact, Lamon is sometimes credited with filling the Wigwam (site of the Republican party convention) with Lincoln supporters by arranging for an extra printing of tickets and instructing friends to present their forged tickets early.

After Lincoln's election, Lamon became his unofficial bodygurad. On that strange train trip from Baltimore to Washington, amidst rumors of an assassination plot, Lamon was constantly at Lincoln's side. The burly bodyguard was well armed: he carried two revolvers, two pistols, and two big knives.

President Lincoln occasionally sent Lamon on special missions and gave him a fancy title, United States Marshal of the District of Columbia. Sometime in October, 1863, Lamon took a trip to Gettysburg, ostensibly to visit the battlefield. Evidently, he met David Wills at that time.

Wills, perceptive, recognized Lamon's special relationship with President Lincoln and decided to involve him in the dedication ceremonies — easing the way for Lincoln's involvement too. On October 30, Wills wrote to Lamon, telling him of the progress in establishing the cemetery. Wills anticipated "a very large concourse of people." There would be an impressive procession and there was need for someone to be in charge of the events. "We have agreed upon you as the proper person," Wills's letter said, "and therefore extend to you an invitation to act as Marshall [sic] of the procession on that day."[62]

Lamon discussed the invitation with the President. "He told me," Lincoln said, "and I told him I thought that, in view of his relation to the Government and me, he could not well decline."[63]

Lamon was an excellent choice and he promptly set to work. He composed a circular letter inviting all United States marshals in the eastern half of the country to serve as "assistant marshals" at the ceremonies to be held at Gettysburg on November 19. He also wrote a letter to each of the eighteen governors whose states had lost sons at Gettysburg to appoint two "assistant marshals."[64] He received permission for free use of the telegraph line for all matters "touching the arrangements for the celebration at Gettysburg."[65] General George H. Stoneman authorized the sending of thirty horses from Washington to Gettysburg — provided that Lamon arranged the transportation.[66]

Lamon received advice from several quarters. General George Cadwalader, for example, insisted that military units "lead" the procession: "The Military parade placed in advance [of the procession] gives *effect* and ensures more *regularity* . . . and I think on this occasion it would be particularly appropriate."[67]

Marshal Lamon, with David Wills's approval, decided that his corps of assistant marshals be attired in a distinctive manner. He spelled out "the proper attire" in detail:

1. Plain black suit (preferably a frock coat), black hat, and white gloves.
2. White satin scarf, five inches wide, to be worn over the right shoulder and carried across the breast and back to the left hip, and there fastened with a rosette, the ends to be fringed, and to extend to the

knee. At the center on the shoulder the scarf should be gathered and mounted with a rosette.

3. Rosette, four inches and raised in center to be made of black and white ribbon, the outer circle only to be white.

4. Rosette of red, white, and blue on left breast. The initials of state in center for identification. The saddle cloths on their horses, of white cambric bordered with black.[68]

On Friday, November 13, Lamon again went to Gettysburg, this time to finalize details.[69] There would be three divisions to the procession: the military, the marshal's (which included the dignitaries), and the civic. Lamon and Wills decided to put the principals on horses, rather than in carriages. The fact that Lincoln's bodyguard was a good horseman may have had something to do with the decision.

As chief marshal, Lamon would oversee activities on the platform as well as the procession. He accepted the responsibility for the printing of the programs, securing horses for the dignitaries and assistant marshals, and the assignment of the principals, the organizations, and state delegations to a place in the procession.

By Monday, November 16, Lamon was back in Washington.[70] He asked two dozen friends to serve as "aides" — insuring, for them, a free trip to Gettysburg aboard the President's special train.[71] He arranged for the printing of the program. That night, he held a meeting of his "aides."[72] It was a chance to plan and talk and drink.

The following morning, at 11:30 o'clock, Lamon entrained for Gettysburg. He remained there until after the dedication ceremonies.[73]

Lamon, along with David Wills, Edward Everett, and the band of the 5th New York Artillery, met the President's train when it arrived at Gettysburg. The welcoming party accompanied Lincoln to the Wills's house. Each then went his own way. " . . . our party," one of the President's secretaries wrote in his diary, "broke like a drop of quicksilver spilled."[74]

Earlier, Lamon had scheduled a meeting of his assistant marshals and aides for eight p.m., November 18, at the courthouse. Lamon explained the duties of his assistants and designated on which street corner each state's delegation would assemble next morning and what place each would have in the procession.[75]

Marshal Lamon had a difficult assignment next morning. The crowd in downtown Gettysburg swelled to "immense proportions."[76] It was difficult, almost impossible, for the assistant marshals to transform the throng into a procession. Fortunately, the distinctive dress of the assistant marshals and the fact that they were on horseback made the task easier.

Shortly before ten o'clock, the scheduled time for the procession to begin its half-mile and southward trek toward Cemetery Hill, President Lincoln emerged from the Wills's house. He was dressed in black, wearing a frock coat and his well-known stovepipe hat, which had a wide mourning band around it. He also carried white riding gloves.

Scores crowded around the President. Some wanted to shake his hand, others to study his facial features from a nearby place. The crowd prevented Lincoln from getting to his horse. It was necessary for Lamon, serving again as the President's bodyguard, to push the crowd back and lead Lincoln to his black steed. After the President mounted his horse, another collection of well-wisher moved forward. Once more it was necessary for Marshal Lamon to come to Lincoln's rescue.

It was nearly eleven o'clock before Lamon put the show on the road. Several bands, taking turns playing marching music led the way. Rather pompously, Lamon led the Marshal's division. He rode at the President's left. Other notables included three members of Lincoln's cabinet, five generals and their staffs, eight governors, three foreign ministers, Lamon's aides, the members of the cemetery commission, and other guests of honor.

After Lamon directed the seating of the dignitaries on the $12' \times 20'$ platform, he took a position on the left side. After the first two musical numbers, Lamon read some regrets, including brief letters from General George G. Meade, General Winfield Scott, and Secretary of the Treasury Salmon P. Chase. Then Marshal Lamon introduced the day's orator most briefly: "Ladies and Gentlemen, the Honorable Edward Everett."

After the oration, a chorus of twelve chanted the hymn composed by Benjamin B. French. Lamon stepped front and center again, this time to introduce Lincoln. The introduction was brief and proper: "Ladies and Gentlemen, the President of the United States."[77] Then Lamon returned to his chosen spot on the platform to be a witness to Lincoln's rendezvous with destiny.

After a brief benediction by the Reverend Henry L. Baugher, president of Gettysburg College, Lamon stepped forward for the last time. He stated that the formal program was over. But he invited all who were interested to attend a special Ohio-sponsored program to be held at the Presbyterian Church at five p.m.[78] Marshal Lamon and his assistants then re-formed the procession and directed it back to Gettysburg.

Lamon did not return that evening on the President's special train to Washington. There was still work to be done. On November 21, Lamon met with his assistants for the last time. Their final act was to adopt a resolution which Lamon had drafted:

> *Resolved,* That we tender our heartfelt thanks to the Ladies and Gentlemen of Gettysburg for their generous hospitality and for the many acts of courtesy and kindness extended to us during our sojourn in the city.[79]

After Lamon returned to Washington, he resumed his duties as United States Marshal for the District of Columbia. Meanwhile, the war of attrition, waged by Northern armies, wore out the reserve of Southern manpower. On Sunday, April 9, 1865, Lee surrendered the remnant of his once noble army to Grant. Lamon was on a special mission to Richmond on the night that President Lincoln was assassinated at Ford's Theatre.

After returning to Illinois, Lamon sloughed the veneer of respectability which the Washington environment had imposed upon him. He felt free to tell lies and concoct myths. He put statements into Lincoln's mouth — fabricating quotations. Referring to the Gettysburg Address, Lamon wrote: "He said to me on the stand, immediately after concluding the speech, 'Lamon, that speech won't *scour*. It is a flat failure, and the people are disappointed.' "[80] Soon after, Lamon concocted another quotation and attributed it to his benefactor: "Mr. Lincoln said to me after our return to Washington, 'I tell you Hill, that speech fell on the audience like a wet blanket. I am distressed about it. I ought to have prepared it with more care.' "[81]

Lamon repaid his patron for all of his favors in a rather shabby fashion. He acquired material (much of it from William H. Herndon)[82] to write a biography of Lincoln. Lacking the self-discipline which such a task entailed, he hired Chauncey F. Black, the son of President James Buchanan's attorney general, to ghost-write it for him. Lamon's *The Life of Abraham Lincoln* appeared in 1872. The book depicted Lincoln rather badly — one historian said with "shocking realism."[83] At times, it was more a contribution to mythology than history. It implied that Lincoln was born out of wedlock. It pictured Thomas Lincoln, Abe's father, as "a lazy vagabond" and "shiftless rover." It furthered the myth that Anne Rutledge was Abraham Lincoln's one and only true love and that, in anguish, he threw himself over her fresh grave. It portrayed Mary Todd Lincoln as "a shrew," a "Hell-cat," and a millstone about Lincoln's neck. It suggested that Lincoln had left her at the altar the first time they planned to be married. And it contended that Lincoln relished smutty stories, that he was an infidel, and that he was a brash opportunist. If Ward Hill Lamon knew the meaning of the words "gratitude" or "deference," they held no place in his heart. Truly, Lamon was an interesting witness, albeit not a reliable one.

John George Nicolay, who also occupied a chair on the $12' \times 20'$ platform at Gettysburg, was still another witness — the fifth in this series — to Lincoln's famous address.

Nicolay, like Lincoln, was a son of the Illinois prairie. Young Nicolay was a half-orphan when his father brought him from Bavaria (Germany), first to St. Louis and then to Pike County, Illinois. The new American environment overpowered his German culture. He picked up the English language readily but retained some German traits — a willingness to work hard and long, an interest in literature, and a determination to get ahead. In his early teens he left the family farm and went to Pittsfield to work as a printer's devil in the shop of the *Pike County Free Press*. "The printing shop became his school and year by year he advanced himself until, before he was twenty-one, he was not only editor of the paper but also an important cog in county politics."[84]

There, in Pittsfield, Nicolay moved into the camp of the Whigs and became an admirer of Lincoln, then only an aspiring politician. During the 1850's both moved out of the dying Whig party and into the newly born Republican party.

Nicolay's work in the political vineyards — plus a pleasant personality — bore fruit in the form of a clerkship in the office of the Secretary of State as well as Keeper of the Library in the State House.

Nicolay's removal to Springfield gave him a chance to further his relationship with Lincoln. Nicolay helped Lincoln handle the constantly swelling correspondence after Lincoln was first nominated, then elected president. Impressed with Nicolay's ability, the President-elect asked him to be his personal secretary. The twenty-eight-year-old accepted the honor and the responsibility. Nicolay, called "Nico" by his friends, recruited John Hay, a twenty-two-year-old friend known as "Dapper John" as his assistant. The two became an inseparable and dependable team, devoted to Lincoln and to each other. They added a touch of humor to their obligations. Unbeknown to the President, they referred to him endearingly as "Tycoon" or "the Exec" or "the Ancient."

Their admiration for Lincoln evolved into adulation as the months passed by. Once Hay wrote to Nicolay, "There is no man in the country so wise, so gentle, and so firm. I believe the hand of God placed him where he is." A month later Hay wrote, "The old man sits here and wields like a backwoods Jupiter the bolts of war and the machinery of government with a hand equally steady and equally firm."[85] Nicolay agreed with every word.

After Ward Hill Lamon agreed to serve as Marshal during the dedication proceedings at Gettysburg, he consulted Nicolay frequently. Eventually, he asked Nicolay to serve as an "aide."

Both Nicolay and Hay accompanied the President on the special train to Gettysburg on the afternoon of November 18. After an evening meal at the Wills's house, the two secretaries parted company. Hay took a walk about Gettysburg and Nicolay attended a meeting of Lamon's assistant marshals and aides at the court house.

Later in the evening, Nicolay, Hay, and John W. Forney (then secretary of the United States Senate and owner of two newspapers) had a party of their own. Hay later jotted down his impressions in his diary: "We went back to F———'s [Forney's] room . . . and drank more whiskey. N——— [Nicolay] sang his little song of the 'Three Thieves' and we then sang John Brown."[86]

The next morning, after breakfast, Nicolay went to Lincoln's second floor bedroom in the Wills's house "to report for duty."[87] He found the President, sitting at a table with a pencil in his hand, rewriting and reworking the last sentence of his address.[88] Nicolay noticed that the first page was in ink and on White House stationery and that the rewritten portion was in pencil on a sheet of bluish-gray foolscap.[89]

Both Nicolay and his sidekick, John Hay, rode in the procession right behind the President on the way to Cemetery Hill.[90] Both had reserved chairs on the 12 ' × 20 ' platform and witnessed the performances of Edward Everett and Abraham Lincoln. Both later commented upon the President's address. Hay's comment, confined to his diary, was brief: " . . . the President, in a firm, free way, with more grace than is his wont, said his half-dozen lines of consecration, the music wailed, and we went home through crowded and cheering streets."[91] Evidently, Hay failed to grasp the significance of the President's words. John Nicolay, on the other hand, recognized that Lincoln had performed well and that his words had an eternal ring. Nicolay put his impressions on paper. First he defended the brevity of Lincoln's address, saying, "It was entirely natural for everyone to expect that this would consist of only a few perfunctory words, the mere formality of official dedication." Then he praised the quality of the address, saying that those carefully chosen words would "carry the concentrated thought of the occasion like a trumpet-peal to the fartherest posterity." For good measure, Nicolay repudiated the myth, already gaining popularity, that Lincoln had written the address on an envelope or bit of wrapping paper while the President's special train was Gettysburg-bound. As a conscientious personal secretary who was constantly at arm's reach, Nicolay wrote, "There is neither record, evidence, nor well-founded tradition that Mr. Lincoln did any writing, or made any notes, on the journey between Washington and Gettysburg."[92] John Nicolay was not only an astute witness, but also a dependable one.

Sometime during the days and weeks that followed the dedication of the soldiers' cemetery at Gettysburg, the President gave John Nicolay the two-page manuscript that he had held in his left hand while reciting the address on the $12' \times 20'$ platform atop Cemetery Hill.[93] It was an historical treasure as well as a reminder of his remarkable services to the Civil War president.

During the postwar years, Nicolay and John Hay collaborated in the writing of a ten-volume work which they entitled *Abraham Lincoln: A History*. The result of twenty years of labor, it was published in 1890. The reverence which Nicolay and Hay had for Lincoln showed in every volume, for the two regarded themselves as "guardians of the Lincoln tradition" and "Lincoln men through and through." "I need not tell you," one of the co-authors wrote to Lincoln's son (this was Robert Todd Lincoln, who loaned the two his father's letters), "that every line has been written in a spirit of reverence and regard."[94] Although John George Nicolay was a perceptive witness, he was far from an objective one.

Chance and circumstance made Benjamin B. French a witness to Lincoln's address at Gettysburg. French was a native of New Hampshire but a resident of Washington. His acquaintanceship with Lincoln dated back to December 7, 1847, when Lincoln came to Washington to begin a two-year term as a congressman. As clerk of the House of Representatives, French presented Lincoln's credentials to the Speaker.[95]

After finishing his term as clerk of the House of Representatives, French resumed his interest in the telegraph and the company that was building the experimental line from Washington to New York City. Earlier, he had been present when Samuel Finley Breese Morse had sent the words "What hath God wrought?" from Washington to Baltimore on May 24, 1844.

After Lincoln gained the presidency, French's friends sought a Washington assignment for Morse's partner. President Lincoln, in turn, appointed French as Commissioner of Public Buildings.[96]

Benjamin B. French developed a favorable relationship with the White House — he liked Lincoln and tolerated the First Lady. Records show that, at the President's request, French purchased $250 worth of books "for the Executive Mansion on August 26, 1862."[97]

Although French had many unpleasant encounters with Mrs. Lincoln, he expressed indignation over the many "vile slanders" and "cruel criticisms" which her enemies put in circulation. Writing to his sister-in-law, French characterized the President's wife as "a kindly, well-meaning woman." Referring to the many "unkind rumors," French wrote, "I *know* many of them to be false."[98]

French also developed a working relationship with Ward Hill Lamon, Lincoln's bodyguard. French, for example, accompanied Lamon to Gettysburg on November 13, when the latter was completing plans for supervising events concerned with the dedication of the soldiers' cemetery.

In Gettysburg, David Wills related some of his problems, including the fact that Longfellow had turned down the invitation to write a special ode or hymn for the dedication program. French, who had dabbled in poetry, offered to work up something that very night and present it for consideration next morning.

Entitling his work "Consecration Hymn," French wrote five stanzas and reworked them time and again before midnight. He incorporated phrases like "holy ground," "sacred blood," "our glorious dead," "widow's tears," and "Freedom's holy cause." By being on the battlefield, he had caught the spirit of the place.

Next morning French handed his five-stanza composition to Wills, who thought it had merit. At least, he decided to incorporate it into the formal program. The two decided to ask the Maryland Musical Association to chant it. It would be rendered after Everett's oration and before the President's remarks of dedication.

After Lamon and French returned to Washington, they remained on amiable terms. Lamon even asked French to be one of his "aides," insuring a free trip to Gettysburg for him. Both Benjamin B. French and his son signed Lamon's list of those wishing to accompany Marshal Lamon to Gettysburg.[99]

French was aboard the President's special train when it departed for Gettysburg at noon on November 18. In Baltimore, twelve members of the Maryland Musical Association clambered aboard, bound for Gettysburg.

Next day French rode in the procession, in the same section as President Lincoln, David Wills, Marshal Lamon, and John Nicolay. French was honored by being assigned one of the chairs in the front row on 12 ' × 20 ' platform. He was, of course, a most interested witness. He listened carefully to Everett's long oration, knowing, of course, that his ode would be the next number on the program. He watched as the twelve-man chorus, members of the Maryland Musical Association, took a place near the front of the platform and readied themselves to chant French's ode. He listened with rapt attention as they chanted the words he had composed several days earlier:

'Tis holy ground —
This spot, where, in their graves
We place our Country's braves,
Who fell in Freedom's holy cause
Fighting for Liberties and Laws —
Let tears abound.

Here let them rest —
And Summer's heat and Winter's cold,
Shall glow and freeze above this mould —
A thousand years shall pass away —
A nation still shall mourn this clay,
Which now is blest.

Here, where they fell,
Oft shall the widows' tears be shed,
Oft shall fond parents mourn their dead,
The orphans here shall kneel and weep,
And maidens, where their lovers sleep,
Their woes shall tell.

Great God in Heaven!
Shall all this sacred blood be shed —
Shall we thus mourn our glorious dead,
Or shall the end be wrath and woe,
The knell of Freedom's overthrow —
A Country riven?

It will not be!
We trust, Oh, God! Thy gracious Power
To aid us in our darkest hour,
This be our Prayer — "Oh, Father! save
A people's Freedom from its grave —
All praise to Thee."[100]

French should have been pleased with the excellence of the presentation by the Baltimore-based glee club and the appreciative response of the audience. The emotional words fitted the time and place, and the applause was loud and long.[101]

But French did not have long to enjoy the apparent success of his ode. It was time for Lincoln to recite his address and French to be a witness. French noticed that there was a bond of empathy between an intent audience and the bespectacled man waiting for silence and attention. He noticed, too, that the President's brief recitation was interrupted five times by applause and that extremely loud applause followed its completion.

French was much impressed. Later he testified that Lincoln's address had struck a responsive chord: "Anyone who saw and heard, as I did, the hurricane of applause that met his every movement at Gettysburg would know that he lived in every heart. It was no cold, faint shadow of a reception; it was a tumultuous outpouring of exultation from true and loving hearts . . . . It was the spontaneous outburst of the heartfelt confidence of the people in their President."[102]

Benjamin B. French was an observant witness, but his admiration for Lincoln prevented him from being an impartial one.

The seventh and last witness — in this odyssey — was a soldier who is nameless. He occupied a spot directly in front of the platform and followed the program with an intense interest. He had fought in the famous three-day battle and had an empty sleeve because an arm had been amputated. When Lincoln recited the sentence "The world will very little note nor long remember what we say here, but it can never forget what they did here" the soldier's emotions took over. A newspaperman reported the scene:

> . . . a gallant soldier (a stout and stalwart officer bearing a captain's insignia and with one empty sleeve) buried his face in his handkerchief [and] sobbed aloud while his manly frame shook with no unmanly emotion. In a few moments, with a stern struggle to master his emotions, he lifted his still streaming eyes to heaven and in low and solemn tones exclaimed *God Almighty, bless Abraham Lincoln.*[103]

The unknown captain, by his actions, offered tangible evidence that Lincoln's address at Gettysburg stirred the heart and impressed the mind of an appreciative audience.

The seven witnesses, ranging from Edward Everett to the unknown soldier, were participants in an historic event of the first order. Lincoln's Gettysburg Address holds a unique place in the history of American literature and American oratory. Praised by posterity, it has stood the test of time. "It ought to be remembered," one who admired the address wrote, "as long as the language lasts in which it was spoken."[104] That compliment was matched by another: "The oration of Lincoln will never be forgotten. It will live until languages are dead and lips are dust."[105]

Abraham Lincoln was correct when he said that the world would never forget what the Union soldiers did at Gettysburg. He was wrong, however, when he said that "the world would little note nor long remember" what he said there.

Chapter IX

A MILWAUKEEAN WITNESSES LINCOLN'S GETTYSBURG ADDRESS: W. YATES SELLECK AND THE SOLDIERS' CEMETERY AT GETTYSBURG*

W. Yates Selleck had a reserved place on the $12' \times 20'$ platform at Gettysburg during the dedication program of November 19, 1863. In a sense, he had earned that place on the platform by serving as an "assistant marshal" during the procession which preceded the program and by representing the state of Wisconsin on the commission which had been set up to oversee the establishment and governance of the new soldiers' cemetery — created out of 17½ acres of a famous battlefield. He witnessed Edward Everett's oration as well as President Abraham Lincoln's rendezvous with destiny. Forty-five years later he wrote his recollections of the event, composing an important but almost unknown historical document. Selleck's participation in the proceedings at Gettysburg and his narrative about that oft-discussed event have earned him a niche in history.

Little is known about W. Yates Selleck before the American Civil War gave him an opportunity to emerge from obscurity and become a historical figure. His father, Isaac Selleck, brought his family to Milwaukee from New York State in 1842 and made the city his place of residence until his death in 1875 at the age of eighty-one.[1]

Young W. Yates Selleck found employment in the insurance industry and found politics an avocation. He became a friend of John F. Potter,[2] a judge who lived in East Troy and who had political ambitions. Both Selleck and Potter exchanged their battered Whig hats for new Republican ones in the late 1850s. Selleck gloried in Potter's election to Congress in 1856 and then worked for the election of Alexander W. Randall as Republican governor of Wisconsin in 1859. Enthralled by politics, W. Yates Selleck helped establish the Young Men's Republican Club in the city in March of 1860 and became the organization's corresponding secretary.[3] Although originally a zealous William H. Seward sup-

---

*Reprinted (with permission) from the *Milwaukee History*, 2 (Summer 1986), pp. 34-49.

porter in 1860, he accepted Lincoln's nomination and worked hard to bring about a Republican victory.

Selleck's work in the political vineyards brought rewards — a clerk's job in Washington, D.C., at the hands of congressman Potter. Soon after Selleck arrived in Washington, the Fort Sumter affair turned a crisis into a conflict. The Union defeat at First Bull Run shocked the North. Soon after General George B. McClellan's peninsular campaign ended in withdrawal and defeat, Wisconsin residents who held federal appointments in Washington banded together to form the Wisconsin Soldiers' Aid Society. The purpose was to furnish aid and comfort to sick, needy, and wounded soldiers — "more especially to visit the hospitals and see that our soldiers are well cared for." James R. Doolittle, one of the state's two U.S. Senators, served as the organization's president, Selleck as vice-president.[4]

As the war expanded to other sectors, and more Wisconsin regiments became involved, the state legislature provided for "state agents" whose responsibilites attached them to state regiments to serve the soldiers' needs. Duties included distributing mail and goodies sent from home, visiting hospitals to see that soldiers received adequate care, and helping to administer the state's new voting-in-the-field law. Democrats, naturally, contended that the new "state agents" would be "political commissars," interested in "manufacturing Republican votes" from camp and battlefield.[5]

Governor Louis P. Harvey directed that the state agents (more correctly called "State Military Agents") be assigned to areas rather than regiments. W. Yates Selleck became the state's chief agent in the Washington area. After Governor Harvey's tragic death in Tennessee following the Battle of Shiloh, Lieutenant Governor Edward Salomon moved up a chair. Salomon and Selleck, both Milwaukeeans, had worked for Lincoln's election as political allies. Selleck stayed on in Washington. Governor Salomon, aware that Selleck's duties multiplied as more battles were fought, assigned William P. Taylor as a deputy or assistant.

Governor Salomon wrote to Selleck often. Sometimes he asked Selleck to get furloughs for wounded men, sometimes to deliver a new regimental banner, sometimes to check on someone's reported disloyalty.[6] Selleck carried out his duties zealously, earning favor in Madison. Once he felt compelled to defend the state's honor. A correspondent of the *New York Times* had accused the Third Wisconsin Infantry Regiment of cowardice at Second Bull Run. Selleck wrote a sharp rebuttal. In an angry letter to the *Milwaukee Sentinel*, Selleck set the record straight: " . . . *it is a base slander and falsehood, and there is not one word of truth in it.*"[7]

After the invading Confederate forces were turned back in a dramatic three-day battle at Gettysburg, Selleck and his assistant made plans to go there to supervise the needs of Wisconsin's wounded. More than six thousand Wisconsin troops were involved, with the already famous Iron Brigade decimated in the battle. Delayed because of disrupted train schedules, Selleck and his assistant reached Gettysburg on July 8.[8] They visited hospitals and noticed that medical supplies were woefully inadequate. Leaving his assistant to "make out lists of all the killed, wounded, and missing," Selleck rushed back to Baltimore and Washington "to procure supplies." He arrived back in Gettysburg on the afternoon of July 10 with dozens of boxes including "five boxes of underclothing," "three bundles of crutches," and "other hospital stores." He promised Governor Salomon that he would send a list of the killed, wounded, and missing "as soon as possible."[9]

Selleck and his assistant performed their work of mercy well, spending long days in makeshift hospitals and sending some of the walking wounded to camps near Washington. "The Wisconsin wounded at Gettysburg," Selleck's assistant wrote to a friend, "were better attended to and cared for than those of any other state — not even excepting Massachusetts."[10]

Selleck's dedication and diligence attracted the attention of David Wills, the Gettysburger who became the central figure in establishing a soldiers' cemetery out of a portion of the famous battlefield. Wills talked to state agents like Selleck and secured their cooperation in the proposal to buy 17½ acres of the battlefield and establish a soldiers' cemetery, subsidized by the eighteen states that had lost sons at Gettysburg — under the hegemony of Pennsylvania.[11]

Governor Salomon, perhaps on Selleck's recommendation, promised to support Wills's project. In turn, he asked Selleck to work with Wills on the cemetery plans, especially "in reference to the detail of arrangements for removal of the Wisconsin dead [from their scattered graves all over the battlefield] to the Cemetery grounds."[12]

In early August Selleck returned to his Washington base and his chores in the camps and hospitals of the area. In mid-August he entrained for Gettysburg again to meet with David Wills and inquire about progress of the cemetery project. He visited soldiers recuperating in the hospitals or in private homes. He worried about the summer heat and its effect upon the bed-ridden wounded. He reported on his ministrations to those in need and he complimented the people of the Gettysburg area for their concerns. "The people of Gettysburg," Selleck wrote, "are very attentive in supplying the wants and looking after the comforts of the wounded soldiers." He added a sentence about the cemetery project: "I will write you to-morrow respecting the plans and arrangements proposed for laying out of the National Cemetery on the late Battlefield."[13]

After David Wills proposed the establishment of a cemetery commission to oversee the project, Governor Salomon officially designated Selleck as the state's representative — "to act in connection with Mr. Wills and the agents of other States in making the necessary arrangements for completing the work." Since state moneys would be forthcoming, the Governor gave Selleck some sensible advice: "A full report, to be laid before the Legislature will be expected, and you will therefore oblige by preserving all necessary memoranda for the purpose."[14]

Selleck replied promptly, promising to keep all "necessary vouchers and memoranda" and to continue reporting on the progress of the cemetery project[15]

The next day, Selleck, still based in Washington, wrote to David Wills to tell him that he had been officially named Wisconsin's representative on the Gettysburg soldiers' cemetery commission.[16]

While performing his chores in the hospitals and camps of the Washington area, Selleck became concerned about the progress of the cemetery project. He did not hear from Wills for more than a month. Since Selleck was planning a hurried trip to Milwaukee and Madison, he wanted to convey the latest word on progress of the cemetery project to Governor Salomon. His anxiety prompted him to write to Wills. "I intend going to Wisconsin the last day of next week and shall see the governor," Selleck wrote, "and I desire to give him some information in reference to the matter."[17]

Wills replied promptly. He assured Selleck that he was pushing the cemetery project vigorously. For good measure, he enclosed a lengthy personal report as a letter to Governor Salomon.[18]

After his brief visit to Wisconsin, Selleck returned to Washington to continue his work as the state's liaison with its soldiers. The cemetery project, meanwhile, moved forward and Wills continued with plans for a dedication program. He supervised the construction of a 12' × 20' platform close to the new cemetery, "northeast of the outer circle of graves" and "facing to the northwest."[19] After the program plans were practically completed, Wills asked Ward H. Lamon, President Lincoln's bodyguard, whose official title was "United States Marshal for the District of Columbia," to supervise the procession which would precede the program and to serve as master of ceremonies aboard the 12' × 20' platform.[20]

Assuming the title Marshal-in-Chief for events of November 19, 1863, Lamon promptly wrote to every one of the eighteen governors involved in the new soldiers' cemetery. He asked each to appoint a person to serve as an "assistant marshal" during the procession and help supervise events for the day.[21] During a trip to Washington, Governor Salomon asked Selleck to serve as "assistant marshal" on November 19, 1863 — adding this duty to one he already had as Wisconsin's official representative on the Gettysburg cemetery commission.

Selleck, meanwhile, continued his work as state agent effectively and, well, gaining a reputation as a dedicated and responsible worker. The *Milwaukee Sentinel* paid Selleck and his aides a compliment: "Mr. W. Y. Selleck, the State Agent, is again at his post, and he is busy, as is also his faithful assistant, William P. Taylor, Esq., attending to the wants of the wounded Wisconsin men as they come into the hospitals."[22] Even Secretary of War Edwin M. Stanton knew of Selleck's devotion to duty. Reacting to reports that the soldiers' hospital needs were not always met, Stanton appointed Selleck as one of five members of a board "to correct every abuse which they may discover" in the soldiers' hospitals.[23]

As the day of the dedication program approached, Selleck made an effort to meet the dress code for the "assistant marshals" which Marshal-in-Chief Lamon had prescribed:

COURTESY OF THE WISCONSIN STATE HISTORICAL SOCIETY

WILLIAM YATES SELLECK

William Yates Selleck represented Wisconsin on the Gettysburg Cemetery Commission, served as an assistant marshal during the procession, and had a reserved
seat on the 12 ' × 20 ' platform during the dedication ceremonies.

1. Plain black suit (preferably a frock coat), black hat, and white gloves.
2. White satin scarf, five inches wide, to be worn over the right shoulder and carried across the breast and back to the left hip, and there fastened with a rosette, the ends to be fringed, and to extend to the knee. At the center on the shoulder the scarf should be gathered and mounted with a rosette.
3. Rosette, four inches and raised in center to be made of black and white ribbon, the outer circle only to be white.
4. Rosette of red, white, and blue on left breast. The initials of state in center for identification. The saddle cloths on their horses, of white cambric bordered with black.[24]

In addition to recruiting "assistant marshals" from states and among U.S. Marshals in the eastern half of the country, Lamon invited many friends to serve as his "aides" in return for a free train ride to Gettysburg. On the evening of November 16, Lamon met with all available "aides" and "assistant marshals" in a room in the city hall. Selleck was in attendance, anxious for information about the excursion and his responsibilities. Lamon stated that the Baltimore & Ohio Railroad had placed a special car at his disposal, "free of charge." The North Central Railroad had made a similar pledge for the second leg of the journey, from Baltimore to Hanover Junction. The rest of the trip, from Hanover Junction to Gettysburg was still in the negotiation stage. Lamon promised to have all travel details verified and posted in his office by eleven o'clock next morning. The train with its special car would leave Washington for Baltimore at three o'clock on November 17 — two days before the dedication ceremonies.[25] On a sheet of paper, Lamon wrote a heading: "The undersigned wish to signify their intention of accompanying Marshal Lamon to Gettysburg tomorrow — leaving this city at the hour named." The name of "W. Y. Selleck" appeared on that list.[26]

The Baltimore & Ohio train, with Lamon's special car and W. Yates Selleck aboard, was fifteen minutes late in leaving Washington. It arrived at Baltimore about one o'clock. All of the occupants of Lamon's special car repaired to the Eutaw House for an elaborate meal, courtesy of the president of the Baltimore & Ohio Railroad.[27] At three o'clock, Lamon's party, this time in a special car provided by the North Central Railroad, left for Gettysburg. After a tiresome delay in Hanover Junction, Lamon and his entourage arrived in Gettysburg.[28]

Next day, Selleck renewed his acquaintanceship with David Wills, toured some hospitals and a part of the battlefield, and attended Lamon's briefing session for his "aides" and "assistant marshals."[29] Selleck learned of his responsibilities during the next day's procession — on what street corner Wisconsin residents would gather before the procession moved southward toward Cemetery Hill. A horse was provided for his use, making it easier to get the attention of Wisconsin citizens partaking in the procession. Lamon also gave Selleck a ticket which entitled him to a place on the 12′ × 20′ platform.[30] After all, he was a cemetery commissioner as well as an "assistant marshal."

On the morning of November 19, Selleck secured his mount. Dressed in his distinctive uniform, prescribed by Marshal-in-Chief Lamon, Selleck spent some time herding together Wisconsin soldiers and civilians willing to march in the procession. He must have been quite successful, for the state's delegation in the procession impressed some viewers. One newspaperman reported, "Pennsylvania furnished the largest numerical representation, Ohio next, Wisconsin third, and Massachusetts fourth."[31]

The procession, which left Gettysburg for Cemetery Hill about eleven o'clock impressed countless viewers. It was "an impressive sight," many participants carried flags or banners or devices. Everything seemed in perfect order as "the mighty mass rolled on as waves of the ocean."[32]

After the procession reached the top of Cemetery Hill and the site of the $12' \times 20'$ platform, the marchers fanned out to become an audience. The dignitaries, along with some of Lamon's "aides" and "assistant marshals," took designated places on the platform. Lamon was the only Wisconsin resident to have a place on the platform and to witness a historic event — Edward Everett's oration and President Lincoln's most memorable address.[33]

The program was a long and impressive one. Selleck listened, as did thousands of others, as Birgfield's Band (sponsored by the Philadelphia Union League) played an introductory dirge. He heard the Rev. Thomas H. Stockton, chaplain of the House of Representatives in Washington, recite a lengthy invocation — "a prayer which thought it was an oration."[34] Then the Marine Band played Luther's hymn "Old Hundred" impressively — "in all its grand and sublime beauty."[35] Selleck heard Edward Everett's two-hour oration, devoted mostly to a discussion of the separate battles which made up the whole. One critic wrote that the famed orator gave his two-hour recitation with his "accustomed grace" but that it lacked "one stirring thought, one vivid picture, one thrilling appeal."[36] Selleck seemed to agree, for years later he wrote that "but little applause was given" when Everett finished his oration.[37]

During Everett's long recitation many on the platform let their eyes wander from the orator to the scene around them. Scattered over the countryside, as far as the eye could see, were thousands of sightseers touring the expansive battlefield. Some had left the fringe of Everett's audience, either bored by the lengthy oration or despairing of a place within hearing of the speaker.[38]

Those who looked northward could see the deserted city of Gettysburg, half a mile away. It was flag bedecked. In the central square stood a sixty-foot flagpole with its flag at half-mast. A quarter of a mile west of the small city one could see the steeple of a Lutheran church and near it the edifice of the seminary (Pennsylvania College); it was "a chaste specimen of the Doric order, one hundred and fifty feet in length."[39] Near there, and farther to the West, many Wisconsin soldiers had fallen, dead or wounded. The already famous Iron Brigade, facing overwhelming odds, had fought heroically as its regiments were decimated.[40]

To the right, toward the northeast, lay Culp's Hill, "precious in history" and scene of several battles. To the east lay hilltops and valleys which had been spared the destruction of battle. To the south, far in the distance, stood two promontories important in the three-day conflict, Little Round Top and Big Round Top. The huge flag on a tall pole on Big Round Top unfurled in the breeze — someone had forgotten to put it at half-mast.[41]

Far to the west and northwest, hazy and distant, stood majestic South Mountain, forming one dimly defined frame for the whole picture. The lofty chain of mountains swept northward, forming both the western and northern borders of Adams County. Stretching everywhere were the fields and farms and hills which had become a battleground where Mars had sown his seeds of death. Even President Lincoln, when earlier surveying the countryside, had expressed surprise to see so many fields and so little wooded area around Gettysburg.[42]

After Everett finished his oration, it was time for a chorus of twelve members of the Maryland Musical Association to perform. They chanted an ode written especially for the occasion by Benjamin B. French, a friend of the Marshal-in-Chief. French, like Selleck, had ridden to Gettysburg in the special cars provided for Lamon.

After Lamon, again as master of ceremonies, introduced "the President of the United States" all eyes centered on Lincoln. He arose slowly from his chair, took a step forward, adjusted his spectacles, and waited for silence. In his left hand he held a two-page manuscript. Slowly and clearly he began to recite his brief address, without once looking down at the manuscript that he held. Selleck, as well as others, heard the audience interrupt Lincoln's nine-sentence address five times and pay homage with "tremendous applause" when he finished — a fact that time erased from Selleck's memory when he wrote his reminiscences forty-five years later.[43] For good measure, the crowd gave three cheers for Lincoln and three more for the governors.[44]

After Lincoln's oft-praised address, a mixed chorus of Gettysburgers sang a dirge, one of Percival's. Then the Rev. Henry L. Baugher, president of the local Lutheran seminary, recited a brief benediction. Lamon stepped forward for the last time to state that the formal program was over and that it was time to reform the procession and return to Gettysburg. While a battery of the 5th New York Artillery fired a salute of eight rounds, Selleck and the other assistant marshals sought out their horses and urged the audience to become a procession.[45] It was a difficult task, for many were reluctant to leave the site and the magnificent scenes one could see from Cemetery Hill. "Many lingered until the shades of evening approached," one observant newspaperman noted, "seemingly loathe to leave the ground consecrated by the blood of those heroes who fought, and died, and found a grave there."[46]

After the procession reached Gettysburg and dispersed, Lamon assembled his aides and assistant marshals once more in a room in the courthouse. He thanked all for their services.[47] He offered a resolution which he had prepared earlier for their approval:

> *Resolved,* That we tender our heartfelt thanks to the Ladies and Gentlemen of Gettysburg, for their generous hospitality and their many acts of courtesy and kindness extended to us during our sojourn in that town.[48]

After Selleck and others approved the resolution, Lamon submitted it to the local newspapers and it was published by both the *Adams County Sentinel* and the *Gettysburg Compiler*.[49]

Selleck and others who had traveled to Gettysburg aboard special cars provided for Marshal-in-Chief Lamon, returned to Washington on President Lincoln's special train. It left for Baltimore and Washington about seven o'clock in the evening. After an aggravating delay in Hanover Junction, the weary travelers reached Washington long after midnight.[50]

Back in Washington, Selleck again went about his regular duties, visiting camps and hospitals and caring for the Wisconsin soldiers' needs. About a month later he submitted a bill of $30.90 for "expenses in attending the consecration of the National Cemetery at Gettysburg."[51]

On December 17 Selleck took a train to Harrisburg, this time to attend a meeting of the commissioners of the new soldiers' cemetery. David Wills called the meeting to order in a room at the Jones House, a local inn. He stated that the first order of business was to elect officers for the cemetery commission, transforming an informal organization into a formal one. The commissioners elected Wills as "President" and W. Yates Selleck as "Secretary" — the honor bestowed upon Selleck indicated his standing with his peers. Then the commissioners discussed plans for "the protection and preservation of the grounds," including their "proper adornment and care." The commissioners eventually approved five resolutions concerned with "the completion and operation" of the newly established cemetery. Before adjourning, the presiding officer named a five-member committee "to procure designs of a monument to be erected in the cemetery."[52]

With most of the plans for the new cemetery completed, Selleck returned again to Washington and his regular duties as state agent. He took time, however, to write a detailed report on his role in the establishment of the soldiers' cemetery and in Wisconsin's share of the cost. Each state's share depended upon how many representatives it had in the lower house of Congress — it was $420.53 for each such congressman. Since his state had six members in the House of Representatives, Wisconsin's share was $2,523.18. "Nearly all of the remains of the Union Soldiers killed in the battle of Gettysburg," Selleck added, "have been removed to the Cemetery; all of those killed in the first day's fighting have been removed; such, are placed in the lots that are marked *unknown*."[53] Wisconsin, unfortunately, had many of its dead soldiers identifiable by regiment, but not by name.

In March of 1864 David Wills wrote a report to his governor and state legislature. He sent a copy to Selleck. In all, 3,512 Union soldiers had been reburied in the new soldiers' cemetery. Of that number, 73 were Wisconsin soldiers and 20 of these were unknowns.[54]

In late March, 1864, the Pennsylvania State Legislature formalized the project, incorporating the "Soldiers' National Cemetery" — the name was a misnomer, for it was still a cooperative project of the eighteen states that had soldiers buried there. The name of W. Yates Selleck appeared as one of the "corporators."[55]

Slightly more than a year later, the war came to a close. When the armies disbanded, Selleck's work as a "Military Agent for the State of Wisconsin" came to an end. In his letter of resignation, dated May 29, 1865, Selleck stated that he had looked after "the interests and welfare of Wisconsin soldiers" both conscientiously and effectively for more than three years. He was anxious to return to Milwaukee to pursue "private affairs."[56]

Six months after returning to Milwaukee, Selleck accepted an offer from the Travelers' Insurance Company of Hartford, Connecticut. The editor of the *Milwaukee Sentinel* paid a long-time friend a compliment and a farewell: "The duties of the office [Military State Agent] were performed with great faithfulness and tact, and many a hundred of the Badger State's 'boys in blue' will hold his name in grateful remembrance for the valuable service which he had rendered them, and will write with his friends in Milwaukee in wishing him success in the new horizon in which he is now to labor."[57]

There was a pot of gold at the end of the rainbow of Selleck's new horizon — first in Hartford, then in Philadelphia and Washington, D.C. He became "a well-to-do businessman." Later he served the United States as a vice-consul at Bradford, England, and "held other positions of trust under the Government."[58]

In the summer of 1906, W. Yates Selleck made a return trip to Milwaukee to visit his daughter and sister as well as old friends of Civil War days.[59] The editor of the *Evening Wisconsin* urged Selleck to write his recollections of his role in the dedication of the soldiers' cemetery at Gettysburg and as a witness to Lincoln's famous address. Eventually, Selleck wrote an 1800-word account, inadvertently composing an invaluable historical document. It appeared in the February 9, 1909 issue of the *Evening Wisconsin*. His "narrative" follows:

> On the 17th of November, 1863, Col. Ward H. Lamon, United States marshal of the District of Columbia, who had been selected to act as marshal-in-chief to conduct the ceremonies of the dedication of the Soldiers' National Cemetery at Gettysburg, left Washington, accompanied by nine gentlemen to act as his aides and to arrange plans for conducting the dedication ceremonies and for the reception of President Lincoln and his party.
>
> The train bearing President Lincoln and those who accompanied him arrived at Gettysburg shortly after dark on the evening of the 18th, and the President was met by Col. Lamon, Col. John Hay and others of the marshal's aides, and conducted to the residence of David Wills, a little over a block from the railroad station. The members of the President's cabinet who were present, and other distinguished guests were conducted to the homes of residents of Gettysburg who had volunteered to entertain them.
>
> As the evening advanced, quite a number of men assembled in front of McClelland's hotel and were addressed by Secretary Seward, Edward McPherson and others. At length Mr. Lincoln was serenaded and called upon for a speech. He replied by saying:

"I appear before you, fellow citizens, merely to thank you for this compliment. The inference is a very fair one that you should hear me for a little while, at least, were I to commence to make a speech. I do not appear before you for the purpose of doing so; and for several substantial reasons. The most substantial of these is that I have no speech to make. In my position it is somewhat important that I should not say any foolish things. [A voice: "If you can help it!"] It very often happens that the only way to help it is to say nothing at all. Believing that is my condition this evening, I must beg of you to excuse me from addressing you further."

Later in the evening, Mr. Lincoln, accompanied by David Wills, went to the house where Secretary Seward was a guest to show him the manuscript of the address that he intended to deliver the next day. He shortly after returned to Mr. Wills's house, and the rest of the night was quietly passed.

The morning of the 19th opened cloudy and chilly. There were about fifty thousand people in and around Gettysburg, including several thousand troops in the commands of Gens. Schenck, Stoneman and Stahel, the whole under the command of Gen. Couch. There was some delay in forming the procession and in getting it started to the cemetery. It was about 10 o'clock in the morning when President Lincoln appeared at the door of Mr. Wills's house. Horses had been provided for him and his party, and for several other distinguished personages. The procession was delayed for a time by people pressing forward to shake hands with the President after he was mounted on his horse, which continued until stopped by the marshal-in-chief and his aides. After those already mentioned came the military and civic organizations on foot, followed by the people at large.

On reaching the stand in the cemetery on which seats had been reserved for the President, members of his cabinet, foreign ministers, governors of states, commissioners and a few invited guests, all were soon seated.

At the east end of the stand was a tent, and from it, a short time after all were seated on the stand, came forth Edward Everett, the orator of the day, conducted to his seat on the stand by Gov. Seymour of New York and Mr. David Wills.

The exercises were opened with an invocation by the Rev. Dr. Stockton; after which Mr. Everett commenced his oration. The stand was near the outline of the semi-circle where the graves of the soldiers were placed, and faced the northwest, where the crowd in attendance listened to what took place. The oration of Mr. Everett was listened to with close attention. He was nearly two hours in delivering the address, and but little applause was given.

After Mr. Everett had finished, a hymn composed by B. B. French of Washington, D.C., was sung, following which President Lincoln arose, and, standing erect, with a manuscript in his hand, but without looking at it, delivered his address as follows:

"Fourscore and seven years ago our fathers brought forth upon this continent a new nation, conceived in Liberty, and dedicated to the proposition that all men are created equal. Now we are engaged in a great civil war, testing whether that nation, or any nation so conceived and so dedicated, can long endure. We are met on a great battlefield of that war. We are met to dedicate a portion of it as the final resting-place of those who here gave their lives that that nation might live. It is altogether fitting and proper that we should do this. But in a larger sense we cannot dedicate, we cannot consecrate, we cannot hallow this ground. The brave men, living and dead, who struggled here, have consecrated it far above our power to add or detract. The world will little note nor long remember what we say here, but it can never forget what they did here. It is for us, the living, rather to be dedicated here to the unfinished work that they have thus far so nobly carried on. It is rather for us to be here dedicated to the great task remaining before us — that from these honored dead we take increased devotion to the cause for which they here gave the last full measure of devotion — that we were highly resolve that the dead shall not have died in vain; that the nation shall, under God, have a new birth of freedom, and that the government of the people, by the people, and for the people, shall not perish from the earth.''

It has been repeatedly published that the address was received by the assembled multitude with loud demonstrations of approval. Such was not the case. The immense throng which had stood for two hours in the chilly atmosphere did not seem to comprehend the fullness, force and logic of President Lincoln's address; and the same may be truly said of those who were on the stand. It was not until afterwards, when the address had been read and re-read, that it was appreciated by those who heard it and the public at large.

After President Lincoln's address a dirge was sung by a choir selected for the occasion. Then a benediction was pronounced by the Rev. H. L. Baugher of Gettysburg.

Immediately after the ceremonies a battery of artillery stationed on the high ridge in the cemetery fired a national salute, during which the President and those who accompanied him mounted on their horses, and a procession was formed which returned to Gettysburg, escorted by the marshal-in-chief and his aides.

Shortly after (in the afternoon) the clouds cleared away and the sun shone bright and warm. The remainder of the day was pleasant. At about 2 o'clock the President, in company with Mr. Wills, went to where Secretary Seward was stopping, and shortly thereafter John Burns, ''the hero of Gettysburg,'' was brought in and introduced to them.

A few minutes later the President, Secretary Seward and others issued from the residence, and Mr. Lincoln taking Mr. Burns's right arm while Mr. Seward took his left, followed by an impromptu procession, moved out on the Baltimore pike to the Presbyterian church, a little over a square distant, to listen to an address by the lieutenant-governor of Ohio.

At the close of the address the President returned to Mr. Wills's house, and before dark left Gettysburg by train, accompanied by the party which had attended him from Washington and the marshal-in-chief and his aides.

The following persons were on the stand (12 feet wide and 18 feet long) with President Lincoln when he delivered his address:

William H. Seward, secretary of state; Montgomery Blair, postmaster-general; John P. Usher, secretary of the interior; Edward Everett; the French minister, M. Mercier; the Italian minister, Sig. Bertinati; Gov. Seymour of New York; Gov. Curtin of Pennsylvania; Gov. Todd of Ohio; Gov. Morton of Indiana; David Wills of Gettysburg; Rev. Dr. Stockton; Rev. Dr. Baugher; B. B. French; Col. Clarke E. Carr; Col. Gordon Lofland; Edward McPherson; Mr. McKnight; Wayne McVeagh; Col. John W. Forney; Capt. H. A. Wise, U.S.N., and Mrs. Wise; Ben. Perley Poore; Henry Edwards, George W. Bond; Charles Hale; J.G. Rosengarten; the two Misses Gilbert of Philadelphia; Col. Ward H. Lamon, marshal-in-chief; Col. John Hay; Silas Casey, chief justice United States court of claims; Judge Abarim Olin; Judge George P. Fisher; Judge James Hughes; Dr. Hanscomb; Charles Kent; Benjamin Schnyder; W. Yates Selleck. The last nine were aides to the marshal-in-chief. There were a few others on the stand, whose names are not remembered by the writer.

Comments on Selleck's Reminiscences

Selleck's narrative was written about forty-five years after the event which he described, sometimes in detail. Circumstantial evidence indicates that he had a clipping from the *Washington Daily National Intelligencer* of November 21, 1863 at his elbow while writing his recollections. Selleck's account of Lincoln's impromptu speech when he was serenaded at the Wills's house the evening before the dedication ceremonies match the words credited to the President by a reporter for the *Intelligencer.*

Selleck's reminiscences are an important historical document. His final paragraph which gives the names of thirty-nine persons who had places on the $12' \times 20'$ platform adds facts not known previously. No other list anywhere names half as many.

Selleck errs when he says that Lincoln's Gettysburg address was not received with "loud demonstrations of approval." Contemporary newspaper sources indicate otherwise.

Selleck also errs when he says that the dedication program took place under "cloudy skies." A reporter for the *Washington Daily Morning Chronicle* wrote that November 19, 1863 was "one of the most beautiful Indian Summer days ever enjoyed."[60] A reporter for the *Cincinnati Commercial* stated that Secretary of State Seward, bothered by a shining sun, sat with his arms folded (during Everett's address) and his hat "drawn down over his eyes."[61]

The statement that there "were about fifty thousand people in and around Gettysburg" on the day of the dedication program should be challenged. Ten thousand would be a better guess, with perhaps eight thousand assembled to hear Everett's oration.

Selleck's statement that the platform was 18 ' × 12 ' is also in error. Onetime, earlier, Selleck had written: "The stand on which President Lincoln stood in the National Cemetery at Gettysburg on November 19, 1863 when he delivered his ever to be remembered address was 12 ft. wide and 20 ft. long, and facing the northwest. It was located 40 ft. northeast of the outer circle of soldiers' graves as shown by pencil mark on the Cemetery map in the book to which this memorandum is attached."[62] Interestingly, Selleck puts the stand at a different location than Gettysburg cemetery officials do today.

Despite these descrepancies, Selleck's observations about a most memorable event are newsworthy and a worth-while historical source.

PART FOUR: POSTSCRIPT

These three chapters were written especially for this book.

The story of the six drafts of the Gettysburg Address in Lincoln's own hand could well be the most interesting of the twelve chapters. One section of it, that dealing with the third draft, might also be termed "very controversial." That chapter, by far, is the longest of the twelve.

Chapter XI, dealing with the dispute over the location of the platform on which Lincoln spoke, is also replete with controversy. W. Yates Selleck again emerges as a central figure in the dispute. The topic is timely, for the debate over the location of the platform surfaced again in 1993.

Chapter XII was added as an afterthought. Originally, notes about the musical numbers appearing in the dedication program were to be an Appendix. In time, with research and writing, they evolved into a chapter.

Each of the three chapters is an aspect of the story about the soldiers' cemetery at Gettysburg and Lincoln's address. The word "Postscript" aptly fits these last three chapters.

CHAPTER X

THE SIX COPIES OF THE GETTYSBURG ADDRESS IN LINCOLN'S OWN HAND

1. The First Draft (The Nicolay Copy)

President Abraham Lincoln was beset by a variety of problems as summer gave way to fall in 1863. Union victories at Gettysburg and Vicksburg in early July had made his administration respectable again, but the glow faded with General William S. Rosecrans's defeat at Chickamauga on September 19-20. Still friends began to promote Lincoln's re-election, but he seemed more concerned with the October-scheduled gubernatorial contests in Ohio and Pennsylvania where Democratic candidates Clement L. Vallandigham and George W. Woodward, respectively, were viable contenders.

When Pennsylvania governor Andrew G. Curtin realized that Woodward was a serious challenger, he raced to Washington to see President Lincoln and Secretary of War Edwin M. Stanton to plead that Pennsylvania troops be furloughed so they could go home and vote in the October elections. On August 28, 1863, Governor Curtin had conferences with both Lincoln and Stanton and both were sympathetic to Curtin's cause.

It is likely that, during his conference with Lincoln, the Pennsylvania governor also mentioned the Gettysburg cemetery project, that the governors of eighteen states that had lost sons at Gettysburg would be invited to the dedication ceremonies, and that the president too would receive an invitation.[1] Lincoln would relish a chance to visit the Gettysburg battlefield — he had earlier ridden in an ambulance over the grounds of the Antietam battlefield. Then too, as a pragmatic politician, he would welcome the opportunity to shake hands with the governors and further his re-election possibilities.

Somewhere and in someway the president made a commitment to attend the dedication programs. Exactly a month before the dedication date, editor Henry J. Stahle of the Gettysburg *Compiler*, in the October 19, 1863 issue, stated: "Hon. Edward Everett is to deliver the dedication oration. President

Lincoln will also be present and participate in the ceremonies." On October 30, 1863, David Wills, in charge of the cemetery project, wrote to Lincoln's bodyguard to ask him to serve as marshal-in-chief during the procession and master of ceremonies during the program of November 19.[2] Lincoln's bodyguard, Ward H. Lamon, would not have been asked to "supervise the ceremonies" if the president were not coming. The invitation to Lamon is proof that Lincoln had made a commitment to attend the dedication program before October 30.

On November 2, David Wills formalized the invitation with a letter to Lincoln. "I am authorized by the governors of the different States," Wills wrote, "to invite you to be present and to participate in these ceremonies, which will doubtless be very imposing and solemnly impressive." The next sentence defined the president's role: "It is the desire that, after the oration, you, as Chief Executive, formally set apart these grounds to their sacred use by a few appropriate remarks." Then Wills invited Lincoln to be his house guest while he was in Gettysburg.[3]

During the days that followed, Lincoln occasionally thought about his new responsibility. He was wrestling with his message to Congress, due on December 8, and a proclamation of amnesty and reconstruction. At times phrases or statements that would be appropriate to dedicate the Gettysburg cemetery crossed his mind. He could do his job in just one sentence, saying something like "I hereby set apart these grounds as a soldiers' cemetery" or "I hereby dedicate this part of the battlefield as the final resting place for those who died here." But Lincoln wanted to say more, something worthy of the office and the occasion. "He probably followed his usual habit in such matters," Lincoln's secretary John Nicolay wrote years later, "using great deliberation in arranging his thoughts, and moulding his phrases mentally, waiting to reduce them to writing after they had taken satisfactory form."[4]

Some days before his scheduled appearance at Gettysburg, Lincoln sat down at his desk in the White House to put his thoughts on paper — no evidence indicates the day or the hour. Using a pen and his official White House stationery, he started the first sentence, already formulated in his mind: "Four score and seven years ago our fathers brought forth, upon this continent, a new nation, conceived in liberty, and dedicated to the proposition that all men are created equal." This was vintage Lincoln. The words "eighty-seven years ago" had evolved into "four score and seven years ago," and borrowing phrases or clauses from the Declaration of Independence was his common practice. After all, he had said repeatedly that he got all of his political ideas from the Declaration of Independence and from Thomas Jefferson.[5] Years before Lincoln had been mesmerized by the inspiring words of the second sentence of the Declaration: " . . . all men are created equal; that they are endowed by their Creator with certain unalienable rights; that among these, are life, liberty, and the pursuit of happiness." Lincoln's opening sentence was a subtle justification of his emancipation proclamations, still being criticized by some conservatives, including Democratic spokesmen.

Lincoln's opening sentence of thirty words served as the first paragraph. He began work on the second. Words, phrases, and sentences came together rather easily. The second paragraph took shape — 127 words in seven sentences. His thoughts were expressed with grace and firmness and with a literary flair.

There was one empty line on the ruled first page and he started his third paragraph there: "It is rather for us, the living, to stand here." Then Lincoln ran into a problem as he tried to continue atop page two of White House stationery. His literary muse deserted him and he struggled to complete the sentence and the address. It was a long, long sentence and its exact words will never be known. But we know that Lincoln was not satisfied with page two — it did not meet his high literary standards. At least there was something down on paper and reworking it could be done at a later date.

Three different individuals presented testimony that Lincoln wrote the first draft or most of it in Washington, not on the Gettysburg-bound train nor in his room at the David Wills house in Gettysburg — mythmakers would have you believe otherwise. James Speed, the brother of one of Lincoln's most trusted friends, visited with the president shortly before he left for Gettysburg and later said, "The day before he [Lincoln] left Washington, he found time to write about half of a speech." He also said that Mr. Lincoln was most anxious "to be prepared to say some appropriate thing."[6]

United States Marshal for the District of Columbia, Ward H. Lamon, and Lincoln's bodyguard also affirmed that the president had written his address some time before he left for Gettysburg. Lamon, late in life, wrote: "From his hat (the usual receptacle of his private notes and memoranda) he drew a page of foolscap, closely written, which he read to me . . . . It proved to be in substance, and I think, *haec verba*, what was printed as his Gettysburg speech."[7]

The third witness was a newspaperman, Noah Brooks of the Sacramento *Union*. Brooks, who had once been an Illinois resident, became both a friend and a confident of Lincoln. The Washington-based reporter visited with Lincoln on a Sunday (November 15) while the president had an appointment at Alexander Gardner's picture-taking studio. During their conversation, Lincoln noted that his speech for the Gettysburg cemetery dedication was rather short. "So it is written, is it, then?" Brooks asked. Lincoln, according to Brooks, replied, "It is not finished, anyway . . . and I shall have to give it another lick before I am satisfied. But it is short, short, short."[8] The president, it is evident, was still not satisfied with the last half version of his address — page two need to be reworked, revised, and tuned to perfection.

It is likely that Lincoln carried his composed draft, on two pages of White House stationery, in the left hand pocket of his black frock coat on his trip to Gettysburg on the afternoon of November 18. It is also likely that Lincoln wrote nothing on that train taking him to Baltimore, Hanover, and Gettysburg.[9]

After Lincoln's arrival in Gettysburg as dusk was getting ready to welcome the night, he was escorted to the David Wills house, a three-story rectangular building fronting on "the Diamond," the local term for the central square. After

Executive Mansion,

Washington, _____, 186 .

[1] Four score and seven years ago our fathers brought forth, upon this continent, a new nation, conceived in liberty, and dedicated to the proposition that "all men are created equal"

[2] Now we are engaged in a great civil war, testing whether that nation, or any nation so conceived, and so dedicated, can long endure. [3] We are met on a great battle field of that war. [4] We have come to dedicate a portion of it, as a final resting place for those who died here, that the nation might live. [5] This we may, in all propriety do. [6] But, in a larger sense, we can not dedicate — we can not consecrate — we can not hallow, this ground — [7] The brave men, living and dead, who struggled here, have hallowed it, far above our poor power to add or detract. [8] The world will little note, nor long remember what we say here; while it can never forget what they did here. [9] It is rather for us, the living, ~~to stand here,~~ we here be dedicated

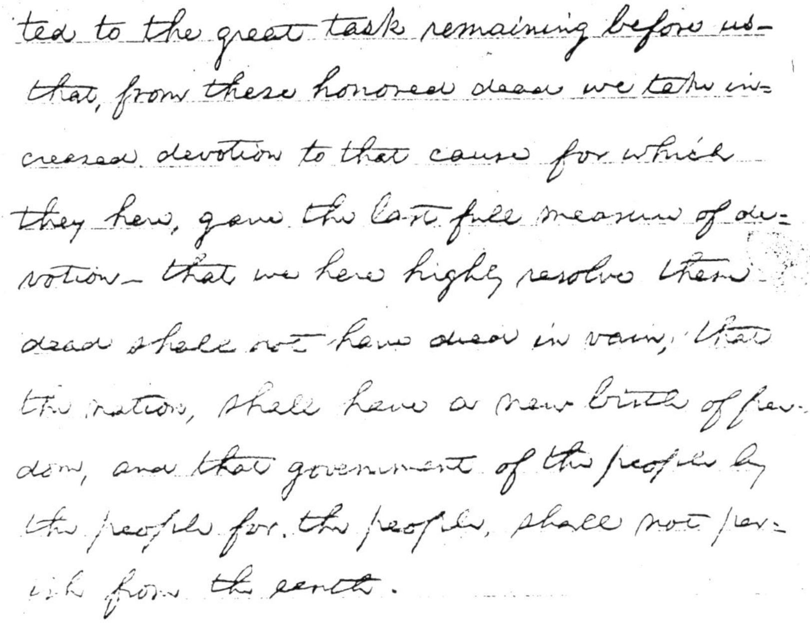

[handwritten manuscript text:]

ted to the great task remaining before us—
that, from these honored dead we take increased devotion to that cause for which
they here, gave the last full measure of devotion— that we here highly resolve these
dead shall not have died in vain, that
the nation, shall have a new birth of freedom, and that government of the people by
the people for the people, shall not perish from the earth.

First Draft (Nicolay Copy)

Note that the first page is on White House stationery. It was written in Washington some time before Lincoln left for Gettysburg. The last sentence of page one in incomplete, carried over to a second page on White House stationery — this second page evidently ended up in a wastepaper basket in Lincoln's room in David Wills's house in Gettysburg. Lincoln revised the second page on 8¼ ″ × 13 ″ lined bluish-gray foolscap provided to Lincoln by Wills. This second page is written in pencil as are the last several words of page one. This second page was written by Lincoln on the evening of November 18, 1863. The first draft consists of 239 words and nine sentences in three paragraphs — the long last sentence has 82 words covering ten lines. This document is in the Library of Congress.

the evening meal Lincoln was serenaded by a band and calls for the president brought him to the front door where he gave a brief impromptu speech.

Later, perhaps about ten o'clock, Lincoln begged to be excused and retired to his second-floor bedroom to redo the second page of his address. With a short pencil in his hand and the two pages of his manuscript before him, he started work on his revision. Soon he instructed his black servant, William Slade, to go downstairs and ask host Wills for some writing paper and pen and ink.[10] Wills sent up some bluish-gray foolscap and the pen and ink.

By the time that servant Slade returned, Lincoln, with a short pencil in his hand, was at work on his revision. He began with the bottom line of page one — the first line of the third paragraph. The line read: "It is for us, the living, to stand here." With his pencil, the president crossed out the last three words and above them wrote "we here be dedica—." Then he continued the sentence, still in pencil, on one of the sheets of foolscap that Wills had provided: "ted to the great task remaining before us — that, from these honored dead we take increased devotion to that cause for which they here, gave the last full measure of devotion — that we here highly resolve these dead shall not have died in vain, that the nation, shall have a new birth of freedom, and that government of the people by the people for the people shall not perish from the earth."[11]

This was better. Not perfect, but better. The opening words of that long last sentence (those on the last line of White House stationery) were ungrammatical. There were commas where none were needed, and there were none where some were needed. That long closing sentence, begun on page one covered eleven lines and included eighty-three words — including "that" four times. But there were some well-turned phrases and some stirring thoughts and noble sentiments. Lincoln anticipated that he would have time next morning to review his composition, finish memorizing it, and perhaps rewrite it. But at least and at last a satisfactory version was down on paper.

It was time to visit his Secretary of State, William H. Seward, and seek his approbation. So Lincoln sent servant Slade to seek out David Wills again. "About eleven o'clock," Wills wrote years later, "he sent for me again, and when I went to his room he . . . asked me if he could see Mr. Seward." Wills told the president that the Secretary of State was staying next door, the guest of Robert G. Harper, editor of the Republican-orientated *Adams County Sentinel*. Wills offered to go next door and "fetch" Seward. "No," Lincoln interjected, "I'll go and see him." Wills accompanied Lincoln to Harper's house and, years later, wrote, " . . . we found Mr. Seward and I left the President with him. In less than half an hour Mr. Lincoln returned with the same paper in his hand."[12] It is likely that Lincoln read his address to Seward and that the Secretary of State approved of its contents and sentiments.

Eventually, Lincoln retired for the night. If sleep was slow in coming it was because his second-floor bedroom window overlooked the central square. A disorganized crowd seemed to be in a "festive mood" as some sang while others cheered or "hallooed."[13]

Early the next morning, Lincoln and Secretary Seward took a buggy ride over part of the battlefield, taking the road west of town and past the Lutheran seminary. It is possible that Lincoln had his two-page manuscript with him, folded in thirds and nestling in the left hand pocket of his black frock coat.[14] Then, after having been served a sumptuous breakfast by Mrs. Wills and visiting with other guests, Lincoln retired to his room to review his address and get ready for the procession and program.

Soon after Lincoln sat down at his table and began looking at his two-page manuscript, his reliable secretary John Nicolay "reported for duty" — calling on his "Boss" to see if he was wanted for some chore or assignment. Nicolay noticed that the president had a pencil in his hand and that two sheets of paper lay before him, the first page being White House stationery and the second "bluish-gray foolscap of large size with wide lines."[15]

The president, it turned out, had no special assignment for his trustworthy secretary and was most anxious to get on with his revision and memorizing. Before Nicolay left he probably asked Lincoln to give him the manuscript sometime after the ceremonies — a request the president later fulfilled.

While perusing the second page of the address, Lincoln noticed that he had inadvertently omitted fourteen words that were on the second page of White House stationery — these words were "here to the unfinished work which they have, thus far, so nobly carried on."

It was probably best to make a new copy of the two-page address so the fourteen words could be put in their proper place in that long last sentence. Furthermore, the first draft was on two different sized sheets, with the sheet of White House stationery much smaller than the page of foolscap — it is much easier to handle a two-page manuscript if both sheets are of the same size. Then too, rewriting is an aid to memorizing and Lincoln wanted to recite his speech rather than read it. If Edward Everett could memorize a two-hour oration the president could do the same for an address of about 240 words. So, with pen in hand and using the foolscap that host Wills had provided, Lincoln rewrote the entire address, making a few slight changes that pleased his ear.

Since Nicolay had asked for the original draft, why not write still another so the president could give the second draft to John Hay, Nicolay's assistant? One for Nicolay, one for Hay — why not one for himself? So Lincoln, at that table in his room at Gettysburg, wrote the third draft — it would become the president's "reading copy." While Lincoln was still rewriting the third draft, Sergeant James A. Rebert of Company B of the 21st Pennsylvania Volunteer Regiment entered the room. Earlier that morning he had been detailed as the president's orderly, and he called to say that he would have Lincoln's assigned horse ready for him when he came down to take part in the procession. Furthermore, Lincoln might have some wish or request. Years later Sergeant Rebert recalled that visit to Lincoln's room:

> He requested me to wait a few minutes until he finished his writing, which I found him engaged in on entering the room. He had several sheets of note paper in front of him written in pencil, and several that

JOHN NICOLAY, PRESIDENT LINCOLN, AND JOHN HAY

President Lincoln and his two secretaries, John Nicolay (sitting) and John Hay (standing). Lincoln gave each a copy of his Gettysburg Address. Photograph by Alexander Gardner.

he was just finishing . . . . After finishing them he folded all together
and placed them in his pocket.[16]

The paper that Lincoln was "just finishing" was the third draft of the Gettysburg Address, the copy that he held in his hand while reciting it early on
the afternoon of November 19, 1863.[17]

After the program, where Lincoln had performed well, was over, and as
dusk again visited Gettysburg, the president took his special train back to
Washington. Soon after, Lincoln gave Nicolay the two-page manuscript (the
first draft in Lincoln's hand) that he had earlier requested. It remained in his
possession during the postwar era. Nicolay mistakenly believed that the
manuscript in his possession was the one that Lincoln had in his hand on the
platform at Gettysburg.

When John Nicolay died in 1901, his copy of Lincoln's address became
the property of his friend and co-worker, John Hay. After Hay's death his
descendants presented it to the Library of Congress. There it resides today
although it goes on exhibit elsewhere occasionally. In 1963, for example, it was
loaned to the Chicago Historical Society for a "centennial exhibit" where it
was shown with four other drafts of the Gettysburg Address — all in Lincoln's
own hand.

2. The Second Draft (The Hay Copy)

Considerable controversy surrounds the second draft, especially when and
where it was written. Some authorities, self-styled or otherwise, contend that
it was written in Washington before Lincoln took his trip to Gettysburg. One,
William H. Lambert, said that this draft "was inadvertently left in
Washington"[18] when President Lincoln hurriedly left for Gettysburg about noon
on November 18. Lambert's supposition was taken seriously by James G. Wilson
who helped to popularize the idea. Since Wilson was both a lecturer and an
author, he was in a position to promote and popularize Lambert's supposition.
In 1913, Wilson stated that theme forthrightly and succinctly: "The Hay copy
[that is, the second draft] is the one he [the president] intended to take to Gettysburg and read; but when he came to leave the White House he could not
find it, and took along instead the rougher draft he afterward gave to Nicolay.[19]

A more popular supposition says that Mr. Lincoln wrote the second draft
or Hay copy in Washington shortly *after* he returned to the capital city from
his Gettysburg pilgrimage. Based upon second-hand information, John Hay
was credited with saying that the second draft was written specifically for Lincoln's second secretary in Washington; John Hay's cousin, a responsible individual, visited the Hay home and later wrote:

. . . the last time I was in the home of my cousin, Col. John Hay, late
Sec. of State, he showed me the original text of this speech [the Get-

tysburg Address] written by the late Pres. himself; and he remarked at that time, that Lincoln wrote it out immediately after his return from Gettysburg and presented it to Mr. Hay, so that it could go down in time in the language that he has then written.[20]

David C. Mearns and Lloyd Dunlap, in their scholarly book, *Long Remembered*, offer two plausible explanations of the same supposition. One is that the second draft is "a copy made shortly after Lincoln's return to Washington." The co-authors added, "Possibly Lincoln made this copy for David Wills in compliance with his request for 'the original manuscript' but gave it instead to John Hay."[21] Earlier, the co-authors had offered a different explanation:

> On November 20 Lincoln received from an eminent source assurance that his address was more than ordinary. On that day, from 225 H Street, Washington, Edward Everett wrote: "Permit me . . . to express my great admiration of the thoughts expressed by you, with such eloquent simplicity & appropriateness, at the consecration of the cemetery. I should be glad, if I could flatter myself that I came as near the central idea of the occasion, in two hours, as you did in two minutes." Such praise raises the possibility that from natural pride in what he said Lincoln desired to preserve a copy. The draft was incomplete, and he prepared a fresh copy based on his recollection and newspaper accounts.[22]

But if Lincoln wrote this copy and based it upon Washington newspapers and his own recall, why was the phrase "under God" not included in this second draft? It was right there before him in the Washington *National Intelligencer*. So it seems logical to say that the second draft was written *before*, not after the dedication program.

The supposition that Lincoln wrote the second draft on the morning of the dedication program was first advanced by Lincoln scholar William E. Barton. In his book, *Lincoln at Gettysburg* (1930), Barton stated his theory:

> About nine o'clock the following morning [November 19], Lincoln arose from the breakfast table in the Wills house and went to his room. There, not long afterwards, John G. Nicolay found him rewriting his address. For this rewriting he used the same kind of paper which he had used for the penciled first draft of his second page.[23]

Barton added that the newly rewritten draft was "wholly in ink," was "without erasure," and was on two pages of "wide-lined paper."[24]

Sergeant Rebert's statement that Lincoln finished writing his address while he waited at the bedroom door seems to give some substance to Barton's contentions. After all, Lincoln *needed* to rewrite to reincorporate those fourteen words unintentionally omitted on the penciled second page and to put the address in ink on two similar-sized sheets of paper. Drafts two and three, most likely, were copied in Gettysburg on the morning of the day on which President Lincoln delivered his address.

There were some differences in wording between the first and second drafts. In Lincoln's opening sentence in the first draft, the word "Liberty" is capitalized

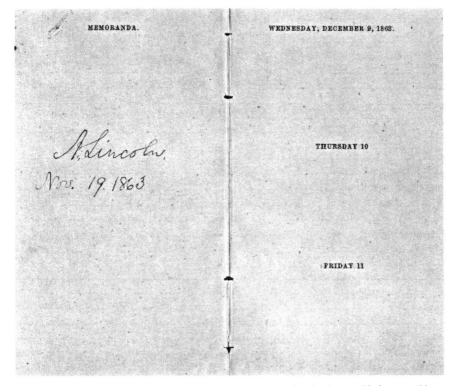

President Lincoln signed an autograph for someone on the day that he gave his famous address — the inscription is in pencil. It is likely that the autograph-seeker approached the president soon after he came out of the Wills house to be part of the procession. A newspaperman noted that the president was literally besieged by well-wishers and Marshal-in-Chief Ward H. Lamon encouraged his protege to mount his horse to escape the crowd. The tactic was only partially successful. This item, never before published, is in the hands of Lloyd Ostendorf and is reproduced here with his permission.

Four score and seven years ago our fathers brought forth, upon this continent, a new nation, conceived in Liberty, and dedicated to the proposition that all men are created equal.

Now we are engaged in a great civil war, testing whether that nation, or any nation, so conceived, and so dedicated, can long endure. We are met here on a great battle-field of that war. We have come to dedicate a portion of it as a final resting place for those who here gave their lives that that nation might live. It is altogether fitting and proper that we should do this.

But in a larger sense we can not dedicate— we can not consecrate— we can not hallow this ground. The brave men, living and dead, who struggled here, have consecrated it far above our poor power to add or detract. The world will little note, nor long remember, what we say here, but can never forget what they did here. It is for us, the living, rather to be dedicated here to the unfinished work, which they have, thus far, so nobly carried on. It is rather

[Handwritten text — Second Draft of the Gettysburg Address:]

for us to be here dedicated to the great task remaining before us,— that from these honored dead we take increased devotion to the cause for which they here gave the last full measure of devotion— that we here highly resolve that these dead shall not have died in vain; that this nation shall have a new birth of freedom; and that this government of the people, by the people, for the people, shall not perish from the earth.

Second Draft (Hay Copy)

The second draft, on the same kind of bluish-gray foolscap as page 2 of the first draft, was written in Lincoln's room in the Wills's house on the morning of November 19, the morning of the dedication ceremonies. It is in ink provided by David Wills. Again there are three paragraphs — the first consisting of one sentence (30 words), the second of four sentences (127 words), and the third of five sentences (166 words). The 268 words compare to the 239 in the first draft. The words "here to the unfinished work which they have, thus far, so nobly carried on" are not in the first draft and appear for the first time in the second. This manuscript shows no fold marks so it could not have been the reading copy. It also resides in the Library of Congress.

— not so in the second draft. In the same first sentence the clause "all men are created equal" appears in quotation marks — not so in the second. The next two sentences were copied verbatim. The fourth sentence saw a change in wording: "We have come to dedicate a portion of it, as a final resting place for those who died here, that the nation might live" became "We have come to dedicate a portion of it as a final resting place for those who here gave their lives that that nation might live." The fifth sentence also underwent change. "This we may, in all propriety do" became "It is altogether fitting and proper that we should do this." The sixth sentence remained exactly the same in both drafts. The seventh sentence had only a one word change as "hallowed it" became "consecrated it." The eighth sentence, the last in the second paragraph, remained the same.[25]

The last line of the first draft on White House stationery started a new sentence — this was the ungrammatical part, so Lincoln revised extensively. Furthermore, the fourteen words ("here to the unfinished work which they have, thus far, so nobly carried on") that Lincoln had inadvertently omitted in his rewrite the evening before found their rightful place in the second draft. The rest of that long last sentence remained quite the same, including "the new birth of freedom" phrase and the closing words where the president supposedly emphasized the word "people" each time instead of the prepositions "of," "by" and "for."

Those who mistakenly argue that it was the second draft (the Hay copy) that Lincoln held in his hand while reciting his address have no satisfactory answer to the claim that the two sheets making up that draft *have no fold marks*. There is undisputable evidence that Lincoln had his reading copy folded and in his pocket both before and after reciting his address.

No one knows exactly where and when Lincoln presented the second draft to John Hay. Strangely, Nicolay seems not to have known that Hay had the second draft in his possession — at least in his article in *Century Magazine* he made no mention of it.

Mearns and Dunlap wrote as a postscript: "The existence of this manuscript [the second draft] was not publicly known until 1906, when William H. Lambert described it in a lecture. It was first published in facsimile for public distribution in 1909. This copy with the First Draft was given to the Library of Congress by the children of John Hay in 1916."[26] With armed guards patrolling the gallery, the second draft was on exhibit with others in the Chicago Historical Library in 1963.

3. The Third or "Lost" Draft (the Wills Copy)

There are more questions than answers regarding the third draft of the Gettysburg Address in Lincoln's own hand. It is logical to assume that both the second and third drafts were written by Lincoln the morning of the dedication program. After all, he spent nearly an hour at the table in his second-floor bedroom that morning and two reliable witnesses saw him sitting there — at work. John Nicolay, who came into the room to ask if the president had some assignment for him, stood right next to Lincoln at the table. Orderly Rebert watched the president finish his writing, fold some papers, and put them in his pocket. Furthermore, the phrase "under God" appears for the first time in the third draft, i.e., the reading copy. It was belatedly inserted, above a caret, between the words "nation" and "shall" — this on page two.

Lincoln had that two-page document, on bluish-gray foolscap and folded in fourths, in his pocket as he rode in the procession and as he sat on the $12' \times 20'$ platform waiting for his turn to shine. When master-of-ceremonies Ward H. Lamon introduced the president, the latter arose from his chair, took the two pages out of the left hand pocket of his black frock coat, unfolded them, and held them in his left hand while he waited for the applause to cease. He had memorized well and did not have to look down at his manuscript as he recited his piece. He was interrupted by applause five times and he received "thunderous applause" at the end.[27]

After the program was over and before Lincoln left the stage, Associated Press reported Joseph L. Gilbert asked the president if he might "borrow" the two-page manuscript to correct his shorthand version. Lincoln obliged, taking the document out of his pocket, unfolding it, and handing it to the newspaperman. After making his corrections or additions, Gilbert handed Lincoln's copy back to him. The president folded it again and put it back in his pocket again.[28] The document, presumably stayed in Lincoln's coat pocket until he got back to Washington about midnight.

On November 23, four days after the dedication ceremony, David Wills wrote a two-paragraph letter to his president:

> On behalf of the States interested in the National Cemetery here, I request of you the original manuscript of the Dedicatory Remarks delivered by you here last Thursday.
>
> We desire them to be placed with the correspondence and other papers connected with the project. Please append your certificate to them.[29]

Note that Wills asked for the "original manuscript" and the president's certification. It should also be noted that Wills made the same request of Edward Everett.

It is logical to assume that Lincoln sent Wills the reading copy (the third draft) as requested. The president cooperated with every other similar request. When Mrs. Daniel P. Livermore asked Lincoln to send her *"the original manuscript of the Proclamation of emancipation,"* saying that it would bring in a sizeable amount of money for the Chicago Sanitary Commission Fair, Lincoln heeded her request[30] — this a month before Wills made his plea. Lincoln replied promptly, writing, "According to the request made in your behalf, the original draft of the Emancipation proclamation is herewith enclosed . . . . I had some desire to retain the paper; but if it shall contribute to the relief or comfort of the soldiers that will be better."[31] Furthermore, Lincoln later heeded three other requests for copies of the Gettysburg Address. Nicolay also wrote, years later, that the president complied with Wills's request,[32] but in this case Lincoln's secretary was an impeachable witness, for he was in New York City when the "please send" request arrived in Washington.[33]

Anyway, in one manner or another, the third draft became "the lost draft." Wills never wrote to Lincoln acknowledging receipt of the document, although such a "thank you" letter might not be viewed as necessary.

The second half of the story of the third or "lost" draft revolves around a respected Dayton, Ohio, resident named Lloyd Ostendorf — and it has a rather bizarre beginning. Ostendorf has a national reputation as a collector, illustrator, and author, and is regarded as the authority on Lincoln photographs. The book, *Lincoln in Photographs: An Album of Every Known Pose* (1963), co-authored with Charles Hamilton, is a remarkable and oft-praised book. Another book, *A Picture Story of Abraham Lincoln* (1962), contains 160 ink drawings (along with many photographs) by Ostendorf; although interesting to the young it intrigues adults as well. Ostendorf has presented scholarly papers at conferences and conventions, and he has six entries in Eugene C. Murdock's *The Civil War in the North: A Selective Annotated Bibliography*. Amateur collectors of Lincolniana or Civil War artifacts frequently seek his advice, freely given, or ask him to appraise items.

In midsummer of 1990, an individual who seeks to remain anonymous, brought Ostendorf "a handwritten page of paper" — most likely the second page of the third or "lost" draft of the Gettysburg Address. Ostendorf asked his caller where he obtained the document, for it seemed to be genuine as to Lincoln's penmanship. The caller, in a matter of fact way, replied that it was between the pages of a book, *The Lincoln Memorial: A Record of the Life, Assassination, and Obsequies of the Martyred President*, published by Bunce & Huntington, 640 Broadway, New York City. The caller said that it was "picked up" at an antique fair in northern Ohio. Ostendorf was skeptical, aware that forged documents were put into old books — a favorite forger's ploy. The caller offered to leave the one-page document with Ostendorf so that he could study it further. The rather nonchalant attitude of the caller intrigued Ostendorf.

The Dayton resident, who had handled many of Lincoln's writings, recognized that this one-page document was really page two of the Gettysburg Address, perhaps half of the "lost" Wills copy. Where was this sheet during its 127 missing years? Why did the caller want anonymity? Why did he seem so unconcerned, and not the least bit nervous? Intrigued, Ostendorf decided to seek to authenticate the document, knowing that this called for "carefully validating historical accuracy, verbal correctness, forensic analysis, and scientific testing."[34]

Seven factors led Lloyd Ostendorf to believe that he might have the authentic page two of the third draft in Lincoln's own hand. In the first place, Osten-

dorf could detect nothing inconsistent in punctuation, wording, spelling, or penmanship — it certainly seemed to be genuine Lincoln. "I had immediately
recognized the little quirks in Lincoln's writing," Ostendorf wrote later, "the
lifting of the pen before certain letters, the upsweep flourish on the line end
of a word, and all the quaint features I had long observed in more than fifty
years of collecting Lincoln items."[35] In the second place, it is the only copy
of page two of the Gettysburg Address with the phrase "under God" above
the line and above a caret inserted between the words "nation" and "shall"
— Lincoln did use the phrase in his oral recitation. In the third place, there
was a small glue stain in the upper left hand corner and Ostendorf knew that,
in Lincoln's day, it was common practice for lawyers to use a tab of glue to
hold two pages together. In the fourth place, this newly discovered sheet of
paper was bluish-gray foolscap and the same kind of paper used by lawyers
during the 1860s. In the fifth place, there was the endorsement or certification:
"For Hon. Judge David Wills, from A. Lincoln, November 19, 1863." Not
only had Wills asked for the "original" document in his letter but he had also
asked the president to certify it. In the sixth place, the newly found page showed slight fold marks as Lincoln's reading copy properly should. And in the
seventh place, the watermark on the page, oval Crown Britannica, showed that
the paper belonged to the Civil War era.

Encouraged by his initial analysis of the document, Ostendorf remarked,
"If authentic, this would be the sixth variant of the Gettysburg Address in Lincoln's hand. It would be only the second one bearing his signature. It would
be the best part of the lost original."[36]

The next step was to show the document to other Lincoln "authorities."
In the fall of 1990 Ostendorf met with Dr. Wayne C. Temple who earned his
Ph.D. in History under Professor James G. Randall at the University of Illinois. Randall, in his day, was considered the country's top Lincoln scholar.
Dr. Temple achieved a reputation of his own as "a Lincoln man." He published extensively and served a stint as editor of the *Lincoln Herald* before moving
to Springfield to become Chief Deputy Director of the Illinois Archives. In that
position he has handled thousands of Lincoln documents. After a careful examination of the page that Ostendorf showed Temple, the latter concluded that
the document was indeed page two of the third draft or the so-called Wills copy.
Everything seemed to fit. Dr. Temple's endorsement was most heartening to
Ostendorf.[37]

Some months later, the fellow who had brought the handwritten page to
Ostendorf in the first place paid his second visit to Dayton. The caller listened
to Ostendorf's suppositions. There was still more verification to be done before
one could say with certainty that this was indeed the second page of the "lost"
draft. But Ostendorf thought it was. The caller listened, then said, "I am not
interested in collecting autographs," and then added abruptly, "Nor do I want
any publicity."[38]

Ostendorf was surprised at the caller's nonchalance and his matter-of-fact
manner. The caller offered to sell the document to Ostendorf then and there,

COURTESY OF LLOYD OSTENDORF

LLOYD OSTENDORF

Mr. Lloyd Ostendorf purchased the second page of Lincoln's third draft (the so-called Wills copy) of the Gettysburg Address in midyear, 1990, from an anonymous fellow.

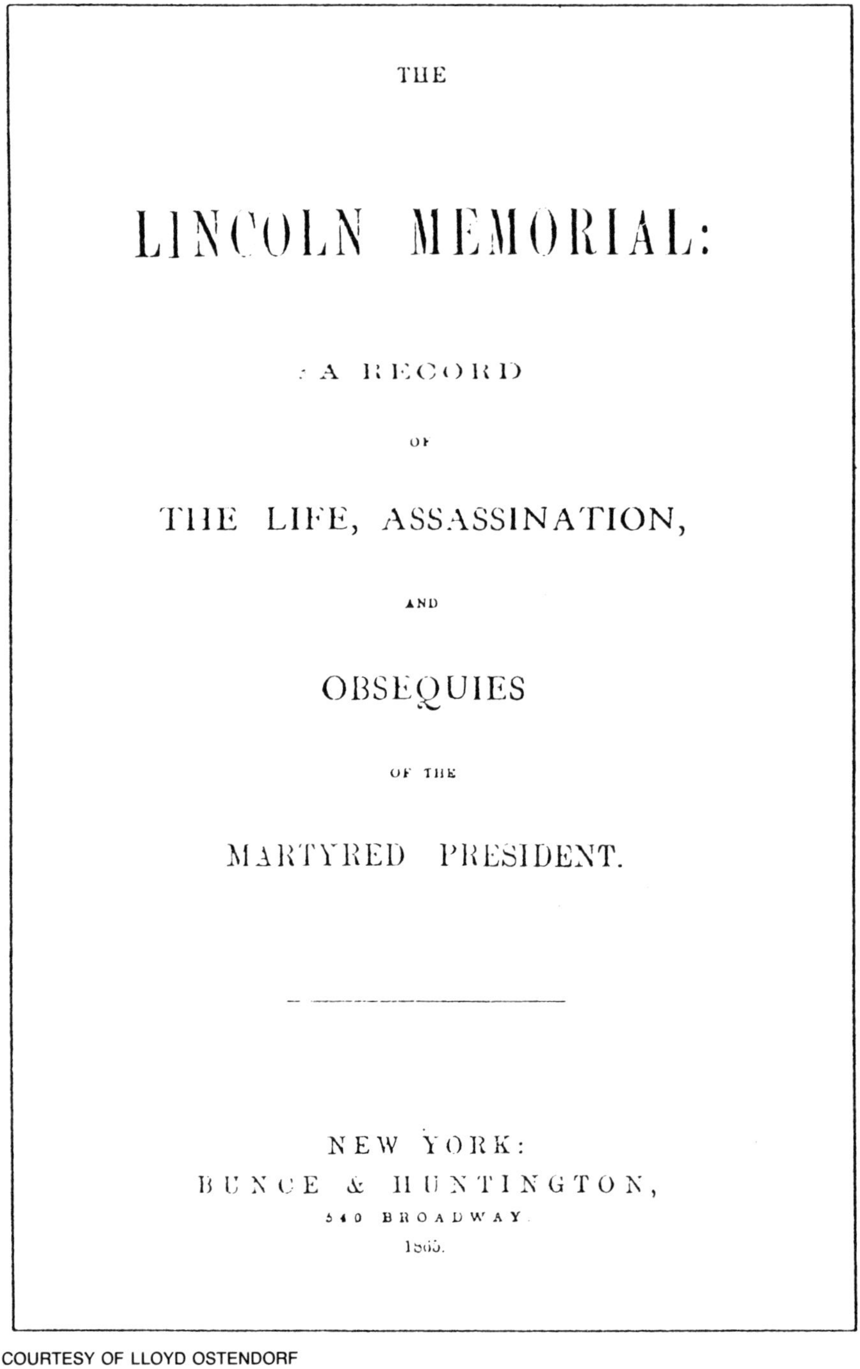

THE

LINCOLN MEMORIAL:

A RECORD

OF

THE LIFE, ASSASSINATION,

AND

OBSEQUIES

OF THE

MARTYRED PRESIDENT.

NEW YORK:
BUNCE & HUNTINGTON,
540 BROADWAY.
1865.

COURTESY OF LLOYD OSTENDORF

The second page of Lincoln's third draft of the Gettysburg Address was tucked between the pages of this book.

for us to be here dedicated to the great task remaining before us—that from these honored dead we take increased devotion to that cause for which they here gave the last full measure of devotion—that we here highly resolve that these dead shall not have died in vain; that this nation, under God, shall have a new birth of freedom; and that this government of the people by the people, for the people, shall not perish from the earth.

This is page two of the draft that Lincoln held in his hand while reciting the Gettysburg Address. Note glue mark in upper left hand corner and the phrase "under God" above a caret on the eighth line.

Lincoln's endorsement on the back of page two of the third draft of the Gettysburg Address. David Wills's letter of November 23, 1863 requested "the original manuscript" of "the dedicatory remarks." Wills added, "Please append your certificate to them." Note that the fold marks show.

Third Draft (Wills Copy)

Page one is missing; page two is in the possession of Mr. Lloyd Ostendorf of Dayton, Ohio. There are still some who question its authenticity. The endorsement (above) appears on the back of page two — David Wills asked Lincoln to sign it when he asked him to send "the original manuscript." Three fold marks show on the document, and it is likely that this was Lincoln's reading copy. Like the second draft, this third copy was written in Lincoln's room in the Wills's house on the morning of the dedication program. The words "under God" (above a caret) appear for the first time, and Lincoln did use the phrase in his recitation. Except for the phrase "under God," the second pages of drafts two and three are so much alike. They should be because Lincoln was copying one from the other.

[Photographic copies courtesy of Lloyd Ostendorf and *Gettysburg Magazine* (January, 1992 issue).]

COURTESY OF LLOYD OSTENDORF

JUDGE DAVID WILLS

Judge David Wills in 1863 at the time he invited President Lincoln to Gettysburg to give a "few appropriate remarks" at the cemetery dedication, November 19, 1863 and the latter decided to take a chance. "You usually get only one chance at opportunities like this," Ostendorf said to himself.[39] Here was a chance for fame or folly.

Before agreeing to a selling price the caller set down some rules. Ostendorf must not release the caller's name — he wanted absolute anonymity without giving a reason. The risk and burden of proof, that is authentication of the document, belonged solely to the buyer. The purchase price included "thousands of dollars in cash" plus four valuable items from Ostendorf's collection of artifacts: (1) an "imperial" photograph of a uniformed General U.S. Grant, signed hy him, (2) a tintype of President Lincoln and his son "Tad," of 1865 vintage, (3) a Brady Gallery composite with pictures of Lincoln and his cabinet members, and (4) one of Lincoln's depositions (written by Lincoln but not signed by him — Lincoln rarely signed legal pages) going back to his partnership days with William H. Herndon. The bargain was sealed with a handshake and the caller departed — into anonymity. Hoping that he had a treasured document, Ostendorf had it insured by Lloyd's of London and its usual resting place was in a safety deposit box in a local bank.[40]

Next Ostendorf sought the opinion of two other Lincoln authorities, Ralph Newman of Chicago and Dr. James T. Hickey of Springfield. Ostendorf met them in Springfield on February 11, 1991 and gave them an opportunity to study and scrutinize the document. Using a magnifying glass, the two studied the document. After a "lengthy consultation" of the one-page draft the two analysts said that they could find no "disqualifying aspects" yet both were reluctant to say that the document was genuine. "If genuine," the two experts agreed, "this is a very important discovery."[41]

It was time, Ostendorf thought, to let the public know of his discovery. With the help of Dr. Temple and several Springfield friends, he arranged for a press conference on February 11, 1991 at the Springfield American Legion Post No. 32. Ostendorf expressed his suppositions and had his document on exhibit. The press conference made headlines.

All the experts whom Ostendorf consulted did not give his suppositions full credence. Dr. Joseph Nickell of the University of Kentucky in Lexington was one. Ostendorf took his document to Lexington and gave the professor a chance to study it at length. In time Dr. Nickell responded with a very cautious critique:

> Under stereo-microscopic examination, the handwriting seemed more shaky than I expected. Forger's tremor came to mind.
>
> The writing is astonishing similar to the Hay copy, word for word, line for line. Also a too-heavy downstroke and pen lift on the loop of the second "p" in "by the people" are duplicated.[42]

Mr. James Gilreath, an expert on rare books, handwriting, and forgery, and associated with the Library of Congress, offered a more negative evaluation than Dr. Nickell. Although Gilreath had not seen Ostendorf's document, he studied a photographic copy of it and compared it to page two of the second draft (the Hay copy). Gilreath made much of the fact that Lincoln usually crossed his "t's" from right to left and not in the customary manner. Many of the "t's" in Ostendorf's copy were crossed left to right.[43] Ostendorf later countered by finding many examples where Lincoln had crossed his "t's" left to right.

Another skeptic, Richard Sloan of New York, also studied Ostendorf's document. A past president of the Lincoln Group of New York City, Sloan laid a transparency of Ostendorf's document over page two of the second draft or Hay copy. He cited some discrepancies — then quickly removed himself from the controversy, saying, "I have no expertise in this area, however."[44]

To those who argued that the newly discovered page was a tracing, Ostendorf had a ready and reasonable answer: " . . . it would be virtually impossible to make a tracing on the *heavy* blue gray legal paper. It is so dark that one cannot see through two sheets of this dark paper, which is thick. The only traced Lincoln forgeries that I have seen are of thin white paper."[45]

Dr. Walter C. McCrone, head of his own research institute in Chicago, gave Ostendorf's document a "high tech" analysis. Applying as much scientific study to Ostendorf's document as he could, McCrone then came to Ostendorf's defense. He wrote a rather lengthy report and came down hard on those who would call Ostendorf's document a tracing. "Both versions [the Hay and Wills versions] show a fluidity and continuity in terms of brush strokes that would be natural to Lincoln and difficult to duplicate by others in a tracing which, by necessity, would be more labored and probably done almost letter by letter."[46]

Next Ostendorf decided to seek an opinion from Mr. Roderick McNeil, a scientist of the Rocky Mountain Research Laboratories in Montana. McNeil had developed a new scientific method of analyzing ink and paper as a means to detect forgeries. McNeil had gained national attention by analyzing Mark Hoffman's "Oath of a Freeman" and declaring it a forgery. Scientific tests, developed by McNeil, could show how long ink had been on paper and discern the difference between inks used on documents. He could associate ink and paper with eras and examine both by "energy dispersive analysis by X-ray." These tests, to no one's surprise were expensive — costing "several thousand dollars." These Rocky Mountain people would give the best scientific analysis available in the United States. Ostendorf was willing to risk the costs to get the best scientific evaluation possible.[47]

The wait for McNeil's report seemed like eternity. Finally, in early November of 1991, McNeil called and his words were like sweet music — "all tests are positive." A long, typewritten report would soon be in the mail.[48]

McNeil's report stated that the document in Ostendorf's possession was made by the Liberty Paperworks of Philadelphia — with an oval Crown Britannica watermark. The paper was consistent with the era. The same could be said about the spot of glue in the upper left hand corner. The ink also was consistent with the era, and most important, the ink used for the text was different than that used on the back, for Lincoln's certification. The ink used for the text had been provided by David Wills; the ink used for the certification was from a White House inkwell. "My overall conclusion," McNeil stated emphatically, "is that it is genuine; that is, that it was created in the time period purported by the document."[49]

After the favorable report from the Rocky Mountain Research Laboratories, Ostendorf decided that it was time for another press conference. Springfield friends, headed by Dr. Temple, arranged for one in the Press Room of the state capitol building on November 19, 1991 — the 128th anniversary of Lincoln's Gettysburg Address. Dr. Temple opened the conference with a review of the Battle of Gettysburg but he also discussed the importance of Ostendorf's discovery, referring to the document as a precious relic. Then it was Ostendorf's turn. He stated his case briefly, firmly, and competently:

> I have done everything possible to authenticate the piece. I have consulted renowned Lincoln experts for their views, both positive and negative. I have given the foremost forensic experts time to study and formulate their professional input, both positive and negative.
>
> I am sure that the Wills copy of the Gettysburg Address, page two, is authentic. I am equally sure that Lincoln wrote it himself. Knowing when the ink was applied to the paper, I have concluded that the Hay draft [the second draft] is an uncorrected version in a similar format; it's the one President Lincoln used to rewrite the Wills draft, line by line as was his habit; it was suitable to bring to the podium at the dedication at Gettysburg, it is the copy he later endorsed to Judge Wills as requested. Judge Wills's request letter and the Hay copy did not surface until the 1900s. So no early forger had these two items as aids. As a historian, I'll keep an open mind to any scholarly challenges.
>
> Having completed my investigation, I'm pleased my original professional judgment was correct. Finding President Lincoln's final reading copy of the treasured Gettysburg Address is indeed a national triumph.[50]

Ostendorf had an array of Lincoln experts in the Middle West supporting his position. Dr. Wayne Temple, the distinguished and erudite Lincoln scholar of the Illinois state archives, is one. David A. Warren, the able editor of *The Lincoln Legacy*, an interesting newsletter, is another. It was Warren who gave Ostendorf a chance to present his case in the newsletter of the Lincoln Group of Illinois. Dr. Walter McCrone of the Chicago-based McCrone Research Institute was an early convert and he was pleased that McNeil's conclusions matched his own. He added one more "Amen:" "I have absolute confidence in the results of Rod McNeil's analysis . . . . I have to believe that no matter how close the two versions [Hay and Wills copies] appear when overlaid, that the Wills version was done by Lincoln . . . . I go along with its being Lincoln's."[51]

Ostendorf then took his case to *The Lincolnian*, the bimonthly newsletter of the Lincoln Group of the District of Columbia. He prepared a reasoned and worthy presentation — it deserves to be reprinted here:

> I have noted in *The Lincolnian* during the past year occasional comments about my newly discovered page of the sixth known copy of the Gettysburg Address in Abraham Lincoln's handwriting. The

document is signed and dated for Judge David Wills, Lincoln's host at Gettysburg in 1863.

I think it is time some conclusive facts replace a lot of opinionated guesswork and speculation about it on the part of some experts who have never even seen the original document. Now, over eight months of tests and research have proven some revealing facts:

The document is genuine, an original pen and ink writing from the 1860's. Highly expensive and sophisticated tests at the Roderick McNeil Rocky Mountain Research Labs in Polson, Montana have proven just how long the ink has been applied to the paper — 1869 — 10 years one way or the other, written in Lincoln's own time.

The ink is old, the paper is old, the watermark is of old milled paper.

Granted, the written document is quite similar to — but not a tracing of — the John Hay copy (the second known draft). It has a similar format as one page copied from another. Those of us who have long studied Lincoln's writing habits realize that Lincoln often wrote out his own file copy to keep, and sent out the other letter or document to where it was intended.

When copying one manuscript from the other, Lincoln often made minor changes and corrections. The Hay draft shows five crossed-out and changed words, while Lincoln's reading copy for Gettysburg is a more correct manuscript. This corrected reading copy used at Gettysburg is a legal-size page, folded three times so he could place it in his pocket. A number of eye-witnesses at the dedication ceremony at Gettysburg on Nov. 19, 1863 observed Lincoln taking his document from his pocket, speaking, and returning the papers to his pocket.

The late historian David C. Mearns, along with Lloyd A. Dunlap, wrote in 1963 that the Hay copy "had never been folded." Thus, the Hay copy was the filing copy and could not have been the reading copy on the battlefield.

The very first known draft of the Address, known as the Nicolay copy, was only Lincoln's preliminary draft. It was partly written at the White House on Executive Mansion stationery in ink. Its second page was written in pencil with several words crossed out. The Nicolay copy contains changes and incomplete text when compared to later copies, and is without folds. For these reasons it was unsuitable for a reading copy.

All the other three previously known copies — the Everett, Bancroft, and Bliss copies, as they are known — were written for specific request in 1864, long after the Gettysburg Address event. To qualify for being the original draft the document would have to have been folded. This newly found sixth copy does qualify in this respect.

A few days after the Gettysburg event Judge Wills did write to President Lincoln and requested "the original manuscript," asking him to "please append your certificate to them." This sixth signed copy fits the request completely. Lincoln obliged the judge just as he obliged all three other requests. He was an obliging person.

Lincoln endorsed the back fold of the document, and signed and dated it for Judge Wills. It is highly significant that the old inks used and tested by the McNeil laboratory prove the ink on the body of the manuscript is of different composition than the ink used on the back endorsement, which was obviously penned at a different time and place.

No self-respecting or knowledgeable expert has ever seriously questioned the handwriting on the document — all agree it looks very strongly like Lincoln's penmanship. Certain detractors have conveniently ignored the beautiful Lincolnesque endorsement on the back. The Hay copy has no such endorsement. Thus, the endorsement on the newly found sixth copy was not copied or traced from anything else.

No Lincoln scholar or student has questioned the Lincoln signed endorsement, making this copy one of the only *two* signed by Lincoln. Lincoln was asked to sign this one. Lincoln was also specifically asked to sign the Bliss copy, the official standard (fifth) version of his Gettysburg Address.

There are only a few qualified Lincoln writings experts living today — men who spent years examining and handling hundreds of *original* Lincoln documents — men like Dr. Wayne C. Temple and Dr. James T. Hickey of Springfield, Ill. Both have told me they have seen too many original file copies of Lincoln writings turn up. They have no problem with these look-alike writings, such as the Hay copy and the newly found Wills copy of Lincoln's address. They contend that these "duplicates" (file copies) are not tracings, not forgeries, but original similar file copies. After all, in Lincoln's day they did not have our modern carbon copies, xeroxes or fax copies — you simply had to write it out yourself, or have a secretary do it.

Lincoln often made his own copies himself. Seasoned Lincoln document experts recognize this fact. Unfortunately, many manuscript experts — no matter how good they are in their fields — are not necessarily Lincoln document experts. And it shows.

Given the results of the McNeil positive forensic tests, as well as months of previous testings by old-ink-and-paper experts yielding supporting conclusions, the burden of proof against the new sixth original copy of the Gettysburg Address now rests with the few detractors.

This sixth copy — the Wills draft page in Lincoln's handwriting, the paper held by Lincoln at Gettysburg — is the ultimate Lincoln collector's top treasure, and I thank God for letting it come my way.

Those who wish to believe otherwise will have to live with this fact: the Hay copy, Lincoln's file copy, was never revealed by John Hay during the 19th century — he did not let it become known to the public until 1906.[52]

There were skeptics who used the columns of *The Lincolnian* to express their dissent. James Gilreath of the Library of Congress said the so-called scientific tests could be fallible, that the "t's" were crossed wrong, and that he still believed Ostendorf's document was a tracing.[53] Richard Sloan of the Lincoln Group of New York wrote to say that Ostendorf's supposed second page of the Gettysburg Address was "a forgery — a tracing."[54] Richard Seddelmeyer, an Eastern lawyer, offered the opinion that the most "plausible theory" was that "Lloyd Ostendorf has in his possession a contemporaneous tracing of the Hay copy, endorsed and sent to Wills by Lincoln himself."[55] Thomas Budnik, who wrote that he was "a manuscript collector for nearly 25 years" offered the unkindest cut of all. After ridiculing "the lab work" and implying that Ostendorf's document was a forgery, Budnik wrote, "Mr. Ostendorf would be well served to drop this document in the garbage where it belongs and give us another one of his great books on Lincoln photographs."[56]

Because the two newsletter, *The Lincolnian* and *The Lincoln Legacy* had a limited readership, Ostendorf took his case to two historical journals with a national circulation. Ostendorf's article "Turning the Pages of History: A New Draft of the Gettysburg Address Discovered" was published in the January, 1992 issue of *The Gettysburg Magazine*. Most of Ostendorf's contentions that were earlier stated in *The Lincolnian* were repeated here. The Daytonian's article "Lost Copy of the Gettysburg Address Comes to Light" appeared in the *Lincoln Herald* (Spring, 1992 issue), a quarterly with a long and worthy history. Ostendorf ended this brief article with two forthright statements: "Despite . . . the fact that this document was somehow lost for all these years, this physical article [the one-page document] speaks for itself quite boldly. I believe it is indeed a top treasure and of great value."[57]

Throughout the game of provenance, Lloyd Ostendorf showed toleration of his critics and played his cards cautiously and skillfully. As the game nears its end, Ostendorf holds the trump cards. In time, as the skeptics retreat, it will be recognized that the document which an anonymous caller showed Ostendorf in midyear 1990 is indeed the second page of the third draft of Lincoln's Gettysburg Address — the Wills or "lost" copy. This is the very page that the President held in his hand while reciting his lines on the 12 ' × 20 ' platform atop Cemetery Hill. It is the first copy with the phrase "under God" in the text and Lincoln remembered to use it in dramatic fashion in his recitation.

Still questions outnumber answers. If everything was on the up-and-up, why did the fellow who sold the document to Ostendorf demand anonymity? Exactly when, where, how, and why did he obtain it? Where was it between the years 1863 and 1990? Will it, eventually, as a national treasure, find a place in some exhibit, preferably in Gettysburg? And what happened to page one?

4. The Fourth Draft (the Everett Copy)

Soon after his return to Washington from Gettysburg, the president was confined to bed with an illness called varioloid, a variation of smallpox. With pillows as a prop, he worked on affairs of state. Thinking of all the favor-seekers, Lincoln remarked that now he had something that he could give to everybody.[58]

The president finished work on his annual message to Congress, in time for the December session. Good news came from Chattanooga, where Maj. Gen. Ulysses S. Grant decisively defeated Confederate forces on November 24-25, and Lincoln now wrestled with the idea of bringing him to Washington and putting him in charge of all Union armies. On December 13, Lincoln issued a proclamation of amnesty and reconstruction, a document later criticized by many Radical Republicans. Then there were the many requests for appointments or favors. U.S. Senators John Sherman and Benjamin F. Wade, for example, called on the president and verbally asked for the copy of the proclamation of amnesty and reconstruction; it would be auctioned off at the Cincinnati-based Great Western Sanitary Fair for the benefit of soldiers and sailors.[59] Christmas would be less cheerful this year, for it would be the first White House Christmas without "Willie" who had died the previous February.

An interesting request, dated January 30, 1864 came from Edward Everett. He wrote that he had promised to give the manuscript of his oration to the New York governor's wife (Mrs. Hamilton Fish) who was head of the Ladies' Committee of the New York City-based Metropolitan Fair. Everett added, "It would add very greatly to its value, if I could bind up with it your dedicatory Remarks, if you happen to have preserved them."[60]

Lincoln could not send Everett the "original" manuscript, that is, the copy that he held in his hand while reciting the address, because he had already sent it to David Wills the previous November. Furthermore, the president had already given the first draft to John Nicolay and the second draft to John Hay. So Lincoln asked one of his secretaries to make a copy of the address as it appeared in a Washington newspaper. Then Lincoln used this copy and his own recall to compose his fourth draft, the one to be sent to Everett. In his brief accompanying letter, the president wrote, " . . . I send herewith the manuscript of my remarks at Gettysburg, which . . . you are at liberty to use for the benefit of our soldiers as you have requested."[61] Some time later, Everett wrote to Lincoln: "I have this day received your letter of the fourth of February kindly transmitting the manuscript of your remarks at Gettysburg . . . . I feel very sensible your goodness in having found time amidst your occupations and cares to attend to so small a matter."[62]

Everett had promised that his manuscript and Lincoln's would be bound together in time to be auctioned off at the Metropolitan Fair, but he evidently failed to have his own manuscript ready — at least, "there is no record that it was ever sold at the Metropolitan Fair."[63] Some time later, however, it was sold to Carlos Pierce, a merchant prince of Boston, for one thousand dollars.[64]

Mr. Pierce died in Canada in 1870 and the bound documents became the property of his wife. In 1877 Mrs. Pierce sold "the packet" to her deceased husband's sister, Mrs. Henry Keyes. It remained in the Keyes family for a long time, shared by Isabella F. Keyes and her brother Henry W. Keyes. In 1918 the latter was elected, as a Republican, to the U.S. Senate, where he served for eighteen years, until January 3, 1937.

On February 12, 1920 Senator Keyes received widespread publicity by reading the Gettysburg Address to the U.S. Senate, holding in his hand the manuscript then in the possession of his family. In February, 1930 an autograph dealer named Thomas A. Madigan purchased the document from the Keyes' and later sold it to James C. Ames for $150,000. Charles B. Pike, a friend of Ames, urged him to place the document on exhibit at the Chicago Historical Society. Ames acquiesced, and in February of 1955 it came into the care of that historical society — but still owned by Ames.

Meanwhile, some civic-minded Illinois citizen began a campaign to purchase this copy of the Gettysburg Address so it could become the property of

5,

Four score and seven years ago our fathers brought forth upon this continent, a new nation, conceived in Liberty, and dedicated to the proposition that all men are created equal,

Now we are engaged in a great civil war, testing whether that nation, or any nation so conceived, and so dedicated, can long endure, We are met on a great battle-field of that war. We have come to dedicate a portion of that field, as a final resting place for those who here gave their lives, that that nation might live. It is altogether fitting and proper that we should do this.

But, in a larger sense, we can not dedicate— we can not consecrate— we can not hallow— this ground, The brave men, living and dead, who struggled here, have consecrated it, far above our poor power to add or detract. The world will little note, nor long remember, what we say here, but it can never forget what they did here. It is for us, the living, rather, to be dedicated here to the unfinished work which they who fought here, have, thus far, so nobly advanced. It is rather for us to be here dedicated to the great task remaining before

*no — that from these honored dead we take increas-
ed devotion to that cause for which they here gave
the last full measure of devotion — that we here
highly resolve that these dead shall not have
died in vain — that this nation, under God,
shall have a new birth of freedom — and that
government of the people, by the people, for the
people, shall not perish from the earth.*

Fourth Draft (Everett Copy)

This copy was written in the White House early in March of 1864, in response to Edward Everett's written request of March 3. Everett expected that this draft, bound with the original manuscript of his own oration, would be auctioned off at the Metropolitan Soldiers' and Sailors' Fair in New York City. The phrase "under God" appears in its place in the last sentence. Tradition says that the President no longer had drafts one, two, or three in his possession and had to depend on newspaper accounts and his own memory to write out this fourth copy. This manuscript is in the Illinois State Historical Library in Springfield with page two mounted below rather than beside page one.

the "Land of Lincoln," the state of Illinois. Aided by a generous donation by Marshall Field, the purchase fund accumulated quite a sum, but still $60,000 short of the set amount. An effort to get the state legislature to contribute that amount came to naught. Then some imaginative citizens came up with the idea of raising the $60,000, via "a school campaign." School children would donate pennies, nickels, and dimes to help buy a treasure for the state. The campaign was launched on October 12, 1943 and by March 21, 1944 the $60,000 was raised and the purchase of the Everett copy was made the same day. The next day the fourth copy of the Gettysburg Address in Lincoln's own hand was transferred to the Illinois State Historical Library and put on exhibit with the second page mounted below the first.[65]

The wording of the so-called Everett copy differs but little from that of the second, the Hay copy. The phrase, "under God," above a caret in the third draft (the Wills copy) appears now in its rightful place in a sentence of the fourth draft.

This fourth draft (the Everett copy), like the others, was on exhibit at the Chicago Historical Society as a means of commemorating the 100th anniversary of President Lincoln's most famous document.

5. The Fifth Draft (the Bancroft Copy)

A Baltimore resident, Colonel Alexander Bliss, and a Massachusetts man, George Bancroft, teamed up to play an important role in the story of the fifth draft of the Gettysburg Address in Lincoln's own hand. Bliss was a member of a committee responsible for collecting manuscripts that would be put together in a volume as facsimiles entitled *Autograph Leaves of Our Country's Authors*. This book would be sold for the benefit of soldiers and sailors as one of the promotions of the Baltimore Sanitary Fair. The committee decided that Francis Scott Key's "Star Spangled Banner" would be the first facsimile-document in the book and it wanted Lincoln's "Gettysburg Address" as the second. Colonel Bliss accepted the assignment of obtaining a copy of the address from the president.

Colonel Bliss recruited his stepfather, George Bancroft, to help him. Bliss reasoned that Bancroft's reputation would help — Lincoln would be more likely to heed Bancroft's request than Bliss's.

Bancroft was a nationally known American. Like other Boston Brahmins he was a graduate of Exeter Academy and Harvard University. After five additional years at European universities, including Gottingen, he returned to Massachusetts to teach in a prep school in Northampton that he helped found, 1823-1830. After moving to Boston, and as a disciple of Jacksonian Democracy, Bancroft began the first volume of *The History of the United States*, a work that eventually reached ten volumes. Every volume, someone remarked years later, was "a vote for Andrew Jackson." Anyway, the first volume appeared in 1834 and the author suddenly found that he was famous. As a Democratic party activist, he received a sinecure (collector of the Port of Boston) at the hands of President Martin Van Buren. Democrats nominated him as their gubernatorial candidate in 1844 but he lost the election. But there was a reward, for President James K. Polk named Bancroft as his Secretary of the Navy in 1845. After the start of the Mexican War Bancroft ordered the Navy to seize Californian ports, thus helping to win that coveted land for his country. He was also credited with establishing the U.S. Naval Academy. He resigned from the cabinet in 1846 in order to become minister to Great Britain where he served until 1849. After returning to the U.S. Bancroft resumed work on *The History of the United States.*

After the Civil War broke out Bancroft supported the war and Lincoln's policies vigorously, breaking with the lukewarm Democrats. Bancroft felt compelled to write a letter, dated November 18, 1861, to his president:

> Your administration has fallen upon hard times, which will be remembered as long as human events find a record. I sincerely wish you the glory of perfect success. Civil war is the instrument of Divine Providence to root out social slavery; posterity will not be satisfied with the result, unless the consequences of the war shall effect an increase of free states. This is the universal expectation and hope of men of all parties.[66]

Lincoln, of course, wrote a "thank you" letter to Bancroft. Its last sentence read, "The main thought in the closing paragraph of your letter is one which does not escape my attention, and with which I must deal in all due caution, and with the best judgment I can bring to it."[67]

The Lincoln-Bancroft relationship was off to a good start. Bliss was right when he anticipated that Bancroft's plea would receive a friendly hearing in the White House. In February of 1864, Bancroft visited the White House to make his personal request for a copy of the Gettysburg Address in behalf of his stepson and for the Baltimore-based soldiers' and sailors' fair. Would the president provide a copy of the Gettysburg Address to become a facsimile in *Autograph Leaves of Our Country's Authors*?

Lincoln willingly acquiesced. He wrote out his fifth draft of the Gettysburg Address, adding a one sentence note: "Herewith is the copy of the manuscript which you did me the honor to request."[68] Ironically, this fifth copy and the one made for Edward Everett were mailed on the same day.

There were several slight variations in the Bancroft copy from the Everett copy. In the first sentence, "upon" became "on" with a comma preceding it. "Two other changes," one historian wrote, "were in the removal of commas, one after 'it' following the words 'have consecrated it,' another was dropped after 'remember,' and three in the clause beginning 'who fought here' after the words 'here,' 'have,' and 'for'."[69] But there was one remarkable difference. Instead of being written on two sheets of paper like all the previous drafts, it was written on both sides of a single sheet of paper.

Four score and seven years ago our fathers brought forth, on this continent, a new nation, conceived in Liberty, and dedicated to the proposition that all men are created equal.

Now we are engaged in a great civil war, testing whether that nation, or any nation so conceived, and so dedicated, can long endure. We are met on a great battle-field of that war. We have come to dedicate a portion of that field, as a final resting-place for those who here gave their lives, that that nation might live. It is altogether fitting and proper that we should do this.

But, in a larger sense, we can not dedicate— we can not consecrate— we can not hallow— this ground. The brave men, living and dead, who struggled here, have consecrated it far above our poor power to add or detract. The world will little note, nor long remember what we say here, but it can never forget what they did here. It is for us the living, rather, to be dedicated here to the unfinished work which they who fought here have thus far so nobly advanced. It is rather for us to be here dedicated to the great task remaining be=

fore us— that from these honored dead we take in-creased devotion to that cause for which they here gave the last full measure of devotion— that we here high-ly resolve that these dead shall not have died in vain— that this nation, under God, shall have a new birth of freedom— and that government of the people, by the people, for the people, shall not perish from the earth.

Fifth Draft (Bancroft.Copy)

George Bancroft, a noted Massachusetts historian, attended a White House reception on February 23, 1864 and there asked Lincoln for a copy of the Gettysburg Address — he made his request in the name of his stepson, Colonel Alexander Bliss, who was a member of a committee (of the Baltimore Soldiers' and Sailors' Fair) collecting manuscripts for a lithographed volume of facsimiles to be entitled ''Autograph Leaves of Our Country's Authors.'' Lincoln made this copy, perhaps on February 29, 1864 for that was the date of the letter accompanying the document. The copy became the property of George Bancroft and eventually ended up as the gift of a donor to Cornell University.

The copy requested by Bancroft reached the desk of John Pendleton Kennedy, editor of *Autograph Leaves of Our Country's Authors*, on March 3. It was not suited for that volume of facsimiles for it lacked sufficient margins and it needed both a heading and Lincoln's signature. Editor Kennedy wrote to the president, asking him to "appropriate another quarter hour to the making of another copy for us."[70] Nicolay, writing for the president, asked for specifications. Colonel Bliss replied for Kennedy, enclosing specifications and several sheets of paper. He also returned the other copy of the Gettysburg Address "with great regret." He asked that it be returned to him "with the new copy." He had promised it, he said, to his stepfather (none other than George Bancroft).[71] Lincoln complied.

The Massachusetts historian had Lincoln's fifth draft in his possession until his death in 1891. It then passed into the hands of his son, John C. Bancroft. The executors of the estate permitted the Library of Congress to make photographic copies. In 1935 an autograph dealer named Thomas F. Madigen purchased it and sold it to Mrs. Nicholas H. Noyes of Indianapolis some years later. In 1940 she presented it to her deceased husband's alma mater, Cornell University. Authorities at Cornell loaned it to the Chicago Historical Society in 1963 for that widely publicized centennial exhibit.

6. The Sixth Draft (the Bliss Copy)

The final and sixth copy of the Gettysburg Address in Lincoln's own hand was written according to specifications laid down by John Pendleton Kennedy and on lined paper provided by Colonel Alexander Bliss. Kennedy, as editor of *Autograph Leaves of Our Country's Authors*, wanted margins of a certain width and paper of a certain size as well as a title and Lincoln's signature.

Lincoln obliged, writing his sixth draft shortly after March 7. It reached the hands of Colonel Bliss on March 11.[72]

The sixth draft carried over to a third sheet — it is the only three-page copy. It has a heading "Address delivered at the dedication of the Cemetery at Gettysburg," is signed "Abraham Lincoln," and is dated ("November 19, 1863"). The president, evidently wrote that draft with great care for it covered six more lines than the others. It differed from the Bancroft version with the omission of the word "here" in the clause "they here gave." Lincoln also dropped two commas, one after the word "conceived" and the other after "lives;" he added one comma, inserted after the three words "have consecrated it."

That sixth draft of Bliss copy was popular with writers of history textbooks for it had a title as well as the president's signature. The move to have one of the drafts declared the official copy came from various individuals as well as members of congress. Congressmen were concerned because they wanted the same text used in national parks or on national monuments. An 1895 act of

Address delivered at the dedication of the
Cemetery at Gettysburg.

[1] Four score and seven years ago our fathers
brought forth on this Continent, a new nation, conceived in Liberty, and dedicated
to the proposition that all men are created equal.
[2] Now we are engaged in a great civil war,
testing whether that nation; or any nation
so conceived and so dedicated, can long
endure. [3] We are met on a great battle-field
of that war. [4] We have come to dedicate a
portion of that field, as a final resting
place for those who here gave their lives,
that that nation might live. [5] It is altogether fitting and proper that we should
do this.
[6] But, in a larger sense, we can not dedi-

cate — we can not consecrate — we can not hallow — this ground. [6]The brave men, living and dead, who struggled here, have consecrated it, far above our poor power to add or detract. [7]The world will little note, nor long remember what we say here, but it can never forget what they did here. [8]It is for us the living, rather, to be dedicated here to the unfinished work which they who fought here have thus far so nobly advanced. [9]It is rather for us to be here dedicated to the great task remaining before us — that from these honored dead we take increased devotion to that cause for which they gave the last full measure of devotion — that we here highly resolve that these dead shall not have died in vain — that this nation, under God, shall have a new birth of freedom — and that government of the people,

by the people, for the people, shall not per-
ish from the earth.

Abraham Lincoln.

November 19, 1863,

Sixth Draft (Bliss Copy)

The Fifth Draft (Bancroft Copy) did not suit the editor of ''Autograph Leaves of Our Country's Authors'' because it had no title, nor Lincoln's signature, nor the proper margins; so he asked for another copy to meet his specifications. Colonel Alexander Bliss sent Lincoln's secretary
(John Nicolay) the paper and specifications. So Lincoln made this last-known copy early in March
of 1864. This is the only copy with a title and the signature ''Abraham Lincoln.'' Eventually, the
U.S. government designated this the ''standard copy.'' Bliss was the owner after it was reproduced
to facsimile, but this document eventually ended up in the Lincoln room of the White House.

Congress mandated a standard version. Most persons favored the sixth draft. Robert Lincoln, the son of the martyred president and a Chicago businessman, wrote to the congressional committee: "The Baltimore fair version represents my father's last and best thought as to the address and the corrections in it were legitimate for an author, and I think there is no doubt they improve upon the version as written out by Col. Hay."[73] Eventually, the final decision was put into the hands of Secretary of State Richard Olney and he approved the Bliss version as the standard one — to be used on "all tablets to be erected in national cemeteries and parks."

After being used to make that book of facsimiles, Lincoln's last draft of the Gettysburg Address became the property of Colonel Bliss. After his death, a son, William G. A. Bliss, acquired the rights to the valuable document. After the son's death his widow and a daughter had possession of it. In 1949 the Parke-Bernet Auction Galleries of New York City offered it for sale. On April 27, it was purchased by Oscar B. Cintas of Havana, Cuba, for $54,000. Cintas, a former ambassador to the United States and a successful businessman, was an admirer of Lincoln and he possessed a real reverence for the Gettysburg Address. After Fidel Castro took over control of Cuba, Cintas became a refugee and took his copy of the Gettysburg Address with him to the United States and the city of New York. After Cintas' death, Castro claimed his property, including the copy of the Gettysburg Address. But Cintas, in his will, bequeathed the document to the United States with the stipulation that it be exhibited in the Lincoln Room of the White House. It was loaned to the Chicago Historical Society for that 1963 centennial commemoration and then returned to Washington and the White House.

Chapter XI

The Dispute Over the Site of the Platform

Several days before the dedication ceremonies took place on November 19, 1863, David Wills supervised the building of a $12' \times 20'$ speakers' platform. Wills, responsible for planning both the procession and the program, heeded the recommendation of Edward Everett, who wanted a good-sized platform rather than a small one. But after the ceremonies of November 19 were over, "though the memories linger on," that platform was demolished, and a hundred years later a dispute arose over its exact location.

Tradition as well as substantial evidence put the location of the platform in front of the semicircle of graves — at the spot where the national monument now stands. William Saunders, who laid out the cemetery plan, wanted a monument exactly at that spot, and a committee of the soldiers' cemetery commission carried out his wishes and endorsed plans for a magnificent monument, worthy of the scene and situation.

The cornerstone of the monument was laid during ceremonies in 1865 with Major General Oliver O. Howard reading Lincoln's Gettysburg Address as part of the program. Then in 1869 the completed monument was dedicated with more in attendance than were present to hear Lincoln speak. The 1865 and 1869 ceremonies were held at the site of the national monument — as they should have been — and many assumed that the $12' \times 20'$ platform preceded the monument at that exact spot. Tradition took over.

When the federal government acquired control of the state-sponsored cemetery in 1895, Congress also directed that "a Lincoln Speech Memorial" be erected at the cemetery — it must consist of a bust of Lincoln and two bronze tablets, one containing the words of the Gettysburg Address and the other containing the words in Wills's letter inviting the president to the dedication ceremonies. Instead of locating this speech monument right next to the cemetery — or at the exact spot where Lincoln spoke — the committee in charge had it placed on a higher bit of ground some distance away. This caused confusion as to where Lincoln gave that memorable address, so in 1912 federal authorities

added a third tablet to the Lincoln Speech Memorial: "Lincoln Memorial . . . .
The address was delivered about 300 yards from this spot along the Upper
Cemetery Drive. That spot is now marked by the Soldiers' National Monument."
So a tablet endorsed tradition.

Three authors also gave their endorsement to tradition. Clark E. Carr,
onetime member of the soldiers' cemetery commission and a master of misstatements, was the author of *Lincoln at Gettysburg*, published in 1906. "It
was upon the ground in the center reserved for the monument," Carr stated
in his popular book, "that the platform upon which the addresses was delivered
was placed."[1] Eleven years later, Orton H. Carmichael made a similar statement in his book *Lincoln's Gettysburg Address* (1917).[2] Author F. Lauriston
Bullard, in a book published in 1944, endorsed the same supposition. This work,
popular with Lincoln cultists, has an illustration of the Soldiers' National Monument on one page and across from it are the words: "This impressive monument marks the site of the platform from which President Lincoln delivered
his immortal address."[3]

Documents challenging the concept that the $12' \times 20'$ platform was located
where the monument now stands came into the possession of the Lincoln National Life Foundation in Fort Wayne, Indiana, in 1960. The two documents
were once in the possession of W. Yates Selleck.

David Wills, the central figure in the story of the soldiers' cemetery in Gettysburg, showed his respect for co-worker Selleck by sending him an autographed
copy of the second edition of the *Revised Report of the Select Committee of
the Soldiers' National Cemetery*, published in 1865 — it came to Selleck with
the "compliments of David Wills." At the top of page 51 was the "official
map" of the cemetery as planned by William Saunders in 1863. It carried a
designation: "Map of the Grounds and Design for the Improvement of the
Soldiers' National Cemetery, Gettysburg, Pa., 1863." Sometime later, with a
pencil in hand, Selleck drew a rectangle on that map, marking the spot where
the $12' \times 20'$ platform was located. Selleck's rectangle was outside the semicircle
of graves. Then Selleck, with pen in hand, wrote out the location of the platform on some paper and pasted his notation on page 52, opposite the marked
map. Selleck's handwritten note read:

> The stand on which President Lincoln stood in the National Cemetery
> at Gettysburg on November 19, 1863 when he delivered his ever to be
> remembered address was 12 ft. wide and 20 ft. long, and facing to the
> North West — it was located 40 ft. North East of the outer circle of
> Soldiers' Graves as shown by pencil mark on the Cemetery Map in the
> book to which this memorandum is attached.[4]

The Selleck documents came into the hands of Louis A. Warren, former
director of the Lincoln Museum and Library, founded and funded by the Lincoln National Life Foundation.[5] Warren, a self-trained historian, accepted
Selleck's contention as to the location of the $12' \times 20'$ platform at face value
and he decided to incorporate that information into the last chapter of his book,
Lincoln's Gettysburg Declaration: "A New Birth of Freedom" (1964).

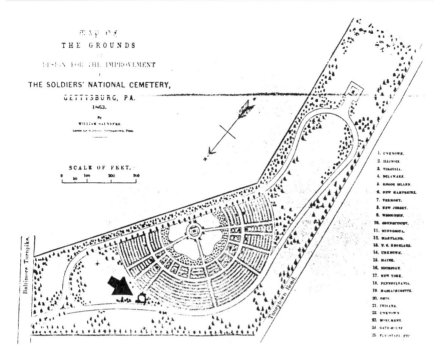

FROM THE LINCOLN NATIONAL LIFE FOUNDATION

The small arrow points to the rectangle or square drawn on the map by W. Yates Selleck to indicate the location of the speakers' platform from which Lincoln delivered the Gettysburg Address.

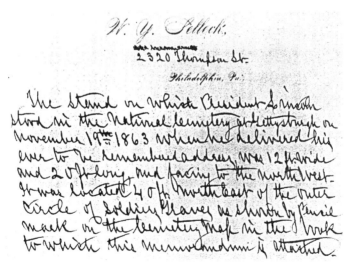

FROM THE LINCOLN NATIONAL LIFE FOUNDATION

The note of explanation written in ink by W. Yates Selleck relative to the location of the speakers' platform and appended to page 152 (opposite the map) of the second edition of the *Revised Report of the Select Committee of the Soldiers National Cemetery*, 1865.

COURTESY OF LINCOLN MUSEUM, FORT WAYNE, IND.

Dr. Louis A. Warren examining a file in the Lincoln Museum. Dr. Warren endorsed the Selleck-designated site of the 12' × 20' platform at the dedication exercises.

Warren's credentials, as well as the reliability of Selleck, are important, for they have a bearing on the controversy that followed.

Warren's life was a Horatio Alger story. Born in Holden, Massachusetts, on April 23, 1885, he became the family breadwinner after the early death of his father — quitting school and working "some fifty-five hours a week in a grocery store to support his mother and a younger brother."[6] After the younger brother got a job, Louis A. Warren headed west with forty dollars in his pocket. He went to Lexington, Kentucky and enrolled in the academy connected to Transylvania University — graduating at the age of twenty-six from the high school. He continued his formal education at the university, graduating with a Bachelor of Theology degree in 1916. He became an ordained minister in the Disciples of Christ Church, and promptly accepted a pastorate in Hodgenville, Kentucky — Abraham Lincoln's birthplace. The spirit of Lincoln soon made him a prisoner and he spent endless hours in research in county courthouses, seeking wills, surveys, land deeds, tax records — anything associated with Abraham Lincoln and his ancestors. He found nuggets of gold here and there and decided to incorporate his findings in a book. The Century Company published Warren's *Lincoln's Parentage and Childhood* in 1926. The self-trained historian received accolades, even in academia. Professor Milo M. Quaife, for example, wrote: "We do not know whether Mr. Warren ever belonged to a seminar in history, but he has produced a work which may profitably be conned by every neophite of the art of historical research. In every chapter and on almost every page the handiwork of a keen and capable investigator is disclosed."[7]

Warren started his climb up the ladder. He became "the lecturer" for the Indiana Lincoln Union.[8] Arthur Hall, president of the Lincoln Life Insurance Company in Fort Wayne, heard one of Warren's lectures and promptly decided "to bring him into the company." Hall's idea was vague, merely "to establish something to pay the company's debt to Lincoln." Competent, personable, and energetic, Warren transformed Hall's dream into the Lincoln Museum and Library with its marvelous collection of books, manuscripts, and memorabilia. Warren, in due time, founded *Lincoln Lore*, a four-page monthly newsletter that quickly developed a nation-wide circulation. He edited that grab-bag of Lincoln information for more than two decades and authored another book, *Lincoln Youth... 1816-1830* (1960), dealing with the Civil War president's Indiana years. In the process, Louis A. Warren became the most famous "Lincoln man" in the country.[9]

Warren investigated Selleck's reliability before crawling out on a limb and challenging tradition regarding the location of the 12 ′ × 20 ′ platform on the day of the cemetery's dedication. Warren had every reason to believe that W. Yates Selleck was an astute observer, a competent participant in the dedication ceremony, and an honest and reliable individual.

In the 1850s William Yates Selleck was a young Milwaukeean with insurance work as a vocation and politics as an avocation. He was one of the founders of the Young Men's Republican Club in March of 1860 and gloried in Lincoln's election that fall. Selleck was rewarded for his political work with a clerk's job in Washington, largely through the influence of Congressman John F. Potter. Selleck, along with others, organized the Wisconsin Soldiers' Aid Society after the first battle of Bull Run to furnish aid and comfort to sick, needy, and wounded Wisconsin soldiers in Washington area camps and hospitals. Selleck, the youngest member, was named the organization's vice-president.

After the Wisconsin state legislature passed an act authorizing the governor to appoint "state agents" to Wisconsin troops, Selleck gave up his federal clerkship. He visited the sick and wounded in camps and hospitals, secured furloughs, delivered mail and "goodies," and saw to the needs of Wisconsin soldiers. After the battle of Gettysburg, Selleck and an assistant hurried there to take care of the many Wisconsin wounded — three Wisconsin regiments had been decimated in the first day's fighting.[10] Selleck visited the wounded in the makeshift hospitals, made out lists of the dead and wounded for his governor, and became a close friend and co-worker of David Wills, head of the soldiers' cemetery project. "The Wisconsin wounded at Gettysburg," Selleck's aide wrote to a friend, "were better attended to and cared for than those of any other State — not even excepting Massachusetts."[11]

Wisconsin regiments had suffered heavy casualties. Selleck helped fathers locate the graves of their sons and secured coffins from a federal stockpile before the bodies were shipped home. Selleck encouraged David Wills to recommend the establishment of a soldiers' cemetery for those bodies not claimed by relatives. Then when the cemetery project developed, Wisconsin's governor named Selleck to represent the state on the Gettysburg Soldiers' Cemetery Commission.

Occasionally Selleck took a hurried trip to Gettysburg to meet with David Wills and serve the needs of Wisconsin soldiers still there.[12]

After David Wills set November 19, 1863 as the date of the cemetery's dedication, he asked President Lincoln's bodyguard, Ward H. Lamon, to serve as the day's Marshal-in-Chief. In turn Marshal-in-Chief Lamon asked the Northern governors to appoint individuals as assistant marshals. Wisconsin's Governor Salomon appointed Selleck as the state's "assistant marshal." So on November 19, 1863 Selleck would wear three hats: Wisconsin's state agent; commissioner, i.e., member of the Soldiers' Cemetery Commission; and assistant marshal.

On the day of the dedication ceremonies W. Yates Selleck had a reserved place on the platform. If he looked northward, he could see the deserted city of Gettysburg with its flag at half-mast. If he looked westward he could see Seminary Ridge and the valley that Confederate troops crossed in their fatal and futile assault during the third day's fighting. Behind him lay the semicircular cemetery with about one-third of the reburials completed. Selleck heard the bands play, preachers pray, choirs sing or chant, Everett orate, and Lincoln recite.[13]

The next day Selleck returned to Washington to take care of Wisconsin soldiers' needs in the area hospitals and camps. But on December 17, 1863 Selleck was back in Gettysburg to attend the first meeting of the Gettysburg Cemetery Commission. The twelve commissioners elected David Wills as president and

W. Yates Selleck as secretary — his peers respected the energetic and personable commissioner from Wisconsin. The commissioners, in addition to other business, appointed a committee "to procure designs of a monument to be erected at the cemetery."[14]

At the war's end, Selleck returned to Milwaukee and later did well financially in both Philadelphia and Washington, D.C. In his recollections Selleck made a comment regarding the location of the 12' × 20' platform: "The stand was near the outline of the semi-circle where the graves of the soldiers were placed, and faced the northwest, where the crowd in attendance listened to what took place."[15] — which supplements the handwritten notation acquired by the Lincoln Museum.

Warren did not know of the existence of Selleck's published recollections when he was writing his book, *Lincoln's Gettysburg Declaration: "A New Book of Freedom"* (1964). But he did incorporate Selleck's holograph into the text in his last chapter. He followed it with another paragraph:

> Mr. Selleck's diagram places the platform location about 350 feet almost due north of the Soldiers' National Monument, and forty feet from a point in the outer circle of lots where the Michigan and New York sections are separated by a path. With this arrangement the soldiers' graves would be at the rear of the platform, thereby protecting the burial areas from trespassers during the exercises. The thousands of visitors stood in the open spaces which gradually sloped away from the front of the speakers' stand.[16]

Intentionally or otherwise, Warren fired his opening shot at tradition and the contentions contained in the brochures and materials handed out at the Gettysburg National Military Park.

R. Gerald McMurtry, director of the Lincoln National Life Foundation and a friend and ally of Warren fired the second shot. McMurtry, who had once edited the *Lincoln Herald* and was "universally regarded as an authority on the life and times of Abraham Lincoln," presented Warren's case in *Lincoln Log* (October, 1965 issue), published by the Lincoln Savings and Loan Association. McMurtry provided a three-page article entitled "Lincoln Stood Here." McMurtry argued that the magnificent national monument "could not mark the place where Lincoln stood":

> Such a location would hardly be logical with some 15,000 people trampling the burial area as they listened to the exercises of November 19, 1863. Such thoughtless planning would not have been tolerated then or today. It was necessary that the crowd congregate in an area adjacent to but not actually on the cemetery site.
>
> The area designated on the original burial ground for the erection of a soldiers' monument is surrounded with graves. The Union soldiers who fell at Gettysburg are interred on all three sides (a 197° circle) of the monument site, while the area behind is the Evergreen Cemetery, the public burial ground. With such an array of facts to disprove the monument site as the location of the speakers' platform, it is difficult to understand how the area could have been almost unanimously accepted.[17]

Then the author of the article "Lincoln Stood Here," dependent upon McMurtry for quotes and documentation, made mention of the Selleck holograph and incorporated it into the text — a photograph of it is an illustration on page 3. Common sense and the Selleck holograph, McMurtry implied, repudiate the contention that the 12 ′ × 20 ′ platform was located where the national monument now stands.[18]

McMurtry sought a wider audience for the proposition that Lincoln spoke at the Selleck-designated site. National publicity would put the spotlight upon his foundation and its Lincoln Museum and Library. So far the discussion had been confined to two paragraphs in Warren's latest book and to a newsletter published by a savings-and-loan association. McMurtry, therefore, contacted Neal Ashby, associate editor of *Parade Magazine*, a syndicated supplement in Sunday newspapers. McMurtry sent Ashby a copy of *Lincoln Log* with its article "Lincoln Stood Here," suggested that Ashby contact Gettysburg park officials for a response, and suggested "The New Battle of Gettysburg" as an appropriate title.[19]

The November 14, 1965 issue of *Parade Magazine* contained McMurtry's suggestion as a short news-story, appropriately entitled "The New Battle of Gettysburg." Ashby, author of the article, quoted from the article that had appeared in *Lincoln Log:*

"This location [the monument site] could hardly have been logical," declares R. Gerald McMurtry, director of the Lincoln National Life Foundation of Fort Wayne, Ind., and a Lincoln historian. "The 15,000 soldiers and civilians who gathered for the ceremonies could only have drawn near enough to hear Lincoln by trampling over the burial ground."[20]

Ashby also incorporated Selleck's holograph into his article and he repeated the assertion that the speakers' stand was located "about 350 feet almost due north of the Soldiers' National Monument." Then Ashby quoted McMurtry again: "With this arrangement, the soldiers' graves would be at the rear of the platform, thereby protecting the burial area from trespassers during the exercises."[21]

Associate Editor Ashby devoted the last half of his article to a rebuttal by Gettysburg park authorities. Kittridge A. Wing, superintendent of Gettysburg National Military Park, spoke first. He was certain that "the Soldiers' National Monument stands where Lincoln stood." He dismissed McMurtry's contentions bluntly and in only three sentences: "We're as satisfied as we're ever going to be. In response to the raising of this doubt, we assigned our official historian to make a thorough study last spring. He worked on it for a month and presented a report that fully confirms the monument site."[22]

Frederick Tilberg, the official park historian, summarized his case:

I haven't been able to see how Dr. Warren could accept that hand-written statement. He couldn't have made a very thorough investigation, particularly in newspapers of the time.

I studied accounts of the ceremonies in approximately 20 different newspapers. The Cincinnati *Gazette* specifically reported a monument was to be built where the speakers' platform stood. Others spoke of the high elevation of the spot and the panoramic view. The site advanced by the dissenting side is not on high ground.[23]

Park historian Tilberg had a ready answer to the question of the trampling of the graves by asserting that only about 1000 bodies had been reburied in the semicircular cemetery at the time of the dedication ceremonies. "Marshals were on hand to keep the crowds clear of them." Evidence in old photographs, Tilberg asserted, proves that the monument location is correct. The park historian concluded his rebuttal by saying that he could find no proof that W. Yates Selleck "was present for the ceremonies."[24]

McMurtry and co-worker Warren seemed to think that the *Parade Magazine* article was shaded in favor of the point of view of the officials of the Gettysburg park, so they collaborated in countering their adversaries. Their article entitled "The Precise Location Where Lincoln Delivered the Gettysburg Address" took up all four pages of the January, 1966 issue of *Lincoln Lore*. McMurtry stated that their "treatise" was "an answer to the claims set forth in *Parade Magazine*" and that the treatise was "largely the work of Dr. Warren."[25]

Warren stated Selleck's qualifications as a competent and capable witness. Selleck's handwritten statement and one sentence from his recollections provided the foundation that Warren used to build his case. Then Warren developed three other arguments in behalf of the Selleck-designated site. The first pertained to the marching instructions given for two different events: the dedication of the cemetery (1863) and the laying of the cornerstone of the National Monument (1865). The instuctions for the line of march for the dedication of the cemetery read: "The route will be up Baltimore Street, to the Emmitsburg Road, thence to the junction of the Tareytown Road, thence to the Cemetery." On the other hand, the instructions for the line of march for the laying of the cornerstone of the monument read: "The head of the column will move at precisely ten o'clock a.m. up Baltimore Street to the Cemetery."[26] The instructions were different, Warren reasoned, because the destinations were different. Warren argued:

> The Tareytown Road furnished part of the western boundary of the cemetery. The destination of this parade [for the dedication of the cemetery] could not have been the site of the monument; if so, it would have continued straight out Baltimore Street. This exhibit alone should be sufficient to nullify the tradition that the programs for the dedication of the cemetery, and the laying of the cornerstone, were both conducted from a platform located on the same site.[27]

Warren's second argument dealt with "the desecration of the graves" — if the 12' × 20' platform were located where the National Monument now stands. By November 19, 1863, Warren said, over 1000 soldiers' bodies had been reburied in the new semicircular cemetery. More than a thousand markers were over these graves. Then Warren drove home his point: "Not only would it be prohibitive for thousands of people to assemble in the area, but the desecration of the graves by a throng of persons standing upon them would be inconceivable."[28]

Warren's third argument centered around a photograph taken of the crowd at the dedication ceremonies:[29]

The Adams County *Sentinel* of November 19, 1863 stated: "A flagpole was raised in the National Cemetery yesterday near the stand prepared for the world's renowned orator, Hon. Edward Everett." At the rear of the platform a tent was erected at the request of Dr. Everett. The photographs show the great crowd of people in front of the speakers' stand, and also extending to both the right and the left. The flagpole mentioned by the newspaper may be observed, and also the tent is plainly visible. In the far distant background the gateway of Evergreen Cemetery can be seen. It was not far from the Soldiers' Monument site. The photographs reveal that the terrain had not been disturbed by the preparations for burials and is free from any impediments. There is a general rise of the land up to the location of the speakers' platform. No such photograph could have been made of an audience facing a stand located on the site where the Soldiers' Monument was to be erected.[30]

After having made his case, Warren suggested that "a memorial in keeping with the significance of the event" be erected to mark "the precise location where the world renowned address was delivered."

Frederick Tilberg, although retired at this time, felt compelled to take up the cudgel again. The former park historian at Gettysburg wrote his rebuttal to Warren's treatise in *Lincoln Lore* as an article, "The Location of the Platform From Which Lincoln Delivered the Gettysburg Address" in *Pennsylvania History*, a scholarly quarterly.[31]

Tilberg's opening shot seemed to have been based upon scorn rather than scholarship as he referred to Warren's cornerstone evidence as "a holograph purported to have been written by W. Yates Selleck."[32] The word "purported" subtly challenged Warren's reputation as well as Selleck's respectability. Then Tilberg proceeded to ignore the document's validity — but no one, except perhaps David Wills, was better qualified to state the exact site of the 12 ' × 20 ' platform atop Cemetery Hill. Instead, Tilberg's first rebuttal argument dealt with the number of reburials as an answer to Warren's concern about desecration of the graves by "a trampling crowd." Tilberg wrote that only 1,258 had been reburied in the semicircular cemetery by the dedication date of November 19, 1863. " . . . of the 582 reinterments . . . 554 were placed in the plot east of the monument site, and only 27 in the plot west of it."[33] In other words, there was room for the audience in front of the platform without much trampling on the graves. Nor were Tilberg's answers relative to the line of march of the procession very satisfactory.

But Tilberg did have some good arguments, although many of his newspaper quotations had nothing to do with the location of the 12 ' × 20 ' platform and were little more than diversionary fluff and filler. Newspaperman J. Whitelaw Reid of the Cincinnati *Daily Gazette* provided Tilberg with his best ammunition. The speakers' stand, Reid wrote, "was erected on the spot where the monument is to be built, in front of which are two semi-circular sections with portions set apart for each state.''⁻⁴ But, overall, Tilberg's rebuttal beat around the bush and his many footnotes lent little credence to his supposed arguments.

Three years later Warren and Tilberg continued the debate in a very short article in the July, 1976 issue of *Civil War Times Illustrated*. The editor gave the article a long title, "Have We Done Lincoln Justice at Gettysburg? No, Says Dr. Louis Warren; Yes, Says Dr. Frederick Tilberg."

Warren simply restated the arguments that he had presented in the January, 1966 issue of *Lincoln Lore*, but he was more precise and more concise. Selleck's two statements, the 67-word holograph and the one-sentence statement in his recollections, again formed Warren's central theme. Warren only devoted three sentences to the marching orders given the 1863 and 1865 processions — different for the laying of the monument's cornerstone than for the cemetery's dedication. Warren's three-sentence statement follows:

> The official parade route for the dedication ceremonies recorded in *Official Report of the Cemetery Commission* (1867) wound "up Baltimore Street, to the Emmitsburg Road, thence to the junction of the Tareytown Road, thence to the latter road to the Cemetery." But in the same report marching orders for laying the cornerstone to the Soldiers' National Monument in 1865 read: "The head of the column will move . . . up Baltimore Street to the Cemetery grounds . . . ." Two different routes can mean only one thing — that there were two separate destinations.³⁵

Warren also restated the argument that if the speakers' stand were located at the monument site, graves would be "desecrated" and "trampled upon" by the audience/crowd. "With newly made graves and wooden markers [over 1000] over the entire field," Warren said, "there would hardly have been room at the soldiers' monument location to accommodate the thousands who gathered . . . ."³⁶

As in his *Lincoln Lore* article, Warren also referred to photographs taken on the day that the cemetery was dedicated. "All things considered," Warren argued, "a photographer stationed behind the crowd could never have caught this scene had he been facing in the direction of the future monument."³⁷

In closing, Warren expressed the wish that someday the "correct site" of the 12′ × 20′ platform would be properly and "accurately memorialized."³⁸

Tilberg, in his half of the article, countered Warren's contentions as best he could. His first sentence showed that he was sure of himself: "I take sharp issue with the Warren claim."³⁹

This time Tilberg did not try to discredit Selleck as a worthy witness — he just ignored him and his statements completely. But Tilberg did try to refute Warren's contentions that graves would be desecrated and trampled upon if the speakers' platform were at the monument site. "The cemetery design," Tilberg stated, "provided a space of 150 feet between the centrally indicated monument site and the first line of graves." Quite a number of people could gather in that space, fronting the platform. "The large number of marshals, aides, and a military cordon stationed among and around the standing multitude," Tilberg added, "formed the dual purpose of preserving order in the crowd assembled in front of the platform and for adequate protection of graves."[40]

Then Tilberg turned to press reports for his most compelling arguments. Joseph L. Gilbert, the competent AP reporter, saw the assembled throng as one " . . . of magnitude . . . gathered within a circle of great extent around the [speakers'] stand which is located on the highest point of ground."[41] The monument site was ten feet higher than the Selleck-designated site.

Tilberg, then, quoted the reporter for the Philadelphia *Daily Evening Bulletin* who wrote about the distant hills — "Round Top with forest covering and Little Round Top half-veiled in Indian Summer haze." "The Round Tops," Tilberg asserted, "cannot be seen from the Selleck site on the northern slope of Cemetery Hill."[42] But Tilberg's favorite reporter, J. Whitelaw Reid of the Cincinnati *Daily Gazette*, provided the best quotation — the park historian had incorporated it into his article in *Pennsylvania History*. The speakers' stand, reporter Reid wrote, "was erected on the spot where the monument is to be built, in front are two semi-circular sections with portions set apart for each state."[43]

Ironically, one of Tilberg's successors as park historian has suggested a third site as the location of the platform from which Lincoln spoke. That suggested site, championed by park historian Mrs. Kathleen G. Harrison, is on the grounds of the Evergreen Cemetery, adjacent to the soldiers' burial ground. In 1982 Mrs. Harrison "took the two key photographs of the crowd in the cemetery [i.e., at the dedication of November 19, 1863] — one taken facing the Evergreen Cemetery gateway, the other taken from the second story of that gatehouse — and tried to align every identifiable feature in the pictures with remaining features."[44]

Garry Wills, in his book *Lincoln at Gettysburg* (1992), explains Mrs. Harrison's suppositions and seems to endorse them:

> According to Harrison's reading of the photos, a flagpole had been erected at what is now the monument site. In the photo facing the gateway, the pole is seen to the left of the gate, with bits of Cemetery Hill visible beyond it. Most of the graves lie outside the picture to the left. To the *right* of the gateway — even farther up a slope than the flagpole — is the platform and the tent raised for Everett, with Culp's Hill seen beyond (out to the right of) them. In the picture taken *from* the gateway, these positions are naturally reversed — platform on the left, flagpole almost in the center, grave area to the right. The site makes sense. The later fences between the cemeteries did not exist. The crowd was bound to treat the two as one general area. The Harrison site had no graves on or around it at the time, nor any between the platform and the flagpole. Once the stand was moved up the slope, a space was created above the graves, looking down on them, in which the crowd could be fitted without impinging on the burial area. In the photo facing the gateway, the crowd ends in a generally straight line just at the flat side of the hemispherical scheme.
>
> The results fit those newspaper accounts that emphasized the height of the position and view commanded from it. On both counts the Harrison site is actually better than the monument site, in better accord

with the Associated Press report that "the stand . . . was located at the highest point of ground on which [the section of] the battle was fought.[45]

Since the Harrison site lay outside the boundaries of the soldiers' cemetery and inside the grounds of the Evergreen Cemetery, doubts were cast against it. Furthermore, Mr. David McConaughy, an official of the Evergreen Cemetery Association, had a running feud with David Wills. McConaughy had hoped to gain the post of "state agent" that Governor Andrew G. Curtin gave to Wills — in matters having to do with the removal of Pennsylvania's dead from the battlefield. Then, when a special soldiers' cemetery was proposed, McConaughy and other officers of the Evergreen Cemetery Association tried to have the soldier reburials on grounds owned by that organization. Their proposal was that a stipulated price be paid to the cemetery association for each soldier reburied there. Next they tried to have both cemeteries "within one enclosure," supervised and controlled by the cemetery association.[46] Furthermore, both McConaughy and Wills were trying to buy the same plots of land, confusing the sellers and driving up the price. It seems rather incredible that David Wills, therefore, would build the speakers' stand on ground owned by the Evergreen Cemetery Association.

Author Garry Wills goes overboard with his contentions regarding the Harrison site:

> The Harrison site seems securely established. The author of the best book on Gettysburg photographs, William A. Frassanito, has been convinced and says he will alter the next edition of his book to accept Harrison's reading of the pictures. At least one small battle of Gettysburg has, finally, been won.[47]

Disciples of Louis A. Warren and Frederick Tilberg disagree.

CHAPTER XII

THE MUSIC AT GETTYSBURG

Music played an important role in the story of the dedication of the soldiers' cemetery at Gettysburg. Bands played and people sang the evening before the dedication — President Lincoln was serenaded twice. The dedication program itself included four musical numbers, two band and two choral pieces. Four bands marched in the procession that preceded the program and then provided plenty of music after the dedication and before the day was done. "Music," the editor of a Gettysburg newspaper wrote two days before the dedication, "is the most delightful rational entertainment that the human mind can possibly enjoy."[1] But in this case, enjoyment was out of order, and the musical numbers, as dirges or hymns or funeral marches were intended to stir the soul and add to the solemnity of the occasion.

The Marine Band, scheduled to play the hymn "Old Hundred" as part of the formal program, was based in Washington and was a favorite of President Lincoln. It had performed admirably at his inauguration, impressing both the president and the First Lady. Directed by Francis Scala and composed of excellent musicians, the Marine Band had an enviable reputation. Scala's poverty-to-respectability story had its beginnings in Naples, Italy, in 1841. It was there that young Scala, a clarinet player, joined the U.S. Navy to play in the band of the frigate *Brandywine*. Later he gained a transfer to the Marine Corps as "a field musician." The Marine Band rested in limbo, for the corps excused the musicians from field service while Congress, unwittingly perhaps, paid them as field musicians. The ten or twelve-member band was ill-organized, supposedly under the leadership of a lieutenant anxious to turn over responsibilities to someone else. Years later, Scala wrote: "Soon I secured a place in the Marine Band. It wasn't much of an organization then. Congress had made no provisions for the Band, so that the ten or twelve members were enlisted as fifers or drummers, there being no leader, a Fife Major and a Drum Major served as leaders."[2] Showing both leadership and musicianship, Scala was put in charge of the band about 1850 on a trial basis. Under his direction, the band "at once began to improve" and "succeeded so well that he has kept the place without much difficulty."[3] Scala's band played regular concerts and took part in presidential functions. Once there were some complaints that the band played too much Italian music at its concerts and not enough American airs. But Scala deserved accolades for transforming the band into an excellent musical organization.

The members of the Marine Band boarded President Lincoln's special train, Gettysburg-bound, about noon, on the day before the cemetery dedication exercises were scheduled. The Washington-to-Baltimore leg of the journey was uneventful, ending at the Baltimore & Ohio station at one end of the city. Horses dragged the railroad cars, one by one, to the station and tracks of the Northern Central Railroad for the second leg of the trip — to Hanover Junction and then Gettysburg. During this time-consuming process, the Marine Band entertained both the travelers and the townsmen attracted by the music.

In Baltimore, the Second United States Artillery Regiment Band from Fort McHenry boarded the train. Several extra cars were added to the train, including one carrying city officials as well as twelve "well-trained singers," from the National Union Musical Association of Baltimore. They were scheduled to chant a "Consecration Hymn," sandwiched between Edward Everett's oration and President Lincoln's address. Their "Baltimore car," a sleeper provided for the occasion, was well decorated. An American flag covered nearly the length of the ceiling with bunting and banners everywhere. A buffet, well stocked with food and refreshment, and the bunk beds, would mean that the Baltimore authorities — except for the choristers — would not need to rely on Gettysburgers for sustenance and lodging.

Occasionally, as the train rumbled on toward Hanover Junction, the twelve-man chorus broke out in song. It sang ballads and hymns and patriotic numbers, but once they rendered a humorous song that began with the words

>We were there all the while
>At the siege of Carlisle —

It was a song of about fifty verses, each a sort of repetition of the previous one.

At every station stop — and there were many — President Lincoln spoke briefly and the Baltimore chorus sang well-known airs with "The Battle Cry of Freedom" and "We Are Coming, Father Abraham" as two of the favorites. Usually there was time for one of the bands on the train to play a number or two.

Lincoln's train reached Gettysburg about dusk. He was met as he dismounted by David Wills, Ward H. Lamon, and Edward Everett; Wills had planned the next day's dedication program and had issued the invitation to Lincoln to attend; Ward H. Lamon, Lincoln's bodyguard, would serve as marshal-in-chief during the next day's proceedings; and Everett, of course, was scheduled to give next day's oration. The three, assisted by a company of soldiers from the Invalid Corps, escorted the president to the Wills house where he would spend the night. No one, evidently, thought of asking the Marine Band or the 2nd United States Artillery Band to lead the way.

The oft-praised band of the Fifth New York Artillery Regiment had arrived in Gettysburg earlier in the day. Late in the afternoon it had played an hour-long concert in the city's central square, called "the Diamond" by local residents. In the evening that band returned to the central square and found the Marine Band and the band of the 2nd United States Artillery Band already there. The three bands took turns playing patriotic tunes, hymns, or funeral dirges. The evening air was filled with constant band music and the ever growing crowd seemed to be in a jovial mood, saving solemnity for the morrow.

During the dinner hour the Fifth New York Artillery Band gathered in front of the Wills house to serenade the president. Once he left the dinner table to go to the front door to acknowledge the serenade. He bowed a time or two to the band and the assemblage before returning to finish his meal. The crowd grew larger, the band played louder, there were constant cheers, and there were occasional calls for the president. The president reappeared at the front door and responded this time with a short speech of seven sentences.[4]

The band and many of the serenaders then moved next door to the home of Robert G. Harper, Republican editor of the (Gettysburg) *Adams County Sentinel* and the evening's host for Secretary of State William H. Seward. The band played and there were calls for Mr. Seward. The Secretary of State appeared at the front door, acknowledged the honor conferred on him by the serenaders, and gave a good speech — emotional and patriotic. Then the band moved to the front of the house where Governor Horatio Seymour of New York was a guest for the night. Seymour too came to the front door and repaid the revelers with a three-minute speech.[5]

The twelve members of the National Union Musical Association of Baltimore, about an hour later, also wished "to pay their respect" to the president. When it was reported that Lincoln had walked over to the Harper house, the choristers hustled there and began to sing, starting with "We Are Coming, Father Abraham" and following it with "Our Army Is Marching On."[6] After Lincoln finished his conference with Secretary of State Seward, Harper escorted him to the front door and introduced him to the crowd. Lincoln bowed time and again but refused to give another impromptu speech.[7] "The crowd seemed satisfied," a historian wrote years later, "and gave a tremendous cheer."[8]

After the serenade, it was time for the Baltimore singers and their director to retire for the night. Their sleeping arrangements were far from the ideal — the parlor floor in the house of James MacCreary. The three bands also left the central square to spend the night in makeshift quarters.

The central square, however, was still filled with people and most were in a festive mood. There were shouts and cheers and spontaneous songs. Benjamin B. French, who had composed an ode that would be chanted as part of next day's program, occupied a second-floor room in the Robert G. Harper home fronting on the central square. Kept awake by the noisy revelers, he wrote later: "Among other things they sang, in full chorus and admirably, the whole of that well known production whose refrain is — "We are coming Father Abraham, three hundred thousand and more.""[9]

Birgfield's Band of Philadelphia, scheduled to open the dedication program next day with a dirge, did not take a part in the activities of the evening of November 18 in Gettysburg. Those band members were aboard Governor Andrew G. Curtin's special train, delayed on its way from Harrisburg to Gettysburg by a balky engine. The troubled train took nearly four hours to cover the thirty-three miles and did not reach Gettysburg until some time before midnight.

The Philadelphia-based band, partially sponsored by the city's Union League, was named after Adolph Birgfield, founder and director of that musical organization. Most of the band members were German-Americans and local Philadelphia citizen's sometimes referred to it as Birgfield's German Band. Birgfield was also the director of the city's Academy of Music. His musicians played public concerts and at operatic performances when they were needed there.[10] Birgfield was truly a talented musician, adept at arranging and composing. He composed the dirge "Homage d'un Heros" that would be the opening number in the dedication program scheduled at the Gettysburg soldiers' cemetery.

Earlier, Birgfield's Band received accolades for its performance at Philadelphia's victory celebration following Union military victories at Gettysburg and Vicksburg. The city's Union League organized the affair. First there was a parade from Union League headquarters to Independence Square, with Birgfield's Band leading the way. After an appropriate invocation, there were several patriotic speeches. Then the band, settled in the steeple of Independence Hall, played a dirge or two and several patriotic songs, including "Battle Hymn of the Republic." The unique location of the band and its music caused a sensation; the audience was thrilled and patriotism engendered. "John Brown's Body" was one of the numbers the band played while leading the parade back to Union League headquarters. The band's stellar performance was the talk of the town for a week or more.

Governor Curtin invited Birgfield's Band to partake in the dedication ceremonies, perhaps at the suggestion of John W. Forney, owner of the Philadelphia *Press* and the Washington *Daily Morning Chronicle* — also clerk of the United States Senate, confidant of President Lincoln, and friend of Ward H. Lamon who helped David Wills plan the dedication program.

Birgfield's bandsmen took a train to Harrisburg where they would transfer to the special train that Governor Curtin had provided for many guests, including five governors and Major General Darius Couch, a Pennsylvanian commanding the Department of the Susquehanna.

The "Governor's Special," with about 400 aboard, left Harrisburg about one o'clock p.m., scheduled to meet President Lincoln's train in Hanover Junction. But after engine troubles caused delay after delay, generating considerable discontent, much grumbling, and dampened sentiment. Birgfield's Band came to the rescue, proceeding "to discourse music of the most entertaining description."[11] When the train made a rather lengthy stop in Goldsboro, halfway between Harrisburg and York, the bandsman detrained, set up their music stands, and then played one number after another. It was lively music and many of

(Telegram.)

Navy Department,
13 November, 1863.

Sir:

Marshall Lamon has telegraphed from Gettysburg to know if the Marine Band can be sent there on the 19th instant. Telegraph immediately to David Wills, at Gettysburg, whether you can send the Band or not.

Gideon Welles,
Sect. of the Navy

Col. John Harris
Comdt. Marine Corps.
Head Quarters
Washington, D.C.

The above is a telegram sent by the Secretary of the Navy to the Commander of the Marine Corps relative to securing the services of the Marine Band for the dedication program at the Gettysburg Soldiers' Cemetery.

The librarian of the Marine Band sent this item to Dr. Nicholas Contorno (of the Marquette University faculty) who, in turn, gave it to the author.

From Muster Roll of Marine Barracks, Washington, D. C., November 1863, in the National Archives:

Personnel known to have been assigned to duty at the consecration and dedication of the cemetery at Gettysburg, Pa., 19 Nov 1863:

****

Captain Alan Ramsay, Commanding
Second Lieutenant Henry C. Cochrane

Musicians, Marine Band (27):
    Arth, George M.
    Arth, Jacob
    Bigler, Philip
    Bonini, John
    Boll, Paul
    Baptista, Antonio
    Desimoni, Louis
    Douch (or Donch), Henry
    Grillo, Scipione
    Hilton, Francis
    Krause, Julius
    Lapini, John
    Mazzulli, John
    Noziglio, Angelo
    Noro (or Novo), Joseph
    Prosperi, Charles
    Prosperi, Frederick
    Pistori, Nicholas
    Petrola, Salvadore
    Poller, Henry
    Pons, Antonio
    Raffa, Pasquale
    Schroeder, Augustus
    Sousa, Antonio
    Wagener, Frederick
    Windus, Caspar
    Weber, Louis

The name of Francis Scala, director of the Marine Band, is missing from this list. Scala directed his 27 bandsmen in the playing of "Old Hundred," the second musical number of the program which dedicated the soldiers' cemetery at Gettysburg.

Note that more than half of Scala's musicians have Italian names. Joining the Marine Band was a means to U.S. citizenship.

Note too that the name of Antonio Sousa appears on the list of musicians assigned to go to Gettysburg. Antonio Sousa was the father of John Phillip Sousa, then a nine-year old.

Dr. Nicholas Contorno, Director of Marquette University Bands, obtained this page from MGySgt Mike Ressler, Chief Librarian, U.S. Marine Band.

COURTESY SCALA COLLECTION, MUSIC DIVISION, LIBRARY OF CONGRESS

FRANCIS SCALA

Francis Scala, director of the Marine Band. At the dedication ceremonies, Scala's band played "Old Hundred" as the second musical number of the formal program.

WALTER DIGNAM COLLECTION, MANCHESTER (N.H.) HISTORICAL SOCIETY

Page 68 of "Instruments Parts Book 1st E^b Cornet, 2nd Sett"

The two lines were played over again and again. "Old Hundred" was the second musical number of the dedication program and was performed admirably by the Marine Band, directed by Francis Scala.

Secured from the Dignam Collection by Dr. Nicholas J. Contorno for the author.

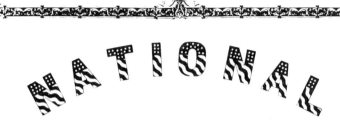

CONSECRATION CHANT

OR

H Y M N.

The following beautiful lines were chanted at the dedication of the National Cemetery, Gettysburg, Pa., Nov. 19, 1863,
by the National Union Musical Association of Baltimore, at the close of Mr. Everett's Oration, and just
before President Lincoln's Address. The deep pathos of the poetry—the words of which,
being clearly enunciated, were distinctly heard by the assembled thousands—
the occasion, and surroundings, made it a solemn feature of
the day, moving very many to tears.

Respectfully Dedicated

TO

THE MEMORY OF THE FALLEN HEROES OF GETTYSBURG.

WORDS BY | MUSIC ARRANGED BY
MAJ. B. B. FRENCH. | WILSON G. HORNER.

PRICE, 25 CTS.

BALTIMORE:

PUBLISHED BY HENRY McCAFFREY, 205 BALTIMORE STREET.

Entered, according to Act of Congress, in the year One Thousand Eight Hundred and Sixty Four, by W. G. Horner, in the Clerk's Office of the District Court of Maryland.

COURTESY OF THE CLEMENTS LIBRARY, UNIVERSITY OF MICHIGAN.

Benjamin B. French's "Consecration Hymn," chanted by a twelve-man chorus, made up of members of the National Union Musical Association of Baltimore. This was the third musical number of the dedication program.

To his Excellency,
ANDREW G. CURTIN.
Governor of Pennsylvania

DIRGE

SUNG AT THE CONSECRATION

——— OF THE ———

Soldiers' Cemetery at Gettysburg:

(NOV: 19TH 1863)

Composed and arranged for Four Voices,

——— BY ———

ALFRED DELANEY.

Philadelphia. LEE & WALKER, 722 Chesnut St.

This dirge was the last of the four musical numbers of the dedication ceremony. It was sung by a mixed chorus of Gettysburgers, accompanied by Birgfield's Band. The original copy is in the Brown University Library.

THANKS TO MS. RUTH COOK OF THE LINCOLN MUSEUM, FORT WAYNE, INDIANA, FOR OBTAINING COPIES OF THE TITLE PAGE AND THE MUSIC.

DIRGE

SUNG AT THE CONSECRATION

OF THE

SOLDIER'S CEMETERY

GETTYSBURG, PA.

The words by Jas. G. Percival.   Music by Alfred Delaney

O! it is great for our Country to die, whose ranks are con-tending,

O! it is great for our Country to die, whose ranks are con-tending,

fade, nev_er O !   never   a _ _ way !

fade, nev_er O !   never   a _ _ way !

2

O ! It is sweet for our Country to die, how softly reposes
Warrior youth on his bier, wet by the tears of his love,
Wet by a mother's warm tears; they crown him with garlands of roses,
Weep, and then joyously turn, bright where he triumphs above.

3

Not in Elysian fields, by the still oblivious river,
Not in the Isles of the blest, over the blue rolling sea;
But on Olympian heights shall dwell the devoted forever;
There shall assemble the good, there the wise, valiant, and free.

4

O ! then how great for our Country to die, in the front rank to perish,
Firm with our breast to the foe, Victory's shout in our ear;
Long they our statues shall crown, in songs our memory cherish!
We shall look forth from our heaven, pleased the sweet music to hear.

the village's residents "gathered round" and applauded. After arriving in Gettysburg, the bandsmen settled for uncomfortable sleeping quarters.

Before ten o'clock next morning the parade marshals, mounted on horseback and distinctively dressed, began to organize the various musical organizations, civic and fraternal groups, and the many civilians into a procession. The Marine Band stood ready to lead the way and the other three bands were inserted into the procession in various places, all bound for Cemetery Hill. As the procession moved southward along Baltimore Street the bands took turns playing marches or funeral dirges. The holiday spirit, so manifest the night before, gave way to a mantle of solemnity as the paraders trudged southward to take part in ceremonies honoring the soldiers who had given their lives in the three-day battle of Gettysburg. The music echoed over the valley where Pickett's charge cost the Confederate army many, many lives.

Five places in front of the $12' \times 20'$ speakers' platform had been staked out as stations for the four bands and the Baltimore choir.[12] Eventually, the parade marshals transformed the half-mile long procession into a half-circle audience in front of the speakers' stand. Meanwhile, the bands took turns playing favorite or selected musical numbers, chosen for this now solemn occasion. After Lincoln and other notables were seated, all was in readiness for the program to begin. But where was Edward Everett, the honored orator for the occasion? He was still in his tent (that had been set up specifically at his request) in the rear of the platform. Eventually Everett appeared and he was escorted to his front-row chair, between Lincoln's and Secretary of State Seward's.

Marshal-in-Chief Lamon, who was supposed to serve as master-of-ceremonies, was away from his selected spot on the platform, so his first assistant, Benjamin B. French, had the good sense to step forward and signal Director Birgfield that it was time to begin the formal program. His band, well prepared and primed for the occasion, responded with an excellent rendition of "Homage d'un Heros."

Compliments were commonplace. A reporter for the Chicago *Tribune* wrote that the dirge played by Birgfield's Band was "magnificent" — "a piece eloquently suited for the occasion" and "performed with pre-eminent skill."[13] Editor Isaac Jackson Allen of the (Columbus) *Ohio Daily State Journal* wrote about "the solemn and dirge-like music."[14] The reporter for Forney's Washington *Daily Morning Chronicle* characterized the rendition "an introductory dirge, solemn and suitable for the occasion."[15] There were other compliments and the characterizations were quite similar: "a solemn piece of music;" "a funeral military dirge;" "a grand funeral march;" and "a funeral dirge."[16] There was limited applause, for most part members of the audience seemed to think that funeral-like music should be followed by prayerful silence rather than hand-clapping.

Marshal-in-Chief Lamon was back on the platform and he nodded to Rev. Thomas H. Stockton that it was time for his invocation. The stern-faced Presbyterian preacher, Washington-based and chaplain to the House of

Representatives, arose and recited a rather long prayer. It brought tears to some eyes and even Lincoln showed the emotion.[17]

It was time for the second musical number, and the Marine Band was ready. Director Francis Scala raised his baton, and the band played the popular hymn, "Old Hundred," as it had been arranged by Walter Dignam.[18] During the Civil War era, "Old Hundred" was probably played and sung more than any other hymn — there were various sets of words and a contemporary commentator called it the Te Deum of America.[19] It was sung by all — at home, in churches, and in the army camps. A soldier who had participated in a songfest the previous year (at Yorktown in April of 1862), singing "Old Hundred" several times, wrote his impressions:

> There was a silence for a moment, and then there was wafted across the air the music of that glorious anthem, "Old Hundred," in which it seemed [that] a thousand voices were participating . . . . Never before had we heard anything so magnificently grand as that same "Old Hundred," sung by soldiers of the Union army on the plains of Yorktown. The air was made vocal with music, and the woods around reverberated with the mighty strain. Beneath the canopy of heaven, the soldier gazed upward into the starlight sky and sang unto God, "from whom all blessings flow," an anthem that stirred the heart of man with the best and holiest emotions.[20]

Many in the audience were stirred emotionally by the Marine Band's rendition of "Old Hundred." It was played "with great effect, in all its grand and sublime beauty," according to the report of a newspaperman working for the Washington *Daily Morning Chronicle*.[21] Everybody else seemed to agree.

As the echoes of "Old Hundred" resounded over the valley separating Cemetery Ridge and Seminary Ridge, it was time for Edward Everett to recite his two-hour oration. The gray-haired, seventy-year old Everett performed creditably. The reviews were mixed. Robert G. Harper of the (Gettysburg) *Adams County Sentinel* wrote words of praise: "Every word is memorized; there is no hesitation; the stream of eloquence flows steadily on; and there is the gesture, once observed but never forgotten, when the orator rises to some climax, and the arms outspread and the fingers quivering and fluttering as one said, like the pinions of an eagle, there seems to reign down upon the audience the emotions with which they vibrate."[22] James Gordon Bennett who originated the penny newspaper and pioneered non-partisan journalism, was less complimentary; he called Everett's presentation "milk and water;" "utterly inadequate, although his sentences were as smooth as silk and his metaphors as white as snow."[23] The Democratic editor of the Philadelphia *Age*, predictably critical, thought that Everett's many words had "no heart" and that his rhetoric was "as scentless and as lifeless as wax flowers" and his style "as cold as Croton ice."[24]

With Everett's two-hour oration out of the way, it was time for another musical number, Benjamin B. French's "Consecration Hymn." Lamon's printed program listed it simply as "Music," without mentioning the author, arranger, or the choir that would chant it. The "Programme of Arrangements" listed it as "*Music*, Hymn composed by B. B. French, Esq." In his 1864 report, David Wills called it an "Ode."

French's hymn dated back to the evening of November 13, 1863. Lamon and French, his first assistant, came to Gettysburg at Wills's request to finish planning the procession and program for the dedication of the soldiers' cemetery. Wills, in an evening conference, states some of his disappointments, including the fact that Henry Wadsworth Longfellow, John Greenleaf Whittier, William Cullen Bryant, and George H. Boker, in that order, had turned down his invitation to compose a special ode or hymn for the occasion. French, without modesty to hamper his ambitions, then and there offered to compose an appropriate hymn and submit it to his fellow committee members next morning. "My muse volunteered" he wrote unabashedly in his journal the next day.[25] Actually, French had the right to volunteer to write something, for some of his poems had been published in newspapers and literary journals. Anyway, either that night or early next morning he composed a five-stanza poem or ode that he entitled "Consecration Hymn." French presented it to Wills and Lamon next morning and it seemed suitable for the dedication program. Someone in someway put French's composition into the hands of Wilson G. Horner, the young and able director of the National Union Musical Association of Baltimore. Horner, in turn, "composed appropriate music, set the words to the music, and . . . introduced the piece to his singers."[26] Then the Baltimore singers were scheduled to chant French's "Consecration Hymn" as one of the four musical numbers of the dedication program.

After Everett finished his two-hour oration, he received compliments from both Lincoln and Seward before he sat down again in his chair. Lamon then called on Horner to put his chorus in action. Horner, always dramatic, used a small American flag as a baton and directed his singers through the hymn's five verses:

> *'Tis holy ground —*
> *This spot, where, in their graves*
> *We place our Country's braves,*
> *Who fell in Freedom's holy cause*
> *Fighting for Liberties and Laws —*
> *Let tears abound.*
>
> *Here let them rest —*
> *And Summer's heat and Winter's cold,*
> *Shall glow and freeze above this mould —*
> *A thousand years shall pass away —*
> *A nation still shall mourn this clay,*
> *Which now is blest.*
>
> *Here, where they fell,*
> *Oft shall the widows' tears be shed,*

Oft shall fond parents mourn their dead,
The orphans here shall kneel and weep, '
And maidens, where their lovers sleep,
Their woes shall tell.

Great God in Heaven!
Shall all this sacred blood be shed —
Shall we thus mourn our glorious dead,
Or shall the end be wrath and woe,
The knell of Freedom's overthrow —
A Country riven?

It will not be!
We trust, Oh, God! Thy gracious Power
To aid us in our darkest hour,
This be our Prayer — "Oh, Father! save
A people's Freedom from its grave —
All praise to Thee."[27]

Replete with emotional phrases like "holy ground," "Country's braves," "widow's tears," "sacred blood," and "our glorious dead," and supplemented by superior choral work, the "Consecration Hymn" restored the spirits of an already tired audience — most had been standing for three hours.

Compliments included terms like "in fine style," "with excellent effect," and "in a manner that elicited the admiration of all."[28] A Baltimore reporter, rightfully proud of the excellent performance, wrote, "The Glee Club of Baltimore conspicuously participated in the ceremonies of the dedication, their musical talent and patriotism contributing not a little to give *eclat* to the occasion."[29]

French had every right to be as proud as the reporter for the Baltimore *American*. Somewhat apprehensive earlier, he must have gloried in both the music and the prolonged applause. He recorded his pride and pleasure: "I can say *here* that I was never so flattered at any production of my own, as in relation to that same Hymn. All who heard it seemed to consider it more appropriate and most happily conceived."[30]

After French's hymn stirred the soul of the assemblage, it was time for President Lincoln to play his part in the day's ceremonies. His assignment, stated in a letter written by David Wills, was to dedicate a portion of the battlefield into sacred burial grounds with "a few appropriate remarks."[31]

Lamon gave Lincoln the traditional introduction: "Ladies and Gentlemen, the President of the United States." Lincoln rose to the occasion admirably. His nine-sentence recitation met the test. He was interrupted by applause five times so that his two-minute speech lasted about three. At its conclusion there was prolonged applause. Then the enamored audience gave three cheers for Lincoln and three more for the governors.[32]

Joseph L. Gilbert, the Associated Press reporter known for his shorthand skills, was one of the many scribes who incorporated the word "Applause" five times within his copy of the nine-sentence address and the words "Long continued applause" at the end of his text. Gilbert found Lincoln's public speeches easy to report. "His lucid thinking and distinct articulation — qualities in a speech which most delight a reporter — and his natural unaffected delivery," Gilbert once said, "make him the orator par excellence for a shorthand novice like myself."[33] Reminiscing forty-four years later, Gilbert offered a second compliment: "No one of the many orators whom, in after years, I had heard repeat the address, ever made it sparkle with light and meaning as its great author did...."[34]

After President Lincoln acknowledged the applause and received Everett's and Seward's compliments, he sat down again. Lamon then called on a local mixed choir to present its number, a dirge composed especially for the occasion — with the words written by James G. Percival and the music devised by Alfred Delaney. It was dedicated to Pennsylvania's governor, Andrew G. Curtin. The choir was composed of volunteers, most of whom belonged to their own church's choral groups. There were twice as many women as men in that mixed choir. They rehearsed several times, even with Birgfield's Band accompanying them, so they did well. The four verses follow:

O! it is great for our Country to die,
Whose ranks are contending,
Bright is the wreath of our fame;
Glory awaits us for aye;
Glory that never is dim
Shining on with a light never ending,
Glory that shall never fade,
Never O! never away.

O! it is sweet for our Country to die,
how softly reposes
Warrior youth on his bier,
wet by the tears of his love,
Wet by a mother's warm tears;
they crown him with garlands of roses,
Weep, and then joyously turn,
bright where he triumphs above.

Not in Elysian fields,
by the still oblivious river,
Not in the Isles of the blest,
over the blue rolling sea;
But on Olympian heights

shall dwell the devoted forever;
There shall assemble the good,
   there the wise, valiant, and free.

O! then how great for our Country to die,
   in the front rank to perish,
Firm with our breast to the foe,
   victory's shout in our ear;
Long they our statues shall crown,
   in songs our memory cherish;
We shall look forth from our heaven,
   pleased the sweet music to hear.[35]

A reporter for the Philadelphia *Bulletin* called that musical number "a beautiful dirge."[36] The Republican editor of the local newspaper was quite complimentary, perhaps because some of the singers were friends or neighbors or subscribers. It was, editor Harper said, "an exquisite performance, and has rarely been excelled on such an occasion."[37]

After a brief benediction, by Rev. Henry L. Baugher, head of the local college and Lutheran seminary, Lamon took center stage once more. In behalf of Governor David Tod, Lamon invited all who were interested in a special "Ohio Program" at five o'clock in the local Presbyterian Church. Then he announced that the dedication ceremonies were over and he instructed the marshals to form a procession for the return to Gettysburg. A battery of the Fifth New York Artillery fired a salute of eight rounds and its regimental band played a lively number as the Marine Band moved forward to the head of the line. Lincoln and the other dignitaries started to go down the platform's steps to take their place in the Marshal-in-Chief's section of the parade. After descending the steps, Lincoln detoured to shake hands with some of the wounded veterans, saying to their chaplain, "The men upon their crutches were orators; their very appearance spoke louder than tongues."[38] The president also shook hands with some members of the mixed chorus; one of them recalled her handshaking experience many years later.[39]

The Marine Band escorted the procession back to town. Lincoln, Everett, and nine governors were guests at the Wills house where a dinner was served to "a very large company" about three o'clock. The four bands, preempting places in the central square, alternated playing "lively music" and "kept the air resonant with melody until sunset."[40]

After dinner, Wills turned his house into a hospitality center and hundreds filed through, first shaking their president's hand and then their governor's. Lincoln expressed a desire to meet the local seventy-year old cobbler who, dressed in his Sunday best, had taken his musket and joined the Union troops fighting the invaders west of Gettysburg — he was slightly wounded three different times in the first day's encounter.[41] Wills sent someone to hunt up John Burns and bring him to the house. When he arrived, the president shook his hand and listened to some of his story. Then, shortly before five o'clock, Burns, flanked by Lincoln and Seward, walked over to the Presbyterian Church for "the Ohio Program" escorted by the Marine Band.

After the program was over, Lincoln returned to the Wills house to pick up his carpetbag, say his "thank yous," and walk to the railroad station. The Marine Band again led the way.

A large crowd had already assembled at or near the railroad station, many waiting for their excursion trains to come off the spur — but none could leave until the president's train departed. Bands relieved some of the tension with their music and even the twelve-man chorus from Baltimore did its part in livening up the evening. It sang "a constant succession of patriotic and popular songs."[42]

With the departure of the trains and the bands, life was quiet again in Gettysburg — "the imposing ceremonies of the day having been completed in admirable order and without being marred in any respect."[43] Editor Harper termed the day's activities "a perfect success."[44] The bands and the music, an important part of the formal dedication program, contributed considerably toward making the affair a memorable event and a perfect success.

APPENDIX A

GETTYSBURG (A NEWSPAPERMAN'S DESCRIPTION)

The Town of Gettysburg

(The following account appeared in the Washington <u>Daily National Intelligencer,</u> November 24, 1863. The reporter who wrote the description of Gettysburg was a member of Marshal-in-Chief Ward H. Lamon's traveling party and spent two days in the city.)

Gettysburg, so called after Mr. James Getty, formerly a property-holder of the township, is a plain but neat and well built town of Adams county, Pennsylvania, situated on elevated ground, at the intersection of several important turnpike roads, and surrounded by a delightful and well-cultivated country. It contains the usual country buildings — a Bank, an Academy, Presbyterian, Seceder, Methodist, and German Lutheran Churches — a Theological Seminary, and the Pennsylvania College, both under the patronage of the Lutheran denomination.

The society of the place is highly respectable and intelligent. It was formerly noted for its extensive manufacture of coaches, but the business has declined with the change of the times. Gettysburg is one hundred and fourteen miles from Philadelphia, thirty-six from Harrisburg, and fifty-two from Baltimore. The principal trade of the region is carried on with Baltimore, to which place there is an excellent turnpike road.

The Presbyterian Church at this place was the first erected in the county, but the old edifice has been destroyed, and another built on a different site. The old "Hill Church" of the Seceders is of nearly equal antiquity.

The Seminary edifice, situated about one-fourth of a mile from Gettysburg, is a four-story brick building, one hundred feet by forty, and was erected in 1831. At a short distance on each side are the dwellings of the professors, also of brick. The library numbers between seven and eight thousand volumes, and consists of works of almost every age and language.

The edifice of the Pennsylvania College is a chaste specimen of the Doric order. It is one hundred and fifty feet in length, and contains seventy-five apartments, fifty-four of which are designed for the lodging of students. This college, erected in 1832, had its origins in the wants of the German portion of the community, and especially of the Theological Seminary. Its library is well selected and regularly increased.

DOCUMENTS RELATING TO THE PROCESSION AND PROGRAM

ORDER OF PROCESSION
for the
Consecration of the National Cemetery at Gettysburg, PA.,
on the 19th of November, 1863

Military, under command of Major General Couch.
Major General Meade and Staff,
and the Officers and Soldiers of the Army of the Potomac.
Officers of the Navy and Marine Corps of the United States.
Aids.   Chief Marshal.   Aids.
PRESIDENT OF THE UNITED STATES.
Members of the Cabinet.
Assistant Secretaries of the several Executive Departments.
General-in-chief of the Army, and Staff.
Lieutenant General Scott and Rear-Admiral Stewart.
Judges of the United States Supreme Court.
Hon. Edward Everett, Orator of the Day, and the Chaplain.
Governors of the States, and their Staffs.
Commissioners of the States on the Inauguration of the Cemetery.
Bearers with the Flags of the States.
Vice President of the United States and
Speaker of the House of Representatives.
Members of the two Houses of Congress.
Officers of the two Houses of Congress.
Mayors of Cities.
Gettysburg Committee of Arrangements.
Officers and Members of the United States Sanitary Commission.
Committees of different Religious Bodies.
United States Military Telegraphic Corps.
Officers and Representatives of Adams Express Company.
Officers of different Telegraph Companies.
Hospital Corps of the Army.
Soldiers' Relief Associations.
Knights Templar.
Masonic Fraternity.
Independent Order of Odd Fellows.
Other Benevolent Associations.
Literary, Scientific and Industrial Associations.
The Press.
Officers and Members of Loyal Leagues.
Fire Companies.
Citizens of the State of Pennsylvania.
Citizens of other States.
Citizens of the District of Columbia.
Citizens of the several Territories.

PROGRAMME

The Military will form at 9 o'clock, A.M., on Carlisle street, North of the Square, its Right resting on the Square, opposite McClellan's Hotel.

The Marshals will assemble in the Public Square at the same hour.

All the Civic Processions, except the States, will assemble according to the printed Programme, on York street, at the same hour.

The Pennsylvania Delegation will form on Chambersburg street, its Right resting on the Square, and the other Delegations, in their order, will form on the same street, in rear of the Pennsylvania Delegation.

The Marshals of the several States are charged with seeing that their several Delegations are duly formed, and that they wheel into the Column of March, in their proper order.

The head of the Column will move at precisely ten o'clock, A.M. Its route will be up Baltimore street, to the Emmittsburg road, thence to the junction of the Taneytown road, thence by the latter road to the Cemetery, where the Military will form in Line, as the General in Command may order, and present arms, when the President of the United States, and all who are to occupy the Stand, will pass in front to the Stand.

The Military will then close up and occupy the space on the left of the Stand. The Civic Procession will then advance and occupy the area in front of the Stand, the Military leaving sufficient space, between them and the line of graves, for the Civic Procession to pass.

The Ladies will occupy the right of the Stand, and it is desirable that they be upon the ground as early as ten o'clock,

Silence having been ordered, the Exercises will take place, as follows:

MUSIC.

PRAYER.

MUSIC.

ORATION.

MUSIC.

DEDICATORY REMARKS,

By the President of the United States.

DIRGE.

BENEDICTION.

After the Benediction, the Procession will be dismissed, and the Marshals will form on Baltimore street and return to the Court House, where a meeting of the Marshals will be held.

WARD H. LAMON,
Marshal-in-Chief

REV. THOMAS H. STOCKTON'S "INVOCATION"

O God our Father, for the sake of Thy Son our Saviour, inspire us with Thy Spirit, and sanctify us to the right fulfilment of the duties of this occasion.

We come to dedicate this new historic centre as a National Cemetery. If all departments of the one government which Thou hast ordained over our Union, and of the many governments which Thou has subordinated to our Union, be here represented — if all classes, relations, and interests of our blended brotherhood of people stand severally and thoroughly apparent in Thy presence — we trust that it is because Thou hast called us, that Thy blessing awaits us, and that Thy designs may be embodied in practical results of incalculable and imperishable good.

And so, with Thy holy Apostle, and with the Church of all lands and ages, we unite in the ascription, "Blessed be God, even the Father of our Lord Jesus Christ, the Father of mercies, and the God of all comfort, who comforteth us in all our tribulation, that we may be able to comfort them which are in any trouble, by the comfort wherewith we ourselves are comforted of God."

In emulation of all angels, in fellowship with all saints, and in sympathy with all sufferers, in remembrance of Thy works, in reverence of Thy ways, and in accordance with Thy word, we laud and magnify Thine infinite perfections, Thy creative glory, Thy redeeming grace, Thy providential goodness, and the progressively richer and fairer developments of Thy supreme, universal and everlasting administration.

In behalf of all humanity, whose ideal is divine, whose first memory is Thine image lost, and whose last hope is Thine image restored, and especially of our own nation, whose history has been so favored, whose position is so peerless, whose mission is so sublime, and whose future is so attractive, we thank thee for the unspeakable patience of Thy compassion and the exceeding greatness of Thy loving kindness. In contemplation of Eden, Calvary, and Heaven, of Christ in the Garden, on the Cross, and on the Throne; nay, more, of Christ as coming again in all-subduing power and glory, we gratefully prolong our homage. By this Altar of Sacrifice, on this Field of Deliverance, on this Mount of Salvation, within the fiery and bloody line of these "munitions of rocks," looking back to the dark days of fear and trembling, and to the rapture of relief that came after, we multiply our thanksgivings, and confess our obligations to renew and perfect our personal and social consecration to Thy service and glory.

Oh, had it not been for God! For lo! our enemies, they came unresisted, multitudinous, mighty, flushed with victory, and sure of success. They exulted on our mountains, they revelled in our valleys; they feasted, they rested; they slept, they awaked; they grew stronger, prouder, bolder, everyday; they spread abroad, they concentrated here; they looked beyond this horizon to the stores or wealth, to the haunts of pleasure, and to the seats of power in our capital and chief cities. They prepared to cast a chain of Slavery around the form of Freedom, binding life and death together forever. Their premature triumph was the mockery of God and man. One more victory, and all was theirs! But behind these hills was heard the feebler march of a smaller, but still pursuing host. Onward they hurried, day and night, for God and their country. Foot-sore, wayworn, hungry, thirsty, faint — but not in heart — they came to dare all, to bear all, and to do all that is possible to heroes. And Thou didst sustain them! At first they met the blast on the plain, and bent before it like the trees in a storm. But then, led by Thy hand to these hills, they took their stand upon the rocks and remained as firm and immovable as they. In vain were they assaulted. All art, all violence, all desperation, failed to dislodge them. — Baffled, bruised, broken, their enemies recoiled, retired, and disappeared. Glory to God for this rescue! But oh, the slain! In the freshness and fulness of their young and manly life, with such sweet memories of father and mother, brother and sister, wife and children, maiden and friends, they died for us. From the coasts beneath the Eastern star, from the shores of Northern lakes and rivers, from the flowers of Western prairies, and from the homes of the Midway and the Border, they came here to die for us and for mankind. Alas, how little we can do for them! We come with the humility of prayer, with the pathetic eloquence of venerable wisdom, with the tender beauty of poetry, with the plaintive harmony of music, with the honest tribute of our Chief Magistrate, and with all this honorable attendance: but our best hope is in thy blessing, O Lord, our God! O Father, bless us! Bless the bereaved, whether present or absent; bless our sick and wounded soldiers and sailors; bless all our rulers and people; bless our army and navy; bless the efforts for the suppression of the rebellion; and bless all the associations of this day and place and scene forever. As the trees are not dead, though their foliage is gone, so our heroes are not dead, though their forms have fallen. In their proper personality they are all with Thee. And the spirit of their example is here. It fills the air; it fills our hearts. And, long as time shall last, it will hover in the skies and rest on this landscape; and the pilgrims of our own land, and from all lands, will thrill with its inspiration, and increase and confirm their devotion to liberty, religion, and God.

Our Father, who art in Heaven, hallowed by thy name. Thy kingdom come. Thy will be done on earth as it is in Heaven. Give us this day our daily bread. And forgive us our debts, as we forgive our debtors. Lead us not into temptation, but deliver us from evil. For Thine is the kingdom, the power, and the glory, forever. *Amen.*

EDWARD EVERETT'S ORATION,
"THE BATTLES OF GETTYSBURG"

Standing beneath this serene sky, overlooking these broad fields now repos-
ing from the labors of the waning year, the mighty Alleghenies dimly towering
before us, the graves of our brethren beneath our feet, it is with hesitation that
I raise my poor voice to break the eloquent silence of God and Nature. But
the duty to which you have called me must be performed; — grant me, I pray
you, your indulgence and your sympathy.

It was appointed by law in Athens, that the obsequies of the citizens who
fell in battle should be performed at the public expense, and in the most
honorable manner. Their bones were carefully gathered up from the funeral
pyre, where their bodies were consumed, and brought home to the city. There,
for three days before the interment, they lay in state, beneath tents of honor,
to receive the votive offerings of friends and relatives, — flowers, weapons,
precious ornaments, painted vases, (wonders of art, which after two thousand
years adorn the museums of modern Europe,) — the last tributes of surviving
affection. Ten coffins of funeral cypress received the honorable deposit, one
for each of the tribes of the city, and an eleventh in memory of the unrecogniz-
ed, but not therefore unhonored, dead, and of those whose remains could not
be recovered. On the fourth day the mournful procession was formed; mothers,
wives, sisters, daughters led the way, and to them it was permitted by the simplicity of ancient manners to utter aloud their lamentations for the beloved and the
lost; the male relatives and friends of the deceased followed; citizens and
strangers closed the train. Thus marshalled, they moved to the place of interment in that famous Ceramicus, the most beautiful suburb of Athens, which
had been adorned by Cimon, the son of Miltiades, with walks and fountains
and columns, — whose groves were filled with altars, shrines, and temples, —
whose gardens were kept forever green by the streams from the neighboring
hills, and shaded with the trees sacred to Minerva and coeval with the foundation of the city, — whose circuit enclosed

> "the olive Grove of Academe,
> Plato's retirement, where the Attic bird
> Trilled his thick-warbled note the summer long," —

whose pathways gleamed with the monuments of the illustrious dead, the work
of the most consummate masters that ever gave life to marble. There, beneath

the overarching plane-trees, upon a lofty stage erected for the purpose, it was ordained that a funeral oration should be pronounced by some citizens of Athens, in the presence of the assembled multitude.

Such were the tokens of respect required to be paid at Athens to the memory of those who had fallen in the cause of their country. For those alone who fell at Marathon a peculiar honor was reserved. As the battle fought upon that immortal field was distinguished from all others in Grecian history for its influence over the fortunes of Hellas, — as it depended upon the event of that day whether Greece should live, a glory and a light to all coming time, or should expire, like the meteor of a moment; so the honors awarded to its martyr-heroes were such as were bestowed by Athens on no other occasion. They alone of all her sons were entombed upon the spot which they had forever rendered famous. Their names were inscribed upon ten pillars, erected upon the monumental tumulus which covered their ashes, (where after six hundred years, they were read by the traveler Pausanias,) and although the columns, beneath the hand of time and barbaric violence, have long since disappeared, the venerable mound still marks the spot where they fought and fell, —

> "That battle-field where Persia's victim horde
> First bowed beneath the brunt of Hellas' sword."

And shall I, fellow citizens, who, after an interval of twenty-three centuries, a youthful pilgrim from the world unknown to ancient Greece, have wandered over that illustrious plain, ready to put off the shoes from off my feet, as one that stands on holy ground, — who have gazed with respectful emotion on the mound which still protects the dust of those who rolled back the tide of Persian invasion, and rescued the land of popular liberty, or letters, and of arts, from the ruthless foe, — stand unmoved over the graves of our dear brethren, who so lately, on three of those all-important days which decide a nation's history, — days on whose issue it depended whether this august republican Union, founded by some of the wisest statesmen that ever lived, cemented with the blood of some of the purest patriots that ever died, should perish or endure, — rolled back the tide of an invasion, not less unprovoked, not less ruthless, than that which came to plant the dark banner of Asiatic despotism and slavery on the free soil of Greece? Heaven forbid! And could I prove so insensible to every prompting of patriotic duty and affection, not only would you, fellow citizens, gathered many of you from distant States, who have come to take part in these pious offices of gratitude — you, respected fathers, brethren, matrons, sisters, who surround me — cry out for shame, but the forms of brave and patriotic men who fill these honored graves would heave with indignation beneath the sod.

We have assembled, friends, fellow citizens, at the invitation of the Executive of the great central State of Pennsylvania, seconded by the Governors of seventeen other loyal States of the Union, to pay the last tribute of respect to the brave men, who, in the hard fought battles of the first, second and third days of July last, laid down their lives for the country on these hill sides and the plains before us, and whose remains have been gathered into the cemetery which we consecrate this day. As my eye ranges over the fields whose sods were so lately moistened by the blood of gallant and loyal men, I feel, as never before, how truly it was said of old that it is sweet and becoming to die for one's country. I feel as never before, how justly, from the dawn of history to the present time, men have paid the homage of their gratitude and admiration to the memory of those who nobly sacrifice their lives, that their fellow men may live in safety and in honor. And if this tribute were ever due, when, to whom, could it be more justly paid than to those whose last resting place we this day commend to the blessing of Heaven and of men?

For consider, my friends, what would have been the consequences to the country, to yourselves, and to all you hold dear, if those who sleep beneath our feet, and their gallant comrades who survive to serve their country on other fields of danger, had failed in their duty on those memorable days. Consider what, at this moment, would be the condition of the United States, if that noble army of the Potomac, instead of gallantly and for the second time beating back the tide of invasion from Maryland and Pennsylvania, had been itself driven from these well contested heights, thrown back in confusion on Baltimore, or trampled down, discomfited, scattered to the four winds. What, in that sad event, would not have been the fate of the Monumental city, of Harrisburg, of Philadelphia, of Washington, the capital of the Union, each and every one of which would have lain at the mercy of the enemy, accordingly as it might have pleased him, spurred by passion, flushed with victory, and confident of continued success, to direct his course?

For this we must bear in mind, it is one of the great lessons of the war, indeed of every war, that it is impossible for a people without military organization, inhabiting the cities, towns, and villages of an open country, including, of course, the natural proportion of non-combatants of either sex, and of every age, to withstand the inroad of a veteran army. What defence can be made by the inhabitants of villages mostly built of wood, of cities unprotected by walls, nay, by a population of men, however high-toned and resolute, whose aged parents demand their care, whose wives and children are clustering about them, against the charge of the war-horse whose neck is clothed with thunder — against flying artillery and batteries of rifled cannon planted on every commanding eminence — against the onset of trained veterans led by skillful chiefs? No, my friends, army must be met by army, battery by battery, squadron by squadron; and the shock of organized thousands must be encountered by the firm breasts and valiant arms of other thousands, as well organized and as skillfully led. It is no reproach, therefore, to the unarmed population of the country to say, that we owe it to the brave men who sleep in their beds of honor before us, and to their gallant surviving associates, not merely that your fertile fields, my friends of Pennsylvania and Maryland, were redeemed from the presence of the invader, but that your beautiful capitals were not given up to threatened plunder, perhaps laid in ashes, Washington seized by the enemy, and a blow struck at the heart of the nation.

Who that hears me has forgotten the thrill of joy that ran through the country on the 4th of July — auspicious day for the glorious tidings, and rendered still more so by the simultaneous fall of Vicksburg — when the telegraph flashed through the land the assurance from the President of the United States that the army of the Potomac, under General Meade, had again smitten the invader? Sure I am, that, with the ascriptions of praise that rose to heaven from twenty millions of freemen, with the acknowledgements that breathed from patriotic lips throughout the length and breadth of America, to the surviving officers and men who had rendered the country this inestimable service, there beat in every loyal bosom a throb of tender and sorrowful gratitude to the martyrs who had fallen on the sternly contested field. Let a natlon's fervent thanks make some amends for the toils and sufferings of those who survive. Would that the heartfelt tribute could penetrate these honored graves!

In order that we may comprehend, to their full extent, our obligations to the martyrs and surviving heroes of the army of the Potomac, let us contemplate for a few moments the train of events, which culminated in the battles of the first days of July. Of this stupendous rebellion, planned, as its originators boast, more than thirty years ago, matured and prepared for during an entire generation, finally commenced because, for the first time since the adoption of the Constitution, an election of President had been effected without the votes of the South, (which retained, however, the control of the two other branches of the government,) the occupation of the national capital, with the seizure of the public archives and of the treaties with foreign powers, was an essential feature. This was, in substance, within my personal knowledge, admitted, in the winter of 1860-61, by one of the most influential leaders of the rebellion; and it was fondly thought that this object could be effected by a bold and sudden movement on the 4th of March, 1861. There is abundant proof, also, that a darker project was contemplated, if not by the responsible chiefs of the rebellion, yet by nameless ruffians, willing to play a subsidiary and murderous part in the treasonable drama. It was accordingly maintained by the Rebel emissaries in England, in the circles to which they found access, that the new American Minister ought not, when he arrived, to be received as the envoy of the United States, inasmuch as before that time Washington would be captured, and the capital of the nation and the archives and muniments of government would be in the possession of the Confederates. In full accordance also with this threat, it was declared, by the Rebel Secretary of War, at Montgomery, in the presence of his Chief and of his colleagues, and of five thousand hearers, while the tidings of the assault on Sumter were traveling over the wires on that fatal 12th of April, 1861, that before the end of May "the flag which then flaunted the breeze," as he expressed it, "would float over the dome of the Capitol at Washington."

At the time this threat was made, the rebellion was confined to the cotton-growing States, and it was well understood by them, that the only hope of drawing any of the other slaveholding States into the conspiracy, was in bringing about a conflict of arms, and "firing the heart of the South" by the effusion

of blood. This was declared by the Charleston press, to be the object for which
Sumter was to be assaulted; and the emissaries sent from Richmond, to urge
on the unhallowed work, gave the promise, that, with the first drop of blood
that should be shed, Virginia would place herself by the side of South Carolina.

In pursuance of this original plan of the leaders of the rebellion, the capture of Washington has been continually had in view, not merely for the sake
of its public buildings, as the capital of the Confederacy, but as the necessary
preliminary to the absorption of the border States, and for the moral effect
in the eyes of Europe of possessing the metropolis of the Union.

I allude to these facts, not perhaps enough borne in mind, as a sufficient
refutation of the pretence, on the part of the Rebels, that the war is one of
self-defence, waged for the right of self-government. It is in reality, a war
originally levied by ambitious men in the cotton-growing States, for the purpose of drawing the slaveholding border States into the vortex of the conspiracy,
first by sympathy — which, in the case of South-Eastern Virginia, North
Carolina, part of Tennessee, and Arkansas, succeeded — and then by force
and for the purpose of subjagating Maryland, Western Virginia, Kentucky,
Eastern Tennessee, and Missouri; and it is a most extraordinary fact, consider-
ing the clamors of the Rebel chiefs on the subject of invasion, that not a soldier
of the United States has entered the States last named, except to defend their
Union-loving inhabitants from the armies and guerillas of the Rebels.

In conformity with these designs on the city of Washington, and notwithstanding the disastrous results of the invasion of 1862, it was determined
by the Rebel Government last summer to resume the offensive in that direction. Unable to force the passage of the Rappahannock, where General Hooker,
notwithstanding the reverse at Chancellorsville, in May, was strongly posted,
the Confederate general resorted to strategy. He had two objects in view. The
first was by a rapid movement northward, and by maneuvering with a portion
of his army on the east side of the Blue Ridge, to tempt Hooker from his base
of operations, thus leading him to uncover the approaches to Washington, to
throw open to a raid by Stewart's cavalry, and to enable Lee himself to cross
the Potomac in the neighborhood of Poolesville and thus fall upon the capital.
This plan of operations was wholly frustrated. The design of the Rebel general
was promptly discovered by General Hooker, and, moving with great rapidity
from Fredericksburg, he preserved unbroken the inner line, and stationed the
various corps of his army at all the points protecting the approach to
Washington, from Centreville up to Leesburg. From this vantage-ground the
Rebel general in vain attempted to draw him. In the mean time, by the vigorous
operations of Pleasanton's cavalry, the cavalry of Stuart, though greatly superior
in numbers, was so crippled as to be disabled from performing the part assigned it in the campaign. In this manner, General Lee's first object, namely, the
defeat of Hooker's army on the south of the Potomac and a direct march on
Washington, was baffled.

The second part of the Confederate plan, which is supposed to have been
undertaken in opposition to the views of General Lee, was to turn the demonstra-

tion northward into a real invasion of Maryland and Pennsylvania, in the hope, that, in this way, General Hooker would be drawn to a distance from the capital, and that some opportunity would occur of taking him at disadvantage, and, after defeating his army, of making a descent upon Baltimore and Washington. This part of General Lee's plan, which was substantially the repetition of that of 1862, was not less signally defeated, with what honor to the arms of the Union the heights on which we are this day assembled will forever attest.

Much time had been uselessly consumed by the Rebel general in his unavailing attempts to out-manoeuvre General Hooker. Although General Lee broke up from Fredericksburg on the 3d of June, it was not till the 24th that the main body of his army entered Maryland. Instead of crossing the Potomac, as he had intended, east of the Blue Ridge, he was compelled to do it at Shepherdstown and Williamsport, thus materially deranging his entire plan of campaign north of the river. Stuart, who had been sent with his cavalry to the east of the Blue Ridge, to guard the passes of the mountains, to mask the movements of Lee, and to harass the Union general in crossing the river, having been severely handled by Pleasanton at Beverly Ford, Aldie, and Upperville, instead of being able to retard General Hooker's advance, was driven himself away from his connection with the army of Lee, and cut off for a fortnight from all communication with it — a circumstance to which General Lee, in his report, alludes more than once, with evident displeasure. Let us now rapidly glance at the incidents of the eventful campaign.

A detachment from Ewell's corps, under Jenkins, had penetrated, on the 15th of June, as far as Chambersburg. This movement was intended at first merely as a demonstration, and as a marauding expedition for supplies. It had, however, the salutary effect of alarming the country; and vigorous preparations were made, not only by the General Government, but here in Pennsylvania and in the sister States, to repel the inroad. After two days passed at Chambersburg, Jenkins, anxious for his communications with Ewell, fell back with his plunder to Hagerstown. Here he remained for several days, and then having swept the recesses of the Cumberland valley, came down upon the eastern flank of the South mountain, and pushed his marauding parties as far as Waynesboro. On the 22d, the remainder of Ewell's corps crossed the river and moved up the valley. They were followed on the 24th by Longstreet and Hill, who crossed at Williamsport and Shepherdstown, and, pushing up the valley, encamped at Chambersburg on the 27th. In this way the whole rebel army, estimated at 90,000 infantry, upwards of 10,000 cavalry, and 4,000 or 5,000 artillery, making a total of 105,000 of all arms, was concentrated in Pennsylvania.

Up to this time no report of Hooker's movements had been received by General Lee, who, having been deprived of his cavalry, had no means of obtaining information. Rightly judging, however, that no time would be lost by the Union army in the pursuit, in order to detain it on the eastern side of the mountains in Maryland and Pennsylvania, and thus preserve his communications by the way of Williamsport, he had, before his own arrival at Chambersburg, directed Ewell to send detachments from his corps to Carlisle

and York. The latter detachment, under Early, passed through this place on
the 26th of June. You need not, fellow-citizens of Gettysburg, that I should
recall to you those moments of alarm and distress, precursors as they were of
the more trying scenes which were so soon to follow.

As soon as Gen. Hooker perceived that the advance of the Confederates
into the Cumberland valley was not a mere feint to draw him away from
Washington, he moved rapidly in pursuit. Attempts, as we have seen, were made
to harass and retard his passage across the Potomac. These attempts were not
only altogether unsuccessful, but were so unskilfully made as to place the entire Federal army between the cavalry of Stuart and the army of Lee. While
the latter was massed in the Cumberland valley, Stuart was east of the mountains, with Hooker's army between, and Gregg's cavalry in close pursuit. Stuart
was accordingly compelled to force a march northward, which was destitute
of strategical character, and which deprived his chief of all means of obtaining
intelligence.

Not a moment had been lost by General Hooker in the pursuit of Lee. The
day after the Rebel army entered Maryland, the Union army crossed the Potomac
at Edward's Ferry, and by the 28th of June lay between Harper's Ferry and
Frederick. The force of the enemy on that day was partly at Chambersburg,
and partly moving on the Cashtown road in the direction of Gettysburg, while
the detachments from Ewell's corps, of which mention has been made, had
reached the Susquehanna opposite Harrisburg and Columbia. That a great battle
must soon be fought, no one could doubt; but in the apparent and perhaps
real absence of plan on the part of Lee, it was impossible to foretell the precise
scene of the encounter. Wherever fought, consequences the most momentous
hung upon the result.

In this critical and anxious state of affairs, General Hooker was relieved,
and General Meade was summoned to the chief command of the army. It appears to my unmilitary judgment to reflect the highest credit upon him, upon
his predecessor, and upon the corps commanders of the army of the Potomac,
that a change could take place in the chief command of so large a force on
the eve of a general battle — the various corps necessarily moving on lines
somewhat divergent, and all in ignorance of the enemy's intended point of con-
centration — and that not an hour's hesitation should ensue in the advance
of any portion of the entire army.

Having assumed the chief command of the 28th, General Meade directed
his left wing, under Reynolds, upon Emmitsburg, and his right upon New Windsor, leaving General French with 11,000 men to protect the Baltimore and Ohio
railroad, and convoy the public property from Harper's Ferry to Washington.
Buford's cavalry was then at this place, and Kilpatrick's at Hanover, where
he encountered and defeated the rear of Stuart's cavalry, who was roving the
country in search of the main army of Lee. On the Rebel side, Hill had reached
Fayetteville on the Cashtown road on the 28th, and was followed on the same
road by Longstreet on the 29th. The eastern side of the mountain, as seen from

Gettysburg, was lighted up at night by the camp-fires of the enemy's advance, and the country swarmed with his foraging parties. It was now too evident to be questioned, that the thunder-cloud, so long gathering blackness, would soon burst on some part of the devoted vicinity of Gettysburg.

The 30th of June was a day of important preparation. At half-past eleven o'clock in the morning, General Buford passed through Gettysburg, upon a reconnoissance in force, with his cavalry, upon the Chambersburg road. The information obtained by him was immediately communicated to General Reynolds, who was, in consequence, directed to occupy Gettysburg. That gallant officer accordingly, with the First Corps, marched from Emmitsburg to within six or seven miles of this place, and encamped on the right bank of Marsh's creek. Our right wing, meantime, was moved to Manchester. On the same day the corps of Hill and Longstreet were pushed still further forward on the Chambersburg road, and distributed in the vicinity of Marsh's creek, while a reconnoissance was made by the Confederate General Pettigrew up to a very short distance from this place. — Thus at nightfall, on the 30th of June, the greater part of the Rebel force was concentrated in the immediate vicinity of two corps of the Union army, the former refreshed by two days passed in comparative repose and deliberate preparation for the encounter, the latter separated by a march of one or two days from their supporting corps, and doubtful at what precise point they were to expect an attack.

And now the momentous day, a day to be forever remembered in the annals of the country, arrived. Early in the morning, on the 1st of July, the conflict began. I need not say that it would be impossible for me to comprise, within the limits of the hour, such a narrative as would do anything like full justice to the all-important events of these three great days, or to the merit of the brave officers and men, of every rank, of every arm of the service, and of every loyal State, who bore their part in the tremendous struggle — alike those who nobly sacrificed their lives for their country, and those who survive, many of them scarred with honorable wounds, the objects of our admiration and gratitude. The astonishingly minute, accurate, and graphic accounts contained in the journals of the day, prepared from personal observation by reporters who witnessed the scenes, and often shared the perils which they describe, and the highly valuable "notes" of Professor Jacobs, of the University in this place, to which I am greatly indebted, will abundantly supply the deficiency of my necessarily too condensed statement.*

---

*Besides the sources of information mentioned in the text, I have been kindly favored with a memorandum of the operations of the three days, drawn up for me by direction of Major General Meade, (anticipating the promulgation of his official report,) by one of his aids, Colonel Theodore Lyman, from whom also, I have received other important communications relative to the campaign. I have received very valuable documents relative to the battle from Major General Halleck, Commander-in-Chief of the army, and have been much assisted in drawing up the sketch of the campaign, by the detailed reports, kindly transmitted to me in manuscript from the Adjutant General's office, of the movements of every corps of the army, for each day, after the breaking up from Fredericksburg commenced. I have derived much assistance from Colonel John B. Bachelder's oral explanations of his beautiful and minute drawing (about to be engraved) of the

General Reynolds, on arriving at Gettysburg, in the morning of the 1st, found Buford with his cavalry warmly engaged with the enemy, whom he held most gallantly in check. Hastening himself to the front, General Reynolds directed his men to be moved over the fields from the Emmittsburg road, in front of M'Millan's and Dr. Schmucker's under cover of the Seminary Ridge. Without a moment's hesitation, he attacked the enemy, at the same time sending orders to the Eleventh Corps (General Howard's) to advance as promptly as possible. General Reynolds immediately found himself engaged with a force which greatly outnumbered his own, and had scarcely made his dispositions for the action when he fell, mortally wounded, at the head of his advance. The command of the First Corps devolved on General Doubleday, and that of the field on General Howard, who arrived at 11.30 with Schurz's and Barlow's divisions of the Eleventh Corps, the latter of whom received a severe wound. Thus strengthened, the advantage of the battle was for some time on our side. The attacks of the Rebels were vigorously repulsed by Wadsworth's division of the First Corps, and a large number of prisoners, including General Archer, were captured. At length, however, the continued reinforcement of the Confederates from the main body in the neighborhood, and by the divisions of Rodes and Early, coming down by separate lines from Heidlersberg and taking post on our extreme right, turned the fortunes of the day. Our army, after contesting the ground for five hours, was obliged to yield to the enemy, whose force outnumbered them two to one; and toward the close of the afternoon General Howard deemed it prudent to withdraw the two corps to the heights where we are now assembled. The greater part of the First Corps passed through the outskirts of the town, and reached the hill without serious loss or molestation. The Eleventh Corps and portions of the First, not being aware that the enemy had already entered the town from the north, attempted to force their way through Washington and Baltimore streets, which in the crowd and confusion of the scene, they did with a heavy loss in prisoners.

---

field of the three day's struggle. With the information derived from these sources, I have compared the statements in General Lee's official report of the campaign, dated 31st July, 1863, a well written article, purporting to be an account of the three days' battle, in the *Richmond Enquirer* of the 22d of July, and the article on "The Battle of Gettysburg and the Campaign of Pennsylvania," by an officer, apparently a colonel in the British army, in *Blackwood's Magazine* for September. The value of the information contained in this last essay may be seen by comparing the remark under date 27th June, that "private property is to be rigidly protected," with the statement in the next sentence but one, that "all the cattle and farm horses having been seized by Ewell, farm labor had come to a complete stand still." He, also, under date of 4th July, speaks of Lee's retreat being encumbered by "Ewell's *immense train of plunder*." This writer informs us, that, on the evening of the 4th of July, he heard "reports coming in from the different *Generals* that the enemy [Meade's army] was *retiring*, and had been doing so all day long." At a consultation at head-quarters on the 6th, between Generals Lee, Longstreet, Hill, and Wilcox, this writer was told by someone, whose name he prudently leaves in blank, that the army had no intention at present, of retreating for good, and that some of the enemy's dispatches have been intercepted, in which the following words occurr: "The noble, but unfortunate army of the Potomac has again been obliged to retreat before superior numbers!" He does not appear to be aware, that in recording these wretched expedients, resorted to in order to keep up the spirits of Lee's army, he furnishes the most complete refutation of his own account of its good condition. I much regret that General Meade's official report was not published in season to enable me to take full advantage of it, in preparing the brief sketch of the battles of the three days contained in this address. It reached me but the morning before it was sent to the press.

General Howard was not unprepared for his turn in the fortunes of the day. He had, in the course of the morning, caused Cemetery Hill to be occupied by General Steinwehr, with the second division of the Eleventh Corps. About the time of the withdrawal of our troops to the hill, General Hancock arrived, having been sent by General Meade, on hearing of the death of Reynolds, to assume the command of the field till he himself could reach the front. In conjunction with General Howard, General Hancock immediately proceeded to post troops and to repel an attack on our right flank. This attack was feebly made and promptly repulsed. At nightfall, our troops on the hill, who had so gallantly sustained themselves during the toil and peril of the day, were cheered by the arrival of General Slocum with the Twelfth Corps and of General Sickles with a part of the Third.

Such was the fortune of the first day, commencing with decided success to our arms, followed by a check, but ending in the occupation of this all-important position. To you, fellow-citizens of Gettysburg, I need not attempt to portray the anxieties of the ensuing night. Witnessing, as you had done with sorrow, the withdrawal of our army through your streets, with a considerable loss of prisoners — mourning as you did over the brave men who had fallen — shocked with the wide-spread desolation around you, of which the wanton burning of the Harman House had given the signal — ignorant of the near approach of General Meade, you passed the weary hours of the night in painful expectation.

Long before the dawn of the 2d of July, the new Commander-in-Chief had reached the ever-memorable field of service and glory. Having received intelligence of the events in progress, and informed by the reports of Generals Hancock and Howard of the favorable character of the position, he determined to give battle to the enemy at this point. He accordingly directed the remaining corps of the army to concentrate at Gettysburg with all possible expedition, and breaking up his head-quarters at Taneytown at ten P.M., he arrived at the front at one o'clock in the morning of the 2d of July. Few were the moments given to sleep, during the rapid watches of that brief midsummer's night, by officers or men, though half of our troops were exhausted by the conflict of the day, and the residue wearied by the forced marches which had brought them to the rescue. The full moon, veiled by thin clouds, shone down that night on a strangely unwonted scene. The silence of the grave-yard was broken by the heavy tramp of alarmed men, by the neigh of the war-horse, the harsh rattle of the wheels of artillery hurrying to their stations, and all the indescribable tumult of preparation. The various corps of the army, as they arrived, were moved to their positions, on the spot where we are assembled and the ridges that extended south-east and south-west; batteries were planted and breastworks thrown up. The Second and Fifth Corps, with the rest of the Third, had reached the ground by seven o'clock A.M.; but it was not till two o'clock in the afternoon that Sedgwick arrived with the Sixth Corps. He had marched thirty-four miles since nine o'clock on the evening before. It was only on his arrival that the Union army approached an equality of numbers with that of the Rebels, who were posted upon the opposite and parallel ridge, distant from a mile to a mile and a half, overlapping our position on either wing, and probably exceeding by ten thousand the army of General Meade.*

And here I cannot but remark on the providential inaction of the Rebel army. Had the contest been renewed by it at daylight on the 2d of July, with the First and Eleventh Corps exhausted by the battle and the retreat, the Third and Twelfth weary from their forced march, and the Second, Fifth and Sixth not yet arrived, nothing but a miracle could have saved the army from a great disaster. Instead of this, the day dawned, the sun rose, the cool hours of the morning passed, the forenoon and a considerable part of the afternoon wore away, without the slightest aggressive movement on the part of the enemy. Thus time was given for half of our forces to arrive and take their place in the lines, while the rest of the army enjoyed a much needed half day's repose.

At length, between three and four o'clock in the afternoon, the work of death began. A signal gun from the hostile batteries was followed by a tremendous cannonade along the Rebel lines, and this by a heavy advance of infantry, brigade after brigade, commencing on the enemy's right against the left of our army, and so onward to the left centre. A forward movement of General Sickles, to gain a commanding position from which to repel the Rebel attack, drew upon him a destructive fire from the enemy's batteries, and a furious assault from Longstreet's and Hill's advancing troops. After a brave resistance on the part of his corps, he was forced back, himself falling severely wounded. This was the critical moment of the second day; but the Fifth and part of the Sixth Corps, with portions of the First and Second, were promptly brought to the support of the Third. The struggle was fierce and murderous, but by sunset our success was decisive, and the enemy was driven back in confusion. The most important service was rendered toward the close of the day, in the memorable advance between Round Top and Little Round Top, by General Crawford's division of the Fifth Corps, consisting of two brigades of the Pennsylvania Reserves, of which one company was from this town and neighborhood. The Rebel force was driven back with great loss in killed and prisoners. At eight o'clock in the evening a desperate attempt was made by the enemy to storm the position of the Eleventh Corps on Cemetery Hill; but here, too, after a terrible conflict, he was repulsed with immense loss. Ewell, on our extreme right, which had been weakened by the withdrawal of the troops sent over to support our left, had succeeded in gaining a foothold within a portion of our lines, near Spangler's spring. This was the only advantage obtained by the Rebels to compensate them for the disasters of the day, and of this, as we shall see, they were soon deprived.

Such was the result of the second act of this eventful drama, — a day hard fought, and at one moment anxious, but, with the exception of the slight reverse

---

*In the Address as originally prepared, judging from the best sources of information then within my reach, I assumed the equality of the two armies on the 2d and 3d of July. Subsequent inquiry has led me to think that I underrated somewhat the strength of Lee's force at Gettysburg, and I have corrected the text accordingly. General Halleck, however, in his official report accompanying the President's messages, states the armies to have been equal.

just named, crowned with dearly earned but uniform success to our arms, auspicious of a glorious termination of the final struggle. On these good omens the night fell.

In the course of the night General Geary returned to his position on the right, from which he had hastened the day before to strengthen the Third Corps. He immediately engaged the enemy, and, after a sharp and decisive action, drove them out of our lines recovering the ground which had been lost on the preceding day. A spirited contest was kept up all the morning on this part of the line; but General Geary, reinforced by Wheaton's brigade of the Sixth Corps, maintained his position, and inflicted very severe losses on the Rebels.

Such was the cheering commencement of the third day's work, and with it ended all serious attempts of the enemy on our right. As on the preceding day, his efforts were now mainly directed against our left centre and left wing. From eleven till half-past one o'clock, all was still — a solemn pause of preparation, as if both armies were nerving themselves for the supreme effort. At length the awful silence, more terrible than the wildest tumult of battle, was broken by the roar of two hundred and fifty pieces of artillery from the opposite ridges, joining in a cannonade of unsurpassed violence — the Rebel batteries along two-thirds of their line pouring their fire upon Cemetery Hill, and the centre and left wing of our army. Having attempted in this way for two hours, but without success, to shake the steadiness of our lines, the enemy rallied his forces for a last grand assault. Their attack was principally directed against the position of our Second Corps. Successive lines of Rebel Infantry moved forward with equal spirit and steadiness from their cover on the wooded crest of Seminary Ridge, crossing the intervening plain, and, supported right and left by their choicest brigades, charged furiously up to our batteries. Our own brave troops of the Second Corps, supported by Doubleday's division and Stannard's brigade of the First, received the shock with firmness; the ground on both sides was long and fiercely contested, and was covered with the killed and the wounded; the tide of battle flowed and ebbed across the plain, till, after "a determined and gallant struggle," as it is pronounced by General Lee, the Rebel advance, consisting of two-thirds of Hill's corps and the whole of Longstreet's — including Pickett's division, the *elite* of his corps, which had not yet been under fire, and was now depended upon to decide the fortune of this last eventful day — was driven back with prodigious slaughter, discomfited and broken. While these events were in progress at our left centre, the enemy was driven, with a considerable loss of prisoners, from a strong position on our extreme left, from which he was annoying our force on Little Round Top. In the terrific assault on our centre, Generals Hancock and Gibbon were wounded. In the Rebel army, Generals Armistead, Kemper, Pettigrew, and Trimble were wounded, the first named mortally, the latter also made prisoner, General Garnett was killed, and thirty-five hundred officers and men made prisoners.

These were the expiring agonies of the three days' conflict, and with them the battle ceased. It was fought by the Union army with courage and skill, from the first cavalry skirmish on Wednesday morning to the fearful route of the enemy on Friday afternoon, by every arm and every rank of the service, by officers and men, by cavalry, artillery, and infantry. The superiority of numbers was with the enemy, who were led by the ablest commanders in their service; and if the Union force had the advantage of a strong position, the Confederates had that of choosing time and place, the prestige of former victories over the army of the Potomac, and of the success of the first day. Victory does not always fall to the lot of those who deserve it; but that so decisive a triumph, under circumstances like these, was gained by our troops, I would ascribe, under Providence, to the spirit of exalted patriotism that animated them, and the consciousness that they were fighting in a righteous cause.

All hope of defeating our army, and securing what General Lee calls "the valuable results" of such an achievement, having vanished, he thought only of rescuing from destruction the remains of his shattered forces. In killed, wounded and missing, he had, as far as can be ascertained, suffered a loss of about 37,000 men — rather more than a third of the army with which he is supposed to have marched in Pennsylvania. Perceiving that his only safety was in rapid retreat, he commenced withdrawing his troops at daybreak on the 4th, throwing up field works in front of our left, which, assuming the appearance of a new position, were intended probably to protect the rear of his army in their retreat. That day — sad celebration of the 4th of July for an army of Americans — was passed by him in hurrying off his trains. By nightfall, the main army was in full retreat on the Cashtown and Fairfield roads, and it moved with such precipitation, that, short as the nights were, by day-light the following morning, notwithstanding a heavy rain, the rear guard had left its position. The struggle of the last two days resembled in many respects the battle of Waterloo; and if, in the evening of the third day, General Meade, like the Duke of Wellington, had had the assistance of a powerful auxiliary army to take up the pursuit, the rout of the Rebels would have been as complete as that of Napoleon.

Owing to the circumstances just named, the intentions of the enemy were not apparent on the 4th. The moment his retreat was discovered, the following morning, he was pursued by our cavalry on the Cashtown road and through the Emmittsburg and Monterey passes, and by Sedgwick's corps on the Fairfield road. His rear guard was briskly attacked at Fairfield; a great number of wagons and ambulances were captured in the passes of the mountains; the country swarmed with his stragglers, and his wounded were literally emptied from the vehicles containing them into the farm houses on the road. General Lee, in his report makes repeated mention of the Union prisoners whom he conveyed into Virginia, somewhat overstating their number. He states, also, that "such of his wounded as were in a condition to be removed" were forwarded to Williamsport. He does not mention that the number of his wounded *not* removed, and left to the Christian care of the victors, was 7,540, not one of whom failed of any attention which it was possible, under the circumstances of the case, to afford them, not one of whom, certainly, has been put upon Libby prison fare — lingering death by starvation. Heaven forbid, however, that we should claim any merit for the exercise of common humanity.

Under the protection of the mountain ridge, whose narrow passes are easily held even by a retreating army, General Lee reached Williamsport in safety, and took up a strong position opposite to that place. General Meade necessarily pursued with the main army by a flank movement through Middletown, Turner's Pass, having been secured by General French. Passing through the South mountain, the Union army came up with that of the Rebels on the 12th, and found it securely posted on the heights of Marsh run. The position was reconnoitred, and preparations made for an attack on the 13th. The depth of the river, swollen by the recent rains, authorized the expectation that the enemy would be brought to a general engagement the following day. An advance was accordingly made by General Meade on the morning of the 14th; but it was soon found that the Rebels had escaped in the night, with such haste the Ewell's corps forded the river where the water was breast-high. The cavalry, which had rendered the most important services during the three days, and in harassing the enemy's retreat, was now sent in pursuit, and captured two guns and a large number of prisoners. In an action which took place at Falling Waters, Gen. Pettigrew was mortally wounded. General Meade, in further pursuit of the Rebels, crossed the Potomac at Berlin. Thus again covering the approaches to Washington, he compelled the enemy to pass the Blue Ridge at one of the upper gaps; and in about six weeks from the commencement of the campaign, General Lee found himself again on the south side of the Rappahannock, with the probable loss of about a third part of his army.

Such, most inadequately recounted, is the history of the ever-memorable three days, and of the events immediately preceding and following. It has been pretended, in order to diminish the magnitude of this disaster to the Rebel cause, that it was merely the repulse of an attack on a strongly defended position. The tremendous losses on both sides are a sufficient answer to this misrepresentation, and attest the courage and obstinacy with which the three day's battle was waged. Few of the great conflicts of modern times have cost victors and vanquished so great a sacrifice. On the Union side there fell, in the whole campaign, of generals killed, Reynolds, Weed and Zook, and wounded, Barlow, Barnes, Butterfield, Doubleday, Gibbon, Graham, Hancock, Sickles and Warren; while of officers below the rank of General, and men, there were 2,834 killed, 13,709 wounded, and 6,643 missing. On the Confederate side, there were killed on the field or mortally wounded, Generals Armistead, Barksdale, Garnett, Pender, Pettigrew and Semmes, and wounded, Heth, Hood, Johnson, Kempter, Kimball and Trimble. Of officers below the rank of general, and men, there were taken prisoners, including the wounded, 13,621, an amount ascertained officially. Of the wounded in a condition to be removed, of the killed and the missing, the enemy has made no return. They are estimated, from the best data which the nature of the case admits, at 23,000. General Meade also captured 3 cannon, and 41 standards; and 24,978 small arms were collected on the battlefield.

I must leave to others, who can do it from personal observation, to describe the mournful spectacle presented by these hill-sides and plains at the close of the terrible conflict. It was a saying of the Duke of Wellington, that next to a defeat, the saddest thing was a victory. The horrors of the battle field, after the contest is over, the sights and sounds of woe, — let me throw a pall over the scene, which no words can adequately depict to those who have not witnessed it, on which no one has witnessed it, and who has a heart in his bosom, can bear to dwell. One drop of balm alone, one drop of heavenly, life-giving balm, mingles in this bitter cup of misery. Scarcely has the cannon ceased to roar, when the brethren and sisters of Christian benevolence, ministers of compassion, angels of pity, hasten to the field and the hospital, to moisten the parched tongue, to bind the ghastly wounds, to soothe the parting agonies alike of friend and foe, and to catch the last whispered messages of love from dying lips. "Carry this miniature back to my dear wife, but do not take it from my bosom till I am gone." "Tell my little sister not to grieve for me; I am willing to die for my country." "Oh, that my mother were here!" When since Aaron stood between the living and the dead was there ever so gracious a ministry as this? It has been said that it is characteristic of Americans to treat women with a deference not paid to them in any other country. I will not undertake to say whether this is so; but I will say, that, since this terrible war has been waged, the women of the loyal States, if never before, have entitled themselves to our highest admiration and gratitude, — alike those who at home, often with fingers unused to the toil, often bowed beneath their own domestic cares, have performed an amount of daily labor not exceeded by those who work for their daily bread, and those who, in the hospital and the tents of the Sanitary and Christian Commissions, have rendered services which millions could not buy. Happily, the labor and the service are their own reward. Thousands of matrons and thousands of maidens have experienced a delight in these homely toils and services, compared with which the pleasures of the ball room and the opera house are tame and unsatisfactory. This on earth is reward enough, but a richer is in store for them. Yes, brothers, sisters of charity, while you bind up the wounds of the poor sufferers — the humblest, perhaps, that have shed their blood for the country — forget not WHO it is that will hereafter say to you, "Inasmuch as ye have done it unto one of the least of these my BRETHREN, ye have done it unto me."

And now, friends, fellow-citizens, as we stand among these honored graves, the momentous question presents itself, Which of the two parties to the war is responsible for all this suffering, for this dreadful sacrifice of life, the lawful and constitutional government of the United States, or the ambitious men who have rebelled against it? I say "rebelled" against it, although Earl Russell, the British Secretary of State for Foreign Affairs, in his recent temperate and conciliatory speech in Scotland, seems to intimate that no prejudice ought to attach to that word, inasmuch as our English forefathers rebelled against Charles I. and James II., and our American fathers rebelled against George III. These certainly are venerable precedents, but they prove only that it was just and proper to rebel against oppressive governments. They do not prove that it was just and proper for the son of James II. to rebel against George I., or his grandson

Charles Edward to rebel against George II.; nor as it seems to me, ought these dynastic struggles, little better than family quarrels, to be compared with this monstrous conspiracy against the American Union. These precedents do not prove that it was just and proper for the "disappointed great men" of the cotton growing States to rebel against "the most beneficent government of which history gives us any account," as the Vice President of the Confederacy, in November, 1860, charged them with doing. They do not create a presumption even in favor of the disloyal slaveholders of the South, who, living under a government of which Mr. Jefferson Davis, in the session of 1860-61, said that it was "the best government ever instituted by man, unexceptionably administered, and under which the people have been prosperous beyond comparison with any other people whose career has been recorded in history," rebelled against it because their aspiring politicians, himself among the rest, were in danger of losing their monopoly of its offices. — What would have been thought by an impartial posterity of the American rebellion against George III., if the colonists had at all times been more than equally represented in parliament, and James Otis, and Patrick Henry, and Washington, and Franklin, and the Adamses, and Hancock, and Jefferson, and men of their stamp, had for two generations enjoyed the confidence of the sovereign and administered the government of the empire? What would have been thought of the rebellion against Charles I., if Cromwell, and the men of his school, had been the responsible advisers of that prince from his accession to the throne, and then, on account of a partial change in the ministry, had brought his head to the block, and involved the country in a desolating war, for the sake of dismembering it and establishing a new government south of the Trent? What would have been thought of the Whigs of 1688, if they had themselves composed the cabinet of James II., and been the advisers of the measures and the promoters of the policy which drove him into exile? The Puritans of 1640, and the Whigs of 1688, rebelled against arbitrary power in order to establish constitutional liberty. If they had risen against Charles and James because those monarchs favored equal rights, and in order themselves, "for the first time in the history of the world," to establish an oligarchy "founded on the corner-stone of slavery," they would truly have furnished a precedent for the Rebels of the South, but their cause would not have been sustained by the eloquence of Pym, or of Somers, nor sealed with the blood of Hampden or Russell.

I call the war which the Confederates are waging against the Union a "rebellion," because it is one, and in grave matters it is best to call things by their right names. I speak of it as a crime, because the Constitution of the United States so regards it, and puts "rebellion" on a par with "invasion." The constitution and law not only of England, but of every civilized country, regard them in the same light; or rather they consider the rebel in arms as far worse than the alien enemy. To levy war against the United States is the constitutional definition of treason, and that crime is by every civilized government regarded as the highest which citizen or subject can commit. Not content with the sanctions of human justice, of all the crimes against the law of the land it is singled out for the denunciations of religion. The litanies of every church in Christendom whose ritual embraces that office, as far as I am aware, from the metropolitan cathedrals of Europe to the humblest missionary chapel in the islands of the sea, concur with the Church of England in imploring the Sovereign of the Universe, by the most awful adjurations which the heart of man can conceive or his tongue utter, to deliver us from "sedition, privy conspiracy and rebellion." And reason good; for while a rebellion against tyranny — a rebellion designed, after prostrating arbitrary power, to establish free government on the basis of justice and truth — is an enterprise on which good men and angels may look with complacency, an unprovoked rebellion of ambitious men against a beneficent government, for the purpose — the avowed purpose — of establishing, extending and perpetuating any form of injustice and wrong, is an imitation on earth of that first foul revolt of "the Infernal Serpent," against which the Supreme Majesty of heaven sent forth the armed myriads of his angels, and clothed the right arm of his Son with the three-bolted thunders of omnipotence.

Lord Bacon, in "the true marshalling of the sovereign degrees of honor," assigns the first place to "the *Conditores Imperiorum*, founders of States and Commonwealths;" and, truly, to build up from the discordant elements of our nature, the passions, the interests and the opinions of the individual man, the rivalries of family, clan and tribe, the influences of climate and geographical position, the accidents of peace and war accumulated for ages — to build up from these oftentimes warring elements a well-compacted, prosperous and powerful State, if it were to be accomplished by one effort or in one generation, would require a more than mortal skill. To contribute in some notable degree to this, the greatest work of man, by wise and patriotic counsel in peace and loyal heroism in war, is as high as human merit can well rise, and far more than to any of those to whom Bacon assigns this highest place of honor, whose names can hardly be repeated without a wondering smile — Romulus, Cyrus, Caesar, Ottoman, Ismael — is it due to our Washington, as the founder of the American Union. But if to achieve or help to achieve this greatest work of man's wisdom and virtue gives title to a place among the chief benefactors, rightful heirs of the benedictions, of mankind, by equal reason shall the bold, bad men who seek to undo the noble work, *Eversores Imperiorum*, destroyers of States, who for base and selfish ends rebel against beneficent governments, seek to overturn wise constitutions, to lay powerful republican Unions at the foot of foreign thrones, to bring on civil and foreign war, anarchy at home, dictation abroad, desolation, ruin — by equal reason, I say, yes, a thousandfold stronger, shall they inherit the execrations of the ages.

But to hide the deformity of the crime under the cloak of that sophistry which strives to make the worse appear the better reason, we are told by the leaders of the Rebellion that in our complex system of government the separate States are "sovereigns," and that the central power is only an "agency" established by these sovereigns to manage certain little affairs — such, forsooth, as Peace, War, Army, Navy, Finance, Territory, and Relations with the native tribes — which they could not so conveniently administer themselves. It happens, unfortunately for this theory, that the Federal Constitution (which has been adopted by the people of every State of the Union as much as their own State constitutions have been adopted, and is declared to be paramount to them) nowhere recognizes the States as "sovereigns" — in fact, that, by their names, it does not recognize, them at all; while the authority established by that instrument is recognized, in its text, not as an "agency," but as "the Government of the United States." By that Constitution, moreover, which purports in its preamble to be ordained and established by "the People of the United States," it is expressly provided, that "the members of the State legislatures, and all executive and judicial officers, shall be bound by oath or affirmation to support the Constitution." Now it is a common thing, under all governments, for an agent to be bound by oath to be faithful to his sovereign; but I never heard before of sovereigns being bound by oath to be faithful to their agency.

Certainly I do not deny that the separate States are clothed with sovereign powers for the administration of local affairs. It is one of the most beautiful features of our mixed system of government; but it is equally true, that, in adopting the Federal Constitution, the States abdicated, by express renunciation, all the most important functions of national sovereignty, and, by one comprehensive, self-denying clause, gave up all right to contravene the Constitution of the United States. Specifically, and by enumeration, they renounced all the most important prerogatives of independent States for peace and for war, — the right to keep troops or ships of war in time of peace, or to engage in war unless actually invaded; to enter into compact with another State or a foreign power; to lay any duty on tonnage, or any impost on exports or imports, without the consent of Congress; to enter into any treaty, alliance, or confederation; to grant letters of marquee and reprisal, and to emit bills of credit — while all these powers and many others are expressly vested in the General Government. To ascribe to political communities, thus limited in their jurisdiction — who cannot even establish a post office on their own soil — the character of independent sovereignty, and to reduce a national organization, clothed with all the transcendent powers of government, to the name and condition of an "agency" of the States, proves nothing but the logic of secession is on a par with its loyalty and patriotism.

Oh, but "the reserved rights!" And what of the reserved rights? The tenth amendment of the Constitution, supposed to provide for "reserved rights," is constantly misquoted. By that amendment, "the *powers* not delegated to the United States by the Constitution, nor prohibited by it to the States, are reserved to the States respectively, or to the people." The "powers" reserved must of course be such as could have been, but were not delegated to the United States, — could have been, but were not prohibited to the States; but to speak of the *right* of an *individual* State to secede, as a *power* that could have been, though it was not delegated to the *United States*, is simple nonsense.

But waiving this obvious absurdity, can it need a serious argument to prove that there can be no State right to enter into a new confederation reserved under a constitution which expressly prohibits a State to "enter into any treaty, alliance, or confederation," or any "agreement or compact with another State or a foreign power?" To say that the State may, by enacting the preliminary farce of secession, acquire the right to do the prohibited things — to say, for instance, that though the States, in forming the Constitution, delegated to the United States and prohibited to themselves the power of declaring war, there was by implication reserved to each State the right of seceding and then declaring war; that, though they expressly prohibited to the States and delegated to the United States the entire treaty-making power, they reserved by implication (for and express reservation is not pretended) to the individual States, to Florida, for instance, the right to secede, and then to make a treaty with Spain retroceding that Spanish colony, and thus surrendering to a foreign power the key to the Gulf of Mexico, — to maintain propositions like these, with whatever affected seriousness it is done, appears to me egregious trifling.

Pardon me, my friends, for dwelling on these wretched sophistries. But it is these which conducted the armed hosts of rebellion to your doors on the terrible and glorious days of July, and which have brought upon the whole land the scourge of an aggressive and wicked war — a war which can have no other termination compatible with the permanent safety and welfare of the country but the complete destruction of the military power of the enemy. I have, on other occasions, attempted to show that to yield to his demands and acknowledge his independence, thus resolving the Union at once into two hostile governments, with a certainty of further disintegration, would annihilate the strength and the influence of the country as a member of the family of nations; afford to foreign powers the opportunity and the temptation for humiliating and disastrous interference in our affairs; wrest from the Middle and Western States some of their great natural outlets to the sea and of their most important lines of internal communication; deprive the commerce and navigation of the country of two-thirds of our sea coast and of the fortresses which protect it; not only so, but would enable each individual State — some of them with a white population equal to a good sized Northern county — or rather the dominant party in each State, to cede its territory, its harbors, its fortresses, the mouths of its rivers, to any foreign power. It cannot be that the people of the loyal States — that twenty-two millions of brave and prosperous freemen — will, for the temptation of a brief truce in an eternal border war, consent to this hideous national suicide.

Do not think that I exaggerate the consequences of yielding to the demands of the leaders of the rebellion. I understate them. They require of us not only all the sacrifices I have named, not only the cession to them, a foreign and hostile power, of all the territory of the United States at present occupied by the Rebel forces, but the abandonment to them of the vast regions we have rescued from their grasp — of Maryland, of a part of Eastern Virginia and the whole of Western Virginia; the sea coast of North and South Carolina, Georgia, and Florida; Kentucky, Tennessee, and Missouri; Arkansas, and the larger portion of Mississippi, Louisiana, and Texas — in most of which, with the exception of lawless guerrillas, there is not a Rebel in arms, in all of which the great majority of the people are loyal to the Union. We must give back, too, the helpless colored population, thousands of whom are perilling their lives in the ranks of our armies, to a bondage rendered tenfold more bitter by the momentary enjoyment of freedom. Finally, we must surrender every man in the Southern country, white or black, who has moved a finger or spoken a word for the restoration of the Union, to a reign of terror as remorseless as that of Robespierre, which has been the chief instrument by which the Rebellion has been organized and sustained, and which has already filled the prisons of the South with noble men, whose only crime is that they are not the worst of criminals. The South is full of such men. I do not believe there has been a day since the election of President Lincoln, when, if an ordinance of secession could have been fairly submitted, after a free discussion, to the mass of the people in any single Southern State, a majority of ballots would have been given in its favor. No, not in South Carolina. It is not possible that the majority of the people, even of that State, if permitted, without fear or favor, to give a ballot on the question, would have abandoned a leader like Petigru, and all the memories of the Gadsdens, the Rutledges, and the Cotesworth Pinckneys of the revolutionary and constitutional age, to follow the agitators of the present day.

Nor must we be deterred from the vigorous prosecution of the war by the suggestion, continually thrown out by the Rebels and those who sympathize with them, that, however it might have been at an earlier stage, there has been engendered by the operations of the war a state of exasperation and bitterness which, independent of all reference to the original nature of the matters in controversy, will forever prevent the restoration of the Union, and the return of harmony between the two great sections of the country. This opinion I take to be entirely without foundation.

No man can deplore more than I do the miseries of every kind unavoidably incident of war. Who could stand on this spot and call to mind the scenes of the first days of July with any other feeling? A sad foreboding of what would ensue, if war should break out between North and South, has haunted me through life, and led me, perhaps too long, to tread in the path of hopeless compromise, in the fond endeavor to conciliate those who were predetermined not to be conciliated. But it is not true, as is pretended by the Rebels and their sympathizers, that the war has been carried on by the United States without entire regard to those temperaments which are enjoined by the law of nations, by our modern civilization, and by the spirit of Christianity. It would be quite easy to point out, in the recent military history of the leading European powers, acts of violence and cruelty, in the prosecution of their wars, to which no parallel can be found among us. In fact, when we consider the peculiar bitterness with which civil wars are almost invariably waged, we may justly boast of the manner in which the United States have carried on the contest. It is of course impossible to prevent the lawless acts of stragglers and deserters, or the occasional unwarrantable proceedings of subordinates on distant stations; but I do not believe there is, in all history, the record of a civil war of such gigantic dimensions where so little has been done in the spirit of vindictiveness as in this war, by the Government and commanders of the United States; and this notwithstanding the provocation given by the Rebel Government by assuming the responsibility of wretches like Quantrell, refusing quarter to colored troops and scourging and selling into slavery free colored men from the North who fall into their hands, by covering the sea with pirates, refusing a just exchange of prisoners, while they crowd their armies with paroled prisoners not exchanged, and starving prisoners of war to death.

In the next place, if there are any present who believe that, in addition to the effect of the military operations of the war, the confiscation acts and emancipation proclamations have embittered the Rebels beyond the possibility of reconciliation, I would request them to reflect that the tone of the Rebel leaders and Rebel press was just as bitter in the first months of the war, nay, before a gun was fired, as it is now. There were speeches made in Congress in the very last session before the outbreak of the Rebellion, so ferocious as to show that their authors were under the influence of a real frenzy. At the present day, if there is any discrimination made by the Confederate press in the affected scorn, hatred and contumely with which every shade of opinion and sentiment in the loyal States is treated, the bitterest contempt is bestowed upon those at the North who still speak the language of compromise, and who comdemn those measures of the administration which are alleged to have rendered the return of peace hopeless.

No, my friends, that gracious Providence which overrules all things for the best, "from seeming evil still educing good," has so constituted our natures that the violent excitement of the passions in one direction is generally followed by a reaction in an opposite direction, and the sooner for the violence. If it were not so — if injuries inflicted and retaliated of necessity led to new retaliations, with forever accumulating compound interest of revenge, then the world, thousands of years ago, would have been turned into an earthly hell, and the nations of the earth would have been resolved into clans of furies and demons, each forever warring with his neighbor. But it is not so; all history teaches a different lesson. The Wars of the Roses in England lasted an entire generation, from the battle of St. Albans in 1455 to that of Bosworth Field in 1485. Speaking of the former, Hume says: "This was the first blood spilt in that fatal quarrel, which was not finished in less than a course of thirty years; which was signalized by twelve pitched battles; which opened a scene of extraordinary fierceness and cruelty; is computed to have cost the lives of eighty princes of the blood; and almost entirely annihilated the ancient nobility of England. The strong attachments which, at that time, men of the same kindred bore to each other, and the vindictive spirit which was considered a point of honor, rendered the great families implacable in their resentments, and widened every moment the breach between the parties." Such was the state of things in England under which an entire generation grew up; but when Henry VII., in whom the titles of the two Houses were united, went up to London after the battle of Bosworth Field, to mount the throne, he was everywhere received with joyous acclamations, "as one ordained and sent from heaven to put an end to the dissensions" which had so long afflicted the country.

The great rebellion in England of the seventeenth century, after long and angry premonitions, may be said to have begun with the calling of the Long Parliament in 1640, and to have ended with the return of Charles II. in 1660 — twenty years of discord, conflict and civil war; of confiscation, plunder, havoc; a proud hereditary peerage trampled in the dust; a national church overturned, its clergy beggared, its most eminent prelate put to death; a military despotism established on the ruins of a monarchy which had subsisted seven hundred years, and the legitimate sovereign brought to the block; the great families which adhered to the king proscribed, impoverished, ruined; prisoners of war — a fate worse than starvation in Libby — sold to slavery in the West Indies; in a word, everything that can embitter and madden contending factions. Such was the state of things for twenty years; and yet, by no gentle transition, but suddenly, and "when the restoration of affairs appeared most hopeless," the son of the beheaded sovereign was brought back to his father's blood-stained throne, with such "unexpressible and universal joy" as led the merry monarch to exclaim, "he doubted it had been his own fault he had been absent so long, for he saw nobody who did not protest he had ever wished for his return." "In this wonderful manner," says Clarendon, "and with this incredible expedition did God put an end to a rebellion that had raged near twenty years, and had been carried on with all the horrid circumstances of murder, devastation and parricide that fire and sword, in the hands of the most wicked men in the world," (it is a royalist that is speaking,) "could be instruments of, almost to the desolation of two kingdoms, and the exceeding defacing and deforming of the third . . . . By these remarkable steps did the merciful hand of God, in this short space of time, not only bind up and heal all those wounds, but even made the scar as undiscernible as, in respect of the deepness, was possible, which was a glorious addition to the deliverance."

In Germany, the wars of the Reformation and of Charles V. in the sixteenth century, the Thirty Years' war in the seventeenth century, the Seven Years' war in the eighteenth century, not to speak of other less celebrated contests, entailed upon that country all the miseries of intestine strife for more than three centuries. At the close of the last named war — which was the shortest of all, and waged in the most civilized age — "an officer," says Archenholz, "rode through seven villages in Hesse, and found in them but one human being." More than three hundred principalities, comprehended in the Empire, fermented with the fierce passions of proud and petty States; at the commencement of this period the castles of robber counts frowned upon every hilltop; a dreadful secret tribunal, whose seat no one knew, whose power none could escape, froze the hearts of men with terror throughout the land; religious hatred mingled its bitter poison in the seething caldron of provincial animosity; but of all these deadly enmities between the States of Germany scarcely the memory remains. There are controversies in that country, at the present day, but they grow mainly out of the rivalry of the two leading powers. There is no country in the world in which the sentiment of national brotherhood is stronger.

In Italy, on the breaking up of the Roman Empire, society might be said to be resolved into its original elements — into hostile atoms, whose only movement was that of mutual repulsion. Ruthless barbarians had destroyed the old organizations, and covered the land with a merciless feudalism. As the new civilization grew up, under the wing of the church, the noble families and the walled towns fell madly into conflict with each other the secular feud of Pope and Emperor scourged the land; province against province, city against city, street against street, waged remorseless war with each other from father to son, till Dante was able to fill his imaginery hell with the real demons of Italian history. So ferocious had the factions become, that the great poet-exile himself, the glory of his native city and of this native language, was, by a decree of the municipality, condemned to be burned alive if found in the city of Florence. But these deadly feuds and hatreds yielded to political influences, as the hostile cities were grouped into States under stable governments; the lingering traditions of the ancient animosities gradually died away, and now Tuscan and Lombard, Sardinian and Neapolitan, as if to shame the degenerate sons of America, are joining in one cry for a united Italy.

In France, not back to the civil wars of the League in the sixteenth century and of the Fronde in the seventeenth; not to speak of the dreadful scenes throughout the kingdom, which followed the revocation of the edict of Nantes; we have, in the great revolution which commenced at the close of the last century, seen the blood-hounds of civil strife let loose as rarely before in the history of the world. The reign of terror established at Paris stretched its bloody Briarean arms to every city and village in the land, and if the most deadly feuds which ever divided a people had the power to cause permanent alienation and hatred, this surely was the occasion. But far otherwise the fact. In seven years from the fall of Robespierre, the strong arm of the youthful conqueror brought order out of this chaos of crime and woe; Jacobins whose hands were scarcely cleansed from the best blood of France met the returning emigrants, whose estates they had confiscated and whose kindred they had dragged to the guillotine, in the Imperial antechambers; and when, after another turn of the wheel of fortune, Louis XVIII. was restored to his throne, he took the regicide Fouche, who had voted for his brother's death, to his cabinet and confidence.

The people of loyal America will never ask you, sir, to take to your confidence or admit again to a share in the government the hard-hearted men whose cruel lust of power has brought this desolating war upon the land, but there is no personal bitterness felt even against them. They may live, if they can bear to live after wantonly causing the death of so many thousands of their fellowmen; they may live in safe obscurity beneath the shelter of the government they have sought to overthrow, or they may fly to the protection of the governments of Europe — some of them are already there, seeking, happily in vain, to obtain the aid of foreign powers in furtherance of their own treason. There let them stay. The humblest dead soldier, that lies cold and stiff in his grave before us, is an object of envy beneath the clods that cover him, in comparison with the living man, I care not with what trumpery credentials he may be furnished, who is willing to grovel at the foot of a foreign throne for assistance in compassing the ruin of his country.

But the hour is coming and now is, when the power of the leaders of the Rebellion to delude and inflame must cease. There is no bitterness on the part of the masses. The people of the South are not going to wage an eternal war, for the wretched pretexts by which this Rebellion is sought to be justified. The bonds that unite us as one people — a substantial community of origin, language, belief, and law, (the four great ties that hold the societies of men together;) common national and political interests; a common history; a common pride in a glorious ancestry; a common interest in this great heritage of blessings; the very geographical features of the country; the mighty rivers that cross the lines of climate and thus facilitate the interchange of natural and industrial products, while the wonder-working arm of the engineer has levelled the mountain-walls which separate the East and West, compelling your own Alleghanies, my Maryland and Pennsylvania friends, to open wide their everlasting doors to the chariot-wheels of traffic and travel; these bonds of union are of perennial force and energy, while the causes of alienation are imaginary, factitious, and transient. The heart of the people, North and South, is for the Union. Indications, too plain to be mistaken, announce the fact, both in the East and the West of the States in rebellion. In North Carolina and Arkansas the fatal charm at length is broken. At Raleigh and Little Rock the lips of honest and brave men are unsealed, and an independent press is unlimbering its artillery. When its rifled cannon shall begin to roar, the hosts of treasonable sophistry — the mad delusions of the day — will fly like the Rebel army through the passes of yonder mountain. The wary masses of the people are yearning to see the dear old flag again floating upon their capitols, and they sigh for the return of the peace, prosperity, and happiness, which they enjoyed under a government whose power was felt only in its blessings.

And now, friends, fellow-citizens of Gettysburg and Pennsylvania, and you from remoter States, let me again, as we part, invoke your benediction on these honored graves. You feel, though the occasion is mournful, that it is good to be here. You feel that it was greatly auspicious for the cause of the country, that the men of the East and the men of the West, the men of nineteen sister States, stood side by side, on the perilous ridges of the battle. You now feel it a new bond of union, that they shall lie side by side, till the clarion, louder than that which marshalled them to the combat, shall awake their slumbers. God bless the Union; it is dearer to us for the blood of brave men which has been shed in its defence. The spots on which they stood and fell; these pleasant heights; the fertile plain beneath them; the thriving village whose streets so lately rang with the strange din of war; the fields beyond the ridge, where the noble Reynolds held the advancing foe at bay, and, while he gave up his own life, assured by his forethought and self-sacrifice the triumph of the two succeeding days; the little streams which wind through the hills, in whose banks in after-times the wondering ploughman will turn up, with the rude weapons of savage warfare, the fearful missiles of modern artillery; Seminary Ridge, the Peach Orchard, Cemetery, Culp, and Wolf Hill, Round Top, Little Round Top, humble names, henceforward dear and famous — no lapse of time, no distance of space, shall cause you to be forgotten. "The whole earth," said Pericles, as he stood over the remains of his fellow-citizens, who had fallen in the first year of the Peloponnesian war, "the whole earth is the sepulchre of illustrious men." All time, he might have added, is the millennium of their glory. Surely I would do no injustice to the other noble achievements of the war, which have reflected such honor on both arms of the service, and have entitled the armies and the navy of the United States, their officers and men, to the warmest thanks and the richest rewards which a grateful people can pay. But they, I am sure, will join us in saying, as we bid farewell to the dust of these martyr-heroes, that wheresoever throughout the civilized world the accounts of this great warfare are read, and down to the latest period of recorded time, in the glorious annals of our common country there will be no brighter page than that which relates THE BATTLES OF GETTYSBURG.

APPENDIX E

PRESIDENT LINCOLN'S "DEDICATORY ADDRESS" (NEWSMAN JOSEPH L. GILBERT'S VERSION)

(The text below is the handiwork of Joseph L. Gilbert, the Associated Press reporter renowned for his shorthand skills. He had a place on the platform from which Lincoln spoke. After the program ended, Gilbert asked President Lincoln for his two-page manuscript so he could "correct" his text. After Gilbert made his "corrections" he returned the manuscript to the president. Note that the word "Applause" appears five times within Gilbert's text which appeared in many Northern newspapers.)

Fourscore and seven years ago our fathers brought forth upon this continent a new nation, conceived in Liberty, and dedicated to the proposition that all men are created equal. [Applause]

Now we are engaged in a great civil war, testing whether that nation, or any nation so conceived and so dedicated, can long endure. We are met on a great battle-field of that war. We are met to dedicate a portion of it as the final-resting place of those who here gave their lives that that nation might live. It is altogether fitting and proper that we should do this.

But in a larger sense we cannot dedicate, we cannot consecrate, we cannot hallow this ground. The brave men, living and dead, who struggled here, have consecrated it far above our power to add or detract. [Applause] The world will little note nor long remember what we say here, but it can never forget what they did here. [Applause] It is for us, the living, rather to be dedicated here to the unfinished work that they have thus far so nobly carried on. [Applause] It is rather for us to be here dedicated to the great task remaining before us, — that from these honored dead we take increased devotion to the cause for which they here gave the last full measure of devotion, — that we here highly resolve that the dead shall not have died in vain [Applause], that the nation shall, under God, have a new birth of freedom, and that the government of the people, by the people, and for the people, shall not perish from the earth. [Long continued applause]

REV. HENRY L. BAUGHER'S "BENEDICTION"

Rev. Henry L. Baugher, D.D.
President of Pennsylvania College, Gettysburg

O Thou King of kings and Lord of lords, God of the nations of the earth, who by Thy kind providence has permitted us to engage in these solemn services, grant us Thy blessing.

Bless this consecrated ground, and these holy graves. Bless the President of these United States, and his Cabinet. Bless the Governors and the representatives of the States here assembled with all needed grace to conduct the affairs committed into their hands, to the glory of Thy name, and the greatest good of the people.

May this great nation be delivered from treason and rebellion at home, and from the power of enemies abroad. And now may the grace of our Lord Jesus Christ, the love of God our Heavenly Father, and the fellowship of the Hold Ghost, be with you all. *Amen.*

INTRODUCTION

[1]Earl Schenck Miers, ed., *Lincoln Day By Day: A Chronology, 1809-1865* (Washington: Lincoln Sesquicentennial Commission, 1960), 220-22.

[2]Louis A. Warren, *Lincoln's Gettysburg Declaration: "A New Birth of Freedom"* (Fort Wayne: Lincoln National Life Foundation, 1964), 119.

[3]Warren, 54.

[4]Letter, David Wills to Abraham Lincoln, November 2, 1863, Robert Todd Papers, Library of Congress. Quoted in Warren, 45.

[5]Quoted in William E. Barton, *Lincoln at Gettysburg* (Indianapolis: Bobbs-Merrill, 1930), 114-5.

[6]Quoted in Warren, 145.

[7]William Roscoe Thayer, *The Life and Letters of John Hay*, Vol. 1, 4th ed. (Boston: Houghton-Mifflin, 1908), 206.

[8]Warren, 124-5.

[9]Joseph H. Barrett, *The Life of Abraham Lincoln* (New York: 1865), 458.

[10]First quotation found in Warren, 145. Second quotation in Josiah G. Holland, *The Life of Abraham Lincoln* (Springfield: 1865), 423.

[11]All quotations found in Mary Raymond Shipman Andrews, *The Perfect Tribute* (New York: Charles Scribner's Sons, 1906), 3-17.

[12]*Lincoln Lore*, No. 408 (February 1, 1937), 1. The book was republished as a paperback booklet in 1987, 1988, and 1990 under the title *Lincoln Got No Applause at Gettysburg: "The Perfect Tribute,"* by Ads Press, P.O. Box 5837, Springfield, Illinois, 62705.

[13]Warren, 62.

[14]Warren, 63.

[15]Metro Goldwyn Mayer was the first to produce a film based on the story with a one-reel motion picture in 1935, starring Charles (Chic) Sales as Lincoln. Jason Robards played Lincoln in the made-for-television movie, "The Perfect Tribute," which aired over ABC on April 21, 1991.

[16]Henry Sweetser Burrage, *Gettysburg and Lincoln* (New York: G. P. Putnam's Sons, 1906), vi.

[17]Orton H. Carmichael, *Lincoln's Gettysburg Address* (New York: The Abingdon Press, 1917), 9-10, 111.

[18]See Paul M. Angle, *A Shelf of Lincoln Books* (New Brunswick: Rutger's U.P., 1946), 94-5 and Benjamin P. Thomas, *Portrait For Posterity: Lincoln and His Biographers* (New Brunswick: Rutger's U.P., 1947), 242.

[19]Mark E. Neely, Jr., *The Abraham Lincoln Encyclopedia* (New York: McGraw-Hill, 1982), 20.

[20]Barton, 10.

[21]Thomas, 242.

[22]*Ibid.*

[23]*Ibid.*

[24]Arnold Gates, review of *Lincoln's Gettysburg Declaration: "A New Birth of Freedom,"* by Louis A. Warren, *Lincoln Lore*, No. 1519 (September, 1964): 1.

[25]Warren served as editor of *Lincoln Lore* from April 15, 1929 (issue 1) until June 25, 1956 (issue 1421). The issues he committed to the Gettysburg Address are numbers 130, 182, 240, 293, 343, 396, 408, 493, 562, 762, 781, 894, 911, 919, 924, 1232, 1284, 1400. Many other issues refer to the address. The two booklets he authored are *Little Known Facts About the Gettysburg Address* (Fort Wayne: Lincoln National Life Insurance Co., 1938) and *Abraham Lincoln's Gettysburg Address: An Evaluation for America's New Dedication Day* (New York: Charles E. Merrill Co.,

1946). After sixty-one years and four different official names, the research center changed its name again to The Lincoln Museum in 1990.

[26]Philip B. Kunhardt, Jr., *A New Birth of Freedom: Lincoln at Gettysburg* (Boston: Little, Brown and Co., 1983), vii.

[27]William Miller, review of *A New Birth of Freedom: Lincoln at Gettysburg*, by Philip B. Kunhardt, Jr., *Lincoln Herald*, Vol. 87, No. 3 (Fall, 1985): 104.

[28]Harold Holzer, review of *Lincoln at Gettysburg: The Words That Remade America*, by Garry Wills, *Chicago Tribune*, May 31, 1992, section 14: 9.

[29]*Ibid.*

[30]Steven K. Rogstad interviews Frank L. Klement, audio cassette, Milwaukee, Wisconsin, May 15, 1988 (Cassette in possession of author).

[31]*Ibid.*

[32]*Lincoln Herald*, Vol. 94, No. 1 (Spring, 1992): 10.

[33]Letter, Michael Pinkston to Frank L. Klement, October 25, 1984 (original in possession of Frank L. Klement).

[34]Mark E. Neely, Jr., *The Fate of Liberty: Abraham Lincoln and Civil Liberties* (New York: Oxford U.P., 1991), 229.

[35]David C. Mearns and Lloyd A. Dunlap, *Long Remembered: The Gettysburg Address in Facsimile* (Washington: Library of Congress, 1963), 1.

[36]William Jennings Bryan quoted in Louis A. Warren, *A Man for the Ages: Tributes to Abraham Lincoln* (Fort Wayne: Louis A. Warren Lincoln Library and Museum, 1978), 37.

CHAPTER I

[1]Harrisburg *Daily Telegraph*, July 9, 1863.

[2]*Ibid.*

[3]Letter of Henry W. Bellows (n.d.) excerpted in (Madison) *Wisconsin Daily Patriot*, July 22, 1863.

[4](Madison) *Wisconsin Daily Patriot*, July 14, 1863.

[5](Gettysburg) *Adams County Sentinel,* August 25, 1863.

[6]Ellen Meade to "My dear Mrs. Dean," August 12, 1863, Lucius Fairchild Papers, State Historical Society of Wisconsin (Madison).

[7]Harrisburg *Daily Telegraph*, July 10, 1863.

[8]After graduating from Pennsylvania College in 1851, Wills read law in the office of Thaddeus Stevens in Lancaster. After receiving his certificate to practice law, he moved to Gettysburg to hang up his shingle and become active in political, educational, and social circles.

[9]*Adams County Sentinel*, July 28, 1863.

[10]*Ibid.*

[11]Andrew B. Cross, head of the Christian Commission of Pennsylvania, in an appeal entitled "To the Patriotic of the Land — A Cemetery for those who Fell at Gettysburg," published in Harrisburg *Daily Telegraph*, July 29, 1863.

[12]*Ibid.*

[13]Wills to Curtin, July 24, 1863, Curtin Letterbooks, Executive Correspondence, 1861-1865, Pennsylvania State Archives (Harrisburg). Although Louis A. Warren, *Lincoln's Gettysburg Declaration: "A New Birth of Freedom"* (Fort Wayne, Ind., 1964) is considered the last word regarding the dedicatory program and Lincoln's address, the author failed to use the governors' correspondence in the Pennsylvania State Archives.

[14]David Wills, report, dated March 21, 1864, published in *Report of the Select Committee Relative to the Soldiers' National Cemetery, Together with the Accompany Documents, as Reported to the House of Representatives of the Commonwealth of Pennsylvania,* March 31, 1864 (Harrisburg: Singerly & Myers, State Printers, 1864), 7.

[15]Harrisburg *Daily Telegraph,* July 29, 1863. It could be added that the *Daily Telegraph* of November 3, 1863, erroneously credited Governor Curtin with "the idea of establishing a National Cemetery at Gettysburg."

[16]*Adams County Sentinel,* August 25, 1863.

[17]Wills, report of March 21, 1864, in *Report of the Select Committee . . . ,* 7.

[18]*Ibid.* Also see David McConaughy's card/proposition, in Harrisburg *Daily Telegraph,* September 7, 1863. For a time both Wills and McConaughy were trying to buy the same plots of land, confusing the sellers and the public and driving up the price.

[19]Wills to Curtin, July 31, 1863, Curtin Letterbooks, Executive Correspondence, 1861-1865. The author expresses his indebtedness to Miss Patricia Hosey, who as a graduate student and a research assistant, perused the Pennsylvania State Archives and took invaluable notes from the Curtin Letterbooks.

[20]Wills to Edward G. Salomon, August 1, 1863, Telegrams, 1861-1865, Executive Department (Administration), Archives Section, State Historical Society of Wisconsin; Wills to David Tod, August 1, 1863, David Tod Papers, Ohio Historical Society; Wills to Austin Blair, August 1, 1863, Austin Blair Papers, Burton Historical Collection, Detroit Public Library.

[21]Wills, report of March 21, 1864, in *Report of the Select Committee . . . ,* 5-9.

[22]Wills to Curtin, August 11, 1863, Curtin Letterbooks, Executive Correspondence, 1861-1865.

[23]"Specifications," dated October 15, 1863, published in *Revised Report of the Select Committee . . . ,* 14-15.

[24]Wills, report of March 21, 1864, in *Report of the Select Committee . . . ,* 8.

[25]Circular letter, signed by Wills as agent for Governor Curtin and dated August 12, 1863, in David Tod Papers.

[26]Wills to Tod, August 12, 1863, Tod Papers.

[27]Wills to "His Excellency, A. G. Curtin," August 17, 1863, published in *Report of the Select Committee . . . ,* 67-68.

[28]*Ibid.*

[29]Report of William Saunders in *Revised Report of the Select Committee Relative to the Soldiers' National Cemetery, Together with the Accompany Documents, as Reported to the House of Representatives of the Commonwealth of Pennsylvania,* (Harrisburg: Singerly & Myers, State Printers, 1865), 37-38.

[30]Curtin to Wills, August 31, 1863, published in Gettysburg *Compiler,* September 14, 1863.

[31]*Ibid.*

[32]Gettysburg *Compiler,* November 2, 1863.

[33]Wills to "Hon. Edward Everett," September 23, 1863, published in *Report of the Select Committee . . . ,* 68-69.

[34]Wills to David Tod, September 15, 1863, mentioned in Tod to Wills letter of September 18, 1863, published in *Documents Accompanying the Governor's Message of January, 1864* (Columbus, 1864), 160.

[35]Everett to "My dear Sir" [Wills], September 26, 1863, in *Report of the Select Committee . . . ,* 69-70.

[36]Harrisburg *Daily Telegraph,* October 9, 1863.

[37]Gettysburg *Compiler,* October 12, 1863; Wills to Austin Blair, October 13, 1863, Blair Papers; Wills to Tod, October 13, 1863, Tod Papers.

[38]"Specifications," dated October 15, 1863, published in *Revised Report of the Select Committee . . . ,* 14-15.

[39]Report, Wills to Curtin, March 21, 1864, published *Report of the Select Committee . . . ,* 8-9. In his letter of October 23 to Curtin, Wills spelled the name Beisecker. In his report of March 21, 1864, he spelled it Biesecker.

[40]*Ibid.*

[41]*Adams County Sentinel*, October 27, 1863. Robert G. Harper, editor of the *Sentinel*, lived next door to Wills.

[42]Wills to Curtin, October 23, 1863, Curtin Letterbooks, Executive Correspondence, 1861-1865.

[43]*Ibid.* Wills's first contact with Lincoln seems to have been through Ward H. Lamon, U.S. Marshal for the District of Columbia and onetime Lincoln's law partner. One of the myths surrounding the dedication ceremonies is that the invitation to Lincoln was an eleventh hour affair.

[44]Gettysburg *Compiler*, October 19, 1863.

[45]*Ibid.*

[46]*Ibid.*

[47]Daniel W. Brown to David Tod, October 28, 1863, Tod Papers.

[48]*Ibid.*

[49]Wills to Lincoln, November 2, 1863, Robert Todd Lincoln Papers, Library of Congress. It should be pointed out that Wills invited William H. Seward, Secretary of State, to give the dedicatory remarks if Lincoln could not attend; see Wills to Seward, November 14, 1863, Gideon Welles Papers, Library of Congress. As early as November 9, 1863, Lincoln wrote to his former law partner, Stephen T. Logan, suggesting meeting him in Gettysburg at "the occasion of dedicating the Cemetery" — an indication that Lincoln planned to attend the ceremonies; see Lincoln to "Dear Judge" [Logan], November 9, 1863, published in Roy P. Basler, Marion D. Pratt and Lloyd A. Dunlap, eds. *The Collected Works of Abraham Lincoln* (9 vols., New Brunswick, N.J., 1953), VII, 7.

[50]Wills to Lincoln, November 2, 1863, Robert Todd Lincoln Papers.

[51]Wills to Curtin, November 7, 1863, published in the *Adams County Sentinel*, November 10, 1863.

[52]*Adams County Sentinel*, November 17, 1863.

[53]*Ibid.*

[54]Meade to Wills, November 13, 1863, and Scott to Wills, November 19, 1863, both published in *Report of the Select Committee . . . ,* 70-71.

[55]Stewart to Wills, November 21, 1863, *ibid.,* 71.

[56]Chase to Wills, November 16, 1863, *ibid.*

[57]Gettysburg *Compiler*, July 20, November 23, 1863.

[58]The best secondary accounts of Lincoln's and Everett's stay in Gettysburg are in Louis A. Warren, *Lincoln's Gettysburg Declaration* and David C. Mearns and Lloyd A. Dunlap, *Long Remembered: Notes and Comments on the Preparation of the Address* (Washington, D.C., 1963).

[59]New York *Daily Tribune*, November 20, 1863; Philadelphia *Inquirer*, November 21, 1863.

[60]David Wills to John G. Nicolay (typewritten enclosure), dated January 19, 1894, published in *Lincoln Lore*, No. 1437. Seward was a guest of Robert G. Harper, Wills's neighbor who edited/published the *Adams County Sentinel*.

[61]Tyler Dennett, ed., *Lincoln and the Civil War in the Diaries and Letters of John Hay* (New York, 1938), 199-120.

[62]Washington (D.C.) *Daily Morning Chronicle*, November 20, 1863.

[63]Gettysburg *Compiler*, November 23, 1863.

[64]The Cincinnati *Daily Commercial*, November 21, 23, 1863, and the Washington *Daily Morning Chronicle*, November 20, 23, 1863, published the most complete reports on the day's program and are indispensable sources.

[65]John Russell Young, *Men and Memories: Personal Reminiscences* (New York, 1901), 71.

[66]Cincinnati *Daily Commercial*, November 21, 1863.

[67](Columbus) *Daily Ohio State Journal*, November 23, 1863.

[68]Washington *Daily Morning Chronicle*, November 21, 1863.

[69]Cincinnati *Daily Commercial*, November 23, 1863.

[70]Boston *Morning Journal*, November 20, 1863.

[71]*Adams County Sentinel*, November 23, 1863.

[72]Gettysburg *Compiler*, November 23, 1863.

[73]Samuel Weaver to William Weaver, November 25, 1863, published in *Civil War Times*, II, 10-11 (November, 1960).

[74]Wills to Tod, December 3, 1863, Tod papers. Also see Tod's letter of December 7 to Wills and Tod's letter of December 12 to Daniel W. Brown and Gordon Lofland (Ohio's two commissioners), in *Documents Accompanying the Governor's Message of January, 1864*, 163-164.

[75]Report, dated March 19, 1864, published in *Report of the Select Committee . . .* , 39-41.

[76]Wills to Yates, December 19, 1863, Richard Yates Papers, Illinois State Historical Library.

[77]Report, Samuel Weaver to David Wills, March 19, 1864, published in *Report of the Select Committee . . .* , 39-41.

[78]Report, Wills to "Committee of the House of Representatives of the Commonwealth of Pennsylvania, on the Soldiers' National Cemetery, at Gettysburg," March 21, 1863, published in *Report of the Select Committee . . .* , 6-9.

CHAPTER II

[1]Ward Lamon, *Recollections of Abraham Lincoln, 1847-1865* (Chicago: A. C. McClurg & Co., 1895), 14-15 (hereafter cited as *RAL*).

[2]Lamon, *RAL*, 14-15.

[3]Lincoln to "Hon. Attorney General" [Edward Bates], April 6, 1861, published in Roy P. Basler, ed. *The Collected Works of Abraham Lincoln*, 9 vols. (New Brunswick, N.J.: Rutgers University Press, 1953), 4:323 (hereafter cited as *CWAL*).

[4]Authorization, signed by Lincoln on August 26, 1862, and Lincoln to French, August 26, 1862, *CWAL* 5:394; Benjamin P. Thomas, *Abraham Lincoln, A Biography* (New York: Alfred A. Knopf, 1952), 299; petition, signed by Van Riswick and eleven others, April 2, 1861, *CWAL* 4:319n; manuscript entitled "The undersigned wish to signify their intention of accompanying Marshal Lamon to Gettysburg tomorrow — leaving this city at the hour named" (undated), Ward H. Lamon Papers, Huntington Library, San Marino, California.

[5]Governor Curtin to Wills, August 31, 1863, published in *Gettysburg Compiler*, September 14, 1863; Wills to Lincoln, November 2, 1863, Robert Todd Lincoln Papers, Library of Congress, Washington, D.C.; Wills to Hon. Edward Everett, September 23, 1863, published in *Report of the Select Committee . . .* , 68-69. Wills's role in the establishment of the cemetery and planning the program is treated at length in Frank L. Klement, " 'These Honored Dead': David Wills and the Soldiers' Cemetery at Gettysburg," *Lincoln Herald* 74 (Fall 1972): 123-35. Wills to Lamon, October 30, 1863, Lamon Papers.

[6]Lincoln to Stephen T. Logan, October 30, 1863, *CWAL* 7:7. Lincoln also suggested to Judge Logan that he come to the Gettysburg ceremonies and bring Mrs. Lamon with him. Lincoln added, "It will be an interesting ceremony, and I shall be very glad to see you." This statement offers evidence that Lincoln had assured Wills that he would attend the ceremonies before receiving the written invitation dated November 2, 1863.

[7]Circular letter, dated November 5, 1863, Lamon Papers.

[8]U.S. marshals' letters declining the invitation were surprisingly numerous and are in the Lamon Papers. The governor of Minnesota was one of several who wrote that Lamon's letter did not reach his desk until the ceremonies were over.

[9] John Dean Caton to Col. Anson Stager, November 15, 1863, Lamon Papers.

[10] Wills to Lamon, November 10, 1863, Lamon Papers; General Stoneman to Col. Andrew J. Alexander, November 10, 1863, Lamon Papers; Maj. Gen. George Cadwallader to Lamon, November 6, 1863, Lamon Papers.

[11] Wills to Lamon, November 10, 1863, Lamon Papers.

[12] *Washington Daily Morning Chronicle*, November 13, 1863; Wills to Governor Curtin, November 7, 1863, published in *Washington Daily Morning Chronicle;* the Lamon-directed order was published in various newspapers. See, for example, the *Washington Daily National Intelligencer*, November 17, 1863.

[13] [Gettysburg] *Adams County Sentinel*, November 16, 1863.

[14] *Washington Daily Morning Chronicle*, November 17, 1863; W. Yates Selleck reminiscences, published in the *Milwaukee Evening Wisconsin*, February 6, 1909. Some of the aides (other than Selleck) whom Lamon recruited included John Hay (an assistant secretary to President Lincoln), Judge Silas Casey, Judge Abarim Olin, Judge George P. Fisher, Judge James Hughes, Dr. L. P. Hanscomb, Henry O. Kent (not Charles Kent as listed), and Benjamin Schnyder.

[15] *Washington Daily Morning Chronicle*, November 17, 1863; updated document, Lamon Papers. Thirty-one names appear on the list, some aides and many friends.

[16] *Washington Daily Morning Chronicle*, November 18, 1863.

[17] *Washington Daily Morning Chronicle*, November 21, 1863. Writing about the platform and the principals, the reporter for the *Chronicle* wrote, "Those who had tickets took their seats upon it."

[18] *Adams County Sentinel*, November 23, 1863; *Washington Daily National Intelligencer*, November 21, 1863; entry of November 18, 1863, "Diary" (microfilm copy), John Hay Papers, Library of Congress; *Gettysburg Compiler*, November 23, 1863.

[19] *Washington Daily Morning Chronicle*, November 21, 1863.

[20] John G. Nicolay, "Lincoln's Gettysburg Address," *Century Magazine* 47 (February 1894): 601.

[21] *Cincinnati Commercial*, November 23, 1863; *Washington Daily Morning Chronicle*, November 21, 1863.

[22] *Washington Daily Morning Chronicle*, November 21, 1863.

[23] *Washington Daily National Intelligencer*, November 21, 1863; *Boston Journal*, November 23, 1863.

[24] *Boston Journal*, November 23, 1863; [Springfield] *Illinois State Journal* (n.d.), quoted in Louis A. Warren, *Lincoln's Gettysburg Declaration: "A New Birth of Freedom"* (Fort Wayne, Ind.: Lincoln National Life Foundation, 1964), 79.

[25] *Washington Daily Morning Chronicle*, November 21, 1863.

[26] No single source lists the ten occupants of the front-row chairs. The information listed here on the ten occupants comes from newspaper accounts, reminiscences, and diaries. One newspaper report indicates that Gov. David Tod of Ohio had a second-row seat.

[27] Selleck, reminiscences, published in the *Milwaukee Evening Wisconsin*, February 6, 1909, lists thirty-nine people who had places on the platform and he adds, "There were a few others on the stand, whose names are not remembered by the writer."

[28] Everett to Wills, November 5, 1863, David Wills Papers, Library of Congress.

[29] General Scott to David Wills, November 13, 1863, published in *Report of the Select Committee . . .* , 71, (hereafter cited as *RSNC*); General Meade to Wills, November 13, 1863, *RSNC*, 70; Salmon P. Chase to Dear Sir [Wills], November 16, 1863, *RSNC*, 72.

[30] French to "Editors of the National Intelligencer," November 21, 1863, published in *Washington Daily National Intelligencer*, November 23, 1863; *Washington Daily Morning Chronicle*, November 21, 1863.

[31]Entry of November 20, 1863, "Diary" (microfilm copy), Hay Papers; *Washington Daily National Intelligencer*, November 21, 1863.

[32]*Washington Daily Morning Chronicle*, November 21, 1863.

[33]*Harper's Weekly*, December 5, 1863; Henry C. Robinson to Gen. George B. McClellan, June 17, 1864, George B. McClellan Papers, Library of Congress.

[34]Impressions of Martin D. Potter, in *Cincinnati Commercial*, November 23, 1863.

[35]*Washington Daily Morning Chronicle*, November 21, 1863.

[36]*Washington Daily Morning Chronicle*, November 21, 1863.

[37]*Washington Daily National Intelligencer*, November 24, 1863.

[38]Selleck, reminiscences, published in the *Milwaukee Evening Wisconsin, February 6, 1909; Cincinnati Commercial*, November 23, 1863.

[39]*Cincinnati Commercial*, November 23, 1863; Columbus *Ohio State Journal*, November 23, 1863; *Washington Daily Morning Chronicle*, November 21, 1863; *Washington Daily National Intelligencer*, November 21, 1863.

[40]*Washington Daily Morning Chronicle*, November 21, 1863. Ohio's special program as well as the state's participation in establishment and dedication of the new Gettysburg cemetery is detailed in Frank L. Klement, "Ohio and the Dedication of the Soldiers' Cemetery at Gettysburg," *Ohio History* 79 (Spring 1970): 76-100.

[41]*Washington Daily Morning Chronicle*, November 21, 1863.

[42]*Adams County Sentinel*, November 23, 1863. A copy of the resolution, in Lamon's own hand, is in the Lamon Papers.

[43]*Washington Daily National Intelligencer*, November 21, 1863; Selleck, reminiscences published in the *Milwaukee Evening Wisconsin*, February 6, 1909.

[44]*Adams County Sentinel*, November 23, 1863; *Gettysburg Compiler*, November 23, 1863.

[45]French to "Editors of the National Intelligencer," November 23, 1863, published in *Washington Daily National Intelligencer*, November 23, 1863.

[46]William B. Webb to Lamon, December 25, 1863, Lamon Papers.

[47]Usher to Lamon, May 20, 1865, published in Lamon, *RAL*, Preface, iii-iv.

[48]Lamon, *RAL*, 171.

[49]Lamon, *RAL*, 172. Lamon's position on the speaker's platform would have put him out of hearing of comments made by Everett and Seward to each other. Furthermore, evidence is conclusive that Everett paid the president an oral compliment after his address and a written one after Lincoln returned to the White House.

[50]Lamon, *RAL*, 173.

[51]The myths are debunked in Frank L. Klement, "Lincoln, the Gettysburg Address, and Two Myths," in *Blue & Gray Magazine* 2 (November 1984): 7-11.

CHAPTER III

[1]Entry of November 22, 1863, "Journal," Benjamin B. French Papers (microfilm), Library of Congress.

[2]Entry of December 7, 1847, *Ibid*.

[3]Benjamin B. French to "My Dear Brother" (Henry F.), November 23, 1851, French Papers.

[4]French to Franklin Pierce, June 30, 1855, French Papers. It is usually said that he was fired for his involvement with the Know-Nothing Party.

[5]Entry of March 1, 1861, "Journal," French Papers.

[6]Entry of March 4, 1861, *Ibid.*

[7]*Ibid.* Each of the thirty-four girls represented one of the thirty-four states, even those that had claimed to have seceded.

[8]French to "My Dear Brother" (Henry F.), April 5, 1861, French Papers.

[9]Entry of April 16, 1861, "Journal," French Papers.

[10]Early in his administration, President Lincoln nominated William S. Wood as Commissioner of Public Buildings and sent his name belatedly to the U.S. Senate on July 15, 1861. The Senate refused to confirm the appointment because Wood's firm printed government securities. Lincoln asked French to take Wood's place in early September, 1861. The President, however, did not send French's name to the Senate until December 15, 1861. French, meanwhile, resigned his position as clerk of the Court of Claims and began his work as Commissioner of Public Buildings.

[11]Entry of September 8, 1861, "Journal," French Papers.

[12]French to "My Dear Judge," October 13, 1863, French Papers. Benjamin B. often addressed a half-brother as "My Dear Judge" in letters, as he held a judicial position in New Hampshire.

[13]Entries of December 8 and 18, 1861, "Journal," French Papers.

[14]French to "My Dear Sister Pamela," December 24, 1861, French Papers.

[15]Entry of March 2, 1862, "Journal," French Papers.

[16]French to "My Dear Judge," March 23, 1862, French Papers.

[17]Entry of June 18, 1862, "Journal," French Papers.

[18]Lincoln to Salmon P. Chase, August 26, 1862, published in Roy P. Basler, editor, *Collected Works of Abraham Lincoln* (9 vols., New Brunswick, NJ 1953), V, 394.

[19]Notation, Lincoln to Secretary of War Edwin M. Stanton, October 14, 1862, *Ibid.*, 463.

[20]French to "My Dear Sister" (Pamela), December 24, 1861, French Papers.

[21]Ward H. Lamon, *Recollections of Abraham Lincoln 1847-1865* (Chicago, 1895), 14-15.

[22]Entry of December 18, 1861, "Journal," French Papers.

[23]Entry of November 6, 1863, "Journal," French Papers.

[24]Ellen Meade to "My Dear Mrs. Dean," August 12, 1863, Lucius Fairchild Papers, State Historical Society of Wisconsin, Madison.

[25]Wills to Gov. Andrew G. Curtin, July 24, 1863, Curtin Letterbooks, Executive Correspondence, 1861-1865, Pennsylvania State Archives, Harrisburg.

[26]Most of the letters exchanged between Wills and Governor Curtin, and other relevant documents, are published in *Revised Report of the Select Committee* . . . . Wills's letter to Lamon of October 30, 1863, is in the Ward H. Lamon Papers, Huntington Library.

[27]Wills's role in the story of the soldiers' cemetery at Gettysburg is related in detail in Frank L. Klement, " 'These Honored Dead': David Wills and the Soldiers' Cemetery at Gettysburg," *Lincoln Herald*, LXXIV (Fall, 1972), 123-135.

[28]Lincoln to Stephen T. Logan, October 30, 1863, published in Basler, *Collected Works*, VII, 7.

[29]Lamon's part in the events on November 19, 1863 is discussed at length in Frank L. Klement, "Ward H. Lamon and the Dedication of the Soldiers' Cemetery at Gettysburg," *Civil war History*, XXXI (December, 1985), 293-308.

[30]Entry of November 14, 1863, "Journal," French Papers; *Washington Daily Morning Chronicle*, November 13-16, 1863; *Washington Daily National Intelligencer*, November 17, 1863.

[31]Entry of November 14, 1863, "Journal," French Papers. Longfellow, Bryant and Whittier are well-known today. Boker is an unknown, but in his day he had received considerable recognition. He was a Philadelphia patrician who was a poet, playwright, and patriot and one of the founders of the Union Club of Philadelphia in 1862. *Poems of War*, published in 1864 enhanced his reputation. After the war he became a renowned diplomat, first in Turkey and then in Russia.

[32] *Ibid.*

[33] Undated document (November 16, 1863, "The undersigned wish to signify their intention of accompanying Marshall [*sic*] Lamon to Gettysburg tomorrow — leaving this city at the hour named"), Lamon Papers. Thirty-one names, all in Lamon's hand, are listed; some were aides, others friends.

[34] Entry of November 22, 1863, "Journal," French Papers.

[35] *Ibid.*

[36] *Ibid.*

[37] *Ibid.*

[38] *Ibid.*; (Gettysburg) *Adams County Sentinel*, November 23, 1863; entry of November 18, 1863, "Diary" (microfilm), John Hay Papers, Library of Congress.

[39] Entry of November 22, 1863, "Journal," French Papers.

[40] *Ibid.*

[41] *Washington Daily Morning Chronicle*, November 21, 1863, John W. Forney, editor of the *Chronicle*, was one of the first to urge Lincoln's re-election in 1864. The term "next president" referred to Lincoln.

[42] *Boston Journal*, November 23, 1863.

[43] Entry of November 22, 1863, "Journal," French Papers.

[44] Quoted in Louis A. Warren, *Lincoln's Gettysburg Declaration: "A New Birth of Freedom"* (Fort Wayne, Indiana, 1964), 79.

[45] See Frank L. Klement, "The Ten Who Sat in the Front Row on the Platform During the Dedication of the Soldiers' Cemetery at Gettysburg," in *Lincoln Herald*, LXXXVIII (Winter, 1985), 106-113.

[46] Entry of November 20, 1863, "Diary," Hay Papers.

[47] Entry of November 22, 1863, "Journal," French Papers.

[48] *Ibid.*; *Washington Daily Morning Chronicle*, November 21, 1863.

[49] Entry of November 22, 1863, "Journal," French Papers.

[50] *Harper's Weekly*, December 3, 1863.

[51] Henry C. Robinson to Gen. George B. McClellan, June 17, 1864, in George B. McClellan Papers, Library of Congress.

[52] This ode or "Consecration Hymn," in French's own hand, is in the November 22, 1863 entry in his "Journal," French Papers. It has been published in such works as Warren, *Lincoln's Gettysburg Declaration*, pages 91-92, and Frank L. Klement, *Seven Who Witnessed Lincoln's Gettysburg Address*, Historical Bulletin No. 40, Lincoln Fellowship of Wisconsin (Madison, 1985), 20.

[53] Entry of November 22, 1863, "Journal," French Papers.

[54] *Cincinnati Commercial*, November 23, 1863; *Washington Daily National Intelligencer*, November 21, 1863.

[55] Entry of November 22, 1863, "Journal," French Papers.

[56] *Adams County Sentinel*, November 23, 1863. A copy of the resolution, in Lamon's own hand, is in the Lamon Papers.

[57] Entry of November 22, 1863, "Journal," French Papers.

[58] *Ibid.*

[59] *Ibid.*

[60] French to "Editors of the *National Intelligencer*," November 21, 1863, published in the *Washington Daily National Intelligencer*, November 23, 1863.

[61] French to "My Dear Brother (Henry F.), January 31, 1864, French Papers.

[62] French to "My Dear Pamela (sister), September 4, 1864, French Papers.

[63] French to "My Dear Sister Pamela," May 21, 1865, French Papers.

CHAPTER IV

[1]The following Ohio organizations, totaling 4327 men, took part in the three-day Battle of Gettysburg: Companies A and C of the First Ohio Cavalry; ten companies of the Sixth Ohio Cavalry; Batteries H, I, K, and L of the First Ohio Light Artillery; and the Fourth, Fifth, Seventh, Eighth, Twenty-Fifth, Twenty-Ninth, Fifty-Fifth, Sixty-First, Sixty-Sixth, Seventy-Third, Seventy- Fifth, Eighty-Second, and One Hundred Seventh Infantry regiments. Only three states, New York, Pennsylvania, and Massachusetts, had more troops at Gettysburg than Ohio. The total number of Federal troops engaged was 88,289, with 23,049 casualties — a ratio considerably lower than Ohio's. *Report of the Gettysburg Memorial Commission* (Columbus, 1887), 63-68; Mark Mayo Boatner, III, *Civil War Dictionary* (New York, 1959), 339.

[2]Daniel Brown to Tod, October 28, 1863, David Tod Papers, Ohio Historical Society. The letter is printed in full in the *Ohio State Journal*, November 2, 1863.

[3]David Wills to Gov. Andrew Curtin, July 24, 1863, in "Curtin Letterbooks," Executive Correspondence, 1861-1865, Pennsylvania State Archives, Harrisburg; "Report of David Wills," *Report of the Select Committee . . .* , 6-9. David Wills was a lawyer, superintendent of schools, and the town's leading Republican at age 32.

[4]Telegram, David Wills to David Tod, August 1, 1863. *Documents Accompanying the Governor's Message of January, 1864* (Columbus, 1864), 158.

[5]Tod to Wills, August 23, 1863, *ibid.*, 160.

[6]Circular letter, signed by David Wills as agent for Governor Andrew Curtin, dated August 12, 1863, *ibid.*, 158-159; Wills to Tod, August 12, 1863, *ibid.*

[7]Tod to Brown, October 25, 1863, *ibid.,* 160.

[8]In all Wills purchased five different lots: two at $225 per acre, one at $200, one for $150, and one for $135. The five lots, totaling seventeen acres, cost $2,475.87. "Report of David Wills," 5-9.

Samuel Weaver reported that he made a list of all items found with the bodies, putting them in a vault before reinterring the bodies. In his "List of Articles," Weaver recorded the following on four of the thirteen Ohio soldiers examined: "Lewis Davis, Company D, 75th Ohio Infantry Regiment, Testament and letters; Asa O. Davis, Company G, 4th Regiment, gun wrench, comb and ring; Thomas Doman, Company K, 25th Regiment, $4 and gold locket; and Serg. John Pierce, Company C, 25th Regiment, pipe." "Report of Samuel Weaver," *Report of the Select Committee . . .* , 15-33, 39-41.

[9]Wills to Curtin, August 17, 1863; Curtin to Wills, August 31, 1863; Wills to Edward Everett, September 23, 1863; Everett to Wills, September 26, 1863, *ibid.*, 181-184; Wills's letter to Tod, September 15, 1863, is noted in the letter of Tod to Wills, September 18, 1863; Tod to Wills, October 25, 1863, *Documents Accompanying the Governor's Message*, 160, 161.

[10]Tod to Daniel Brown, October 25, 1863, *ibid.*, 160; Brown to Tod, October 28, 1863, David Tod Papers. The other three agents were John F. Seymour (brother of Governor Horatio Seymour) of New York, Colonel W. George Geary of Vermont, and Levi Scobey of New Jersey.

[11]*Ibid.*

[12]Circular letter, dated October 25, 1863, signed by Governor Tod, *Documents Accompanying the Governor's Message*, 160.

[13]"Names of Persons Accepting Governor's Invitation to Visit Gettysburg," dated November 19, 1863, in David Tod Papers. The list also included such notables as S. G. Harbaugh (Librarian, State Library), Hon. Levi Sargent (Board of Public Works), Earl Bill (U.S. Marshal), Oviath Cole (State Auditor), John H. Klippart (Corresponding Secretary, State Board of Agriculture), and David Taylor (Treasurer, State Board of Agriculture). Ex-Governor William Dennison attended the ceremonies, but apparently not at state expense. Most of the newspapermen who accepted the free ride were Republicans. They included Martin D. Potter, Cincinnati *Commercial*; L. A. Hine, Cincinnati *Gazette*; W. B. Thrall, Columbus *Express*; Isaac Jackson Allen, *Ohio State Journal* (Columbus); John G. Shryock, Zanesville *Courier*; William D. Bickham, Dayton *Journal*; and George A. Benedict, Cleveland *Herald*. However, John S. Stephenson, editor of the Democratic Cleveland *Plain Dealer*, also accepted.

[14]Cleveland *Herald*, November 19, 1863; Columbus *Daily Express*, November 20, 1863; T. W. Kennard to Tod, November 5, 1863, David Tod Papers. Tod's promise to attend the Gettysburg ceremonies meant he had to forego the "Cleveland Celebration." Congressman-elect James A. Garfield, however, apparently did not attend either event. His correspondence of the period indicates that he was detained at home "for the saddest of reasons" — the illness and death of his four-year-old daughter. Corydon E. Fuller, *Reminiscences of James A. Garfield* (Cincinnati, 1887), 344.

[15]George L. Converse to Tod, October 31, 1863, David Tod Papers.

[16]*Crisis* (Columbus), November 4, 1863; Hillsboro *Weekly Gazette*, November 26, 1863.

[17]*Daily Ohio Statesman* (Columbus), November 20, 1863; Cincinnati *Daily Enquirer*, November 9, 1863; Stark County *Democrat* (Canton), November 18, 1863; no editorial comment appeared in the Circleville *Democrat*, the *Ohio Eagle* (Lancaster), or the Holmes County *Farmer* (Millersburg); Hon. J. H. Putnam to Tod, November 4, 1863, Otto Dressel to Tod, November 2, 1863, and Thomas Beer to Tod, November 10, 1863, David Tod Papers.

[18]George P. Sentin to Tod, November 10, 1863, Martin Welker to Tod, November 7, 1863, Samuel Galloway to Tod, November 12, 1863, and Isaac Jackson Allen to Tod, November 4, 1863, *ibid.*

[19]Brown to Tod, October 28, 1863, *ibid.*

[20]"Report of Samuel Weaver," 162-163.

[21]Tod to Charles Anderson, October 27, 1863, *Documents Accompanying the Governor's Message*, 161-162; Anderson to Tod, November 5, 1863, David Tod Papers.

[22]Tod to Brown, November 6, 1863, *Documents Accompanying the Governor's Message*, 161.

[23]Ward H. Lamon, an old friend from Lincoln's Springfield days and once a law partner, held a patronage post in Washington, being commissioned United States Marshal for the District of Columbia. See form letter, Ward H. Lamon to Tod, November 5, 1863, David Tod Papers.

[24]Wills to Lincoln, November 2, 1863, Robert Todd Lincoln Papers, Library of Congress.

[25]Gideon Welles, *Diary of Gideon Welles, Secretary of the Navy under Lincoln and Johnson*, introduction by John T. Morse, Jr. (Boston, 1911), I, 480; Chase to Wills, November 16, 1863, in Cincinnati *Commercial*, November 23, 1863; Lincoln to Chase, November 17, 1863, Salmon P. Chase Papers, Grosvenor Library, Buffalo, New York.

[26]Lincoln to Stanton [November 17, 1863], in Roy P. Basler, ed., *Collected Works of Abraham Lincoln* (New Brunswick, N.J., 1953), VII, 16.

[27]Springfield *Republic*, November 20, 1863; Cleveland *Herald*, November 20, 1863.

[28]Cincinnati *Commercial*, November 23, 1863; Cleveland *Herald*, November 24, 1863.

[29]"The Ohio Delegation at Gettysburg," *Documents Accompanying the Governor's Message*, 162-163; Springfield *Republic*, November 27, 1863.

[30]*Ibid.*, Cincinnati *Commercial*, November 23, 1863; "Report of David Wills," 8.

[31]Washington *Daily Morning Chronicle*, November 21, 1863; Cincinnati *Commercial*, November 21, 1863.

[32]*Ibid.*, November 23, 1863.

[33]*Ibid.*, Some have mistakenly attributed the Gettysburg dispatches in the *Commercial* to Murat Halstead rather than Martin D. Potter. Halstead was with General Meade's army in November of 1863. Halstead earlier, when the war was going badly, had called Lincoln a blockhead and Grant a drunkard. The proprietor of the *Commercial* used good judgment in sending Potter rather than Halstead to Gettysburg. *Ohio State Journal*, November 23, 1863.

[34]*Ibid.*

[35]*Ibid.*

[36]*Ibid.*

[37]*Ibid.*

[38]Columbus *Express*, November 21, 1863. Democrats had a different view of Schenck. The Stark County *Democrat*, October 28, 1863, stated: "Schenck, the tyrant of Baltimore, will leave the army and take his seat in Congress at the approaching session. A good 'riddance' for the army, but what an infliction on Congress and the decent men in it."

[39]The Cabinet members were Seward, Usher, and Blair. Lincoln's two personal secretaries, flanking him, were John Hay and John Nicolay. William T. Coggeshall, editor of the Springfield *Republic*, had a seat on the platform even though his name was not on the list of those "Accepting Governor's Invitation." Springfield *Republic*, November 30, 1863.

[40]Cincinnati *Commercial*, November 21, 1863; John Russell Young, *Men and Memories: Personal Reminiscences* (New York, 1901), 59. Potter of the *Commercial*, after looking around him, concluded that the platform held a greater number of distinguished men than ever before assembled on one platform in the country. Eight governors, including Horatio Seymour and Tod, occupied seats in the first two rows.

[41]The conversation was reported in the Washington *Morning Chronicle*, November 21, 1863. Could the reference have been to Thomas Corwin, onetime governor, then minister to Mexico?

U.S. Marshal Earl Bill apparently had been added to the marshal corps when he arrived in Gettysburg.

[42]*Ibid*. Seward was Secretary of State, Usher, Secretary of the Interior, and Blair, Postmaster-General.

[43]Cincinnati *Commercial*, November 21, 1863. The band, from Philadelphia, was sponsored by the Union League. Its inclusion in the program was a concession to John W. Forney, ex-Philadelphian and editor of the Washington *Chronicle*.

[44]John Hay, diary entry of November 20, 1863, in Tyler Dennett, ed., *Lincoln and the Civil War in the Letters and Diaries of John Hay* (New York, 1938), 119-120. Coggeshall of the Springfield *Republic*, November 30, 1863, characterized the opening prayer as "eloquent."

[45]Young, *Men and Memories*, 71.

[46]Cincinnati *Commercial*, November 23, 1863. The Union Musical Association of Maryland was listed in some reports as the Baltimore Glee Club.

[47]A myriad of myths about Lincoln's "Gettysburg Address" have developed. All interested in the ceremonies should read Louis A. Warren, *Lincoln's Gettysburg Declaration: "A New Birth of Freedom"* (Fort Wayne, 1964) and *Long Remembered: Facsimiles of the Five Versions of the Gettysburg Address in the Handwriting of Abraham Lincoln*, with Notes and Comments on the Preparation of the Address by David C. Mearns and Lloyd A. Dunlap (Library of Congress, Washington, 1963). See also John Y. Simon, ed., "Reminiscences of Isaac Jackson Allen," *Ohio History*, LXXIII (Autumn 1964), 225-226.

[48]*Ibid*., Washington *Morning Chronicle*, November 21, 1863; *Ohio State Journal*, November 23, 1863.

[49]Washington *Morning Chronicle*, November 21, 1863.

[50]Springfield *Republic*, November 30, 1863.

[51]Cincinnati *Commercial*, November 23, 1863; Columbus *Express*, November 21, 1863.

[52]Cincinnati *Commercial*, November 23, 1863.

[53]During the afternoon reception at the Wills's house, Lincoln had expressed a desire to meet John Burns, the seventy-year-old local constable-cobbler, veteran of the War of 1812, who, when hearing that the rebels were outside of Gettysburg, grabbed his musket and first joined the One Hundred and Fiftieth Pennsylvania volunteers and later fought with the Iron Brigade, trying futilely to hold the line against the overwhelming attack of the Confederate forces west of Gettysburg the first day of battle. David Wills hunted up the gray-haired fellow and introduced him to Lincoln, and the President then took him over to the Presbyterian church to hear Anderson's oration. Bret Harte's ballad, "John Burns of Gettysburg," helps perpetuate some of the myths about Burns. *Ohio State Journal*, November 23, 1863; *Battles and Leaders of the Civil War* (New York, 1884), 276.

[54]Cincinnati *Commercial*, November 23, 1863.

[55]The speech as given in full in *ibid*.; see also Earl W. Wiley, "Colonel Charles Anderson's Gettysburg Address," *Lincoln Herald*, LIV (Fall 1952), 14-21.

[56]Cincinnati *Commercial*, November 23, 1863; *Ohio State Journal*, November 23, 1863; "The Ohio Delegation at Gettysburg," 162. Anderson borrowed heavily from a speech which he had delivered in Xenia on May 2, 1863, and which had subsequently been published as a propaganda document and broadcast over Ohio during the bitter Brough-Vallandigham gubernatorial campaign. Anyone interested in Civil War dissent in general or Vallandigham, see Frank L. Klement, *The Limits of Dissent: Clement L. Vallandigham and the Civil War* (Lexington, 1970).

[57]Cincinnati *Commercial*, November 23, 1863; Simon, "Reminiscences of Isaac Jackson Allen," 226.

[58]Harrisburg *Weekly Press and Union*, November 21, 1863; Cincinnati *Commercial*, November 21, 1863. In the official report, the delay was described as "a little railroad detention." "The Ohio Delegation at Gettysburg," 163.

[59]Cleveland *Plain Dealer*, November 23, 1863.

[60]Cincinnati *Commercial*, November 21, 1863; Cleveland *Plain Dealer*, November 23, 1863.

[61]Columbus *Express*, November 23, 1863.

[62]*Crisis*, November 25, 1863; Circleville *Democrat*, November 27, 1863. No Ohio Democratic editor guessed as badly as the partisan one who edited a Pennsylvania weekly — the Harrisburg *Weekly Patriot and Union*, November 26, 1863 — "We pass over the silly remarks of the President. For the credit of the Nation we are willing that the veil of oblivion shall be dropped over them, or that they shall be no more repeated or thought of."

[63]*Holmes County Farmer* (Millersburg), November 26, 1863. Editor Estill attended the Gettysburg ceremonies, but not as a guest of Tod or the state of Ohio.

[64]Hillsboro *Weekly Gazette*, November 26, 1863.

[65]Cincinnati *Enquirer*, November 28, 1863.

[66]*Ohio State Journal*, November 23, 1863; letter of instruction, Tod to Brown and Lofland, December 12, 1863. *Documents Accompanying the Governor's Message*, 163-164.

[67]*Ibid*. The ceremony for the laying of the cornerstone for the national monument was held July 4, 1865.

[68]"Soldiers' National Cemetery, Harrisburg, December 17, 1863," in *Revised Report made to the Legislature of Pennsylvania, Relative to the Soldiers' National Cemetery, at Gettysburg . . .* (Harrisburg, 1876), 17-20. The commissioners decided to divide the $63,500 by 154, the number of congressmen representing "the interested states" in Congress. This amounted to $414.34 per congressman. Since Ohio had nineteen members in the House of Representatives, the state's quota amounted to $7834.47. Governor Tod had generously suggested that a total of $100,000 for the project would not be too much. In later years Ohio appropriated $40,000 additional for monuments honoring the state's units and generals linked to the Battle of Gettysburg. Ohio erected twenty of the more than one hundred memorials which adorn the field.

[69]"Report of Samuel Weaver," 161. Weaver's report states that the total reburied was 3512; Wills's figure is 3564.

[70]Ohio General Assembly, *Senate Journal, 1864*, p. 26; Ohio General Assembly, *House Journal, 1864*, pp. 37-38. The resolution carried by a vote of 69 to 11 in the lower house and a vote of 30 to 3 in the senate. George L. Converse, Thomas J. Kenny and Meredith R. Willett cast the three dissenting votes in the senate. The Spring Grove Cemetery was established through Tod's initiative as a state project.

[71]The ode, or hymn, of five stanzas composed by Benjamin B. French was published in the Cincinnati *Commercial*, November 23, 1863.

CHAPTER VII

[1]Cincinnati *Daily Commercial*, November 23, 1863.

[2]Wills's role is detailed in Frank L. Klement, " 'These Honored Dead': David Wills and the Soldiers' Cemetery at Gettysburg," *Lincoln Herald*, LXXIV (Fall, 1972), 123-135.

[3]David Wills to Andrew Curtin, July 24, 31, 1863, in Curtin Letterbooks, Executive Correspondence, 1861-1865, Pennsylvania State Archives, Harrisburg; Wills, report, March 21, 1864, published in *Report of the Select Committee . . .* , 6-9.

[4]Wills to Edward Everett, September 23, 1863, and Everett to "My dear Sir" [Wills], September 26, 1863, both published in *Report of the Select Committee*, 59-61; Wills to Abraham Lincoln, November 2, 1863, in Robert Todd Lincoln Papers, Library of Congress; Wills to Ward H. Lamon, October 30, 1863, in Ward H. Lamon Papers, Huntington Library, San Marino, California.

[5](Gettysburg) *Adams County Sentinel*, November 24, 1863; Cincinnati *Daily Commercial*, November 23, 1863.

[6]Lincoln's formal paper at the Wisconsin State Fair on September 30, 1859 and his Cooper Union address are given in full in Roy P. Basler (ed.), *The Collected Works of Abraham Lincoln* (9 vols.; New Brunswick, N.J., 1953), III, 471-482, 522-550.

[7]Noah Brooks, "Personal Reminiscences of Lincoln," *Scribner's*, XV (February, 1878), 565.

[8]*Harper's Weekly*, December 5, 1863; Philadelphia *Daily Age*, November 26, 1863.

[9]Quoted in Louis A. Warren, *Lincoln's Gettysburg Declaration: "A New Birth of Freedom"* (Fort Wayne, Indiana, 1964), 99.

[10]John G. Nicolay, "Lincoln's Gettysburg Address," *Century Magazine*, XLVII (February, 1894), 597.

[11]Noah Brooks, *Washington in Lincoln's Time* (New York, 1895), 286.

[12]Statement of David Wills, made twenty years later, and quoted in Warren, *Lincoln's Gettysburg Declaration*, 70.

[13]Nicolay, in *Century Magazine*, 601.

[14]Cincinnati *Daily Commercial*, November 23, 1863.

[15]Everett, quoted in Warren, *Lincoln's Gettysburg Declaration*, 124. Mr. John Morrow, superintendent of schools in Allegheny County, stood at the edge of the platform and attributed these words to Everett.

[16]Everett to Lincoln, November 20, 1863, in Robert Todd Lincoln Papers.

[17]Rev. Henry L. Baugher's benediction is given in entirety in the *Adams County Sentinel*, December 1, 1863.

[18]Cincinnati *Daily Commercial*, November 23, 1863.

[19](Springfield) *Illinois State Journal*, November 23, 1863.

[20]*Adams County Sentinel*, November 24, 1863.

[21]Everett, quoted in *Edward Everett at Gettysburg* (Massachusetts Historical Society: Boston, 1863), 12.

[22]John Hay, Diary (microfilm copy), entry of November 23, 1863, John Hay Papers, Library of Congress.

[23]Lincoln notation dated August 26, 1862, published in Basler (ed.), *The Collected Works of Abraham Lincoln*, V, 394.

[24]French's "Ode" is included in Warren, *Lincoln's Gettysburg Declaration*, 91-92.

[25]William Saunders, report (n.d.), published in *Revised Report of the Select Committee . . .*, 35-38.

[26]Wills to John G. Nicolay (typewritten enclosure), January 19, 1894, published in *Lincoln Lore*, No. 1437.

[27]Springfield (Mass.) *Republican*, November 30, 1863.

[28]Cincinnati *Daily Commercial*, November 23, 1863.

[29]This presumption is also expressed in Warren, *Lincoln's Gettysburg Declaration*, 44-45.

[30]Harrisburg *Evening Telegraph*, November 13, 17, 1863.

[31]Curtin, quoted in William E. Barton, *Lincoln at Gettysburg* (Indianapolis, 1930), 167.

[32]There is no record of this telegram and it may be just another Lincoln myth.

[33]Cincinnati *Daily Commercial*, November 23, 1863; John Russell Young, *Men and Memories: Personal Reminiscences* (New York, 1901), 59. Ohio's participation in the day's affair is given in detail in Frank L. Klement, "Ohio and the Dedication of the Soldiers' Cemetery at Gettysburg," *Ohio History*, LXXIX (Spring, 1970), 76-100.

[34]Washington *Morning Chronicle*, November 21, 1863.

[35]Cincinnati *Daily Commercial*, November 23, 1863; Young, *Men and Memories*, 59.

CHAPTER VIII

[1]Estimates vary as to the size of the audience. A reporter for the *Washington Chronicle* estimated that at least 12,000 came to Gettysburg for the dedication ceremonies and to tour the battlefield. Clark E. Carr, fabricator of many myths about the affair, stated that the attendance totaled 100,000 — a ridiculous estimate. Perhaps seven or eight thousand gathered in a semicircle before the platform when the program began. Those on the outer fringe of the crowd heard little of Everett's oration and drifted elsewhere. By the time Lincoln arose to speak the crowd was considerably smaller, several thousand having wandered off to visit portions of the battlefield.

[2]*Cincinnati Daily Commercial*, November 23, 1863. The scribe was Martin D. Potter.

[3]Wills's role in the story is detailed in Frank L. Klement, " 'These Honored Dead': David Wills and the Soldiers' Cemetery at Gettysburg," *Lincoln Herald*, LXXIV (Fall, 1972), 123-124.

[4]*Harrisburg Daily Telegraph*, July 9, 1863.

[5](Gettysburg) *Adams County Sentinel*, July 7, 14, 21, 1863.

[6]*Harrisburg Daily Telegraph*, July 10, 1863.

[7]*Adams County Sentinel*, July 28, 1863.

[8]Letter, Ellen Mead to "My dear Mrs. Dean," August 12, 1863, in Lucius Fairchild Papers, State Historical Society of Wisconsin (Madison).

[9]Letter, David Wills to Governor Andrew G. Curtin, July 24, 1863, in Curtin Letterbooks, Executive Correspondence, 1861-1865, Pennsylvania State Archives (Harrisburg).

[10]*Adams County Sentinel*, August 25, 1862.

[11]Andrew B. Cross, in an appeal entitled "To the *Patriotic of the Land* — A Cemetery for those who fell at Gettysburg," published in *Harrisburg Daily Telegraph*, July 29, 1863.

[12]*Ibid*. W. Yates Selleck of Wisconsin was one of the state agents who endorsed the cemetery project. Selleck's work as stage agent and his role in the cemetery project is related in Frank L. Klement, "Governor Edward Salomon, W. Yates Selleck, and the Soldiers' Cemetery at Gettysburg," in *Transactions of the Wisconsin Academy of Sciences, Arts & Letters*, LXI (1973), 11-28.

[13]Letter, Wills to Governor Curtin, July 24, 1863, in Curtin Letterbooks, Executive Correspondence, 1861-1865.

[14]David Wills, Report of March 21, 1864, published in *Revised Report of the Select Committee . . .* , 7.

[15]*Ibid*.

[16]*Ibid*.

[17]Undated report of William Saunders, published in *Revised Report of the Select Committee . . .* , 37-38.

[18]Letter, Wills to Curtin, August 17, 1863, *ibid*.

[19]Letter, Curtin to Wills, August 31, 1863, published in *Gettysburg Compiler*, September 14, 1863.

[20]Letter, Wills to "Hon. Edward Everett," September 23, 1863, published in *Report of the Select Committee . . .* , 7-8.

[21]Letter, Everett to "My dear Sir" (Wills), September 26, 1863, published in *Report of the Select Committee . . .* , 69-70.

[22]Governor Curtin arrived in Washington, D.C., on August 28, 1863, and soon thereafter had a conference with Lincoln. It is likely that Governor Curtin solicited Lincoln's attendance at the Gettysburg cemetery ceremonies during the conference.

[23]*Gettysburg Compiler*, October 19, 1863. Because he was completing a literary project, Longfellow declined the invitation.

[24]Letter, Daniel W. Brown to Gov. David Tod, October 23, 1863, in David Tod Papers, Ohio Historical Society (Columbus). The soldiers' name was Enoch M. Deddy.

[25]Letter, Wills to Lincoln, November 2, 1863, in Robert Todd Lincoln Papers, Library of Congress.

[26]Letter, Wills to Lincoln, November 2, 1863, *ibid*. Both letters were enclosed in the same envelope.

[27]Letter, Wills to Governor Andrew G. Curtin, November 7, 1863, published in *Adams County Sentinel*, November 10, 1863.

[28]John Hay, diary entry of November 21, 1863, in Tyler Dennett, ed., *Lincoln and the Civil War in the Letters and Diaries of John Hay* (New York, 1938), 119-120.

[29]*Cincinnati Daily Commercial*, November 21, 1863.

[30]One newspaper man stated that Everett's oration, although ably given, was without "one stirring thought, one vivid picture, one thrilling appeal." See *Harper's Weekly*, December 2, 1863. Another observer wrote: "Everett's Gettysburg affair was painfully cold . . . with no sunbeam warmth. He seemed the hired mourner — the laureate chanting a funeral dirge to order, with no touch of 'in memorium' about it. His monument was an iron statue with no glow or pulse or passion in it." See letter, Henry C. Robinson to Gen. George B. McClellan, July 17, 1864, in George B. McClellan Papers, Library of Congress.

[31]*Cincinnati Daily Commercial*, November 21, 1863.

[32]*Ibid*.; (Columbus) *Ohio State Journal*, November 23, 1863.

[33]*Boston Morning Journal*, November 20, 1863; *Adams County Sentinel*, November 23, 1863.

[34]*Gettysburg Compiler*, November 23, 1863.

[35]Report, Samuel Weaver to David Wills, March 19, 1864, published in *Report of the Select Committee . . .* , 39-41.

[36]Report of William Saunders, in *Revised Report of the Select Committee . . .* , 37-38.

[37]Letter, Curtin to Wills, August 31, 1863, published in *Gettysburg Compiler*, September 14, 1863.

[38]This inference can also be drawn from Louis A. Warren, *Lincoln's Gettysburg Declaration: "A New Birth of Freedom"* (Fort Wayne Ind., 1964), 44. Cited subsequently as Warren, *Lincoln's Gettysburg Declaration*.

[39]Curtin, quoted in William E. Barton, *Lincoln at Gettysburg* (Indianapolis, 1930), 167.

[40]Everett's diary (no date given), quoted *ibid*., 95.

[41]Letter of introduction, dated September 24, 1862, and signed "Abraham Lincoln," published in Roy P. Basler, editor, *The Collected Works of Abraham Lincoln* (9 vols.; New Brunswick, 1953), V, 437-438. Cited subsequently as Basler, ed., *Collected Works of Abraham Lincoln*.

[42](Springfield) *Illinois State Journal*, September 4, 1863.

[43]Letter, Wills to Everett, September 23, 1863, published in *Report of the Select Committee . . .* , 68-69.

[44]Letter, Everett to Wills, September 26, 1863, *ibid*., 69-70.

[45]*Harrisburg Daily Telegraph*, October 9, 1863.

[46]*Boston Daily Advertiser*, November 19, 1863.

[47]Noah Brooks, "Personal Reminiscences of Lincoln," *Scribner's Magazine*, XV (February, 1878), 565.

[48]Letter, Everett to Wills, November 10, 1863, in David Wills Papers, Library of Congress.

[49]Everett's diary, quoted in Warren, *Lincoln's Gettysburg Declaration*, 96.

[50]Everett, in a dinner statement at Boston on November 15, 1864, *ibid.*, 66.

[51]Everett's diary, quoted *ibid.*, 96.

[52]"Oration of Edward Everett, Gettysburg, Pennsylvania, November 19, 1863," published in entirety in *ibid.*, 185-214. Everett entitled his oration "The Battles of Gettysburg."

[53]*Ibid.*

[54]Quoted in Warren, *Lincoln's Gettysburg Declaration*, 99.

[55]*Ibid.*, 124. Mr. John Morrow, superintendent of schools in Allegheny County, stood at the edge of the patform and attributed these words to Everett.

[56]*Ibid.* The name of the Pennsylvania politician was Wayne MacVeagh. He went to Gettysburg aboard the president's special train.

[57]Letter, Everett to Lincoln, November 20, 1863, in Robert Todd Lincoln Papers.

[58]Letter, Everett to Lincoln, January 30, 1864, *ibid.*

[59]Letter, Lincoln to Everett, February 4, 1864, in Basler, ed., *Collected Works of Abraham Lincoln*, VII, 168. Lincoln did not send the manuscript which he had held in his hand at Gettysburg, but a copy thereof.

[60]Ward Hill Lamon, *Recollections of Abraham Lincoln, 1847-1865* (Chicago, 1895), 14-15.

[61]Quoted in Stephen B. Oates, *With Malice Toward None: The Life of Abraham Lincoln* (New York, 1977), 112.

[62]Letter, Wills to Lamon, October 30, 1863, in Ward Hill Lamon Papers, Huntington Library (San Marino, Calif.). Cited subsequently as Lamon Papers.

[63]Lincoln, quoted in Warren, *Lincoln's Gettysburg Declaration*, 76.

[64]Only about half the governors cooperated with Lamon. Several reported that they received Lamon's request too late — in two cases after the ceremonies were over. For example, see letter written by Henry A. Swift (governor of Minnesota) to Lamon, November 20, 1863, Lamon Papers.

[65]Telegram, Edward T. Stanford (president, American Telegraph Company) to Col. Andrew Stager, November 14, 1863, *ibid.*

[66]Letter, Col. A. J. Alexander to Lamon, November 10, 1863, *ibid.*

[67]Letter, Gen. George Cadwalader to Lamon, November 6, 1863, *ibid.*

[68]*Adams County Sentinel*, November 17, 1863.

[69]*Washington Morning Chronicle*, November 13, 1863.

[70]*Ibid.*, November 17, 1863.

[71]Document [November 17, 1863] entitled "The undersigned wish to signify their intention of accompanying Marshal Lamon to Gettysburg tomorrow — leaving this city at the hour named," Lamon Papers. Thirty-one signed the document.

[72]*Washington Morning Chronicle*, November 17, 1863.

[73]*Ibid.*, November 18, 1863.

[74]Entry of November 18, 1863, John Hay's "Diary" (microfilm copy), in John Hay Papers, Library of Congress.

[75]*Ibid.*

[76]*Gettysburg Compiler*, November 23, 1863.

[77]Witnesses differed as to the introduction. One credited Lamon with saying, "The President will now make a few remarks." Another credited Governor Curtin with introducing Lincoln.

[78]The "Ohio Program" is treated rather extensively in Frank L. Klement, "Ohio and the Dedication of the Soldiers' Cemetery at Gettysburg," *Ohio History*, LXIX (Spring, 1970), 77-100. Among others Lincoln and Secretary of State Seward attended the program.

[79]Manuscript, in Lamon's hand and dated November 21, 1863, in Lamon Papers.

[80]Lamon, *Recollections of Abraham Lincoln, 1847-1865*, 171.

[81]*Ibid.*, 173.

[82]Herndon was Lincoln's last law partner. He conducted interviews and collected material, intending to write a life of Lincoln. But he lacked the self-discipline necessary for such a venture.

[83]Benjamin F. Thomas, *Abraham Lincoln, A Biography* (New York, 1952), 525.

[84]Tyler Dennett, *John Hay: From Poetry to Politics* (Port Washington, N.Y., 1933), 15.

[85]Entries of August 7, September 11, 1863, Hay's "Diary," Hay Papers. The two quotations appear in printed form in *Letters of John Hay and Extracts from Diary*, edited by Mrs. John Hay (3 vols.; New York, 1969), I, 90-91, 102.

[86]Entry of November 18, 1863, *ibid.*

[87]*Ibid.*

[88]John G. Nicolay, "Lincoln's Gettysburg Address," *Century Magazine*, XLVII (February, 1894), 601.

[89]*Ibid.*

[90]Henry Clay Cochrane, "With Lincoln to Gettysburg, 1863," in Military Order of the Loyal Legion of the United States, Commandery of the State of Pennsylvania, *Abraham Lincoln . . . memorial meeting*, February 13, 1907 (Philadelphia, 1907), 4, cited in Warren, *Lincoln's Gettysburg Declaration*, 79.

[91]Entry of November 18, 1863, Hay's "Diary," in Hay Papers. Although Hay wrote about events of the 19th, he incorporated them in the November 18 entry.

[92]Nicolay, "Lincoln's Gettysburg Address," *Century Magazine*, XLVII (February, 1894), 602.

[93]This draft (one of six in Lincoln's hand) has come to be known as the "Nicolay copy." It remained in Nicolay's hands until his death in 1901. Then is passed into the possession of John Hay. In 1916, Hay's children presented it to the Library of Congress.

[94]Letter, John Hay to Robert Todd Lincoln, January 27, 1884, published in *Letters of John Hay and Extracts from Diary*, II, 87.

[95]French was replaced by Thomas J. Campbell of Kentucky on December 7, 1847, when the Thirtieth Congress elected its officials and organized for business at hand.

[96]The appointment, made in April of 1861, was approved by the United States Senate on January 27, 1862.

[97]Authorization, signed by President Lincoln on August 26, 1862, and letter, Lincoln to "Hon. B. B. French," August 26, 1862, both in Basler, ed., *Collected Works of Abraham Lincoln*, V, 394.

[98]French, quoted in Thomas, *Abraham Lincoln*, 299.

[99]Document [November 17, 1863] entitled "The undersigned wish to signify their intention of accompanying Marshal Lamon to Gettysburg tomorrow — leaving this city at the hour named," in Lamon Papers.

[100]"Ode," by Benjamin B. French, published in Warren, *Lincoln's Gettysburg Declaration*, 91-92. There are several slight errors in Warren's version.

[101]*Cincinnati Daily Commercial*, November 23, 1863.

[102]French, quoted in Barton, *Lincoln at Gettysburg* (Indianapolis, 1930), 170.

[103](Columbus) *Daily Ohio State Journal*, November 23, 1863. Isaac Jackson Allen, editor and co-publisher of the newspaper, accompanied his governor to Gettysburg and reported the proceedings there for his newspaper.

[104]Courtland Parker, quoted in Warren, *Lincoln's Gettysburg Declaration*, 175.

[105]Robert G. Ingersoll (one of the noted orators of the post-Civil War era), quoted in *ibid.*, 174.

CHAPTER IX

[1]*Milwaukee Evening Wisconsin*, February 6, 1909. The senior Selleck "became connected with the business department of the *Milwaukee Gazette*," which merged later with the *Milwaukee Sentinel*. He served as "canvasser" in the office of the *Sentinel and Gazette* until he left to become bookkeeper and office manager of a stagecoach company. In later years he was "an esteemed member of the Old Settlers' Club." His wife was a Yates, one of the "first families" of New York State. Isaac Selleck's obituary appears in the *Milwaukee Sentinel*, October 27, 1875.

[2]*Milwaukee Sentinel*, March 22, 1860.

[3]*Ibid.*

[4]*Ibid.*, April 27, June 9, 1862.

[5]Minority report, *Wisconsin Senate Journal*, 1862, Extra Session (Madison, 1862), 22-26; *Madison Daily Patriot*, September 9, November 8, 12, 1862. The subject of soldier-voting is treated at length in Frank L. Klement, "The Soldier Vote in Wisconsin during the Civil War," *Wisconsin Magazine of History*, XXVIII (September, 1944), 37-47.

[6]William H. Watson (Salomon's Military Secretary) to Selleck, August 25, 28, September 10, October 14, 1863, in Letter Books *General*, Executive Deparment (Administration), 1861-1865, Archives Section, State Historical Society of Wisconsin.

[7]Selleck to "Editor," August 14, 1862, published in *Milwaukee Sentinel*, August 20, 1862.

[8]Selleck to Governor Salomon, July 9, 1863, published in (Madison) *Wisconsin State Journal*, July 15, 1863.

[9]*Ibid.*

[10]William P. Taylor to Leonard J. Farwell, July 18, 1863, published in part in *Wisconsin State Journal*, July 24, 1863.

[11]Wills's role in establishing the cooperative state cemetery and planning the dedication program is treated sympathetically in Frank L. Klement, " 'These Honored Dead': David Wills and the Soldiers' Cemetery at Gettysburg," *Lincoln Herald*, LXXIV (Fall, 1974), 123-35.

[12]William H. Wilson to Selleck, July 27, 1863, Letter Books *General*, Executive Department (Administration), 1861-1865.

[13]Selleck to Governor Salomon, August 18, 1863, *ibid.*

[14]Salomon to Selleck, August 24, 1863, *ibid.*

[15]Selleck to Governor Salomon, August 30, 1863, *ibid.*

[16]Selleck to Wills, August 31, 1863, *ibid.*

[17]Selleck to Wills (copy), October 8, 1863, *ibid.*

[18]Wills to Selleck, October 13, 1863, and Wills to Governor Salomon, October 13, 1863, *ibid.*

[19]Selleck, a note of explanation (undated manuscript), in the possession of the Louis A. Warren Lincoln Library and Museum, Fort Wayne, Indiana. It was reproduced in the January, 1966 issue of *Lincoln Lore* (No. 1535), 4.

[20]Letter (copy) Wills to Lamon, October 30, 1863, Ward H. Lamon Paper, Huntington Library, San Marino, California.

[21]Lamon to Governor Salomon, November 5, 1863, Letter Books *General*, Executive Department (Administration), 1861-1865.

[22]*Milwaukee Sentinel*, November 17, 1863.

[23]*Washington Daily Morning Chronicle*, November 21, 1863. The other four members were James C. Westmore of Ohio, Gardiner Tufts of Massachusetts, A. C. Chester of Illinois, and I. C. Rafferty of New Jersey.

[24](Gettysburg) *Adams County Sentinel*, November 11, 1863; *Washington Daily Morning Chronicle*, November 13, 1863.

[25]*Washington Daily Morning Chronicle*, November 17, 1863.

[26]The document, undated, is in the Lamon Papers. Thirty-one names, most in Lamon's hand, appear on that interesting document.

[27]*Washington Daily Morning Chronicle*, November 18, 1863.

[28]*Ibid.*

[29]*Gettysburg Compiler*, November 23, 1863.

[30]*Washington Daily Morning Chronicle*, November 21, 1863.

[31]*Boston Journal*, November 23, 1863.

[32](Springfield) *Illinois State Journal* (n.d.), quoted in Louis A. Warren, Lincoln's Gettysburg Declaration: "A New Birth of Freedom" (Fort Wayne, Ind.: Lincoln National Life Foundation, 1964), 79.

[33]W. Yates Selleck, reminiscences, pubished in the *Milwaukee Evening Wisconsin*, February 6, 1909.

[34]Entry of November 23, 1863 in "Diary" (microfilm), John Hay Papers, Library of Congress.

[35]*Washington Daily Morning Chronicle*, November 21, 1863.

[36]*Harper's Weekly*, December 5, 1863.

[37]Selleck, reminiscences, published in the *Milwaukee Evening Wisconsin*, February 9, 1909.

[38]*Washington Daily Morning Chronicle*, November 21, 1863.

[39]*Washington Daily National Intelligencer*, November 24, 1863.

[40]Every Wisconsin resident interested in the Battle of Gettysburg should read Alan T. Nolan, *The Iron Brigade* (New York, 1961) and Lance J. Herdegen and William J. K. Beaudot, *In the Bloody Railroad Cut at Gettysburg* (Dayton, Ohio, 1990).

[41]*Washington Daily National Intelligencer*, November 24, 1863.

[42]*Washington Daily Morning Chronicle*, November 21, 1863.

[43]Selleck, reminiscences, published in the *Milwaukee Evening Wisconsin*, February 7, 1909.

[44]Reporters for several newspapers, all taking shorthand notes, reported "applause" five times during Lincoln's address. See, for example, *Cincinnati Commercial*, November 23, 1863 and the *Washington Daily Morning Chronicle*, November 21, 1863.

[45]Published in the *Milwaukee Evening Wisconsin*, February 6, 1909.

[46]*Cincinnati Commercial*, November 23, 1863.

[47]*Ibid.*

[48]*Adams County Sentinel*, November 23, 1863.

[49]*Ibid.*; *Gettysburg Compiler*, November 23, 1863.

[50]Selleck, reminiscences, published in *Milwaukee Evening Wisconsin*, February 6, 1909.

[51]William H. Watson to Selleck, December 23, 1863, Letter Books *General*, Executive Department (Administration), 1861-1865. This letter acknowledges receipt of Selleck's bill and states that a $30.90 "Treasury Draft" was enclosed.

[52]Wills to Selleck, December 3, 1863, *ibid.*; report of the commissioners, dated December 17, 1863 and signed by David Wills as "President" and W. Yates Selleck as "Secretary," in David Tod Papers, Ohio Historical Society, Columbus.

[53]Selleck, report to "His Excellency Edward Salomon," dated December 28, 1863, published in *Journal of the Proceedings of the Assembly of Wisconsin . . . 1864* (Madison, 1864), 302-306.

[54]Samuel Weaver, report of March 18, 1864, published in *Report of the Select Committee . . . ,* 39-41.

[55]Report of David Wills, President, and W. Yates Selleck, Secretary, and dated March 31, 1864, *ibid.*, 13, 18.

[56]Selleck to "His Excellency, Jas. T. Lewis, Gov. of Wisconsin," May 29, 1865, published in the *Milwaukee Sentinel*, June 23, 1865.

[57]*Milwaukee Sentinel*, January 26, 1866.

[58]*Ibid.*, October 27, 1875. The obituary of Isaac Selleck included a long paragraph on the career of his son.

[59]His daughter was Miss Adelaide Selleck, his sister Mrs. Isaac P. Rogers.

[60]*Washington Daily Morning Chronicle*, November 21, 1863.

[61]*Cincinnati Commercial*, November 23, 1863.

[62]Selleck, a note of explanation (undated manuscript), in the possession of the Louis A. Warren Lincoln Library and Museum, and reproduced in *Lincoln Lore*, January, 1966 (No. 1535), 4.

CHAPTER X

[1]The supposition that Governor Curtin told President Lincoln about the cemetery project during their conference is shared by others, including Louis A. Waren, *Lincoln's Gettysburg Declaration: "A New Birth of Freedom"* (Fort Wayne, Ind., 1964), 44-45.

[2]Letter (copy), David Wills to Ward H. Lamon, October 30, 1863, Ward H. Lamon Papers, Huntington Library, San Marino, California.

[3]Letter, Wills to Lincoln, November 2, 1863, Robert Todd Lincoln Papers, Library of Congress.

[4]John G. Nicolay, "Lincoln's Gettysburg Address." *Century Magazine*, 47 (February, 1894), 597.

[5]Mark E. Neely, *The Fate of Liberty: Abraham Lincoln and Civil Liberties* (New York, 1991), 7.

[6]James Speed, in an interview published in the (Springfield) *Illinois State Journal*, November 17, 1879, quoted in David C. Mearns and Lloyd Dunlap, *Long Remembered* (Washington, D.C., 1963), 3. After Lincoln's attorney general Edward Bates retired in 1864, the president appointed James Speed to that cabinet post.

[7]Lamon later wrote his recollections and they were published by his daughter, Dorothy Lamon Teillard. See Ward Hill Lamon, *Recollections of Abraham Lincoln, 1847-1865*, edited by Dorothy Lamon Teillard (Washington, D.C., 1911), 172-179. Could Lamon have erred regarding the type of paper, White House stationary rather than foolscap? Time and again, Lamon was not a reliable witness.

[8]Noah Brooks, "Personal Recollections of Lincoln," *Scribner's Magazine*, 15 (February, 1879), 565.

[9]The myth that Lincoln wrote the address on his way to Gettysburg is debunked and discredited in Chapter 6.

[10]According to one account by Wills, Lincoln asked his host to come to his second-floor bedroom and there made the pen and paper request; see *Lincoln Lore*, No. 1437 (November, 1957 issue), 2-3.

[11]*The Collected Works of Abraham Lincoln*, edited by Roy P. Basler (9 vols.; New Brunswick, N.J., 1953), 8:18.

[12]David Wills, typewritten enclosure with letter, Wills to John Nicolay, January 19, 1894, in *Lincoln Lore*, No. 1437 (November, 1957 issue), 1-2.

[13]Washington *National Intelligencer*, November 21, 1863.

[14]According to some who have carefully examined the two-page manuscript, "both pages still show faint traces of once having been folded in thirds." See Mearns and Dunlap, *Long Remembered*, 8.

[15]Nicolay, "Lincoln's Gettysburg Address," 601-602.

[16]Orton H. Carmichael, *Lincoln's Gettysburg Address* (New York, 1917), 87-88.

[17]The question arises regarding the second page of White House stationery on which Lincoln completed that last sentence started at the bottom of page one. Lincoln, seated at the table in his room at Gettysburg reviewed that second page and then realized he had inadvertently omitted fourteen words. It is likely that the second page of White House stationery ended up in a wastepaper basket in his room, being replaced by a sheet of foolscap.

[18] William H. Lambert, "The Gettysburg Address," *Pennsylvania Magazine of History and Biography* 33 (October, 1909), 5-7.

[19] James G. Wilson, quoted in Charles W. Thompson, "Three Versions of Lincoln's Gettysburg Address," in New York *Times*, June 29, 1913.

[20] Letter, Nelson Thomassen to Elihu Root, February 21, 1913, copy with another letter, Clara S. Hay to Helen Nicolay, February 28, 1913, John Nicolay Papers, Library of Congress, quoted in Mearns and Dunlap, *Long Remembered*, 9.

[21] Mearns and Dunlap, *Long Remembered*, 14.

[22] *Ibid.*, 9.

[23] William E. Barton, *Lincoln at Gettysburg* (Indianapolis, 1930), 68-69.

[24] *Ibid.* But Barton erred when he said that this was the draft that President Lincoln held in his hand when he recited his address.

[25] The second draft, like the others, appears in *Collected Works of Abraham Lincoln*, 8:18-19.

[26] Mearns and Dunlap, *Long Remembered*, 18.

[27] Cincinnati *Daily Commercial*, November 23, 1863.

[28] According to Garry Wills, *Lincoln at Gettysburg* (New York, 1992), 192, a New York reporter for the *Tribune* claimed that the sheets that Lincoln had in his hand during the speech had the Executive Mansion letterhead. Was that New Yorker reporter a keen observer or an imaginative fellow? No reporter on the platform was near enough to Lincoln as he recited his piece to see "Executive Mansion" at the top of page one. Gilbert, who had the "reading" copy in his hand could have answered that question, but no one, strangely, sought such information from him.

[29] Wills to Lincoln, November 23, 1863, Robert Todd Lincoln Papers.

[30] Letter, Mrs. Daniel P. Livermore to Lincoln, October 11, 1863, Robert Todd Lincoln Papers.

[31] Lincoln to "Ladies having in charge of the North-Western Fair For the Sanitary Commission," October 26, 1863, *Collected Works of Abraham Lincoln*, 6:539.

[32] Nicolay, "Lincoln's Gettysburg Address," 605. Nicolay added: "In addition to that from Mr. Wills, other requests came to him for autograph copies. The number he made, and for what friends, cannot now be confidently stated, though it was probably half a dozen or more, all written by him with painstaking care to correspond word for word with his revision." Was Nicolay correct? Are there some other copies waiting to be discovered?

[33] Mearns and Dunlap, *Long Remembered*, 9.

[34] David A. Mearns (editor), in *The Lincoln Legacy* (published by the Lincoln Group of Illinois), 4 (Fall, 1990 and Winter, 1991 issues), 7. The entire paragraph borrows extensively from Editor Warren's account.

[35] Lloyd Ostendorf, "Turning the Pages of History: A New Draft of the Gettysburg Address," located in *The Gettysburg Magazine*, January 1992 (Issue No. 6), 107.

[36] Ostendorf, quoted *ibid.*

[37] *The Lincoln Legacy*, 7-8. Rumors of "a lost copy" continued to persist in the post-Civil War era. This prompted Herman Blum of Blumhaven Library and Gallery in Philadelphia to offer a $5,000 reward to anyone bringing in the "lost" copy. No one ever did. The brazen Philadelphian received much publicity for himself and for Blumhaven.

[38] Quoted in *The Lincoln Legacy*, 9.

[39] *Ibid.*

[40] The paragraph borrows much from Editor Warren's account in *The Lincoln Legacy*, 9-10.

[41] Newman and Hickey, quoted, *ibid.*

[42] Dr. Nickell, quoted, *ibid.*, 12.

[43] James Gilreath, quoted, *ibid.*

[44] Mr. Richard Sloan, quoted, *ibid.*

[45]Letter, Lloyd Ostendorf to Frank L. Klement, December 20, 1992 (letter in possession of the author).

[46]McCrone, quoted, *The Lincoln Legacy*, 13.

[47]Warren, in *The Lincoln Legacy*, 13.

[48]*Ibid.*, 14-15.

[49]Roderick McNeil's 600-word report (undated) is published in full in *ibid.*

[50]Ostendorf's announcement, *ibid.*, 15.

[51]McCrone, quoted, *ibid.*, 15-16.

[52]Ostendorf, "The Document Is Genuine," in *The Lincolnian* (January-February, 1992 issue), 4-5. This excellent newsletter, edited by Paul Verduin, is a bimonthly publication of the Lincoln Group of the District of Columbia, Inc.

[53]Gilreath, in *The Lincolnian* (March-April 1992 issue), 4.

[54]Sloan's undated letter, *ibid.*, (May-June 1992 issue), 4.

[55]Seddelmeyer article, *ibid.*, 4-5.

[56]Budnik article, *ibid.*, (July-August 1992 issue), 5.

[57]Lloyd Ostendorf, "Lost Copy of the Gettysburg Address Comes to Light," *Lincoln Herald*, 94 (Spring, 1992), 24-27.

[58]Benjamin P. Thomas, *Abraham Lincoln, a Biography* (New York, 1952), 403.

[59]Letter, John Sherman to George McLaughlin, December 15, 1863, quoted in Mearns and Dunlap, *Long Remembered*, 10.

[60]Letter, Everett to Lincoln, January 30, 1864, Robert Todd Lincoln Papers.

[61]Letter, Lincoln to Everett, February 4, 1864, in *Collected Works of Abraham Lincoln*, 7:167-168.

[62]Letter, Everett to Lincoln, March 3, 1864, Robert Todd Lincoln Papers.

[63]Mearns and Dunlap, *Long Remembered*, 22.

[64]Louis A. Warren, *Lincoln's Gettysburg Declaration*, 165.

[65]*Ibid.*, 165-166; Mearns and Dunlap, *Long Remembered*, 22.

[66]Letter, Bancroft to Lincoln, November 15, 1861, Robert Todd Lincoln Papers.

[67]Letter, Lincoln to Bancroft, November 18, 1861, *Collected Works of Abraham Lincoln*, 5:25-26.

[68]Letter, Lincoln to Bancroft, February 29, 1864, *ibid.*, 7:212.

[69]Warren, *Lincoln's Gettysburg Declaration*, 167.

[70]Quoted in Mearns and Dunlap, *Long Remembered*, 32.

[71]Letter, Colonel Alexander Bliss to John Nicolay, March 7, 1864, quoted, *ibid.*

[72]Mearns and Dunlap, *Long Remembered*, 22.

[73]Robert Todd Lincoln, quoted in Warren, *Lincoln's Gettysburg Declaration*, 169-170.

CHAPTER XI

[1]Clark E. Carr, *Lincoln at Gettysburg* (Chicago, 1906), 16.

[2]Orton H. Carmichael, *Lincoln's Gettysburg Address* (New York, 1917), 12, 33.

[3]F. Lauriston Bullard, *A Few Appropriate Remarks* (Harrogate, Tenn., 1944), 28.

[4]Quoted in *Lincoln Lore*, No. 1535 (January, 1966 issue), 2. It was incorporated in the featured article "The Precise Location Where Lincoln Delivered the Gettysburg Address," written by Louis A. Warren.

[5]Both the museum and the foundation were set up by the Lincoln National Life Insurance Company.

[6]Mark E. Neely, "Louis A. Warren," in *Lincoln Lore*, No. 1733 (July, 1982 issue), 1. Neely's eulogy took over four issues of this monthly four-page newsletter.

[7]Milo M. Quaife, review, in *Mississippi Valley Historical Review*, 13 (March, 1927), 579.

[8]This organization was involved in raising "a million dollars" for a memorial at Nancy Hanks' grave in southern Indiana.

[9]Louis A. Warren was director of the Lincoln National Life Foundation 1928-1956, and emeritus 1956-1982. He edited *Lincoln Lore* 1929-1955. Other works included *Slavery Atmosphere of Lincoln's Youth* (1933); *Little Known Lincoln Episodes* (1934); *Abraham Lincoln, a Concise Biography* (1934); and *Lincoln Bibliography Check List* (1959).

Warren was "the authority" for Lincoln's early years. James G. Randall was "the authority" on Lincoln the president.

[10]The 2nd, 6th, and 7th Wisconsin regiments, along with the 19th Indiana and the 24th Michigan, made up the famous "Iron Brigade," decimated in the first day's fighting. See Alan T. Nolan, *The Iron Brigade: A Military History* (New York, 1961) and Lance J. Herdegen and William J. K. Beaudot, *In the Bloody Railroad Cut at Gettysburg* (Dayton, Ohio, 1990).

[11]Letter, William P. Taylor to Leonard J. Farwell, July 18, 1863, published *ibid.*, July 24, 1863. Massachusetts had a reputation for good "state agents" and excellent soldier care.

[12]Selleck's work as state agent and cemetery commissioner is treated in Frank L. Klement, "Governor Edward Salomon, W. Yates Selleck, and the Soldiers' Cemetery at Gettysburg," *Transactions of the Wisconsin Academy of Sciences, Arts & Letters*, 61 (1973), 11-28.

[13]After returning to Washington, Selleck submitted his bill of $30.90 for "expenses in attending the consecration of the National Cemetery at Gettysburg." See Letter, William Watson to Selleck, December 23, 1863, Letter Books *General*, Executive Department (Administration), 1861-1865, Archives Section, State Historical Society of Wisconsin, Madison.

[14]Report of the Commissioners, dated December 17, 1863, and signed by David Wills as "President" and W. Yates Selleck as "Secretary," in David Tod Papers, Ohio Historical Society, Columbus.

[15](Milwaukee) *Evening Wisconsin*, February 6, 1909.

[16]Louis A. Warren, *Lincoln's Gettysburg Declaration: A New Birth of Freedom"* (Fort Wayne, Ind., 1964), 182-183.

[17]McMurtry, quoted in article "Lincoln Stood Here," in *Lincoln Log*, October, 1965 issue — photocopy, original is in the Lincoln Museum and Library, Fort Wayne. The author is indebted to Steven K. Rogstad for a photocopy.

[18]*Ibid.*

[19]Neal Ashby, "The New Battle of Gettysburg," in *Parade Magazine*, 14. A notation above the title by R. Gerald McMurtry reads: "I was paid $100.00 by *Parade* for this story idea." The author is indebted to Steven K. Rogstad for a photocopy of page 14 of *Parade Magazine*, and Rogstad had previously obtained his copy from the Lincoln Museum and Library, Fort Wayne.

[20]Ashby, in *Parade Magazine*, November 14, 1965 issue, p. 14.

[21]McMurtry, quoted, *ibid.*

[22]Kittridge A. Wing, quoted, *ibid.*

[23]Frederick Tilberg, quoted, *ibid.*

[24]Historian Tilberg failed to consult the right sources. He could have used the columns of the (Milwaukee) *Evening Wisconsin* of February 6, 1909. Better yet, he could have used the Governor Edward Salomon Papers in the Wisconsin State Historical Society, Madison.

[25]"Editorial Note," *Lincoln Lore*, No. 1535 (January, 1966 issue), 1. McMurtry was editor of *Lincoln Lore* at this time.

[26]Both are quoted in *Lincoln Lore, ibid.*, and are taken from the commissioners' report of 1867.

[27]Warren, quoted, *ibid.*, 2.

[28]*Ibid.*, 2-3.

[29]This particular photograph was republished in the *Gettysburg Times*. Centennial Edition, 1863-1963. It was reproduced in *Lincoln Lore, ibid.*, 3.

[30]Warren, quoted, *ibid.*, 3. The photograph was reproduced in *Lincoln Lore*, No. 1535 (January, 1966 issue). This issue of *Lincoln Lore* also included: 1) a line of march map; 2) a picture of W. Yates Selleck; 3) Selleck's map of the cemetery; 4) the Selleck holograph; and 5) an aerial photo of the Gettysburg National Cemetery.

[31]Frederick Tilberg, "The Location of the Platform From Which Lincoln Delivered the Gettysburg Address," *Pennsylvania History*, 40 (April, 1973), 179-189.

[32]*Ibid.*, 179.

[33]*Ibid.*, 182.

[34]Cincinnati *Daily Gazette*, November 23, 1863, quoted, *ibid.*, 188.

[35]Warren, quoted in "Have We Done Lincoln Justice at Gettysburg? No, Says Dr. Louis Warren; Yes, Says Dr. Frederick Tilberg," in *Civil War Times Illustrated* 15 (July, 1976), 12.

[36]*Ibid.*, 14.

[37]*Ibid.*

[38]*Ibid.*

[39]Tilberg, quoted, *ibid.*, 11.

[40]*Ibid.*, 13.

[41]Gilbert, quoted, *ibid.*, 13-14.

[42]Tilberg, quoted, *ibid.*, 14.

[43]Cincinnati *Daily Gazette*, November 23, 1863, quoted, *ibid.*

[44]Garry Wills, *Lincoln at Gettysburg: The Words That Remade America* (New York, 192), 208. These two photographs, taken by unknown persons, are in the Library of Congress. They have been reproduced on pages 118-121 of William A. Frassanito, *Gettysburg: A Journey in Time* (New York, 1975).

[45]*Ibid.*, 209.

[46]David Wills, report of March 21, 1864, in *Revised Report of the Select Committee . . .* , 7.

[47]Wills, *Lincoln at Gettysburg*, 210.

CHAPTER XII

[1] (Gettysburg) *Adams County Sentinel*, November 17, 1863.

[2]Letter, Francis Scala to Louis A. Frothingham [a congressman from Massachusetts], July 27, 1927, in Francis Scala Collection. Library of Congress, quoted in Kenneth E. Olson, *Music and Musket: Bands and Bandsmen of the Civil War* (Westport, Conn., 1981), 15.

[3]Statement, Carl A. Henderson, dated November 19, 1859, Scala Papers, quoted in Olson, *Music and Musket*, 15.

[4]Washington *Daily Morning Chronicle*, November 21, 1863.

[5]*Ibid.*

[6]Kenneth A. Bernard, *Lincoln and the Music of the Civil War* (Caxton Publishers; Caldwell, Idaho, 1966), 168.

[7]Washington *Daily Morning Chronicle*, November 21, 1863.

[8]Bernard, *Lincoln and the Music of the Civil War*, 168.

[9]Entry of November 22, 1863, "Journal," Benjamin B. French Papers, Library of Congress.

[10]Bernard, *Lincoln and the Music of the Civil War*, 171.

[11]Quoted, *ibid.*, 166.

[12]The Washington *Daily Morning Chronicle*, November 21, 1863 says: "Five or six bands were present, among which were the Marine Band of Washington, Birgfield's Band of Philadelphia, the band of the 2nd Regulars [of Fort McHenry], the New York regimental band [Fifth New York Artillery Regiment], and others." What others? Neither of the two local newspapers, the Republican-oriented *Adams County Sentinel* nor the Democratic-minded Gettysburg *Compiler*, made mention of a local band's participation in the day's affairs. None of the two dozen newspapermen, in their various accounts, made mention of any other bands than the four. Furthermore, Bernard, *Lincoln and the Music of the Civil War*, page 171, speaking of Birgfield's Band, says: "It was the only Pennsylvania band at the ceremony, and was given the 'place of honor' on the program by its assignment to play the opening number."

[13]Chicago *Daily Tribune*, November 21, 1863.

[14](Columbus) *Ohio Daily State Journal*, November 21, 1863.

[15]Washington *Daily Morning Chronicle*, November 21, 1863.

[16]Washington *Daily National Intelligencer*, November 21, 1863; Harrisburg *Evening Telegraph*, November 20, 1863, Cincinnati *Daily Commercial*, November 21, 1863; Benjamin B. French, "Journal," entry of November 22, 1863, French Papers.

[17]Cincinnati *Daily Commercial*, November 23, 1863.

[18]Dr. Nicholas Contorno, director of the Marquette University Band and an authority on Civil War music, provided the author with the name of Walter Dignam as arranger.

Dr. Contorno contacted the Manchester Historical Society of New Hampshire and received the following information about the man who arranged the music ("Old Hundred") played by the Marine Band at the Gettysburg cemetery ceremonies: Walter Dignam was born in England on April 3, 1827 in the town of Paddum, near Manchester. At the age of 17 (in 1844) he "emigrated" to the United States, landing in Providence, R.I. After working as a block printer for a time in Providence, he migrated to Manchester, N.H. and worked as a finisher in a printing plant. In 1854 he organized a band that rapidly became one of the best in New England. Popularly called the "Cornet Band," it made a tour of New York, Philadelphia, Baltimore, and Washington, where they were received and complimented by President Franklin Pierce, himself a citizen of New Hampshire — this in December of 1855. Dignam and his "Cornet Band" served in the Civil War with the 2nd New Hampshire Volunteer Regiment. After the 2nd New Hampshire served its term, the "Cornet Band" became affiliated with the 4th New Hampshire Regiment. After the war, and at the great Gilmore Peace Jubilee in Boston, Dignam's "Cornet Band" took third prize. In the postwar years, the band added to its already well recognized fame. Dignam died on April 23, 1891. "Every old Manchester resident speaks with pride of the old 'Cornet Band' as it was called."

[19]Bernard, *Lincoln and the Music of the Civil War*, 152n.

[20]Frank Moore, editor, *The Rebellion Record: A Diary of American Events, with Documents, Narratives, Illustrative Incidents, Poetry, etc.* (12 vols.; New York, 1894-1922), V, 10.

[21]Washington *Daily Morning Chronicle*, November 21, 1863.

[22](Gettysburg) *Adams County Sentinel*, November 24, 1863.

[23]New York *Herald*, November 20, 1863.

[24]Philadelphia *Age* (n.d.), quoted in Louis A. Warren, *Lincoln's Gettysburg Declaration: "A New Birth of Freedom"* (Fort Wayne, Ind., 1964), 100.

[25]Entry of November 14, 1863, "Journal," French Papers.

[26]Bernard, *Lincoln and the Music of the Civil War*, 172.

[27]David Wills, report dated March 21, 1864, and published in *Revised Report of the Select Committee . . .* , 7-10.

[28]Quoted in Bernard, *Lincoln and the Music of the Civil War*, 173.

[29]Baltimore *American*, November 23, 1863, quoted *ibid.* The reporter mistakenly referred to the organization as the Baltimore Glee Club rather than the National Union Musical Association of Baltimore.

[30]Entry of November 23, 1863, "Journal," French Papers.

[31]Letter, David Wills to Lincoln, November 2, 1863, Robert Todd Lincoln Papers, Library of Congress.

[32](Gettysburg) *Adams County Sentinel*, November 24, 1863; Cincinnati *Daily Commercial*, November 23, 1863.

[33]Philadelphia *Bulletin*, November 12, 1940, quoted in Warren, *Lincoln's Gettysburg Declaration*, 139.

[34]Quoted in William E. Barton, *Lincoln at Gettysburg* (Indianapolis, 1930), 33.

[35]Ms. Ruth Cook of the Lincoln Museum, Fort Wayne, Indiana, obtained the words of the four verses for the author, securing them from the Brown University Library.

[36]Philadelphia *Evening Bulletin*, November 20, 1863, quoted in Bernard, *Lincoln and the Music of the Civil War*, 173.

[37](Gettysburg) *Adams County Sentinel*, November 24, 1863.

[38]*Washington National Intelligencer*, November 25, 1863.

[39]Bernard, *Lincoln and the Music of the Civil War*, 174n.

[40]Washington *Daily Morning Chronicle*, November 21, 1863.

[41]John Burns, who had once served as the town's constable developed "a tarnished reputation" because he drank too much too often. He was, one historian wrote, "the only citizen who took part in the battle." There is a John Burns statue on the battlefield.

[42]Washington *Daily Morning Chronicle*, November 21, 1863.

[43]Boston *Morning Journal*, November 20. 1863.

[44](Gettysburg) *Adams County Sentinel*, November 24, 1863.

104, 106, 128, 132, 205; had front row chair, 30; invocation in entirety, 215-216
Stoneman, Gen. George H., 22, 113, 132
Stowe, Harriet Beecher, 86
Stuart, John T., 20

T

Tareytown Road, 187
Taylor, William P., 123, 125
Temple, Wayne C., 155, 161, 163
Thomas, Benjamin P., XII
Tilburg, Frederick, 186-191, 268 (endnote #24)
Tod, David: front row chair, 29, 45, 106; and cemetery dedication, 53-73, 98-99; corresponded with Wills, 54, 55; named a state agent, 55; arranged "Ohio program," 57, 68-70, 99; picture of, 57; composed circular letter, 58; arranged special train, 58, 60-61, 62-63, 70; criticized by Democrats, 58-60, 71-73; complimented, 60; arrived in Harrisburg, 62; arrived in Gettysburg, 63; briefed by Brown, 63; on platform, 65-66, 98-99; dinner guest, 68; returned to Ohio, 70; mentioned, XIV, 6; quoted, 55, 72
Travelers' Insurance Company, 131
Turner, Thomas R., XIII
"Twenty Years Ago," 20

U

Uncle Tom's Cabin, 86
Union Glee Club (Philadelphia), 77
Union Leagues, 71
United States Sanitary Commission, 3, 101
Usher, John P., 33, 62, 66, 68, 134

V

Vallandigham, Clement L., XIII, 54, 65, 71, 99, 139
Van Buren, Martin, 171
Van Riswick, John, 21

W

Wade, Benjamin F., 166
Warren, David A., 163
Warren, Louis A.: wrote Lincoln's *Gettysburg Declaration (1864)*, XII; edited *Lincoln Lore*, XII, 183, 244-245 (endnote #23); early career, 180, 244-245 (endnote #23); acquired Selleck halograph, 180; debated platform site, 185-191; picture of, 182; quoted, 187, 188, 189
Washington, George, 92, 109
Washington *Morning Chronicle*, 27, 88, 134, 195, 206
Washington *National Intelligencer*, 48-49, 134, 148
Weaver, Samuel, 9, 18-19, 60, 253 (endnote #8)
Webster, Daniel, 92
Western Telegraph Company, 22
Whittier, John G., 42, 207

Wills Copy, 152-166
Wills, David: prewar career, 4, 100; and soldiers' cemetery, XIV, 1, 3-19, 41-42, 54, 96, 101-102, 103, 105, 106, 119, 124, 140, 179; as Curtin's agent, 4-19, 22, 41, 54, 56, 61, 74, 101, 104-105, 124; suggests cemetery project, 5, 41, 54, 102; and state agents, 5-6, 8, 10, 16, 56-57; buys cemetery plot, 5-6, 41, 55, 102; writes to governors, 6-9, 41, 75; reburial bids, 9, 102; arranges program, 9, 11, 23, 29, 42, 43, 61, 90, 95, 98, 103, 104, 119; invites Lincoln, 9-10, 91, 103, 110; as Lincoln's host, XI, 11-16, 18, 24, 44, 74, 75, 87, 110, 114, 131, 141, 143n, 144, 193, 210; pictures of, 12, 160; in procession, 16, 29, 117, 119, 128; on platform, 16-18, 101, 104, 134; heard Lincoln's address, 17, 101, 105; reception at house, 18, 105; contacts Lamon, 10, 41, 113, 140; requests copy of address, XV, 159n, 164; Wills house, 12n, 24, 25, 32, 44, 68, 93, 111, 112, 114, 117, 133, 141, 143n, 194, 210; Lincoln's departure, 18; praised for program, 19, 33, 105; and cemetery commission, 18-19, 72, 124, 130; plans procession, 24, 114; received report from Lamon, 23; escorted Everett, 29, 110; escorted Lincoln, 77, 104, 132; invites Everett as orator, 107, 109; quoted, 22, 41, 48, 103, 124, 144; mentioned, XIX-XV, 1, 43, 44, 56, 76, 77, 110, 112, 125, 180, 184
Wills, Garry, XIII-XIV, 190, 191; quoted, 190, 191
Wills house, 12, 16, 18, 44, 48, 56, 68, 75-76, 87
Wills, Mrs. David, 18, 75, 104-105, 107
Wilson, James G., 147
Wing, Kittridge A., 186
Wisconsin and the Civil War (1963), XIII
Wisconsin Soldiers' Aid Society, 123, 184
Wisconsin State Fair of 1859, 92, 109
Wise, Capt. Henry A., 134
Wise, Mrs. Henry A., 134
Woodward, George W., 139
Wright, Joseph A., 107

Y

Yates, Gov. Richard, 6
York Street (Gettysburg), 32, 68, 75